THE ACTING
PRESIDENT

BOB SCHIEFFER
and GARY PAUL GATES

THE ACTING PRESIDENT

E. P. DUTTON NEW YORK

Published in the United States by E. P. Dutton,
a division of Penguin Books USA Inc.,
2 Park Avenue, New York, N.Y. 10016.

Published simultaneously in Canada by
Fitzhenry and Whiteside, Limited, Toronto.

Library of Congress Cataloging-in-Publication Data

Schieffer, Bob
The acting president/
Bob Schieffer and Gary Paul Gates.—1st ed.
p.   cm.
Includes index.
ISBN 0-525-24752-1
1. Reagan, Ronald.   2. United States—Politics and
government—1981–1989.   3. Presidents—United States—Biography.
I. Gates, Gary Paul.   II. Title
E877.S26   1989
973.928'092—dc20   89-7719
CIP

Designed by REM Studio

1   3   5   7   9   10   8   6   4   2

First Edition

This book is for our first ladies—Pat and Phyllis

Actors are like politicians, and politicians are like actors. They both spend time each day contemplating their image. They both have a desire to be loved.

—*Gore Vidal*

Contents

Acknowledgments

Whatever else may be said about it, Ronald Reagan's political career certainly provoked a lot of literary attention. In preparing to write this book, we read numerous others that have been written on the subject over the years, and almost all of them were helpful in one way or another. But there were two in particular that proved to be of invaluable assistance. The first is *Reagan*, Lou Cannon's excellent biography of the pre-Presidential years and Reagan's first year in the White House. For an understanding of how Ronald Reagan, the former actor, became the fortieth President of the United States, Cannon's book is the benchmark against which all other books on the subject must be measured. The second is *Landslide*, Jane Mayer and Doyle McManus's compelling account of the troubles that afflicted Reagan's presidency during his second term. Their meticulous reporting provided a road map through the labyrinth of the Iran-Contra affair, which we consulted at various steps along the way. In the case of both Cannon's book and *Landslide*, we did not always agree with the authors' assessments and interpretations. We do not wish to saddle them—or anyone else—with responsibility for judgments we formed, which were based on our own reporting and research.

Other books deserving of our special thanks are *Gambling with History* by Laurence Barrett; *Reagan's America—Innocents at Home* by Garry Wills; *Wake Us When It's Over* by Jules Witcover and Jack Germond; *The Power Game* by Hedrick Smith, and *Men of Zeal* by senators William S. Cohen and George J. Mitchell. Each of them, in various ways, helped us to round out our portrait of the Reagan presidency. In addition, we are indebted to the spate of insider memoirs, the so-called kiss-and-tell books, that were written by officials who had served in the Reagan administration. As most of the authors of those books are people we deal with in our book, we allude to their recorded observations at appropriate intervals in the narrative.

We also drew information from hundreds of newspaper and magazine articles, not only those that were published during the years of Reagan's presidency but others as well, dating back to his early years in California. In citing these sources, we wish to express our gratitude to our researcher, Teresa Sessoms, whose painstaking efforts in sifting through vast quantities of material made our task immeasurably easier than it otherwise would have been. A warm word of thanks also to our editor, Richard Marek, whose wise counsel and gifted scalpel greatly strengthened our manuscript, and to his able staff of associates at E. P. Dutton who were steadfast in their support and encouragement.

Finally, however, this book could not have been written without the cooperation of primary sources. The scores of interviews we conducted with men and women who served in or dealt with the Reagan administration served as the beacons that guided us from one point to another. Their insights into events they observed or participated in, and their candor in sharing them with us not only furnished a rich vein of information but emboldened us to form judgments that otherwise would have been beyond our reach. We acknowledge these sources by name throughout this book, but in some instances they asked to be spared the honor of direct attribution. Thus, we take this opportunity to thank them all collectively.

Bob Schieffer
Gary Paul Gates

April 1989

THE ACTING PRESIDENT

1

The True Believers

"There *are* simple answers."
—*Candidate Ronald Reagan*

It was a night of triumph and euphoria, one of those rare moments when the past, present, and future blend into one another to form a most perfect union. The occasion itself—an elegant black tie dinner celebrating the twenty-fifth anniversary of *National Review*—was a significant milestone. Long recognized as the bible of the right-wing movement, *National Review* had flourished since its modest beginnings in the mid-1950s, and the high-ranking conservatives gathered at the Plaza Hotel in New York that evening in early December 1980 had ample reason to gloat over the journal's success. But what made that sense of achievement even more exhilarating was the fact that the gala event came just a few weeks after American conservatives had won their greatest victory on the political battlefield: the election of Ronald Wilson Reagan as the fortieth President of the United States.

Presiding over the festive affair was the most articulate advocate of the conservative crusade and founder of *National Review*: his eminence, William F. Buckley, Jr. More than anyone else, he embodied the zeal that crackled through the hotel ballroom that evening. The triumphant glow that emanated from Buckley and his colleagues reflected their buoyant belief that they had finally arrived at *their* destiny. Blessed are the true believers, for they shall inherit the earth—or at least the White House.

The road to that inheritance had been long and arduous. Back in 1955, when Buckley launched *National Review*, those who swore allegiance to the conservative faith were an obscure and embittered sect largely confined to the political catacombs. They had been outcasts ever since 1932, the year Franklin Roosevelt put together the New Deal coalition that completely altered the shape and structure of American politics. Even within their own house, the Republican party, conservatives had been subjected to one humiliating defeat after another. In their effort to cope with the Roosevelt magic, Republican leaders repeatedly turned to centrist or progressive candidates for their presidential nominees: men such as Wendell Willkie, Thomas Dewey, and, most recently, Dwight D. Eisenhower. Eisenhower's election in 1952 put a Republican in the White House for the first time in twenty years, but it gave no joy to Old Guard conservatives, who certainly did not regard the popular war hero as one of their own—and with good reason. Had Eisenhower not decided to enter the race, the Republican nomination would have gone to the far more conservative Robert Taft. During the primaries, Taft's forces had actually accused Eisenhower of being a "New Dealer, beholden to Roosevelt and Truman," and once Ike took office, they complained that many of his largely bipartisan policies were having the subtle effect of giving Republican sanction to the sweeping reforms of the New Deal. Ike may have presided over a Republican White House, but it was a house of many rooms and the Old Guard was consigned to quarters far from the centers of power. And so conservatives continued to chafe in frustration and exile, like so many Romanovs adrift in a world that bore no resemblance to the days of St. Petersburg and the czars.

It was in this bleak atmosphere that Buckley begat his brainchild. He was just twenty-nine at the time and, insofar as he had any reputation at all, was primarily known as the author of a book critical of his alma mater, *God and Man at Yale*. But he had all the breezy self-confidence of a young man on the rise, and he was determined that his new journal of opinion would have an impact.

In a manifesto written for the maiden issue, Buckley proclaimed that *National Review*'s mission would be "to stand athwart history, yelling Stop." Elaborating on that theme, he wrote that "there is a Liberal point of view on national and world affairs . . . a huge propaganda machine engaged in a major sustained assault upon the sanity and upon the prudence and morality of the American people." Then came the vow to keep a "watchful eye" on this parlous state of affairs.

During the first few years of *National Review*'s existence, the public paid little attention. The Eisenhower era was a time of consensus and complacency, and advocates of the far Left and Right were generally dismissed as strident hecklers out of tune with the Muzak mood of what became known as the silent generation. It was John F. Kennedy's call to action on the New Frontier that snapped the country out of its torpor and gave conservatives, as well as liberals, a more receptive forum for their attacks on the status quo. There is a tendency to think of the resurgence of political activism that took place in the early 1960s solely in terms of the Left: the formation of the Students for a Democratic Society (SDS), the civil rights movement, and the other social revolutions that erupted during that raucous decade. But those were also the years when the Right tapped into fresh sources of passion and energy that greatly helped to revitalize its cause. The conservative counterpart of SDS was the Young Americans for Freedom (YAF), and although they were polar extremities, both groups were driven by a profound discontent with the political mainstream.

Yet even the most dedicated army must have a general to march behind and here, too, there was good news, for the conservatives now had a vigorous new leader to rally around. The former heroes of the Old Guard—Taft and Joe McCarthy—had passed into history; by 1960 the battered banner they left behind had been taken up by Senator Barry Goldwater. At that year's Republican convention, conservatives once again felt they had been spurned by the ruling faction of the party, the despised Eastern establishment. Their only moment of satisfaction came toward the end with Goldwater's appearance on the podium. He had been given the token honor of making the nomination of the Nixon-Lodge ticket unanimous, but he seized the opportunity to do more. Venting his own frustration, Goldwater concluded his brief remarks with an exhortation to his troops: "Let's grow up, conservatives! If we want to take this party back, and I think we can some day, let's get to work!"

And so they did. Over the next three years, the political commandos of the conservative movement mobilized the grass roots. They spread their philosophy so successfully that by 1964, they had taken control of the Republican party from the Eastern moderates and were able to secure the presidental nomination for Goldwater. Yet it was a Pyrrhic victory. The Goldwater coup left the Republicans so bitterly divided they had no resources left for the main purpose of the exercise: the general election. Unable to arouse even lukewarm support beyond its narrow base, the Goldwater candidacy led to the Republicans' most crushing defeat since the years of Roosevelt's reign. In the aftermath of that debacle, the conventional wisdom held that never again would the GOP succumb to the folly of embracing a hard-core conservative as its presidential nominee.

A minor footnote to that campaign was a pro-Goldwater television speech delivered by the semiretired actor Ronald Reagan, a onetime liberal Democrat who, in recent years, had become an earnest spokesman for the conservative cause. In the years to come, as the Reagan legend grew, it would be remembered as The Speech, the transcendental moment when Reagan made the leap from concerned private citizen to active politician. It was The Speech, along with the avalanche that buried Goldwater, that put Reagan on the road toward replacing the Arizona senator in the hearts of the stricken conservatives, who now desperately needed a new spokesman. In 1966, Reagan formally became their leader when, in his first run for public office, the former actor was elected governor of California. But the performance that played to standing ovations in California was not yet ready for a national tour. In 1968, when Reagan made his first, half-hearted bid for the presidential nomination, the Republicans were still recovering from the trauma of the 1964 disaster, and even some conservatives were reluctant to pledge their support to a candidate who could so easily be nailed to Barry Goldwater's cross. They were content, on that occasion, to settle for the more pragmatic Richard Nixon. But twelve years later, it was Ronald Reagan who captured the party and the country, and who, in the process, transformed the long-suffering conservative crusade into a victory march.

* * *

Years later, Richard Viguerie, the direct-mail fund-raising wizard who became known as the postmaster general of the New Right, would recall that those were just some of the memories that permeated the conversations in the ballroom at the Plaza Hotel that Friday night in December 1980. Viguerie had taken his whole family to New York, and as he gazed across the ballroom that night, surveying the cross section of conservatives that only Buckley could bring together—the Old Guard, the New Right, the Religious Right—it occurred to him that most of the people who had gathered there had been active through the bleak years of struggle and defeat. Like all combat veterans who had survived the test of battle in a common cause, they were eager to swap war stories, to recall the days when it took courage to preach right-wing philosophy, and to pay tribute to the heroes of the past who were not there.

It is in such settings that the oxygen of righteous victory is most easily inhaled. As Viguerie recalled: "There were a lot of résumés floating through the air that night. Fully a dozen people in that room sincerely thought they were headed for cabinet posts." Some of the old warriors were still in a bellicose mood. In his speech that evening, Buckley's longtime associate William A. Rusher, the publisher of *National Review*, exhorted his colleagues "to stamp out any remaining embers of liberalism." But the prevailing spirit was one of triumph and exultation. The long war was finally over, and they had won. They had broken the sinister spell of liberalism and big government that had been cast over the Republic for so many years and had threatened to destroy it from within; at long last, they had brought the country to its senses.

No one struck the note of vindication more directly than George Will, a former disciple of Buckley at *National Review* who would go on to become a media celebrity in his own right. Billed as the dinner's main speaker, Will took it upon himself to set the historical record straight. "It took approximately sixteeen years to count the vote in the '64 election," he declared, "and Goldwater won!"

This was the message that this crowd wanted to hear, and it responded with hearty applause and a few decorous war whoops. (Nothing unseemly, to be sure; these were, after all, conservative Republicans.) But even though George Will was surrounded by friends and admirers, his presence as the main speaker was a sour reminder of the one regrettable circumstance that tarnished an otherwise perfect evening. For in truth, Will was merely a surrogate. The guest of honor and main speaker that night was supposed to have been President-elect Reagan, who had been a big hit in that role five years earlier when *National Review* observed its twentieth anniversary. It was widely known that *National Review* was Ronald Reagan's favorite magazine, each issue of which he read from cover to cover, a habitual preference he once acknowledged in a personal letter to Bill Buckley. Moreover, in all the advance press accounts of the gala, it was prominently mentioned that Reagan would be there to share in the dual rejoicing over his election victory and the journal's truimph of survival. But a few days before the dinner, Reagan telephoned Buckley to say that because of a conflict in his schedule, he couldn't make it. "Bill," he explained, "I've got this nowhere on my calendar."

The response stunned Buckley. He reminded Reagan that he had accepted the invitation six months earlier and had confirmed that in writing. He then added: "And unless I'm crazy, you told me you were going to put it on your calendar."

The President-elect conceded this was so. Now that Buckley had refreshed his memory, he did indeed recall that he had accepted the invitation back in May, but that in the interim—what with the primaries and the convention and the general election campaign—he had completely forgotten about it, and now he had this other commitment that he just couldn't break. He apologized for the mix-up and muttered something about taking steps to improve his clerical procedures. But Reagan did assure the editor of his favorite magazine that he would be with them in spirit.

Buckley was dismayed. He broke the news to his colleagues, and as they brooded on their disappointment, there passed over them unsettling questions. Was it plausible that Reagan would have forgotten that he had accepted an invitation to such a momentous event, one that so many of his longtime friends and allies were counting on him to attend? Or was the President-elect being less than candid, feigning a lapse of memory to conceal some ulterior motive for not wanting to make an appearance at the *National Review* dinner? Or—a third possibility—was this the handiwork of certain unscrupulous aides who had purposely bollixed up the schedule because they were determined, for ominous reasons of their own, to put distance between Reagan and his most loyal supporters? And if this last were the case, did the President-elect acquiesce in that decision, or was he the innocent victim of zealous deputies who were making moves that were clearly not in the best interests of Reagan or the country?

In the waning years of Ronald Reagan's presidency, similar questions would be raised in a far more disturbing context—the Iran-Contra affair—but at the time, his no-show at the Buckley celebration was dismissed as a mere social gaffe. Buckley and his friends set aside their suspicions and met the crisis of guest of honor in absentia with dignity. Although they rankled at the snub, inadvertent or otherwise, all the after-dinner speakers did their duty and sang the praises of the man who wasn't there. After all, Reagan was still their hero, the aging gunfighter who rode out of the west and outdrew all the urbane city slickers, who, for years, had sneered at him and his cause. Given that heady circumstance, they were more than willing to forgive this snafu, at least for the time being. It wasn't until much later, after many conservatives became disenchanted with certain actions and policies of the Reagan White House, that they would look back on that evening as a melancholy harbinger of the betrayals to come.

To those hard-line conservatives who formed the basis of the Reagan constituency, the election of 1980 was but one part of a right-wing tide sweeping through the Western democracies. They pointed out that Ronald Reagan's victory followed the smashing defeat Margaret Thatcher's Tories had delivered to the British Labour party just a year earlier. Conservatives also were gathering strength in Canada and West Germany, and since 1977, the right-wing coalition cobbled together by Menachem Begin had been in power in Israel. At home and abroad, Reagan conservatives saw growing evidence that their sturdy doctrine was taking hold. But even as the strong conservative winds were blowing, more complex forces were swirling through the American electorate. Examining those forces in retrospect, it is difficult to conclude that ideology was the overriding reason for the Reagan landslide. On the contrary, when one looks back on the state of America in the fall of 1980, and the turmoil that had befallen the country in the two previous decades, it may have been one of the least significant factors.

The elections of John Kennedy in 1960 and Ronald Reagan in 1980 were, in a sense, historical bookends for one of the most turbulent eras in the history of the Republic since the Civil War.

In the course of those two decades, major social revolutions altered and redefined the basic relationships between blacks and whites, men and women, and parents and children, as the national psyche was—on other fronts—subjected to an unprecedented series of shock waves: political assassinations and attempted assassinations, a bitterly divisive war that severely undermined the country's prestige, a political scandal of such magnitude that it plunged the White House into a crisis of impeachment and forced a duly elected President to resign in disgrace, and a soaring inflation that stripped America of its once-impregnable position as the world's greatest economic power. All this was prelude to a new ordeal in 1980. As Reagan campaigned that year, Americans were in the grip of yet another national humiliation: U.S. diplomats being held hostage in Iran and the American flag again being spit on. It had been a twenty-year period when many Americans of all political persuasions saw abundant reasons to ask the question, What is happening to our country, and in effect, what has happened to the presidency?

Part of Reagan's appeal was that, despite being a relative latecomer to politics, he spoke with the voice of experience. At the age of sixty-nine, he could evoke the past in a direct and personal way, with warm, even folksy recollections of a time when the presidency was not only the center of action and power, but a rock of stability. For nearly three decades, from 1933 to 1961, America had only three Presidents—Franklin Roosevelt, Harry Truman, and Dwight Eisenhower—men with a clear sense of command who governed a people with a strong sense of national identity and common purpose. This is not to suggest that the years themselves were serene and untroubled, for indeed, they were marked by tremendous crises: the Great Depression, World War II, the perils of the cold war, and the corrosive effects of McCarthyism. But no matter how grave the situation, most Americans of the thirties, forties, and fifties found refuge in the conviction that the presidency was equal to any challenge. One could despise a specific occupant (as many did despise Roosevelt and Truman), but there was still faith that an American President, whoever he might be, would always somehow lead the nation through the storm and that the Oval Office, in Truman's confident boast, was the place where the buck stopped. Roosevelt, Truman, and Eisenhower had arrived at the White House by widely differing routes, but each, it can be argued, strengthened the office. Equally important, a perception grew during those years—especially during Truman's time—that the office strengthened the man. Power may corrupt, but as Truman's stature grew in office, Americans realized there was another effect of power. It could also ennoble.

The years that followed, the twenty-year stretch from Kennedy to Reagan, provided a stark contrast. No fewer than five presidents would live in the White House in the sixties and seventies and all of them, in one way or another, were defeated by forces that erupted around them. A part of the fallout from the turbulence of those years was the impact on the institution of the presidency and the way Americans came to view it, an impact that, more often than not, served to diminish the office and the men who occupied it. In the span of years between the inaugurations of Kennedy and Reagan, the perception that the institution of the presidency could "make the man," as many felt it had made Truman, began to fade. Rather, the presidency came to be seen as an office that consumed the occupant, raising questions of whether it were a job any man or woman could handle. Certainly, the assassination of John Kennedy did not tarnish his reputation; indeed, the myth that grew out of that tragedy cast a permanent glow over the man. But that violent act forced the country to reassess the presidency and its meaning, and that reassessment was sobering: Presidents were not supermen after all, but as vulnerable as the rest of us, and although the presidency was the highest office in the land and one of enormous power, it was not an invincible sanctuary. This alone was a shattering lesson to absorb, yet it was just the first blow in a series of shocks that forced Americans to reconsider many of the assumptions that had shaped their political experience.

In 1964, when Barry Goldwater was mysteriously winning those millions of votes that went uncounted until George Will discovered them sixteen years later, most of the country was still mourning the death of Kennedy. That grief helped propel Lyndon Johnson to his landslide victory over Goldwater, and in the immediate aftermath, the assassination was seen as an aberration, a savage departure from the normal course of events in a rational and civilized society. Sadly, it was an assumption that proved mistaken. The rifle shots in Dallas would be seen as an omen of a new era of violence in America. By the mid-1960s, black militants were rioting in major cities across the country, and anti–Vietnam War demonstrations were turning ugly and confrontational. The climate of chaos and disorder reached a peak in 1968 when the country was rocked by two more political assassinations. First, Martin Luther King, Jr., was killed; the brutal slaying touched off even more violent rioting. Later that year, Kennedy's brother Robert, in the midst of his own campaign for the presidency, was slain by another gunman. Four years later, yet another Presidential campaign was halted when a would-be assassin severely wounded George Wallace. And there was more: In 1975, a new President, Gerald Ford, found himself the target of two would-be assassins, both of them women.

It is impossible to gauge, at least in the short term, what effect such a period of extended violence has on the spirit of a nation. But there seems little question that the America where Ronald Reagan campaigned in 1980 was a country where the shock level was rising, a nation so bombarded by bad news and traumatic events that, if nothing else, it had become numbed. A year after Reagan had himself been wounded by yet another disturbed loner during his first weeks in office, a Washington reporter was stunned to realize that he could not recall where he had been and what he had been doing when Reagan was shot, yet he could recall in detail where he had been when Kennedy was killed eighteen years earlier.

It was more than the long cycle of violence, however, that aroused confusion and resentment within the electorate. Americans who had come to revere the White House were finding it harder and harder to believe the man who presided there. A new expression was added to the political lexicon during Lyndon Johnson's tenure: "credibility gap." Harking back to the 1964 election, it is worth recalling that Johnson ran that year as a "peace candidate" who pledged not to send "American boys to Vietnam to do the job that Asian boys should be doing," the clear implication being that Goldwater, who was known to have a more combative attitude toward acts of Communist aggression, would be only too willing to escalate the U.S. military commitment in Vietnam. But in the spring of 1965, it was Johnson who ordered the huge buildup of forces that transformed the Vietnam conflict into an American war. Not long after that, Goldwater took perverse delight in beginning his standard speeches with the cutting remark "Remember me? I'm the son of a bitch who wanted to bomb Hanoi." By 1968, the war had so weakened the Johnson presidency that he chose not to seek reelection.

In a less obvious way, the war in Vietnam also brought down the presidency of Richard Nixon. His policy of gradual withdrawal from Vietnam inflamed antiwar critics who wanted an immediate pullout. It was from the confrontational politics of those encounters that an "us-versus-them" mentality took root in the White House; and as time went on, Nixon and his deputies grew to regard outsiders with a suspicion and hostility bordering on paranoia. In that poisonous climate, the infamous "enemies list" was drawn up, the Plumbers Unit was established to tap telephones and perform spy missions, and other clandestine groups were allowed to operate illegally. All those elements, stitched together, formed a pattern that John Mitchell later described as "the White House horrors," and out of that grew the vast and elaborate web of crimes that came to be called "Watergate." By the time Nixon and Henry Kissinger achieved their "peace with honor"—the Paris Accords of January 1973 that finally sent American troops home from Vietnam—the Watergate scandal was a dam waiting to burst, and when the deluge came in the spring of 1973, it put Richard Nixon squarely on the road to impeachment, a fate he escaped only by agreeing to resign.

The problems of Vietnam and Watergate also fell across the brief reign of Nixon's successor, Gerald Ford, the country's only unelected President. After the dour Nixon, Americans embraced Ford with good-natured affection, even forgiving him his penchant for unlikely pratfalls. (One of the brighter lines around Washington in those days was that "Vice President Rockefeller is just a banana peel away from the Oval Office.") But, although Gerald Ford was given credit for allowing the country to catch its breath after Watergate, the fact that he was becoming something of a running joke on comedy programs such as "Saturday Night Live" did add to the feeling that he was something less than an imposing figure, and in this way, too, the office was diminished. The excesses and failures in Vietnam prodded Congress into a rare mood of defiance. Determined to curb future misguided overseas activities, it passed the War Powers Act and subjected the long-sacrosanct CIA to a detailed and chilling examination of its covert actions over the preceding thirty years. Well-intentioned or not, those pressures from Capitol Hill further diminished the prestige of the chief executive, putting the President on the defensive and restricting his authority to act in times of crisis.

Far worse, in terms of Ford's personal aspirations, was his

decision to grant Nixon a "full, free and absolute" pardon, a move that, fairly or not, raised suspicions about his own complicity in the Watergate cover-up. Years later, even some of Ford's friends would say that more than anything else, it was the pardon that prevented Ford from winning a national election in his own right and becoming something more than just a caretaker President.

Ford's blunder proved a blessing to the improbable candidacy of Jimmy Carter, the peanut farmer and one-term Georgia governor who campaigned on a promise that he would "never lie to the American people." Coming after the deceits of the Johnson and Nixon years, Carter's sanctimonious pledge had a refreshing ring. More significantly in retrospect, it revealed just how reduced our expectations had become. In another time, a promise to tell the truth might have been the least that voters would have expected from a candidate seeking any office. But the image of the American presidency had become so tainted by the mid-1970s that such quaint virtues as a winning smile and a vow to tell the truth were cited as formidable assets in the successful candidacy of a rank outsider with no reputation whatsoever in national politics. As the Carter presidency later became mired in the multitude of troubles that would eventually destroy it, an exasperated Democratic congressman would remark, "The problem with Carter is that he's just what he advertised himself to be in the campaign—a person totally lacking in experience."

During the first few months in the White House, the populist image that had carried Carter through the campaign continued to strike a responsive chord. Walking "home" to his new residence after his inauguration and being photographed wearing Levi's and cardigans were clearly calculated gestures, but they drove home the point that "Jimmy" (never James Earl) Carter was determined to resist the trappings of the imperial presidency, which had come into vogue during the Nixon years. But image could carry Carter only so far, and even before he was drawn into the Iran hostage crisis, he was in trouble, in large part because of the economic miseries afflicting the country. To some extent, those problems had been inherited; the roots of the virulent inflation that ravaged the Carter years could be traced back to Lyndon Johnson's "guns *and* butter" policy; both Nixon and Ford had had to contend with fiscal disorders. But the tentative, indecisive steps Carter took to curb the inflation and record-high interest rates of the late 1970s were failures, and in other areas as well he came to be perceived as a well-meaning but ineffectual President who did not lead or inspire. Aware that his support was dwindling, he went on the offensive in the summer of 1979 with a speech bemoaning the "crisis of confidence . . . that strikes at the very heart and soul and spirit of our national will." But many of his countrymen believed that Carter himself was a chief cause of the "malaise" that he so accurately diagnosed. (Oddly enough, although it was instantly labeled "the malaise speech" and is almost always referred to as such, that word did not appear in Carter's remarks.) His presidency by then was already sinking into disrepute, and the ordeal in Iran finished him. The bold rescue mission he ordered in the spring of 1980 was viewed by many as an act of desperation that was not at all in character—a reckless move by an innately cautious man—and when the helicopters went down in the Iranian desert, Carter's hopes for reelection crashed with them.

But should Carter have been there in the first place? Or was he merely the latest link in a chain of accidental presidents extending back to the early 1960s? Take away the Kennedy assassination and there would have been no Johnson presidency. Take away the war in Vietnam and there would have been no Nixon comeback victory in 1968. Take away the Watergate scandal and there would have been no Ford in the White House. Take away the Nixon pardon (and the Watergate fallout in general) and there would have been no opportunity for a political unknown like Carter to win in 1976. Among those who agree with this assessment is Jody Powell, Carter's White House press secretary and one of the former President's closest advisers. In a conversation with an old Washington acquaintance several years after the 1980 election, Powell conceded that "if we hadn't had the pardon, we wouldn't have had Jimmy Carter." He then proceeded to add another link to the chain: "And if we hadn't had Jimmy Carter, we would never have had Ronald Reagan."

This opinion is not universally shared in Washington, but surely the problems that engulfed Carter's presidency, following all the turmoil of the preceding years, provided the perfect climate for Reagan's triumph. For rarely, if ever before, had a candidate been so right for the time. By 1980, as millions of Americans watched yet another presidency fail, a woman in New Orleans talked to a reporter about the impotence that gripped the Carter White House. "What Americans want from this election," she said, "is reassurance that it doesn't always have to be this way." As surveys would later show, Americans in 1980 were not looking for radical new (or revitalized old) ideology. They were hungry for a little good news, for someone who could reassure them that America could again be successful, and, it is no exaggeration to say, that every President did not have to be like Jimmy Carter. (One of the first opinion surveys taken after the Reagan landslide, the CBS News–New York Times Poll, showed that only 11 percent of the sample voted for Reagan because he was a conservative; 38 percent preferred him simply because he was *not* Jimmy Carter.

To an electorate that was now getting most of its information from television, no one at first glance *looked* more like a President than the handsome, genial former actor from California. If Ronald Reagan had not come along, surely Norman Rockwell would have invented him. The man whose "heroes had always been heroes" had the look of a storybook hero himself, the kind of man who could restore to the presidency the power, respect, and credibility it once had. Reagan oozed common sense and preached a simple message that challenged the oft-heard assumption that there are no "simple answers" in the modern world. "There *are* simple answers," he said, "but there are not always easy ones."

Campaigns are won by candidates who correctly sense the political mood of the moment. Back in 1960, John F. Kennedy sensed that the lethargy of the 1950s had run its course and that America was ready to respond to the spirit and vigor of a new challenge. Twenty years later, Reagan addressed a much different electorate, one that had been battered by assassinations, Vietnam, Watergate, social revolutions, severe economic woes, and, as it headed for the polling booths that November, a long year of unrelenting humiliation in Iran. To the voters of 1980, Reagan posed a rhetorical question: "Just ask yourself, are you better off now than you were four years ago?" To critics it was a blatant appeal to selfishness, but Reagan correctly understood that Americans were exhausted after two decades of national trauma. So, just as the youthful Kennedy had struck such a positive contrast to the passive, grandfatherly Dwight Eisenhower, Ronald Reagan seemed strong in contrast to Carter. As much as anything else, that contrast helped transform what was supposed to be a close contest into an electoral landslide.

Thus, in the waning months of 1980, there were differing theories about what it was, precisely, that the voters had wrought. Was the Reagan landslide a triumph of ideology, as his conservative supporters believed? Or was it a triumph of image and personality, as the polls clearly suggested? Those questions spawned others, no less fascinating. Would Reagan, too, fail the test of power and become yet another weak link in the chain of accidental Presidents? Or would he be able to restore some much needed prestige to the Oval Office? Would Reagan initiate policies that would so change the country that its future would be significantly altered? That had been the enduring achievement of Reagan's onetime hero, FDR, and during the 1980 campaign he often cited Roosevelt as the prime example of what strong and creative leadership from the White House could accomplish.

To the conservatives who celebrated the silver anniversary of *National Review*, there was no doubt what the immediate future would bring. Ronald Reagan was their man and he was going to Washington to do their bidding, to launch a revolution on the Right as sweeping and decisive in its way as the New Deal revolution had been a half century earlier. Many of them, having fought so hard for the cause, fully expected to be rewarded. Résumés at the ready, they waited the call to serve. Blessed are the true believers, for they shall inherit the White House. That was the joyous sermon that rang through the congregation that night. Yet in the weeks and months ahead, the hard-line conservatives would be among the first to become disenchanted with Reagan's presidency. In hindsight, they would have been better prepared for the disillusionment to come if they had turned their attention to another passage from Scripture—the parable of the Marriage Feast, the one that ends with the admonition: "Many are called but few are chosen."

2

The Keys to the Cabinet

"People didn't vote for this. People
didn't vote for moderation."
—Terry Dolan

Ronald Reagan's overwhelming victory hit Washington with such
force that overnight the capital became his town. In Washington
only one thing really counts, only one commodity truly matters:
power, and power comes with being a winner. Not only had Reagan established his own powerful mandate by carrying forty-four
states against an incumbent President, he had achieved a victory
strong enough to propel Republicans to a majority in the Senate.
The only Republicans on Capitol Hill who had been there when
their party last controlled either house of Congress were the two
old Arizonans, Barry Goldwater and John Rhodes. That in itself
signaled a significant change, and from the expense-account res-
taurants to the backstairs of the most remote government agency,
the new people were everywhere, talking new talk, making new
plans, and in some cases, planning to right long-festering wrongs.
Washington sensed—and in some cases feared—that this was
going to be more than the normal reshuffling that occurs when

administrations change. Jobs were at stake, and not just the normal changing of the nameplates at the big agencies and Cabinet posts.

The Reagan revolutionaries hit town like a conquering army vowing to repeal the New Deal and to clean out a bureaucracy that they claimed had been peopled for decades with liberal Democrats and moderate Republicans. These firebrands wanted *real* change and not just at the top. They wanted to reach deep into the government and replace the people they saw as faceless, left-leaning Democrats with disciples of the conservative movement, disciples who could survive a Reagan administration as so many New Dealers had survived FDR's.

From California, Reagan announced that William Casey, the old World War II spy master, would get the work under way. Casey had been Reagan's campaign manager and he would chair the transition team, a group of trusted aides who would lay the groundwork for the new administration. Casey would head the effort, but the real work of putting together the new government would be done by Edwin Meese, the portly and good-humored Californian who had served so long at Reagan's side during his days as governor. Never seen without his Adam Smith tie, Meese had passed every test for conservatives. His title would be director of the transition, and he would be the one who set the tone in those months between Reagan's election and his inauguration. "We intend to hit the ground running," he declared on the day after Reagan's landslide. As he and the others around Reagan had envisioned it, the transition period would be active and swiftly decisive. They expected to have Cabinet nominees selected within a month and the broad outlines of what the administration intended to do worked out before Christmas.

Unfortunately, Meese's good intentions soon suffered a head-on collision with Meese's work habits. Meese had never been a skilled administrator and even his friends said he owned a bottomless briefcase. Once reports went into it, they disappeared, never to be seen again. It was also said that Meese had never met a committee he didn't like, and the transition headquarters he set up in a vacant government building near the White House soon became a committee breeding ground. There were committees appointed for every conceivable task: groups to study the Pentagon budget, panels to recommend new directions in foreign policy, committees to study committees. Reagan had remained in California during the first weeks after the election, but by the time he arrived in Washington on his first postelection visit, his government in waiting had become an organization whose growth seemed boundless. The transition office phone book listed more than six hundred people, a force that took up nine floors of office space.

But that was only part of it. With hundreds of other Reagan supporters spreading through Washington on missions to study the federal bureaucracy and make recommendations on how to improve it, the people crowded into the transition offices probably accounted for less than half of those who were devoting their efforts to transition tasks. Press releases and other documents were being churned out in such volume that the photocopying bill alone soon climbed to $50,000. By early December, it was becoming obvious that the transition team had grown so large that it would require far more than the $2 million that Congress had appropriated to pay its bills.

Verne Orr, a longtime Reagan aide from California who was supervising transition spending, announced plans on December 8 for a fund-raising drive to collect at least $1 million from the President-elect's old friends and supporters. That, coupled with more than $100,000 that had been raised earlier to finance an executive search program for potential members of the new administration and about $400,000 in leftover campaign funds, would be used to pay the transition costs. What did not come to light until years later was that the funds were also used to pay healthy retainers to some of Reagan's closest aides: Meese; Mike Deaver; Helen Van Damm, Reagan's longtime personal secretary; and William Clark, a Reagan confidant who later served as one in a long line of national security advisers. No impropriety in the way the funds were dispersed was ever shown, but the $10,000 paid to Meese set off the first questions about personal financial maneuvering that would dog him throughout his years in Washington. Meese's check first bore the inscription "MOVING EXPENSES," a notation later marked out. Meese said the money was a legitimate fee for consulting services, but the marked-out notation became an embarrassment during his confirmation hearings for attorney general because he testified then that he had paid his moving expenses to Washington out of his own pocket.

The financial arrangements that Reagan's top aides had worked out were unknown, of course, in the early weeks of December 1980. At that point, commentators were instead focusing on the first great irony of the Reagan era: the man who had built a political career by railing against government waste and bloated bureaucracies had somehow—in his first action since the election—fathered Washington's fastest-growing agency, his own transition headquarters. Cartoonists were merciless. Reagan, who had preached that only a little common sense was needed to bring federal spending under control, had fallen into the same trap as his predecessor Jimmy Carter; because millions of dollars in federal funds had been available to "smooth the transition between administrations," his operatives had found a way to spend it. And, as had happened to Carter, whose transition aides had fallen into bitter battles over turf and accomplished almost nothing, it appeared that the mighty effort of the transition force was in danger of bringing forth little more than reams of publicity handouts.

Adding to the irony was the fact that Reagan had always been the candidate who insisted that the country's problems usually got worse, not better, when the federal government intervened and tried to solve them. Yet that was exactly what had happened to transitions. They had not taken on elaborate proportions until Congress began appropriating funds to pay for them, and for Reagan that was the real embarrassment: his people had shown no more skill in holding down costs than any of their recent predecessors. In the old days, which Reagan was fond of recalling, transitions were simple affairs. Woodrow Wilson, for example, spent more time after his election winding up his affairs as governor of New Jersey than planning for the presidency. He took such a light approach to the job ahead that he saw no reason to reveal the names of his Cabinet appointees until after he was sworn in.

It was not until Lyndon Johnson's election in 1964 that Congress began to appropriate federal funds to pay transition costs, and since then, costs have spiraled. Johnson billed the government $72,000 but Richard Nixon's transition costs went far beyond that. The government picked up the bill for $450,000 in expenses, and—as Reagan would later—Nixon called in chits from supporters to pay another $1 million in bills that piled up. Congress appropriated $2 million for Carter's use and with more than three hundred people on his transition payroll at various times in the months before he took office, Carter managed to spend all but $300,000 of that allotment. Reagan's aides bristled at the snickering and the charges that they had acquired Washington's runaway spending habits, but Reagan himself handled the criticism as he would handle criticism on other fronts once he became President: he simply laughed it off, and in a matter of weeks it was all but forgotten.

At the transition office, meanwhile, Meese continued his dawn-to-dark schedule of meetings with various committees as the press office issued more news releases announcing formation of new study groups and advisory panels. Yet nothing of consequence appeared to be getting done. Despite plans to have most of the Cabinet named by early December, no appointments were announced, and the transition operation seemed on the verge of paralysis. The headquarters itself had become inundated with job applications from people who wanted to join the new administration. A young volunteer named Scott Faulkner was given the job of sorting through the applications, and he soon learned how popular a person can become in Washington when he is perceived to be in a position of influence. "It was just incredible," he said one day. "Someone even gave my mother a résumé and asked her to pass it on. Another time I was handed a résumé while I was standing in a takeout line at McDonald's."

Outside the headquarters more serious problems were developing. Sending volunteers en masse into the executive departments and agencies had been the idea of William Timmons, a veteran Republican lobbyist who was serving as Meese's deputy. In theory, the teams were to file reports on each federal agency, detailing its purpose, the programs it administered, and recommendations on how the new administration could improve it. Jack Nugent, one of those working for Timmons, told *The New York Times* the aim was simply to shorten the learning curve for the incoming department heads. "In the past," he said, "they had to rely on the people already in the departments and agencies for information and there's a built-in bias there." In reality, said one Reagan staffer years later, creating the teams was no more than a public relations exercise, a way to give campaign supporters a nice title and a feeling that they had become insiders. An even more cynical view held that the real insider, Timmons, had simply found a way to make every trade association lobbyist in Washington beholden to him. Being appointed to a transition task force was invaluable to any lobbyist worth his Guccis. He could call the home office and announce that he was in so tight with the new administration that the key people were already soliciting his advice. The arrangement left the lobbyist beholden to Timmons. Thus, it was likely that if the lobbyist had a problem somewhere down the line that he couldn't solve, Timmons would be the first person he would recommend that his company bring in for consultation (at a healthy fee, of course). There was nothing illegal or underhanded here; it was just an understanding of how the game was played, and if there was one thing to be said for Timmons, he knew how the Washington game was played. The game was his business.

Whether or not Meese and the others around Reagan ever took the teams seriously, many who were appointed to them pursued their tasks with high purpose. As a result their presence soon plunged the bureaucracy into confusion. An official at the Department of Agriculture was asked by one transition team member for the department's files on strategy to toughen regulations for cured pork products. The request was denied when it was learned that the transition volunteer was a professional lobbyist for pork producers. Meese also filled many of the transition team slots with hard-line conservatives who felt they had played a major role in Reagan's election, and that, too, created problems.

After years of having their views either ignored or trivialized, many found it difficult to remain silent. One "official" held a news conference to talk about upgrading diplomatic relations with Taiwan, setting off an uproar in Peking. In Washington, an anonymous transition aide revealed a hit list of "social reformers" who he felt should be removed from key government positions, a list that included the then-ambassador to El Salvador, Robert White. In most undiplomatic language, White termed the transition team "stupid." Still another transition aide predicted a more "nationalistic" foreign policy under Reagan, which would avoid such abstractions as Carter's commitment to human rights. One source, obviously ahead of the news curve, said that once in office the new President would expand the U.S. presence in the Persian Gulf. The declarations set off a flurry of cables from foreign governments and even U.S. diplomats abroad. Who were these people making these announcements? Were they officials of the government? Would they be officials of the next government? By now, the top command at transition headquarters was beginning to realize it had created a political Tower of Babel. There were just too many people involved, and most of them had no hesitation about reading the President-elect's mind and then passing on the information to anyone who cared to listen. The teams that were supposed to be greasing the way for the new administration were instead making the government in waiting look like an exercise in blunder and folly.

Still, none of this hysteria had any lasting impact. While the transition teams in Washington were engaged in a noisy and distracting side show, the real work of forming the government was being carried out in California by a small group of men who seldom talked to the press but talked often to the next President of the United States. This obscure coterie of advisers had been influencing Ronald Reagan for years, and they were the ones who now guided him on the decisions that mattered.

In the late 1950s, Darrell Royal, the football coach at the University of Texas, was asked before a crucial game whether he intended to change strategy. "No," he replied. "We'll dance with who brung us." In the late fall of 1980, a former college football player who also spoke in parables was reserving his big dance for the people who had "brung" him into politics in the first place: the crusty group of California millionaires who made up the Reagan Kitchen Cabinet. Conservatives all, they were among those who had been mesmerized by The Speech Reagan delivered for Goldwater in 1964, and, in the aftermath of the Goldwater debacle, they latched on to him as their leader. The head of the group was Holmes P. Tuttle, an entrepreneur who had developed a string of Ford Motor Company dealerships in Los Angeles into a fortune. Almost as influential was Justin Dart, a wealthy industrialist whose wife had once appeared with Reagan in a movie called *Brother Rat*.

These millionaires were the men who first induced Reagan to run for governor in 1966. Until he had made The Speech, Reagan had evinced no interest in becoming a candidate for public office, and when he made the bold decision to put his untested political appeal on the line in a race to unseat Edmund G. (Pat) Brown, the two-term incumbent of the state's highest office, it was Tuttle and his friends who hired the political experts and technicians, the psychologists and the advertising men, and in every other respect bankrolled the campaign that turned "Citizen Reagan" into a hot political property. It was during Reagan's years as governor that they acquired the title Kitchen Cabinet and became the corps of behind-the-scenes advisers Reagan repeatedly turned to for counsel. They were not the "name" conservatives who had attended Bill Buckley's party or the professional voices of the Right so familiar to Washington. Yet these were the people the President-elect relied on when the time came to put together his official Cabinet, the various department heads who would serve under him in Washington.

The day after the election, the California millionaires met in the office of Los Angeles attorney William French Smith and began sifting through names of possible appointees. A long-standing member of the Kitchen Cabinet, Smith had been Reagan's personal lawyer since the mid-1960s. Smith headed the executive search team, and when he was nominated as the new Attorney General a few weeks later, a member of the transition team wryly observed: "He scoured the country for talent and found himself." But Smith wasn't the only person at that postelection meeting who wound up in the Reagan administration. Caspar Weinberger, who had served as Reagan's finance director in Sacramento, and William Casey, who had managed the recent presidential campaign, were also selected for high-level jobs in the new government: Weinberger as secretary of defense and Casey as director of the Central Intelligence Agency. Unlike Smith, Weinberger and Casey were no strangers to Washington; both men had served in the Nixon administration, Weinberger as secretary of health, education, and welfare and Casey as chairman of the Securities and Exchange Commission. Still another member of the Kitchen Cabinet who followed Reagan to Washington was Charles Wick, a onetime band leader who went on to become a millionaire filmmaker. He was appointed director of the U.S. Information Agency.

Back in Washington, the movement conservatives who had considered themselves in large part responsible for Reagan's victory were holding press conferences almost daily to advise Reagan on how to put together his government. But it was advice that was largely being ignored in the place where it counted most. To their sorrow, the true believers came to realize they were fast becoming the wallflowers of the "Who Brung Us Dance."

As Reagan saw it—and those around him did nothing to dissuade him of the notion—a President was like the chairman of the board of a large corporation and his Cabinet was his board of directors.

That had been his approach to state government and, as he made clear throughout those months before he took office, that was how he intended to run Washington. Reagan was comfortable with generalists and had always felt that expertise could be hired. This was the kind of Cabinet he intended to assemble: a team of generalists, people of common sense who could work as a group. The Department of Defense need not be left to the secretary of defense alone. Rather, problems could be put on the table and debated among *all* the top people. It worked every day in business. It had worked in California. It would work in Washington.

As part of this concept, Reagan and his advisers had envisioned a staff structure in which all members of the Cabinet would operate from offices within the White House, rather than from offices in the departments they were administering. The idea was quickly discarded as impractical, and the concept of Cabinet government—as it had been for a long line of Presidents who had tried it—was pretty much discarded once the new administration settled in. Still, the feeling that the best Cabinet was a Cabinet of generalists figured heavily in the way Reagan put together his team. He had no qualms, for example, about appointing a secretary of defense who had no expertise in defense or foreign policy. Nor did he resist when aides told him it would be politically expedient to hire a dentist to run the Department of Energy.

In Reagan's first postelection trip to Washington, a largely ceremonial affair during which he had paid a courtesy call on congressional leaders, House Speaker Tip O'Neill had irritated Reagan's entourage when he somewhat brusquely dismissed the President-elect's remark that he had always gotten on well with the California legislature and would try to do the same in Washington. "That was the minor leagues," O'Neill had snorted; "you're in the big leagues now." Richard Williamson, a Chicago lawyer who was working on the transition and who had accompanied Reagan on the Capitol tour, said that others in the room were stunned by O'Neill's tone of voice, but whether or not O'Neill's rejoinder had been impolite, there was truth in what he said, as the people closest to Reagan were coming to understand. Washington, they were learning, was a lot more complicated than any of them had realized. As he returned to California, Reagan and his people were beginning to discover that wanting to have someone in the government was no guarantee you could put him there.

Nothing could ever be done in isolation. Everything you did in Washington reverberated in a dozen ways and places.

Choosing a secretary of defense was a case in point. John Tower, the conservative Texas senator who later achieved such notoriety as George Bush's nominee for Defense, had campaigned discreetly for that post in 1980 and, indeed, was on Reagan's short list. When Tower was rejected by a Democratic-controlled Senate in 1989, the Bush White House claimed he was a victim of partisan politics. Yet ironically, what prevented Tower from becoming secretary of defense under Reagan was that in 1981 his *own* party had just regained control of the Senate. The Republican takeover of the Senate that year meant that Tower was in line to become chairman of the Armed Services Committee. If Reagan had named him secretary of defense, it would have meant the Armed Services chairmanship would have gone to Barry Goldwater. No problem there, but if Tower stayed in the Senate, Goldwater was in line to become chairman of the Senate Intelligence Committee. If Tower left, Goldwater's move to Armed Services would mean the Intelligence Committee chairmanship would go to the liberal Maryland Republican, Charles McC. Mathias. The idea of Mathias in charge of Intelligence dismayed Reagan's people, so Tower stayed on Capitol Hill.

Keeping Tower in the Senate also allowed Reagan to solve another sensitive problem: what to do with his old friend Cap Weinberger, whose first job choice was secretary of state, an idea that did not sit well with the other insiders. Among those who opposed naming Weinberger to that post was Bill Casey. He wanted the job for himself. Weinberger just didn't have the credentials: not enough foreign policy experience, he was gently told. That argument, however, did not seem to apply to the Pentagon slot, and thus Weinberger got Defense as a sort of consolation prize. Casey also had to settle for less. When Alexander Haig was nominated for State, Casey went home to New York in anger. But as Bob Woodward relates the story in his book *Veil*, Casey kept in touch with Meese, letting it be known that he still wanted a place in the Cabinet. Meese then offered him the CIA post, which seemed a perfect fit of man and mission, and when Casey suggested elevating the slot to Cabinet rank, Meese agreed. As Woodward told the tale, it was only then that Meese took the idea to Reagan, who responded, "Fine with me." Except for calling Casey with the offer, the President-elect had no involvement in the selection.

The maneuvering that concluded with Haig's getting the post at State made a fascinating tale. We were told by one Cabinet officer as well as Reagan's longtime aide, Mike Deaver, that Reagan decided early on he wanted George Shultz for the job. But there was a mix-up in signals and when Reagan called Shultz and invited him to join the Cabinet, Shultz thought he was being offered the Treasury secretary's post and politely declined. "I was there," Deaver told us. "The President walked back in the room and said, 'Well, you can scratch Shultz off the list.' " Other people who had varying access to Reagan over the years have said the situation was more complicated than that and hold to the belief that it was Richard Nixon who torpedoed Shultz. To be sure, Shultz and Nixon were not friends. Even though the tactiturn Shultz had served Nixon well in three different cabinet posts, including Treasury, the two never really got on and Nixon was quoted at one point as referring to Shultz as a "candy ass." There had also been animosity toward Shultz among several of the members of the Kitchen Cabinet because he had taken very little part in the campaign until its final stages. Shultz himself has never tried to clear up the mystery of whether or not he thought Reagan was offering him a post at Treasury, or in fact whether Reagan called him. But at the time speculation that he *might* be named secretary of state was rampant, Shultz simply told us, "I have not been offered the job."

What there seems no disagreement about is that Richard Nixon wanted Alexander Haig, his old White House chief of staff, to become secretary of state and lobbied hard on Haig's behalf. As it turned out, Reagan was receptive to the idea. Haig had impressed Reagan in several meetings they had before the election. Nor were his chances hurt when Nancy Reagan was overheard to remark that Haig had "star quality." But in an odd twist, it was a Democrat, Robert Byrd, the outgoing majority leader of the Senate, who sewed up the nomination for Haig. With Republicans taking control of the Senate in January, Byrd wanted Republicans to know that he did not intend to be pushed around. When speculation began to float that Haig would probably get the post at State, Byrd promised a rough time for Nixon's old comrade when the Senate held confirmation hearings. Certainly, he said, Democrats intended to explore in detail what Haig's role had been at the Nixon White House. To Reagan, that was like waving a red flag at a bull. Seeing it as the first real test of his leadership, he flashed the word to Howard Baker, the Republican who was about to replace Byrd as majority leader, that he intended to nominate Haig—and there would be no backing off.

What was so striking about the process of selecting Cabinet members was the way that Reagan himself seemed to fade in and out of the deliberations. In cases such as the one involving State, he seemed to take an active interest in the discussions, conferring with various advisers and weighing choices. In other cases such as deciding who would fill the CIA post, he seemed just as happy to let others make the choice. Another example of Reagan's passivity was the way Donald Regan, the chairman of Merrill Lynch, came to be appointed secretary of the treasury.

His team of advisers first considered and then (on the strong recommendation of former President Ford) rejected William Simon for that post. Then Walter Wriston, the New York banker, was thought to have the inside track. But Wriston did not wish to make the financial disclosures required for the job. After that, Reagan's interest in who got the job seemed to wane. Then Meese had lunch one day with Regan, came away impressed, and proposed him for the job. Although Reagan hardly knew him, he acquiesced to the move. Later, when conservatives in the Senate raised objections because they noted that Regan had sometimes made financial contributions to Democratic as well as Republican candidates, Reagan expressed surprise that no one had told him, but said, in effect, that the deed had been done, the job had already been offered to Regan, and it was too late to take it back.

Several of the other Cabinet posts were awarded with similar casualness. When the advisers split over who ought to run Agriculture, Kansas senator Bob Dole went to the President with a map and pointed out that no one from the Midwest had been asked to join the Cabinet. Reagan grinned, and the job went to Illinois farmer John Block, who had also been serving as director of that state's Agriculture Department. The Energy post was expected to go to Michael Halabouty, a Houston oil man, but he, like Wriston, had no wish to make the extensive financial disclosures that would be necessary to join the government. John Connally was also offered the job, but that had been more a gesture of courtesy since all concerned knew Connally had no interest in any posts other than State and Defense. Then Strom Thurmond, the veteran senator from South Carolina, chimed in. Although he didn't go so far as to display a map of the Old Confederacy to make his point, Thurmond let Reagan know that he and other Southerners were annoyed because no one had yet been selected from *their* region. Reagan began looking around for someone who could put Thurmond in a better humor. From his friend Paul Laxalt, the senator from Nevada, came the suggestion of naming James Edwards, the former governor of Thurmond's home state. Edwards agreed and was soon announced as Reagan's choice to head the Department of Energy. Thurmond was pleased, but it was a choice that some of Reagan's most loyal admirers found surprising because Edwards was a dentist by trade and seemed to have no background at all in energy, except for being a champion of nuclear power during his term as governor. Reagan's friends shrugged it off by saying Reagan was planning to do away with the Department of Energy anyway. The frivolity of that appointment was grasped by Edwards himself, who remarked that people who drilled for cavities did have something in common with people who drilled for oil. Education, the other department that Reagan was determined to shut down, went to a professional educator, Terrel H. Bell, the last Cabinet member picked. Reagan, of couse, was unable to eliminate either department, but he paid little attention to Bell's bailiwick and in his memoirs, Bell said it was appropriate that he had been the last member of the Cabinet to be selected because "in this administration, the Department of Education and its concerns were indeed to be last."

A few Cabinet appointments were strictly political payoffs, rewards dispensed in return for past favors. Health and Human Services went to Richard Schweiker, the moderate Pennsylvania senator who had agreed to serve as Reagan's running mate in Reagan's abortive run against President Gerald Ford in 1976, and Transportation was bestowed on Drew Lewis, who had played a key role in the 1980 campaign. Malcolm Baldrige was given Commerce mainly because he was a longtime friend of Vice-President-elect Bush. Raymond Donovan, who would spend most of his years in government being investigated for financial dealings that took place before he came to Washington, was awarded the labor secretary's post mainly because he had been an active fund-raiser.

Determined to have at least one woman and one black in the

top command, Reagan signed on Samuel Pierce to head the Department of Housing and Urban Development and Georgetown professor Jeane Kirkpatrick to be ambassador to the United Nations, a post upgraded to Cabinet rank during Dr. Kirkpatrick's term and immediately downgraded once a male successor was named to replace her. Pierce was a quiet New Yorker whose government career—at least what the public knew of it—seemed to peak with his appointment. He was never one to seek the limelight, and the limelight cooperated fully. Pierce spent the entire two terms of the Reagan presidency largely unknown even within the administration, a fact underscored when the President spotted him once at a Rose Garden ceremony and, mistaking Pierce for a visitor, greeted him as "Mr. Mayor."

James Watt, the most ideological member of the Cabinet, got his job through a political feud that had been left unresolved. It had been decided early on by the President-elect that Senator Laxalt, his close friend and the man he was counting on to serve as his personal envoy to Capitol Hill, would choose the secretary of the interior. To westerners, Interior is a key post because the federal government holds deeds to much of the land in western states. Laxalt (and Reagan as well) wanted Wyoming senator Clifford Hansen for the job, but Hansen didn't want it for several reasons, not the least of which was that it probably meant putting his substantial interests in trust. That seemed to clear the way for the appointment of another westerner, the eminently qualified John Rhodes of Arizona, the longtime Republican leader in the House, who was finally stepping down from his congressional post. Rhodes wanted the Interior job, and because he was one of the most popular figures in Washington, he would have been a powerful voice for Western interests. But there was one problem. He was one of the few people in Washington who did not get along with the equally popular Laxalt, and Interior was Laxalt's call. So it was that Laxalt then turned to Watt, who had built a law practice fighting environmental advocates and who would prove to be one of the major embarrassments of Reagan's first term.

Watt was a staunch conservative and his appointment pleased the true believers, who otherwise did not have much to cheer about. Another favorite of the conservative movement, Richard Allen, was given the post of national security adviser, but Reagan had already indicated that he planned to reduce that office significantly in both scope and prestige. Beyond that, the right-wing ideologues had to settle for a few ambassadorships and midlevel positions throughout the bureaucracy. Almost all the big jobs—the key Cabinet posts—went to moderates, the kind of team that would have been assembled by any mainstream Republican. The hard-line conservatives were quick to grasp what had happened and they responded with anger and dismay. "People didn't vote for this," said Terry Dolan, the head of one of Washington's most conservative lobby groups. "People didn't vote for moderation." Dolan and *his* people had voted for sweeping change, nothing less than a revolution in ideology, and as they saw it, Reagan was reneging on the promise they thought he had made to them.

Other, less impassioned observers were struck by the casual, almost haphazard way that some of the Cabinet members had been selected. The critical post of secretary of state presumably had gone to Al Haig largely because of a breakdown in communication between Reagan and his first choice, George Shultz. Don Regan landed his job at Treasury through conversations with Ed Meese. Other slots, like Agriculture and Energy, were filled rather impulsively in an effort to appease the regional chauvinisms of certain influential senators. How did these and other appointments mesh with the views and desires of the President-elect? Where was Reagan himself in all of this?

Midway through the transition, David Broder, the dean of political journalists in Washington, began getting telephone calls from people in Reagan's own camp who were worried about the pattern of decision making that seemed to be developing. The problem, as some of Reagan's backers saw it, was that the President-elect's extraordinarily detached role in the proceedings was making him look bad—so bad, in their view, that they were urging reporters to write stories about it in the hope that Reagan would mend his ways. Three days before Christmas, Broder began his column on the Op-Ed page of *The Washington Post* by saying that the central question of the transition was "to what extent is Ronald Reagan running the show and to what extent are others preparing to govern in his name?" It was a question that accurately reflected the concerns that one heard over and over in Washington in the closing days of 1980, and it was a question that would be asked many times during Reagan's years in the White House.

Aside from the selection process, some of the Cabinet choices themselves provoked yet another set of questions as Washington insiders studied the new team in an effort to get an early fix on how the Reagan administration would define itself. Would the mercurial Haig, a disciple of Henry Kissinger, be allowed to dictate foreign policy as Kissinger himself had when he served as secretary of state under Nixon and Ford? Or would Haig have to contend with challenges to his authority from high-level aides in the White House, as had been the fate of William Rogers during the early Nixon years and Cyrus Vance under Carter? Why had the Defense portfolio been entrusted to Caspar Weinberger? Not only did he lack experience in that field, but his reputation when he worked for Reagan in Sacramento and later for Nixon in Washington had been that of a vigorous slasher of budgets (he was called "Cap the Knife" in those days), which hardly made him a logical choice to carry out Reagan's promise to beef up the nation's military arsenal. What qualifications did William French Smith have for the office of attorney general, aside from his membership in the Kitchen Cabinet and his years of faithful service as Reagan's personal lawyer? Would Don Regan, the pragmatic man from Wall Street, be given the job of overseeing Reagan's bold new economic program, a doctrine that would soon be labeled "Reaganomics"? Or would that burden fall to youthful David Stockman, the "supply-side" theorist who had been picked to head the Office of Management and Budget? And who, among the remaining Cabinet officers, would emerge to chart Reagan's domestic policy? Or, inasmuch as Reagan had vowed to make drastic cuts in domestic spending and dismantle many of the social programs he had inherited, would there even be a domestic policy—that is, the kind of creative action that Washington had come to expect from previous administrations?

Yet, even as they pondered these and other questions, observers were aware that the principal players in any administration were found not only in the Cabinet but among the advisers who served inside the White House. Because they often had a closer personal relationship with the President and worked directly with him on a day-to-day basis, they were in a position to rival even the most powerful Cabinet officers in deciding the agenda, establishing the prerogatives, and setting the course of executive action. And the man who seemed destined to take on the role of chief adviser in the Reagan White House was Ed Meese.

Meese had his fingerprints all over the numerous moves of the transition, and throughout that interval, he was the one visible link between the quiet deliberations of the Kitchen Cabinet in California and the frantic activity of those under his command in Washington. Moreover, people who were familiar with Reagan's career as governor of California knew that during most of the years in Sacramento, Meese had been his chief deputy, the man who had coordinated policy across a broad range of issues; and he would soon be setting up a similar power base in the White House. It's true that Meese was not being given the post he had expected and wanted—chief of staff. In a surprise move, that position went to an outsider, James Baker, who had managed George Bush's campaign in the early Republican primaries; in fact, that was yet another appointment that rankled the conservatives and deepened their sense of betrayal. But Meese was going into the White House as counselor to the President, a title that was being upgraded to cabinet rank, and he himself clearly implied that of all the top aides who would gather around the Oval Office, he would be the one with the most influence. If, in David Broder's phrase, others were preparing to govern in Reagan's name, the most significant "other" appeared to be Meese. Thus, as Washington insiders prepared for the start of the Reagan presidency, they focused much of their curiosity on the portly aide with the jowly face who had never met a committee he didn't like.

Who was Ed Meese? Where did he come from and how did he hook up with Ronald Reagan in the first place? The answers to these questions were to be found in California, but to pick up the scent at the start of the trail, one did not look to Los Angeles, which was Reagan's home base, or even to Sacramento, where the two men had worked so closely together. To understand Ed Meese, one's gaze had to shift a few miles southwest of the state capital to that fertile region where the city of San Francisco and its environs form a dynamic urban cluster known as the Bay Area.

3

California Dreamin'

"My God, what do we do now?"
—Lyn Nofziger

Mario Savio is a name that blazed briefly across the scorched political landscape of the 1960s, and then passed into obscurity. As a part-time student at the University of California, Savio was the leader of the Free Speech Movement that disrupted campus life at Berkeley in the fall of 1964. Compared to the far more violent demonstrations that exploded on American campuses in the years that followed, the Free Speech Movement was a fairly tame and even frivolous diversion. Its claim to distinction is that it was the Sarajevo of those disorders, the trigger that set off the chain reaction of student protests that persisted, with mounting fury, through the rest of the decade and into the early 1970s. Yet instead of rejoicing over his modest reputation as a pioneer, Savio could boast of a more lasting contribution to political history. For in his role as organizer of the Berkeley Free Speech Movement, Mario Savio was the catalyst, the inadvertent force, that brought Edwin Meese III into Ronald Reagan's line of vision.

At the time, Meese was a deputy district attorney in Alameda

County and the man who orchestrated the law-enforcement measures that brought the student demonstrators to heel. By training
and inclination he was well equipped for the challenge. Beyond
that, he was no stranger to the area; indeed, if anyone could claim
Alameda County as native soil, it was Ed Meese.

Berkeley and the city of Oakland share the territory of Alameda County just across the bay from the sparkle and splendor
of San Francisco, and San Francisco has always looked on Berkeley
with approval. Its strong academic reputation and liberal tradition
made the university a welcome companion, a neighbor worthy of
being situated so close to Baghdad-by-the-Bay. But Oakland—
well, Oakland was another story. Gertrude Stein spoke for many
of San Francisco's self-styled sophisticates when she dismissed
blue-collar Oakland with the remark, "There is no there there."
As far as Edwin Meese III was concerned, there not only was a
there there, but Oakland had been home to his family for four
generations. He was the rarest of native birds: a Californian whose
paternal forebears had never lived anywhere else in America.

His great-grandfather had emigrated from Germany in 1849.
Shortly after he arrived in the United States, he joined a wagon
train headed west, part of that high-spirited and acquisitive horde,
the Gold Rush. He failed to find gold but chose to settle in the
Bay Area. His son, Meese's grandfather, commenced the family
tradition of public service as an Oakland councilman and city
treasurer. And his son, Edwin Meese, Jr., became even more of
a community fixture, serving for twenty-five years as Alameda
County treasurer and tax collector. He also lived long enough to
see his eldest son become a high-ranking official in Ronald Reagan's Washington, first as White House counselor and then as
U.S. attorney general. When Washington reporters visited him in
Oakland, Meese's father, then in his eighties, told them stories of
his childhood in turn-of-the-century California, especially his recollection of the 1906 San Francisco earthquake, as seen through
the eyes of a ten-year-old boy.

"The sky across the bay glowed orange from the fire after
the earthquake struck," he told Martin Schram of *The Washington
Post*.

> San Francisco was ordered closed to outsiders, but my father
> had gotten a pass from the governor to allow him to enter
> and he took me with him. We went over by boat, and as soon

as we landed we went up to Telegraph Hill. We stood there and looked down on what was left of San Francisco. The city was still smoldering and we just stood there and looked at it in silence. That was the first time I ever saw my father with tears in his eyes.

So Ed Meese's roots were firmly embedded in Alameda County. He was raised in the East Bay Hills section of Oakland, a middle-class enclave that was a comfortable economic distance from the black ghettos and blue-collar neighborhoods that formed the dominant ethos of the city. It was a placid *Saturday Evening Post* environment where dogs barked harmlessly at the postman and kids left their bikes outside all night. Absorbing the values of that community and those of his strict Lutheran parents, Meese joined the Boy Scouts and in the early days of World War II, when he was just ten years old, he and his younger brothers put together a mimeographed neighborhood newspaper, "The Weekly Herald," which they sold for a dollar a year. With the profits, they bought a war bond. The four brothers also were obliged to recite the Pledge of Allegiance and say their prayers every night before going to bed.

Meese was a good enough student to win a scholarship to Yale, and after graduating, he worked briefly in an iron foundry before enrolling in law school at Berkeley. As a law student, he became fascinated with police and law-enforcement procedure, developing an interest that would become a lifelong passion. During his years as a deputy district attorney, he liked to spend his off-duty hours riding the city streets at night in a patrol car, often stopping to talk with the cops on the beat. Later, when he was working for Governor Reagan in Sacramento, a favorite form of relaxation at home was listening to the incessant flow of messages on the police radio. Still later, when he had achieved national power in Washington, Meese loved to show off his collection of pigs: figurines and statuettes he kept on display in his den as a symbolic tribute to the cops who were routinely denounced as "pigs" in the street protests of the 1960s. Nor was this merely an impersonal gesture, for in his corner of America, where the rebellious flames of the 1960s burned more fiercely than anywhere else, the militant radicals in Oakland and Berkeley regarded Ed Meese as a pig of the first rank, a head hog.

He obtained his law degree in 1958 and quickly got a job in

the DA's office, but his first six years there were uneventful. While some on the district attorney's staff made swift reputations as trial lawyers, Meese was known as a plodder who concentrated his efforts on administrative duties and the mechanics of law enforcement, pedestrian chores that most of his colleagues tried to avoid. The book on Meese in those days pegged him as steady and reliable, a solid member of the team. But nothing more.

The initial target of the Free Speech Movement at Berkeley was a new rule that university authorities had put into effect in the early fall of 1964. Until then, students had been allowed to hold political rallies outside the Sather Gate entrance to the campus, but those activities were now prohibited. In reaction, Mario Savio launched the Free Speech Movement, and by the end of November the protest had become a boil ready to burst. The climax came on December 3, when more than seven hundred students seized control of the administration building, Sproul Hall, and vowed not to leave until their demands were met. Hundreds of police officers were dispatched to the campus, and the man who took charge of the effort to restore order was Assistant District Attorney Edwin Meese III. Years later, he recalled the moment when Governor Brown telephoned and asked for advice on how to resolve the crisis. "I told him that the people in the building should be arrested and taken out of there. I told him that if they were allowed to stay, there would be another mob scene, even bigger, the next day."

Pat Brown was reluctant to take such drastic action. Many of the student demonstrators were the sons and daughters of prominent California citizens who were not only voters but influential voices in their communities. Meese, however, did not waver in his conviction that the only sure way to restore law and order was to act swiftly and decisively. So Brown acquiesced and, under Meese's supervision, the police were sent in to clear the building. A total of 773 young men and women were taken into custody on charges of trespassing and resisting arrest.

For Brown it was a setback on two fronts. Liberals formed the core of his constituency, and many of them accused the governor of overreacting to what, in their view, was essentially a campus dispute. At the same time, he was attacked by conservatives for his delayed reaction to the crisis. As far as they were concerned, the hero of the day was Ed Meese, who was praised for his militancy and for his influence in persuading the hand-wringing governor to implement his authority.

The mass arrests at Sproul Hall broke the Free Speech Movement, but viewed in the larger context of that decade of protest and revolution, this was just the beginning. As Bob Dylan warned, you didn't need a weatherman to know which way the wind was blowing, and the center of the storm was Alameda County and the Bay Area in general. By the mid-sixties, the civil rights movement had turned confrontational, culminating in the rhetorical excesses of the Black Panthers, who set up their headquarters in Oakland. The rock-and-drug culture transformed thousands of young Americans, many of whom converged on the Haight-Ashbury district of San Francisco and made that urban enclave the capital of hippiedom. And although antiwar demonstrations were held on college campuses across the country, Berkeley was perceived as the mecca of the movement, the unrivaled seat of radical protest.

For Meese, too, it was just the beginning. His moment in the public eye had clearly stamped him as a law-and-order man, a defender of the status quo, and over the next two years he proceeded to build on that reputation with one crackdown after another. In the process, he refined the law-enforcement technique of dealing with unruly demonstrations. When he was confronted with the first wave of anti–Vietnam War protests in 1965 and 1966—disruptive gatherings that featured such rituals as the burning of draft cards—he was able, through quick, on-the-scene intelligence, to isolate the ringleaders and arrest them, with a demoralizing effect on their followers. It was his version of the old Mexican proverb, "Cut off the head and the body dies." Through it all, whether the target was black militants or SDS zealots, pot smokers or draft-card burners, Meese insisted that there was nothing personal in his determination to arrest and prosecute the transgressors; as a law officer responsible to the people of Alameda County, he was merely doing his duty. But there was more to it than that.

As they were to many Americans, the radicals were an affront to everything Ed Meese had been taught to believe. The man who grew up in a white, middle-class neighborhood and later cultivated a romantic affinity with the cop on the beat was not about to tolerate gun-toting Black Panthers who called the police pigs and threatened, in the most violent language, all out war against the "honkie" power structure. The devout Lutheran who said grace before meals and prayers before going to bed was deeply offended by hippies who lived in communes, practiced free love, and, in a variety of other ways, scorned traditional family values. And most of all, the former Boy Scout who sold newspapers to buy a war bond and later interrupted his studies at law school to serve two years in the army as an intelligence officer (and twenty more in the active reserve), was outraged by antiwar protesters who openly defied the country's military commitment to Vietnam and even went so far as to burn American flags. Years later, in looking back on all that from his post in the Reagan White House, Meese would contend in a tone of hard, quiet anger, "Those demonstrations prolonged the war and cost a lot of American lives."

Meese was not alone in the dismay he felt during those divisive years. Yet he also knew that many adult Americans were inclined to indulge and even support the angry young protestors who clamored for black power and an end to the war in Vietnam. This was especially true in San Francisco, a center of political liberalism and social tolerance. From Meese's point of view, San Francisco, that smug and trendy city that had always looked down its nose on Oakland, was infested with amoral dilettantes. It was this group and people like them that one critic would characterize as "radical chic." But to Meese they were something else: people who should be held as objects of contempt. He sensed that the nation was starting to shift away from permissiveness, that a healthy backlash was beginning to surface. Another Californian shared that vision.

Ronald Reagan was also counting on that anticipated backlash to carry him to victory in his first run for public office. In his 1966 campaign against Pat Brown, he promised to "clean up the mess at Berkeley," and he was referring not only to the students who had demonstrated against the war. Reagan denounced the growing sexual revolution, painting a lurid picture of campus life that contained "orgies so vile I cannot describe them to you." There are other factors that could be cited to explain Reagan's stunning and decisive triumph that year, notably an inept campaign by Brown, who became the first in a long line of political opponents who would underestimate and dismiss Reagan, as a lightweight, a has-been actor. But hostile reaction to student protest and other disorders was on the rise in California, and like a gifted surfer, Reagan caught the wave just as it was starting to crest.

Ed Meese had come to the attention of Reagan and his people in 1964 when he quashed the Free Speech Movement in the show-down at Sproul Hall, and since then, they had followed his law-enforcement tactics with approval. Also working in Meese's favor was the fact that he was known to legislators in Sacramento, where, in recent years, he had lobbied on behalf of the state district attorney's association. Thus, when the time came to recruit a team to help Reagan govern the nation's most populous state, Meese's name was on the list and he was offered a job as the governor's legal affairs secretary. It was a modest post, one with a narrow range of responsibilities, but after eight years as deputy DA in Alameda County, Meese was ready for a change. So at the age of thirty-five, Edwin Meese III moved to Sacramento and went to work for Ronald Reagan.

Once in Sacramento, Meese rose quickly in rank and prominence among Reagan's staff, a rise that was a direct result of the unusual way that Reagan himself had come to the governor's mansion. The new governor had no entourage of veteran aides and han-gers-on when he arrived in Sacramento. Thus, Meese soon dis-covered that as a neophyte he would not necessarily be in competition with aides who had served Reagan for years. The reason was simple: Reagan had started at the top. The highest office in the state was the first public office he ever sought, and even then he had done so not out of ambition, but because others had suggested it and because his career as an actor had been in decline. Until he made The Speech for Goldwater in 1964, and received an overwhelmingly positive public reaction, Reagan had never given serious thought to elected office. Once he did enter politics, his public relations team came up with the title "citizen-politician" to describe him, a description that was entirely accurate. Reagan had been active of course in the politics of running the Screen Actors Guild during the years when he was its president, but he had no experience in party politics, no political appara-tus, and no seasoned team of aides schooled in the intricacies of state government and politics. Lyn Nofziger, a former Copley News Service political reporter who had signed on as campaign press secretary, was one of the few operatives who followed

Reagan to Sacramento after the election. Years later, he still spoke with some wonder of those days when they were all just babes in the redwoods.

"Unlike other political personalities, Ronald Reagan materialized out of thin air with no political background, no political cronies, and no political machine," Nofziger said. "He didn't even run his own campaign. His campaign was run by hired people who then walked away and left it. Therefore, when he was elected, the big question was 'My God, what do we do now?' "

Nofziger's remark has been quoted often over the years, but like so many things connected with Reagan it was right only as far as it went. Reagan had no political cronies and no political apparatus in the conventional sense, and as for putting together a staff, he started from ground zero. But there was more to it than that. Reagan did have strong-willed, influential friends. The wealthy men who had convinced him to run had very clear ideas about politics. To be sure, the Justin Darts and the Holmes Tuttles of the world, the men who had convinced Reagan to make the race, had no interest in becoming bogged down in the tedium of running state government, but with a certainty that comes often to the very rich, they knew what needed to be done, knew Reagan shared their views, and had no doubt he was up to the task. Once they had him elected, they were confident that he would be able to do what any good executive would do when confronted with a task: hire someone to take care of it. To men like Dart, Tuttle, and the others, the important point was to make sure the right man was doing the hiring and they had taken care of that.

Ronald Reagan, after all, was one of them. That is a point that is often overlooked or misunderstood in the legend that has grown up about how Reagan came to politics. The Speech for Goldwater had brought Reagan a much wider audience and had made him something of a figure in national politics, but for Tuttle and his friends, Reagan was no overnight discovery. Reagan's speech for Goldwater had been only a minor rewrite of one outlining conservative principles that Reagan had been giving for years on the banquet circuit, and Tuttle had heard it many times. Once it had been televised nationally, the outpouring of support only confirmed what Tuttle already knew: that Ronald Reagan was a natural politician who could become the new leader of the conservative movement, not just in California but across the nation. After the speech, Tuttle said friends told him, Reagan's message was what people wanted to hear, "while Goldwater had been going on the defensive."

Certainly that was what Tuttle had wanted to hear. He had known Reagan since the days when he was building up his string of auto dealerships and had sold him a new Ford, back in 1946. Their paths had crossed often in the 1960s when Reagan was serving as a spokesman for General Electric. Tuttle has told interviewers over the years that it was during that period that Reagan really came to understand and appreciate the free-enterprise system, and that, conversely, businessmen came to understand how well Reagan could articulate their point of view.

As for Dart, who had built a foundering Rexall Drug chain into a company with multibillion-dollar sales, he had known Reagan since his days as an actors' union leader when Reagan was still a Democrat. Like Tuttle, he had no doubts about Reagan's political philosophy or his views on business. He had seen how growing corruption and the threat of Communist influence had caused Reagan to become disenchanted with the labor movement he had once so admired. The Ronnie Reagan whom Dart had come to know had also learned the hard way about high taxes during his high-income days at the movie studios. They didn't have to worry about where he would come down on the issues, certainly not on issues that really mattered: keeping down taxes, standing guard against communism, and, most important, doing whatever needed to be done to create a good climate for business.

Dart and Tuttle would be the Kitchen Cabinet members most often quoted over the years, but the group was rounded out by others of varying degrees of influence. They included Jack Wrather, a hotel and entertainment magnate; Henry Salvatori, an oilman; William French Smith; and about a dozen others. Individualists all, they were remarkably alike in many ways: colorful, rich men who had possessed personal wealth long enough to be accustomed to hiring people when there was work to be done and discharging them when the work was completed. Ronald Reagan was their man; they had no worry that he would have any trouble running the government of California. And just in case, they would always be available to offer advice and counsel.

It was the perfect environment to nurture the career of a tough, hardworking man like Ed Meese. He impressed the people who counted most around Reagan by simply doing his work and treating Reagan with respect while some of the other staffers set about expanding their own authority. Nofziger, for example, took the lofty title of "communications director" and recruited a *Los Angeles Times* reporter, Paul Beck, to serve under him as press secretary. But even though Nofziger was an important staff member in the first few months in Sacramento, he soon lost much of his influence, in large part because he aroused the displeasure of the governor's wife. Nancy Reagan didn't like Nofziger's style, she didn't like his looks, and, most of all, she didn't like the way Nofziger sometimes made her beloved Ronnie the butt of caustic barbs. A heavyset man who often seemed to have slept in his clothes and kept a cigar clenched in his teeth, Nofziger was not the kind of man that image-conscious Mrs. Reagan envisioned as her husband's spokesman.

Nofziger remained in the Reagan camp through the tentative campaign for the Republican presidential nomination in 1968 and then moved to a low-level post in the Nixon White House, where, among other things, he helped John Dean compile the "enemies list." In spite of that blemish on his record and his defects in style and grooming, Nofziger was allowed to return to the Reagan team at various intevals through the 1970s. But he never regained the position of influence he had enjoyed during the early years in California. After another stint as press secretary in the closing months of the 1980 campaign, he served for a year in the White House as Reagan's political director, then left the job to start up his own Washington lobbying firm, a move that eventually swept him into the maelstrom of the Wedtech scandal. In 1987, Nofziger took this place alongside other longtime Reagan associates who fell under the shadow of indictment; he was accused and later convicted of lobbying practices that violated the federal conflict-of-interest laws.

Another early adviser who bungled his chance to become an enduring member of Reagan's inner circle was Philip Battaglia, an energetic and precocious lawyer from Pasadena. Although he was only thirty-one at the time and had no previous experience in politics (aside from serving as student body president at the University of Southern California), Battaglia was given the assignment of managing the gubernatorial campaign. Both Reagan and Tuttle were dazzled by the young man's quick intelligence and air of aggressive self-assurance. For his part, Battaglia was so confident of his value to Reagan that, in the final weeks of the campaign, he invariably positioned himself at the candidate's side and often handed him notes on three-by-five cards. Then, with the conditioned reflex of a veteran actor who long had been accustomed to reading lines written for him by others, Reagan would dutifully repeat, almost verbatim, the comments that had been prepared for him, thereby revealing to those who witnessed these scenes how much he relied on the judgment and advice of his young aide. It was an impressive display of Battaglia's influence, and he carried the habit over into the transition period, when, on one occasion, he handed Reagan a note reminding him to announce Battaglia's appointment as executive secretary, a post comparable to chief of staff and one that would make him the second most powerful figure in the new administration. Reagan promptly made the announcement, proclaiming that "Phil is my strong right arm."

But Battaglia soon began to overplay his hand. He had insinuated himself into the top echelon by declaring his absolute loyalty to Reagan and paying obsequious court to the wealthy patrons who made up the Kitchen Cabinet. Yet others who had to deal with him were put off by his arrogance and freewheeling style, and many came to regard Battaglia as a slick and devious operator who was mainly driven by personal ambition. Hard-line conservatives, in particular, became suspicious of his avowed commitment to the governor's goals and philosophy. "Ronald Reagan was the man who was going to save the world," said one of them to Reagan biographer Lou Cannon, who, at the time, was a California reporter covering the Sacramento beat.

He was the man who was going to get rid of Lyndon Johnson, stop the war in Vietnam and do the things that Barry Goldwater wanted to do but wasn't smart enough to figure out how. And he was the only guy in the United States who could go all the way to the presidency to get that done . . . and lo and behold, the Holy Grail was in the custody of a power-hungry kid.

The more enemies Battaglia made, the more vulnerable he became. His position was also undermined by the blunders and confusion that characterized those first few months in Sacramento as the new team floundered in its efforts to get a grip on the levers of government. Some of the decisions and appointments he made touched off controversies of one kind or another, and helped to set him up as an inviting target. By the late summer of 1967, the "strong right arm" had clearly become a liability, and by then even Reagan realized that Battaglia would have to be dismissed.

The Holy Grail then passed into the custody of William P. Clark, another young lawyer, who had been Reagan's campaign manager for Ventura County. After the election, he was appointed cabinet secretary, and when Battaglia was ousted, he moved up to the position of executive secretary. Bill Clark, who would go on to serve in several high-ranking positions in Ronald Reagan's Washington, provided a welcome contrast to Battaglia's glib and mercurial manner. A rather shy and introspective man, he imposed a beneficial order and stability on the governor's office.

One of his innovations, which he initiated while he was still cabinet secretary, was the "minimemo" prepared for Reagan's perusal. Aware that the governor's natural approach to issues was instinctive and anecdotal and that he had neither the patience nor the inclination to pore through copious written material, Clark instructed all the department heads to boil their policy proposals down to one-page minimemos, each consisting of no more than four paragraphs: one for the statement of the problem, the second for the facts, the third for commentary, and the fourth for a suggested course of action. The minimemos provoked snickers among members of the press and certain legislators, but Clark stoutly defended them. Years later, after he had followed Reagan to Washington, Clark recalled with some relish the negative reaction to his order. But Clark's answer always was that a department head didn't understand his problem if he couldn't boil it down to a page.

In the meantime, Meese was rising quickly. As legal affairs secretary, he worked out of a tiny office and was expected to focus attention on the narrow issues of clemency and extradition. One of the reasons he had been appointed was that he was known to be a strong advocate of the death penalty, and in an early test of that principle he urged the governor to resist public pressure to order a stay in the execution of a man named Aaron Mitchell who had been convicted of killing a policeman. Reagan took the advice and later told Meese how much he appreciated the way he had faced down some other advisers who had recommended leniency. As time went on, Meese gradually expanded his base into a law-enforcement department that included all aspects of criminal justice policy. Moreover, as the radical protests of the sixties continued to escalate, Meese persisted in the crusade that first brought him to Reagan's attention. He became the point man in the governor's relentless law-and-order campaign against student disorders and other acts of civil disobedience, often rushing to the scene of a demonstration to take personal charge of the crackdown, as he had in 1964 at Berkeley. Such decisive displays of leadership steadily strengthened the bond between Meese and Reagan; and in 1969 when Bill Clark was named to a judgeship, the first in a series of judicial appointments that would eventually elevate him to a seat on the California Supreme Court, Meese was picked to replace him as executive secretary.

Meese proceeded to make the most of that opportunity, too. Even more than Clark, he established his authority over the breadth of Reagan's domain, and by the start of the second term in 1971, he had become the chief formulator of policy on nearly every issue that reached the governor's desk. During those years, he was often referred to—not always admiringly—as the "deputy governor." But if there were some who resented his rise to the top of the Reagan hierarchy, Meese was generally praised for his solid grasp of the issues, his thoroughness in guiding a problem through the traps to a solution, and, most of all, his skills as a conciliator. Although he shared Reagan's devotion to the conservative cause, his pragmatic approach to legislation is one reason programs that had languished in stalemate during the first term were later passed into law. Meese took pride in his ability to synthesize opposing points of view, and his willingness to compromise on issues helped to soften resistance to Reagan's proposals; California liberals came to recognize that the governor's right-wing doctrines were not as inflexible as they once had assumed. Bob Moretti, the Democratic speaker of the Assembly who worked out a modus vivendi with the governor's office that reflected well on both factions, gave Meese a large share of the credit for the legislative achievements of the second term. Moretti said Meese's "stick-to-it-iveness" could infuriate people, but he also admitted that "were I in the governor's seat, I would want someone like that on my side."

By the end of the second term, Meese had become indispensible. By then, the only staffer who came close to rivaling Meese was his own hand-picked deputy, Assistant Executive Secretary Michael Deaver. Yet even then, Mike Deaver was a special case. Although Meese clearly outranked him, Deaver had already acquired a certain power and influence, not through the governor himself but through the special relationship he enjoyed with the governor's wife.

Mike Deaver has spent so much of his adult life in the shadow of the Reagans, whom he served with the grateful devotion of an urchin who had been taken in off the streets and given a home, that he hardly seems to have had any identity prior to the day when he answered the call that launched him into their orbit. The footsteps on the trail that led him to Sacramento are so faint that even dedicated Reaganites, who profess a curiosity about the formation of the California team that later wielded so much power in Washington, have been inclined to dismiss Deaver's early years as insignificant. It is a common perception that is altogether accurate.

Deaver grew up in and around the California valley town of Bakersfield. His father made a modest living as a Shell Oil distributor, and although there was always food on the table, the family had to struggle economically. There were times, however, when they were a lot better off than their neighbors. At one point, when the Deavers were living in the migrant-farm community of Arvin, just outside Bakersfield, Mike was the only kid in his fourth-grade class who wore shoes to school. When his grandmother died and left a small inheritance, some of it was set aside to finance piano lessons for Mike. It was money well spent, for in later years his skills at the keyboard proved to be his means to a better life, both socially and professionally. For example, when he was working his way through college at San Jose State, Deaver was admitted into a fraternity mainly because the brothers wanted someone in the house who could play the piano.

During his senior year, he thought perhaps he might have a religious vocation and briefly pondered becoming an Episcopal priest. But instead, after his graduation in 1960, he enrolled in a sales training program at IBM. That didn't work out either; Deaver's interest in the business world was no more serious than his flirtation with the cloth had been. His passion was the piano, and after he dropped out of the IBM program, he earned a living by playing piano in a San Jose cocktail lounge. He managed to save enough money from the wages and tips to set off on a trip around the world. Deaver and a college buddy traveled through Europe; then headed for Africa, where they went on a safari; and flew from there to Australia. The last leg of the journey was supposed to take them through South America, but they never made it. In Australia, their money ran out. Deaver's friend wired home and was sent airfare—for one—and Mike was left behind in Sydney, flat broke. Once again he turned to his trusty piano, playing for his supper at a veterans' club, the Australian equivalent of the American Legion. He eventually made his way back to San Jose and reclaimed his piano-playing gig at the cocktail lounge there.

By this time, Mike Deaver was noticing that other young men his age had become grown-ups. Although he was a college graduate his subsequent pursuits—bumming around the world and working as an itinerant piano player—did not make for the kind of résumé that inspires confidence. Thus, as he contemplated a move toward an adult career, the most painless course open to him was to enter a field where the standards were notoriously low and where there was an indulgent tendency to accept someone with such raffish credentials. A drifter who gave the impression of meandering through life with no apparent sense of purpose can always get a job as a bartender or a blackjack dealer in Las Vegas. Or, if he has the stomach for it, he can go into politics.

Deaver's parents were devout Republicans. (One of his more vivid childhood memories is of his father's banishing him from the dinner table for daring to say something nice about Franklin Roosevelt.) So he was naturally drawn to the Grand Old Party and in 1962 got a job as a party representative in Santa Clara County. The first major campaign he took part in was George Murphy's 1964 race for the U.S. Senate. In California politics, Murphy will always be remembered as Reagan's John the Baptist, the precursor whose conservative message cleared the way for the coming of the real leader of the conservative cause. Murphy was an old Hollywood song-and-dance man, and his upset of Pierre Salinger in that Senate race demonstrated that an aging movie actor who spoke in right-wing platitudes could indeed defeat a liberal Democrat in a statewide race.

Yet Deaver himself was a late convert to the Reagan crusade.

Like many other Republicans, he was devastated by the Goldwater disaster in 1964 and, Murphy's strong victory notwithstanding, he believed the only way the GOP could hope to become the dominant party was to rally around moderate candidates who could appeal to Democrats and voters who claimed to be Independents. He carried that conviction into the 1966 Republican primary race for governor and campaigned for Reagan's opponent, George Christopher, the former mayor of San Francisco. When Christopher lost, Deaver managed to cajole his way into the Reagan operation for the general campaign against Pat Brown and later was invited to work on the transition. When the new team opened for business in Sacramento, he was hired to serve directly under William Clark as assistant cabinet secretary.

Only twenty-eight, Deaver nonetheless was among contemporaries; the fifty-six-year-old governor had surrounded himself with aides who, for the most part, were young enough to be his sons, and most of them had credentials as thin as his own. Like Ed Meese, Deaver couldn't help noticing that there was plenty of opportunity in this company for a young man with ambition. Nor did it take him long to realize that working for Bill Clark gave him an ideal post position in the the Sacramento derby; indeed, when Clark was promoted to executive secretary in the summer of 1967, he took Deaver along as his chief deputy, and that alone was enough to place him close to the center of power. But his biggest break came when Clark entrusted him with the delicate task of dealing directly with Nancy Reagan. Or, to put it less graciously, he was assigned to serve as a buffer between the governor's wife and the governor's office.

Until he began working for Reagan in 1966, Deaver knew almost nothing about the family who would shape and define his existence over the next twenty years. He wasn't much of a movie fan and therefore didn't even "know" Ronald Reagan in the way millions of other Americans had become acquainted with him: as a warm and likeable presence on the screen. Deaver was so out of tune with popular culture that he had never seen a Reagan film in a movie theater, although for years thereafter he kept that secret to himself. He first saw Reagan in the lobby of a Los Angeles hotel in early 1966 when he was working for George Christopher. What struck him most about that first encounter was Reagan's ruddy complexion, and, because Deaver had rather naïve and fanciful notions about the life-styles of Hollywood celebrities, his immediate reaction was, "My God, he has on rouge."

Deaver knew even less about Mrs. Reagan, and what he heard about her during the first few months in Sacramento was not reassuring. The adjustment to living in the Sacramento backwater was far more difficult for her than for her husband. Although he had evolved into a political and ideologicial conservative, the governor was still very much a social democrat, at ease in the company of all kinds of other people. This attractive trait stemmed in part from his own small-town working-class roots in the Midwest and perhaps even more from his naturally sunny disposition. Reagan was a genuinely affable man who enjoyed chatting and swapping stories with acquaintances, or even strangers, regardless of social station. But Nancy Reagan was more discriminating. In her childhood there had been rough moments when her divorced mother, an aspiring actress, had left her in the care of others. But with her mother's remarriage to a rich doctor, Nancy became accustomed to finer things. She had developed a rather patrician attitude that did not please the legislators, lobbyists, and reporters who made up the social and professional fabric of Sacramento. Nancy-sniping became a favorite pastime in the capital. More acerbic critics depicted her as a pernicious harridan—she was referred to as "Governor Nancy" and "the Iron Maiden," as well as less decorous epithets.

Yet Nancy Reagan was never that sinister a force in Sacramento. For all her formidable presence, she made no consistent effort to shape the course of policy or legislative programs. One area over which she did exert tight control was the governor's schedule. More than anyone else, Nancy understood how much rest and leisure time "Ronnie" needed in order to function well. (One of the consistent themes that run through the considerable body of work that has been compiled by journalists who have followed Reagan over the years is his unexplained need for long periods of sleep. It is referred to repeatedly by biographers, some of whom have concluded he was the most rested president since one of his personal heroes, Calvin Coolidge, who was said to have slept twelve hours a day during his time in the White House.) It was Nancy who insisted that her man adhere to a nine-to-five work schedule with weekends off, and she jealously guarded those

private hours away from the office when he could take it easy and
indulge in his favorite forms of relaxation, such as watching television. One of Reagan's favorite programs in those early Sacramento days was "Mission Impossible," a series about a team of
secret agents who undertook missions with the admonition that
if they were found out, "the secretary will disavow any knowledge
of your actions."

However, Nancy Reagan was more than just the shepherdess
of Reagan's private life. She was also a trusted confidant, and her
unvarnished opinions of the various aides who had been recruited
to work for her husband carried considerable weight, as Lyn
Nofziger discovered to his sorrow and as others would during the
Washington years—notably James Watt and Donald Regan. Bill
Clark had nothing to fear on that score, but he wasn't entirely
sure about his position with her. Because he was an introvert who
tended to shy away from social chitchat, he was not altogether
comfortable in the presence of Nancy Reagan, and, in fact, confessed to Deaver that he felt more than a little intimidated by her.
So he assigned his deputy to cover that sensitive flank.

It was an assignment that eventually moved Mike Deaver into
the heart of the inner circle. For the clean little secret about Nancy
Reagan was that she could be as generous with the carrot as she
was unsparing with the stick. Those who were able to make their
way into her good graces found her to be a useful ally, a reliable
source of help and support. In his biography of Reagan, Lou
Cannon recalls how certain reporters in Sacramento became adept
at playing the Nancy card to gain access to the governor or to
confirm leads on stories they were tracking. What was sauce for
the press was even richer sauce for members of Reagan's staff,
and no one benefited more from her approval than Deaver.

His duties included helping Nancy supervise her personal
staff and the family residence in Sacramento, but their friendship
grew out of another, less official connection. One imagines the
joy that must have coursed through the soul of this eager young
man when he discovered that one of Nancy Reagan's favorite
pleasures was to gather with family and friends around a piano
for the cheerful fun of a sing-along. On those occasions, the young
pianist was in his element. Here was a gig worthy of his best efforts
and he made the most of it. To go along with his skill on the
ivories, Deaver had cultivated a gift for the kind of fawning banter

that keeps patrons at a piano bar in a mood to stick around for just one more round of drinks. Thus, he played and charmed his way into the affections of Nancy Reagan, who, in time, became so enamored of his talent to amuse that she even encouraged him to take his act on the road. When the governor ran for reelection in 1970, Nancy arranged to have a portable electric piano put on board the campaign plane so that Deaver could provide some happy-hour diversion at the end of a day on the stump.

The piano was his entrée into the Reagan's family and social life, which Nancy normally kept insulated from the political operatives who worked for her husband. Deaver was unique in that he, alone, was able to move back and forth between the two spheres. As time went on, both Nancy and the governor regarded him almost as a member of the family, a kind of surrogate son. The poor kid from Bakersfield reveled in that role.

There were, to be sure, certain drawbacks in being Mrs. Reagan's pet, not the least of which was the resentment it aroused among some of his colleagues. One member of the governor's staff dubbed Deaver's special assignment "The Mommy Watch," and when that was leaked to the press, and hence into general circulation, it became a popular term of derision in Sacramento. (Everyone in town knew that Reagan's personal endearment for his wife was "Mommy." In private, it was always "Ronnie" and "Mommy," not "Ron" and "Nancy.") Some of his associates took facetious delight in suggesting that even a major romantic decision in Deaver's life had been calculated to please the mistress he served with such devotion. When he courted and rather quickly married a young woman who worked in the governor's office, cynics couldn't resist pointing out that Deaver's bride was a graduate of Smith College, which also just happened to be Nancy Reagan's alma mater.

Yet it would be grossly misleading to imply that Deaver was nothing more than a flattering courtier, a glorified valet, or, in the acid phrase that Pat Buchanan later inflicted on him, "the Lord of the Chamber Pot." Deaver's close association with the family carried over into the governor's office and clearly strengthened his position there. Reagan not only shared his wife's affection for Deaver, but grew to respect his judgment in certain matters as well as his loyalty. Among those who were savvy enough to recognize that the young aide had become special was Ed Meese.

In 1969, when William Clark left the governor's office and Meese was asked to take over as executive secretary, one of his first moves was to call Deaver to tell him that he was accepting the post only on the condition that he, Deaver, stay on as the number-two man. That kid-glove touch was exactly what Deaver needed at that point. Clark had been his mentor and protector, and Deaver was still insecure enough to wonder what his position would be now that a new man was taking over the top job on the executive staff. As for Meese, he shrewdly perceived that it was in his best interest to make an ally of the ingratiating piano player who had become one of the governor's most trusted confidants.

The two men quickly settled into a harmonious working relationship. Deaver took pains not to encroach on those areas that Meese regarded as his domain: matters of policy and dealings with legislators to get Reagan's programs passed into law. Instead, the junior aide chose to concentrate on more nebulous duties that were not so easily defined, such as the care and nurturing of Ronald Reagan. He became Nancy's main ally in the continuous effort to lighten Reagan's work load and give him the leisure time she believed he needed. During office hours, Deaver was guardian of the clock, the man who staggered appointments and kept the governor on a schedule that did not overtax him. He also took charge of the Reagan image. The governor's personal popularity continued to be his most precious political asset, and Deaver became adept at arranging photo opportunities and other PR ploys designed to remind the voters of California how lucky they were to have this genial man of character and principle as their leader.

Yet for all the influence he wielded on the inside, Deaver never acquired the kind of solid reputation that Meese did in Sacramento. Many of the veteran politicians and journalists who came in contact with him found him wary and unsure of himself, someone out of his depth but constantly pretending not to be. The stigma of the "Mommy Watch" played directly into those perceptions. Still, Deaver continued to impress the two people who mattered the most, Ronald and Nancy Reagan. Through the years as others around the Reagans came and went, Deaver maintained his position, marching just behind Meese at the head of the class.

By the time the reign in Sacramento was drawing to a close in 1974, there was little doubt that if Reagan's political career was going to move beyond California, Ed Meese and Mike Deaver would be part of it. The real question was whether Reagan would have that opportunity. It was no secret that Reagan had decided he wanted to make a serious race for the presidency. But now something over which Meese, Deaver, and Reagan himself had no control threatened to destroy that dream. The problem was Watergate, and Reagan and his people had no idea what to do about it.

4

Prophet Without Honor

"Fellas, this just isn't working."
—*Candidate Ronald Reagan*

In May 1974, a young Republican lawyer and former political operative for Richard Nixon boarded an airliner at Dulles Airport on the outskirts of Washington. His name was John Sears, and he was flying to Los Angeles to talk serious politics with Ronald Reagan and some of his people. Richard Nixon had just turned over the transcripts of the White House tapes to the House Judiciary Committee, and talk was growing that Nixon would be impeached by the end of the year. Certainly that was Sears's view, and he wondered as his plane headed west what the Reagan people would say when he told them that; it was not going to be what they wanted to hear, but certainly it was one of the things they would want to talk about.

Ronald Reagan had been one of Richard Nixon's staunchest defenders from the moment the Watergate story broke and, for a political pragmatist such as Sears, it was not difficult to understand why. He knew Reagan's second term as California governor was ending and that Reagan wanted to run for President himself in 1976 when Nixon's second term was due to end. Whatever else Reagan might have thought about Watergate, in purely political terms he wanted Richard Nixon to finish out his term. Otherwise, Gerald Ford, Nixon's appointed Vice President would inherit the presidency and would almost certainly want to run in 1976. For Reagan's timetable that couldn't have been worse, so Sears knew what the Reagan people really wanted to hear from a Washington insider: that somehow or other Nixon was going to survive, else how could their man run for President?

Sears was eager to get back into the action and had worked an invitation to the California meeting through Ronald Walker, an old ally from Nixon's 1968 campaign who now had ties to Reagan. Walker had told him of the gloom that was settling over Reagan and his people. They believed at that point that 1976 was a then or never year for Reagan; but if Ford became President, there would be no way that Reagan could present himself as a challenger in 1976. Once Nixon left, Ford was certain to be seen as the man who would try to heal the Watergate wounds and restore national goodwill. Beyond that, it would be only natural for Gerald Ford to expect all good Republicans to support him, if only out of loyalty to the party. Adding to Reagan's problems was the reality of age. If he did not run in 1976, his chance might never come again. If Ford won in 1976, he would probably want to run again in 1980. If Ford lost in 1976, then the Democratic candidate in 1980 would be an incumbent President. By that time, Ronald Reagan would be six years out of office and sixty-nine years old.

The political meeting was to take place at the governor's Pacific Palisades home, and when Sears arrived there for his first face-to-face meeting with Reagan, he suddenly realized why the age factor was such a major concern. "My overwhelming impression," he recalled, "was how old he looked and how tired. One wondered then if it would be possible for Reagan to mount a serious campaign if he had to wait until 1980." It was shaping up as a dismal weekend.

That was the day Sears also met the members of Reagan's inner circle: Holmes Tuttle, Ed Meese, Mike Deaver, and Lyn Nofziger, who had recently returned to the Reagan fold after his inglorious stint in the Nixon White House. But Sears wasn't the only new face at that meeting. Others on hand who were not part of the California clique included Jim Lake, who worked out of the governor's state lobbying office in Washington; and Ronald Walker, the Washington lawyer who had introduced Sears to the California crowd.

The only person at the meeting who did not not succumb to the pervasive gloom was Sears, who argued forcefully that Reagan should not be deterred from going ahead with his own plans for 1976. Sears prided himself on being able to see things as they were, not as he wished them to be. A onetime admirer of Spiro Agnew, he had nonetheless been one of the first Republicans to predict that Agnew would be forced from office, once the scandal surrounding him came to light. Now he told the Californians he was just as convinced that Nixon would be gone, too, in a matter of months, and that if Ronald Reagan wanted to run for President he should simply face reality: he was going to have to challenge a Republican incumbent. But he advanced another argument as well: Gerald Ford would inherit the presidency, but that did not give him a clear and legitimate claim to the office. After all, he had become vice president not through the proper electoral process, but as an appointee to replace the disgraced Agnew, and now—as the beneficiary of a far more alarming and damaging scandal—he was on the verge of becoming the only unelected President in American history. Given that unprecedented circumstance, there was no reason that Ronald Reagan, or anyone else, should not feel free to challenge Ford in the clean and open combat of the Republican primaries.

This was strong talk that ran counter to Reagan's deeply held belief that Republicans were decent and orderly folks who would never try to dethrone a President when their own party was in power, but Sears was persuasive with his central point: because the present situation was so extraordinary, the ordinary rules of conduct did not apply. Reagan and his lieutenants did not accept the argument immediately. But the seed had been planted and, watered by the strong nutrient of political ambition, it eventually blossomed into an active and vigorous candidacy. For Sears, the meeting was no less significant. He had come to the strategy session as a stranger, a rank outsider, and yet when the time came to mobilize the Reagan presidential campaign, he was the field commander who led the rebellious troops into battle.

Reagan's home overlooking the Pacific was but the latest port of call in the political odyssey of John Patrick Sears, who had discovered his true vocation when he was in college in the early 1960s. A native of upstate New York (he grew up on a prosperous dairy farm near Syracuse) Sears had gone to Notre Dame as a pre-med student with the intention of pursuing a career in psychiatry. But in his senior year there, he managed a friend's successful campaign for class president, and from then on he was enamored of politics. So instead of becoming a doctor, he obtained a law degree from Georgetown and in 1966 joined a prestigious New York firm, where he came to the attention of a senior partner who shared his enthusiasm for political gamesmanship.

The senior partner was Richard Nixon, who already was looking ahead to the next presidential race. Nixon was just starting to recruit a new team to help him launch his comeback run in 1968, and although Sears was only twenty-six, he impressed the old pro with his political sophistication. Starting as an advance man, he quickly rose to become Nixon's chief delegate scout and head counter, and when his precisely calibrated projection came within one vote of the final tally at the convention, John Sears was hailed as the boy wonder of the Nixon campaign. Unfortunately for Sears, the kudos that came his way in 1968 aroused the resentment of Nixon's campaign manager—another senior partner from the New York law firm, John Mitchell—and he began to fall from favor as quickly as he had risen. He remained on the team long enough to land a job in the White House as a special counsel, but by then Mitchell's enmity toward him had rubbed off on the president's increasingly powerful aides, John Ehrlichman and H. R. Haldeman. They felt Sears was a little too cozy in his dealings with the Washington press corps, a transgression that, in their eyes, was tantamount to consorting with the enemy. Eased out of the White House before the end of Nixon's first year in office, Sears returned to private law practice a much wiser man. Never again would he settle for a subordinate role in a campaign, one that would put him at the mercy of envious superiors.

When the Watergate dam broke, Sears surveyed the Republican party and concluded that his future in politics would not be with the new President, Gerald Ford. Ford already had an entrenched team of trusted deputies, sundry aides, and cronies who had gathered around him during his years on Capitol Hill, as well as the new group of advisers he had inherited from Nixon. There would be little chance of a leadership role for Sears among those factions. It was only natural that his thoughts then turned toward the governor of California, and when the opportunity to attend the strategy session in Pacific Palisades arose, he took it.

In the months following that first encounter, Sears continued to impress Reagan and his California cadre. The more dealings they had with him, the more they regarded him as just the man they needed to take charge of the 1976 campaign. Reagan and his band of Californians had never doubted their ability to win elections in their home state, but after the ill-fated run for the presidency in 1968, they were intimidated by the prospect of taking on another national campaign, and they knew of Sears's reputation as a master strategist for Nixon. Beyond that, he had solid credentials in areas where they were wary and inexperienced. Sears had strong connections with the Eastern establishment, not the least of which were the influential media centers in New York and Washington. Unless Reagan and his candidacy were taken seriously there, there was no chance of wresting the Republican nomination from Ford, much less going on to capture the White House. Sears had exactly the kind of expertise that Reagan's people had been so good at finding in the past and, more significant, the manager of Reagan's campaigns in California, Stu Spencer, was not available. He had found himself at cross-purposes with Meese and some of the other insiders and had signed on as a chief operative for Ford.

The defection of Spencer (who would return to the Reagan fold four years later) created the opening at the top that Sears needed. He was chosen to run the 1976 campaign, but he insisted that the campaign be run his way. He would be answerable to no one but the candidate. Sears's original strategy was to win big in the early primaries, thus severely weakening Ford. The strategy backfired when Ford came from behind to win in New Hampshire. To the chagrin of Meese and the California crowd, Ford's victory was engineered by Spencer. Some months earlier Reagan had given a little-noticed speech in Chicago that called for the federal government to transfer many of the services it performed back to the states. As Reagan outlined the plan, it would save the federal government $90 million. It was Spencer who saw the political advantage of stating the obvious: if the states were suddenly required to perform services that had cost the federal government $90 million, it would mean massive increases in state taxes. In

New Hampshire, which prides itself on having no state income tax, the effect was devastating.

Reagan rallied, however, as Sears orchestrated a series of impressive primary victories in the Sunbelt. This kept the campaign alive and allowed Reagan to carry the fight all the way to the convention floor in Kansas City. In the end, the power of incumbency proved too great an obstacle to overcome, yet Ford had to call on all those resources to win a nomination that by any conventional yardstick should have been his in a walk.

Some of Ford's friends still believe he would have beaten Carter that autumn had he not been forced to expend so much time and energy in the primary fight against Reagan. This is debatable, but there is no question Reagan's emerging presence on the political scene in those years had an enormous impact on events. In the beginning, Ford had not taken Reagan seriously as a political threat. He didn't like Reagan, considering him lazy and given to proposing simplistic solutions to complex problems. Despite Reagan's geniality, Ford considered him to be one of the most distant people he had ever met. He observed that Reagan was the only politician he knew who told you more about himself in his speeches than he did in conversation. Yet, once Ford did conclude he had underestimated Reagan, he may have overcompensated. Convinced by the autumn of 1975 that Reagan had to be taken seriously, he tried to head off a Reagan challenge by letting it be known that his running mate in 1976 would be someone other than his vice president, Nelson Rockefeller. Shortly after assuming the presidency, Ford had personally selected Rockefeller to be his vice president, and the four-term New York governor had served loyally for eleven months. Even so, the selection had infuriated conservative Republicans. By taking Rockefeller out of the picture for 1976, Ford thought he could make peace with the right wing and puncture enthusiasm for Reagan's candicacy. The ploy didn't work, nor did it discourage Reagan and the people around him. "I am not appeased," was Reagan's pompous reaction when told that Rockefeller was being dumped.

Ford finally asked Kansas senator Robert Dole to run with him and in the inevitable postmortems, Dole's abrasive style was cited as one cause of Ford's defeat. Whether Rockefeller's presence on the ticket would have overcome the stigma of Ford's pardon of Nixon is a question that political reporters have argued about since. But, at the least, Rockefeller might have carried New York for the ticket, and, barring losses in other states that Ford won, that would have been enough to tilt the election to the Republicans.

Ironically, only a misunderstanding by the usually alert Sears may have prevented Reagan from winding up as Ford's running mate. That misunderstanding occurred on the night that Ford finally won the nomination in Kansas City. The Ford and Reagan camps had agreed that whichever man won the nomination, the other would immediately go to his hotel suite for a show of unity. When Ford went over the top, one of his people, Richard Cheney, was put in touch with Sears and said, "We're ready for the unity visit." Sears responded, "All right, but only on the condition that you don't offer the vice presidency to Reagan. That would put him in an embarrassing position and he doesn't want it." Although he has never commented publicly on the matter, Reagan has since told friends that Sears was wrong. Had Ford offered him the vice presidency, he would have felt duty bound to take it.

To be sure, Ford didn't like Reagan, but sources close to both men say that in all probability Ford would have asked Reagan to be his running mate, had he known Reagan was willing. Had that happened, of course, Reagan might never have been President. If putting Reagan on the ticket with him resulted in tipping the election to Ford, that would have meant Ford would have been eligible to seek reelection in 1980. On the other hand, if Ford had lost, Reagan would have been seen as damaged goods by 1980 and probably could not have mounted a serious campaign.

Although Reagan lost the 1976 nomination to Ford, both he and his campaign manager would be seen as winners in the long term. Until that year, Reagan, the former actor, had been dismissed by many as a California frivolity, who could have succeeded only in a state with a reputation for embracing fads and trendy aberrations. Others saw him as a conservative ideologue, who, like Barry Goldwater before him, would only appeal to a narrow base. There also was a widespread belief that because of his age and the fact that he had taken up politics so late in life, he had neither the stamina nor the campaign savvy to become an effective national candidate. The vigorous race against Ford dispelled all those notions. In the aftermath of Ford's loss to Carter, Reagan emerged as the new party leader and acknowledged front-runner for the GOP presidential nomination of 1980.

As for John Sears, he gained a greatly enhanced reputation as a political strategist. Reporters who were only dimly aware of his work for Nixon eight years earlier now wrote glowing profiles of him and his adroit moves on Reagan's behalf. In addition, thanks to television and numerous photographs in newspapers and magazines, his cherubic face, with his heavy eyelids and sardonic smile, became known to the public. The favorable coverage was no accident. Sears was a smart political operator, and he had an amiable relationship with the press; during the long stretches of idleness on the campaign trail, he often sat around with reporters, trading barbs and swapping anecdotes. That was one reason they liked him. Another was that next to politics, Sears had two enthusiasms that were shared by many members of the working press: a passion for poker and a hearty taste for fine Scotch.

By the time the Reagan challenge was finally repulsed at the convention in Kansas City, John Sears was so firmly identified as the chief strategist behind the Reagan campaign that it seemed to some national reporters that Sears and Reagan had been together for years. It was an easy mistake to make; Reagan seemed to trust Sears completely. What many of us could not appreciate at the time was the way in which Reagan had always been able to put himself firmly in the hands of a hired expert and, as long as the expert's advice worked, do exactly as he was instructed. In that way, Reagan was something of a campaign manager's dream, but as Sears himself later pointed out, Reagan's willingness to follow directions should not have been all that surprising. That was the way it was always done in the movies. The most capable actors were those who were able to place themselves totally in the hands of a director. But those of us who were seeing Reagan in operation for the first time in 1976 did not yet understand how the work habits he had built up over the years would so directly influence his approach to campaigning, and for that matter, governing.

To those closest to Reagan, his trusting nature went beyond old work habits. At its core was his deeply ingrained optimism. As Sears later told us, "Reagan has always trusted life to take care of him, because for the most part it always has." The commitment the two came to share was strengthened by the bond of mutal self-interest. Each man saw the other as his way to the White House. Reagan believed Sears was the professional he needed to structure and implement a winning campaign for the presidency. For Sears, Reagan was the candidate that would carry him back to the political perks and power that should have been his in 1969, and would have been his but for the petty jealousies and paranoia of Richard Nixon's top advisers. Yet already by then, there were signs of friction in the Sears-Reagan alliance, and the time would come when they would burst into open conflict. The ensuing tug-of-war for control of Ronald Reagan's future would, in fact, become so bitter and divisive that before it was finally resolved, some high-ranking members of the Reagan team would be purged and sent into exile, a group of victims that ultimately included John Sears himself.

In the wake of the Bay of Pigs fiasco, John Kennedy had observed that "victory has a hundred fathers and defeat is an orphan." This aptly described the mood that slowly settled over the Reagan operation in the aftermath of the 1976 race. Sears got great notices from the press, but in the inevitable search for a scapegoat, the insiders came to the conclusion that insiders often reach in politics: the outsider had been at fault. Hard-line conservatives in particular complained that Sears was nothing more than an opportunist (*Nixonian* was one adjective leveled at him) who used Reagan to fuel his own ambition. They questioned his loyalty to Reagan and the cause, arguing that because he was not one of them, he could not fully appreciate Reagan's special role as leader of the right-wing crusade.

The prime example of this betrayal, at least the one most frequently cited in those days, was the decision Sears had induced Reagan to make on the eve of the 1976 convention. In a last-ditch attempt to prevent Ford from sewing up the nomination, he persuaded Reagan to name his running mate before the delegates assembled and the balloting began. The man Sears selected to round out the ticket was Richard Schweiker, a liberal Republican senator from Pennsylvania. This unorthodox move, designed to drive a wedge into Ford's mainstream support and prune away some of his delegates, did not achieve its objective. Although the strategem threw the Ford team into temporary confusion, defections to Reagan were minimal and the President was able to secure the nomination on the first ballot. Even so, most impartial observers thought the ploy was a bold and brilliant stroke, and Sears was once again praised for his political creativity. Reagan himself heartily approved the plan, especially after he met with Schweiker and came away satisfied that their views were compatible on most basic issues. But many conservatives denounced the maneuver as a cynical gesture toward accommodation, one that could only compromise Reagan's principles and philosophy. And they were certain that if Sears stayed on as Reagan's manager for the campaign in 1980, he would continue to manipulate their candidate in the interest of expediency. That view would have been reinforced if they had known what Sears had not revealed, even to Reagan. Schweiker had not been his first choice for a running mate. The first choice had been Nelson Rockefeller.

"I really thought about that," Sears told a visitor to his Washington law office in 1987. "I came very close to talking to Nelson about that." The visitor was astonished. Most political observers thought Gerald Ford's decision to make Nelson Rockefeller his vice president had been the one development that finally convinced Reagan to break with Ford and challenge the unelected incumbent for the nomination. When the visitor reminded Sears of this, and of Reagan's statement that he was "not appeased" when Ford later eliminated Rockefeller as a possible running mate, Sears chuckled. "Oh, yes," he said, "but Reagan also sent Rockefeller a warm note of consolation when Ford did that and indeed, Rockefeller called and thanked him for it." When the visitor continued to express incredulity, Sears said simply, "It would have worked. Nelson had enough delegates in New York to give Reagan the nomination." Sears said that in the end he never approached Rockefeller, not because he thought Rockefeller himself would have been unreceptive but because his friends would almost certainly have talked him out of it. Once the news leaked out, as it almost cetainly would have if Rockefeller's friends learned of it, Sears reasoned, it would have been impossible to offer the number-two spot to anyone else and have it play with the desired political effect. The obvious question of course was, even if Rockefeller would have consented, would Reagan have stood for it? "Oh, sure," said Sears without the slightest hesitation. "It would have worked. I didn't do it, but I wish I had."

Once he committed himself to Reagan, Sears devoted all his skills and industry to getting him elected, but his loyalty was strictly that of a technician or strategist. He was conservative, to be sure, but there were times when he betrayed a condescending attitude toward the man he had pledged to serve, and this irritated some of the people around Reagan. Sears was impressed by Reagan's personality, that combination of affable charm and earnest conviction that made him such a superb campaigner, but in the realm of ideas and policy, Sears found his candidate's views on many issues to be so simplistic that he thought it best to shield them from scrutiny. "Reagan was not a stupid man, but he was not a reflective man," Sears said many years later. "It was just a part of his habit to operate on the surface without a plan of how to get from here to there."

In the beginning, this did not bother Sears, who was convinced that the force of Reagan's personality would propel them into the White House, and Sears saw no reason that Reagan should not raise his sights and reach out to all regions and voters. That was the whole point of the Schweiker ploy: to demonstrate that Reagan was not an inflexible right-winger, but rather a truly national candidate whose appeal cut across partisan lines, extending even to the liberal bastions in the East. Reagan, unlike some of his California advisers, had liked Sears's strategy in 1976, and he liked the plan that Sears had drawn up for the 1980 campaign: a plan that again called for planting the Reagan flag early in some Eastern states. So in retrospect, perhaps it should not have been surprising that Reagan fended off conservative complaints about Sears and brought him back once more to run the show in 1980. Reagan had been nettled for years by the patronizing perception of him that permeated the East Coast. His friends said Reagan was keenly aware that plenty of people "back East," as they say in Calfor' ia, still regarded him as either a cowboy actor or a right-wing kook, and he relished the prospect of showing them he could win on their home turf. So, when Sears proposed a plan that would lean hard on winning some big states in what used to be Rockefeller country, Reagan liked it. He liked it a lot.

Emboldened by Reagan's support, Sears began a purge of his right-wing critics within the Reagan entourage as he laid the groundwork for the 1980 campaign. Part of it was revenge for their efforts to undermine him, but he also believed they were a pernicious influence who, if given the chance, would damage the campaign. To a pragmatist like Sears, who had been willing to make a ticket of Ronald Reagan, the darling of the Right, and Nelson Rockefeller, the man the Right hated the most, there was little patience with conservative ideologues. After brushing aside a few minor functionaries, he moved to oust a leading member of Reagan's old guard: Lyn Nofziger.

Nofziger was a dedicated Reagan loyalist and had been since he signed on as press secretary for the first gubernatorial campaign in 1966. But ever since the early months in Sacramento when he wisecracked his way onto Nancy Reagan's get-lost list, his position had been tenuous. Sears had taken his measure in 1976 and had promoted Jim Lake to replace him as press secretary, reassigning Nofziger to the virtually redundant job of running the campaign in California. And now, in the summer of 1979, when he was recruiting the team for the next big effort, Sears decided the time had come to dump him. Mike Deaver was enlisted to sell the dismissal to Reagan and then to break the news to Nofziger, who, after hearing the decision, warned Deaver that Sears was on a full-scale power trip and would not be satisfied until he had picked off all the California deputies, one by one. He went so far as to predict that Deaver himself would be the next one to be shot down. Deaver thought the distraught Nofziger was overreacting and chose to ignore the warning—to his peril.

Sears and Deaver should have been natural allies who understood each other, and, in fact, Deaver thought they did. After all, it had been Deaver who had gone up against Reagan insiders like Paul Laxalt and urged that Sears run the 1980 campaign. Nor was Deaver an ideologue. But as Nofziger had suspected, Deaver was indeed the next one on Sears's hit list. Although Deaver's influence with Nancy Reagan had been in large part responsible for Sears's being brought aboard in the first place, that very influence made the cautious Sears uncomfortable. He was not going to be eased out again as he had been in the Nixon campaign. The problem, Sears contended later, was that Deaver just would not become a part of the team. "It was like an orchestra," Sears said, "and I just couldn't convince Mike to sit down and take an instrument." Whatever the merit of that complaint, Sears intended to exert total control over the campaign, and Deaver stood in the way.

The showdown came at another meeting at Reagan's home in Pacific Palisades on Thanksgiving Day 1979. The California aides and the Sears group had been quarreling for weeks, and the latest problem was Sears's dissatisfaction with the way Deaver was handling fund-raising. Nancy had arranged the meeting and

Sears seized the moment to strike. Arriving before Deaver with his two sidekicks, Jim Lake and Charles Black, Sears unloaded his accumulated grievances against Deaver. Sears insists that he never meant for Deaver to leave the campaign, but by the account of several participants, Mrs. Reagan said to her husband at one point: "Honey, you're going to have to make a choice." In his book, *Behind the Scenes*, Deaver does not mention that line, but says Reagan suggested that the public relations firm Deaver had formed in the mid-1970s had been charging the campaign a huge sum for rent, which Reagan seemed to feel was out of line. Deaver recalls he then said, "If these characters have suggested that I'm ripping you off after all these years, then I'm out. I'm leaving."

Reagan protested that that was not what he wanted, but Deaver said, "I'm sorry, sir, but it is what I want." And with that, he left. Even his critics would admit it had been a classy performance from a man who had entered Reagan's life more than a decade earlier with little more than a smile and a talent to amuse. But Deaver had learned enough from the old actor to know the value of a well-timed exit line, and although he was out—temporarily offstage—he certainly wasn't down. By now, at least, he had a little money. After Reagan left office in 1974, Deaver and another young man named Peter Hannaford had set up a consulting and public relations firm. With Ronald Reagan as their chief client, they had built it into a lucrative business, distributing Reagan's newspaper and radio commentaries and arranging his speaking schedule. Deaver was a wiser man as well, knowing now that Nofziger had been right about Sears. He told friends he now knew it was only a matter of time until the campaign manager would exceed his mandate.

As it turned out, the real loser in the Thanksgiving Day showdown was the presumed winner. Reagan had exploded after Deaver left, remarking with uncharacteristic forcefulness that the "best man in the room" had just walked out. He never forgave Sears for forcing Deaver to leave, and from then until he finally fired Sears three months later, he never spoke to him except in the stiff and formal language of official duty.

Characteristically, Reagan, who normally kept even longtime aides like Deaver at arm's length, never telephoned the man who had devoted most of his adult life to making Ronald Reagan look good. It was Nancy who eventually asked Deaver to rejoin the campaign. Uncharacteristically, in the days after Deaver's departure, Reagan began making cutting remarks about Sears. "I look him in the eye and he looks me in the tie," he confided to aides who, unlike Sears, still laughed at his old movie jokes. Those who were close to Reagan in those days contend that the only reason he didn't get rid of Sears in the waning weeks of 1979 was that he still believed he needed him to win the presidency. "Understand one thing about Ronald Reagan and his wife," a Reagan admirer told us much later. "They will hire anyone who can help them at the moment. If a person can help them, they have short memories about what that person may have done to them or for them in the past." With the critical early tests in Iowa and New Hampshire looming, it was no time to make radical changes in the campaign staff. Later, there would be time enough.

Sears left the Thanksgiving Day encounter convinced that in ousting Deaver he had tightened his grip on the campaign, and he was ready now to get on with it. He dismissed Reagan's frosty attitude toward him as a snit that would fade once he moved into the active phase of his march to the White House, a march that, as choreographed by Sears, resembled a stately procession more than a spirited charge into battle. Part of his strategy was to present Reagan as the inevitable nominee, and to underscore that perception, he counseled the candidate to avoid controversy and conflict and steer clear of complicated issues. Let the less fortunate contenders slug it out; Reagan had nothing to gain by getting into a dispute with them. Sears cited the recent polls, all of which confirmed that Reagan was the clear front-runner; in most of them he was outdistancing his nearest rivals by more than a two-to-one margin. On the basis of that criterion alone, the serene, above-the-battle approach that Sears fostered seemed to make sense. The strategy also reflected the judgment Sears had made at that point: Reagan's strong point was not policy issues. The less he exposed himself in those areas, the better off he would be.

Besides, there was an impressive historical precedent. Dwight Eisenhower was the last old man and political latecomer who had glided into the White House on the strength of an engaging personality and a loftier-than-thou campaign style. Critics at the time complained that Ike's speeches and policy statements were filled with platitudes. But voters had convinced themselves they already knew what Ike stood for—he didn't need to spell it out in speeches—and he crushed both Robert Taft and Adlai Stevenson.

Sears reasoned that what had been good enough for the genial general in the fifties would be good enough for the affable actor in the eighties.

Despite Reagan's growing disenchantment with Sears's style, he dutifully followed his campaign manager's advice as he had always followed the advice of the experts he hired to manage his campaigns. In the early weeks of 1980, Sears was concentrating on the New Hampshire primary. Although the Iowa caucuses were scheduled to take place a month before, he all but ignored them. The polls in Iowa published as recently as December gave Reagan a commanding lead there: 50 percent to a mere 14 percent for his nearest challenger, George Bush, and Sears concluded that even if Iowa were deemed to be important, it would safely fall to Reagan. He was so convinced of that outcome that his campaign schedule called for Reagan to make only a few visits to the farm state. The visits were so brief that one wag characterized them as cameo appearances. In the meantime, Bush was happily boasting that he had spent more days in Iowa than Reagan had hours.

The upshot, of course, was that George Bush scored an upset victory in Iowa that not only necessitated a change in Reagan's front-runner strategy but threatened to destroy his entire candidacy. Bush came flying out of Iowa on the wings of "Big Mo," as he called it. Sears was excoriated not only by his usual critics, the hard-line conservatives, but by all Reaganites. They berated him for failing to take Iowa seriously and for devising a strategy that kept the candidate so tightly under wraps that he was all but invisible. From his vantage point of exile in California, Lyn Nofziger sneered, "If you're going to have a Rose Garden Strategy, you better have a Rose Garden." But the worst insult came in an editorial in the *Manchester Union Leader*, New Hampshire's most influential newspaper. It asserted that Reagan had been "Searscumsized," the dire implication being that because Sears had already gone that far with the knife, more mutilating surgery might be in store.

Sears did not need Nofziger or the *Union Leader* to tell him how badly he had blundered. But his response was that of a pro who had been through these wars before; he shouldered all the blame for the setback in Iowa and did not try to hide behind any excuses. More to the point, Sears did not panic. Yes, he conceded to reporters, they had taken a heavy hit in Iowa, no question about that; but he was ready for New Hampshire, and he was still confident that his many months of preparation in that state would produce a big Reagan victory. That would be enough of a boost to enable Reagan to reclaim his status as front-runner. Then, having demonstrated its strength in the Northeast, the Reagan campaign would go forward with its carefully planned strategy through the rest of the primary states. By the time he won the New York primary in April—a contest that Sears had targeted as the cornerstone of his Eastern strategy—Reagan would have a virtual lock on the nomination and by then the embarrassment in Iowa would be a fading memory.

But New Hampshire was crucial. Another loss to Bush there and his "Big Mo" would indeed be more than a passing enthusiasm. Sears needed a victory in New Hampshire almost as much as Reagan did. He was now under criticism from all quarters and would continue to be unless he and Reagan redeemed themselves in the Granite State. Yet incredibly, it was at this juncture, when he was more vulnerable than he had been at any time since he first went to work for Reagan, that Sears made another ill-advised move to consolidate his power base. Having disposed of two major California deputies, Nofziger and Deaver, he now trained his sights on Ed Meese.

After Reagan had left the governor's office in 1974, Meese had worked in industry and taught at the San Diego Law School, but he maintained his close ties to his old boss and as Reagan geared up for the 1980 race, Meese was put in charge of issues and policy and given the title of campaign chief of staff. Although Sears had full operational control of the campaign, he kept a leery eye on Meese, who enjoyed a close relationship with Reagan. Meese in the beginning had supported the Sears strategy, but like the other Californians, he grew to resent the pushy campaign manager. When he found out what had happened to Deaver at the Thanksgiving Day shootout, Meese went to Reagan and forcefully protested that he had made a serious mistake, then followed that up with a warning that the situation would only get worse if he continued to relinquish so much authority to Sears. Meese could see Sears's growing power and could not help wondering about his own vulnerability. From that point on, Meese and Sears were at such odds that one of them would have to be driven out. Meese won in the end, of course, but it may have been by accident that he pulled the trigger that set off the final sequence of events in the downfall of John Sears.

Two weeks after the debacle in Iowa, an agitated Sears told Nancy Reagan he had accidentally overheard Meese talking on the telephone in an adjoining room at a motel. Sears said he heard Meese tell someone that Sears and his associates, Jim Lake and Charlie Black, would be fired after the New Hampshire primary. Meese has always denied making such a call, but in later years he told Reagan's biographer Lou Cannon that Reagan had promised him the night of the loss in Iowa that "changes would be made." Sears took the line with Mrs. Reagan that it was Meese who should be fired because he was simply out of his depth. The years have not softened Sears's view of Meese, his talents, or what Sears considered the harmful influence that Meese had been able to exert on Reagan. In Sears's version of events, Meese refused to take orders. "People would just show up and say Meese hired me," Sears said. "We wouldn't know who they were." But as Sears tells it, the worst part was Meese's penchant for playing to Reagan's worst side. "He was supposedly helping the candidate become more familiar with the issues," Sears recalled. "Now, he knew very well the candidate didn't know very much about the issues. He also knew the candidate, on his own, wouldn't worry very much about that. He would sit there with us and we would talk about all this—things Reagan needed to know and how we needed to do this or that, but then it wouldn't get done." Sears contends that Meese saw no urgency in performing such assignments because he was confident Reagan would never ask him about them. Reagan just wasn't very interested in substance, Sears said, and he added: "Ed has always realized that and he's taken advantage of it."

Sears's allegations did not sit well with Mrs. Reagan. After Deaver had left the campaign, Nancy Reagan had become as disenchanted with Sears as her husband. Reagan's friends said he had just about come to the conclusion that Sears had to go, but again, it was a well-timed remark from his wife that forced the issue. Sears, still believing he had the upper hand, advanced the idea that William Clark, who had served Reagan so ably in California, should now be brought in to replace Meese. What he did not understand, of course, was that a talent search was already under way to replace him, not Meese, and that ruled out bringing in Clark. For all their disenchantment with Sears, the Reagans had not lost sight of the values that first induced them to hire him; hence, they recognized the need to replace him with someone who had similar contacts and credentials in the East. Several prospects were mentioned, and then Nancy brought up the name of William Casey, whom the Reagans had met at a fund-raising dinner in New York. Like Sears, Casey was a New Yorker, and far more than Sears, he was a member of the Eastern establishment. As the former chairman of the Securities and Exchange Commission, he was tightly tied to Wall Street and other centers of Republican power and influence on the East Coast. So a call went out to Bill Casey, who, after mulling it over, agreed to manage the faltering campaign.

But all of a sudden, it was no longer faltering. In the morning-after gloom of the Iowa defeat, Reagan and Sears agreed that the disengaged, front-runner strategy would have to be scrapped, and the shift from that posture to the role of embattled underdog greatly helped to revive Reagan's candidacy. Ronald Reagan never campaigned more vigorously than he did during the month between the Iowa caucus and the New Hampshire primary, and the long hours and hard work were paying off. Polls revealed a dramatic surge in Reagan's favor. If the forecast proved accurate, then he was headed for a big comeback victory in New Hampshire. That meant the dismissal of Sears would have to be handled with delicacy. To throw him over in the final days of the New Hampshire campaign would only provide the press and the voters with a major distraction, and an unsettling sideshow could seriously disrupt the momentum they seemed to be wresting from Bush. But waiting until after the decisive triumph, a victory that could be attributed in large part to the efforts Sears had made to mobilize the state for his candidate, would make Reagan look like an ingrate—or even worse, a fool. Thus, in a private meeting with his wife and the handful of trusted aides who were in on the secret plan to dump Sears, Reagan made the decision to fire him on primary day, but before the votes were counted. That way, the purge would come late enough to have no adverse impact on the primary campaign, yet early enough to prevent its being directly linked to the outcome.

Late in the morning of primary day, Reagan summoned Sears, Lake, and Black to his hotel suite in Manchester. There, with Nancy and William Casey looking on, he handed each of them a copy of the press release annoucing their resignations from the campaign. "Fellas," he said by way of explanation, "this just isn't working." Sears and Black accepted the news with stoic acquiescence, but Lake couldn't resist a parting shot. "Governor," he warned, "Ed Meese manipulates you; he manipulates you."

The Reagan people had ample reason to be concerned about the timing. A few hours after Sears was sacked, the New Hampshire voters gave Reagan the huge victory his now-former campaign manager had been predicting all along. With that triumph, Reagan recaptured all of the initiative he had lost in Iowa. New Hampshire was the catapult that launched him on his flight through the rest of the primaries and on to a first ballot nomination and a huge victory in November. In the meantime, Sears had returned to his private law practice in Washington, and from that exile he followed the rest of the 1980 campaign with mixed emotions. Even though he was now an outcast, there were several other moments of vindication to be savored along the way.

There was, for example, the success of his Eastern strategy, which many Reaganites had denounced as an ill-considered attempt to transform their hero into a candidate who was trying to be all things to all people. John Sears had been right from the beginning: unlike Barry Goldwater, Ronald Reagan was a conservative who could rally voters of every persuasion, and the victory in the fall underlined that. Sears later confessed amusement, as well, at the irony of the diverting spectacle that had captivated the press for a few hours at the Republican convention that summer. Members of the old Ford crowd had advanced the notion that Reagan should select Ford as his running mate. Given the extended battle Reagan and Ford had waged against each other four years earlier and their deep policy differences, this was a gesture toward expediency if there ever was one. Yet the Reagan people seemed so eager to put together the "dream ticket," as some called it, that they seriously discussed giving to Ford powers greater than had ever been granted to any vice president in history, so great in fact that if put into effect, the arrangement would have probably violated certain tenets of the Constitution. There was even talk of forming a kind of co-presidency with Reagan serving as a lofty chairman of the board and Ford taking on the day-to-day task of running the government. The idea was seen as so unlikely that John Carlson, a onetime press officer in the Nixon and Ford administrations who had been given the task of leaking the information to test the reaction, told us he spent one whole evening at the convention before he could find a reporter who would take him seriously. Several reporters just laughed when Carlson revealed "on background" what was happening behind the scenes and did not report the story, believing that Carlson had been joking. One bemused observer likened the proposal to that of a new groom who invites the best man to come along on his honeymoon.

Sears had thrived on the bold stroke and the grand gesture, as he had demonstrated on the eve of the previous GOP convention when he induced Reagan to accept the liberal Richard Schweiker as his running mate. But that had been a move of desperation. A dream ticket that called for a candidate who had sewn up the nomination to turn over part of the power of the presidency to a former opponent was something else. "I don't think I would have done that," Sears said, the comment followed by the staccatolike chuckle that so often served as punctuation for his remarks. Although the idea was given serious consideration by the Reagan people, it was finally dropped and instead Reagan chose George Bush, a politician he hardly knew but who the polls said would be likely to attract the most votes in a general election.

There is an even deeper irony to be found in the legacy Sears left behind that day when he walked out of Reagan's hotel suite in New Hampshire. Although his motives may have been twisted by personal ambition and the bitter memory of what had happened to him during the Nixon years, his political instincts about Reagan's California deputies had been right. In the months following Sears's downfall, Nofziger and Deaver quietly returned to the campaign, where, reunited with Meese, they resumed their places at the head of the line. Moreover, Reagan later took all three of them with him into the White House, and in the course of their years in Washington, they caused the Reagans great embarrassment. After leaving the White House staff, both Nofziger and Deaver were indicted on charges stemming from illegal lobbying practices, and questions about Meese's personal ethics dogged him throughout his days as a high official in the Reagan administration. Although there is no question that Deaver played a significant role in the success of Reagan's first term and his reelection campaign, Sears could not be blamed for believing that had he been successful in ridding the Reagan entourage of the trio during those early campaign days, Reagan would have been spared some of the trouble that fell on the White House during his second term. Instead, as had happened during the Nixon administration, it was again John Sears's peculiar fate to observe, from the sidelines, the public humiliation of men who had survived as political operatives at his expense and who, in turn, had gone on to tarnish the reputation of a President they had pledged to serve.

5

Master of Finesse

"The President is like the Good Lord:
he's just aware of everything."
—*Larry Speakes*

Once the Reagans fired Sears, Ed Meese felt that he had been restored to his rightful place in the entourage. Bill Casey was to run the campaign, but Meese was the real victor. It was Meese who had engineered Sears's departure, and it was Meese who again was Reagan's most powerful deputy. Immediately, he began to lay plans to maintain that position once Reagan reached the White House.

By the time the fall campaign was under way, the man whose ambition had always been masked by his plodding style began to envision himself as a real Washington power broker. He launched a quiet search for talented people to fill key positions in the coming administration as he began to formulate in his own mind the kind of organization that would best serve Reagan. Meese loved organization charts almost as much as he did committees, and weeks before the election he had already drawn up elaborate diagrams of how the White House would be staffed. Of course, his own name was neatly typed into the slot of White House chief of staff.

Chief of staff was a title Meese never acquired, but as the Reagan people came into Washington after the election, Meese seemed to rank second only to the President. The man who had been called the deputy governor back in Sacramento was already being referred to as the deputy President. Larry Speakes, who later served as White House press spokesman, concluded during the transition that the Reagan administration was shaping up as a one-man show, the one man being Meese. He remembers telling Jim Baker, his acquaintance from the Ford administration, to keep an eye on Meese. "I told him, this guy's going to seize control and you're going to wind up some kind of low level staff guy, but Baker just said, 'Aw don't worry about it.' "

What Speakes did not know was that once Reagan had designated Baker as chief of staff, Baker had begun to fashion an organizational structure for the White House that would make it extremely difficult for Meese to have any real impact on policy without Baker's cooperation. Baker could afford to be nonchalant about the power Meese *seemed* to be acquiring because, as we'll see, he had already induced him to sign a compact severely limiting his ability to maneuver. In retrospect, Meese could not have understood the significance of the pact that Baker convinced him to sign; if he had, he would not have signed it. But Baker did understand it, and the typewritten memo, initialed by both men, was safely locked away among Baker's papers. Knowing nothing of this, Speakes continued to worry about Meese's growing clout. His memory of those days is of a Meese hugely confident, never in doubt about what was on the President's mind or agenda. With a professional spokesman's appreciation, Speakes recalled Meese's responses at briefings when he would rapidly answer reporters, "Yes," "No," "No decision on that yet. . . . Next question."

"It was really something to see," Speakes said years later.

As Reagan settled into the White House, the perception grew that Meese was clearly the first among equals. In power-conscious Washington, it was duly noted that even though Jim Baker had been the surprise choice for chief of staff, the job was obviously being downgraded to an administrative post. It was Meese, Washington noticed, who had been given Cabinet rank and the beautiful corner office in the White House west wing, the prestigious suite once occupied by Henry Kissinger. It was Meese, the organization charts showed, who had direct supervision over the two key components of the White House: the National Security Council, which coordinated the work of the State Department and the Pentagon, and the Domestic Council, which shaped domestic policy. In previous administrations, the national security adviser had always reported directly to the President and men such as Kissinger had used the post to become international celebrities as well as powerful Washington figures. *Congressional Quarterly* quoted a historian who saw Meese's role shaping up as the "fellow who walks about thinking, who always knows what the President wants on any issue." As an old Washington saying goes, that was accurate but not quite true. Like Speakes, most of Washington had not yet realized that it was outsider Baker, not insider Meese, who would become the real power in the early months of the Reagan administration. Baker not only held Meese in check in those early months; he also devised a system to keep the right wing at bay as he engineered a plan that enabled the President to make good on his main campaign promises: a massive buildup in defense coupled with a significant tax cut.

Baker's rise to power in those early months of the administration was no more surprising than Reagan's decision to put him in the job. Conservatives, especially, were dumbstruck. The President-elect did not make the decision public until a week after the election, but word of it spread quickly among the insiders. One of the first to hear of it was Richard Williamson, a young Chicago lawyer and right-wing strategist who had managed Illinois congressman Phil Crane's unsuccessful run for the nomination. He remembers telling the person who passed on the news, "You've got to be kidding."

Williamson eventually admired Baker for his intelligence and his adroit political skills and served ably as a senior member of Baker's White House team, but his reaction that morning reflected the surprise of many Republicans, in and out of the Reagan camp. Baker, after all, had spent most of his time in politics opposing Reagan. He had been Bush's campaign manager and chief strategist in the primaries that year, and he had been on the other side four years earlier when he served as Gerald Ford's campaign manager.

In his memoir, *Behind the Scenes*, Mike Deaver says it was about a week before the election when he first suggested to Reagan that Baker would make a good chief of staff. Reagan found the suggestion "interesting" and shortly after decided that Baker was his man, questioning only whether Baker would be interested. What Deaver did not reveal was the chain of carefully planned moves that had led to his suggestion. In fact, Deaver had been working for months on a plan to get the job for Baker. (Perhaps the plan should more accurately be described as a scheme to prevent Meese from getting it.) "Operation Baker," as some called it, had been the brainchild of Stu Spencer, the shrewd California political strategist who had been hired to run Reagan's first campaign for governor in 1966. Spencer had no use for Meese, and Deaver had reasons of his own for not wanting Meese in the top spot, so at Spencer's instigation during the weeks after the GOP convention, they joined forces with one goal: to prevent Meese from ever becoming chief of staff. Spencer says it was actually he, not Deaver, who first floated the idea of Baker as chief of staff to the Reagans. He brought up Baker's name when he dined with the Reagans at a Dallas hotel in early October. He did not push Baker for the job directly but offered his name as one of several people qualified to run the White House. Spencer was one of the few people whom Nancy Reagan allowed to speak directly to her husband in blunt language, and he remembers telling the couple that night, "You're going to be in a new place and you need someone in there who knows the ropes. Washington is not Sacramento."

Spencer had not played a major role in the 1980 campaign until after the convention in Detroit when Mrs. Reagan feared the campaign was not coming together as it should and urged Spencer to rejoin the team. Her husband was delighted with Spencer's decision to return, but that feeling was not shared by the staff, especially Meese. Meese had always suspected Spencer of trying to get him fired in 1970 when some of Reagan's friends were recommending a wholesale shake-up in the governor's office. (By then some Reagan backers had become disenchanted with Meese, feeling that although he had been competent enough during the time when he had advised Reagan on law enforcement matters, he had proved too disorganized to handle the broader responsibilities he inherited when he was promoted to executive secretary.) Adding to the hard feelings between Spencer and Meese had been Spencer's defection to the Ford campaign in 1976. Spencer had continued to advise Ford into the early months of 1980 as Ford considered the idea of launching yet another run for the presidency.

But Deaver and Spencer shared misgivings about Meese that went far beyond his shortcomings in the administrative area. Meese, in Deaver's view, was "a bumbling idiot," a feeling made worse by several slights Meese had inflicted on Deaver over the years. During their time in Sacramento, Deaver had served as deputy to two men—Meese and Bill Clark—and neither of them ever treated Deaver as an equal, then or later. "To them, Mike was always the guy who carried the suitcases," said one friend, "even after they all got to Washington." The fact that Reagan had allowed Deaver to leave the campaign during the showdown with John Sears, yet stood by Meese when Sears tried to dump him, only deepened Deaver's sense of resentment.

To Spencer, the professional politician, the problem with Meese was not so much personal as practical. It was a business problem, and Spencer's business was politics, specifically offering political advice at a very high fee. Men in such professions build their reputations and practice not only on expertise but on connections. Stu Spencer needed his own guy in Ronald Reagan's Washington, and it was impossible that Ed Meese would ever be that guy. Having Baker running the White House would certainly be in Spencer's best interest, but beyond that, he honestly felt that Baker was far more capable and qualified. Meese just wasn't up to the job, whereas Baker not only knew his way around Washington, but was an expert administrator. Many years later, Spencer chuckled when a visitor brought up the plan he had hatched with Deaver to block Meese. "I always looked on keeping Meese out of that job as my little gift to the health of the Republic," he said.

In the weeks after the convention, Spencer sold the idea to Baker in much the same way he had later presented it to the Reagans. As Baker recalled it, "Stu said he thought it was really important for the governor to have somebody who had been through the 'Washington experience' and he said he was going to talk to Deaver about it and then at one point . . . the three of us talked about it." Baker was definitely interested but was never certain that Reagan would ever take the idea seriously. Deaver, who had rejoined the campaign after Sears was fired, was in the perfect position to activate Spencer's plan. Now in control of Reagan's schedule, Deaver was arranging who saw the candidate and who didn't. Equally important, he always had access to Mrs. Reagan, so it was not difficult for Deaver to see that Baker had plenty of exposure to the Reagans. Intimate dinners were arranged, and Baker was assigned to give the candidate and his wife key briefings.

In truth, selling Jim Baker to the Reagans was not all that difficult a task. Although Baker had never been associated with Reagan's wing of the party (like his patron, George Bush, he had often thought of the Far Right as a group of yahoos), he was the kind of smooth operator who could impress Mrs. Reagan. Baker was a man of many sides and, like Henry Kissinger, had an unerring ability to know which side it was most advantageous to show at a given moment. On a hunting trip to south Texas, Jim Baker was a down-to-earth ""good old boy" who could enjoy a slug of sippin' whiskey without removing the plug of tobacco from his jaw. Yet the other side of Jim Baker was the smooth Princeton-educated sophisticate who moved easily through the boardrooms of the big banks and the country clubs of the Sunbelt. Baker was not just Texas; he was Houston. And he was not just Houston; he was *Old* Houston, the Houston of solid money and understated elegance.

Like many wealthy Texans, Baker had been a conservative Democrat most of his life but had switched to the Republican party in the mid-1960s when his best friend in Houston, George Bush, was first becoming involved in politics. As is often the case with successful men, Baker had always been able to make whatever job he had into a better job. He had used a minor post that Bush had obtained for him in the Ford administration as entrée to a low-level post in Ford's 1976 campaign, but had done such a remarkable job during the primaries that he had wound up running the campaign during the general election. After Bush's campaign had collapsed in the 1980 primaries, he moved on to a low-level position as the Reagan team's liaison with the League of Women Voters (the sponsors of the presidential debates that year). Against the advice of others in the Reagan camp, he had argued forcefully that Reagan should debate Carter. Then, when it seemed at one point that Carter might back out of the debates, he had played a major role in convincing the Carter people to go through with their original plan to meet Reagan face-to-face. Baker had good contacts with the Carter camp because his business interests were often bipartisan. He was involved, for example, in several ventures with fellow Texan Robert Strauss, one of Carter's main advisers. In the view of several political observers, it was the Baker-Strauss friendship that finally cleared the way for the 1980 debates. The debates proved to be a huge success for Reagan, of course, and Baker had been on the right side of that issue. Like Reagan, Baker understood that during the debates demeanor would be as important as content. Baker had put together the team that had prepped Reagan for the encounters, but while others were worrying that Reagan would forget important facts, Baker gave Reagan a card before the first debate with only one word of instruction: "Chuckle." That was the kind of advice that an old Hollywood actor could appreciate.

In all likelihood, Baker would have risen in the Reagans' estimation even without the help of Deaver and Spencer, but perhaps more remarkable than outsider Baker's ascendency was the fact that a longtime insider like Meese never saw it coming. Apparently unaware of the maneuvering, Meese was blindsided by Baker's appointment. He had assumed until the last that he would be the chief of staff. Baker himself has always believed that Meese learned the bad news on election night, but even then, according to Spencer and Deaver, Meese did not know. Baker and Meese met for breakfast the morning after Reagan's landslide victory and after a little conversation about the size of the President's victory, Meese told Baker, "The President's going to talk to you about some things that will involve us working together down the line." He left it at that.

"I'm sure we can, Ed," Baker responded. He, too, left it at that. Baker did not mention that he had received a call from the President just the night before, during which Reagan said he wanted to meet the next day to discuss something of importance. Baker's wife, Susan, had known of the discussions with Deaver and Spencer and surmised that the call could only mean one thing: the President-elect intended to offer her husband the chief of staff job. She burst into tears as Baker hung up the phone and they were not tears of joy. Susan Baker, like her husband, knew a little something about Washington, and she knew the job was a killer. Baker comforted her with the words, "Let's just wait and see."

Susan Baker's suspicions were confirmed the next day. Shortly after Baker's breakfast with Meese, Reagan offered Baker the chief of staff post with the hope that he "would be able to work with Ed Meese." Baker expressed confidence that he could but asked for a little time to think about it. He had already thought about it, of course, but Baker needed to work out exactly how Meese would be handled. He told Reagan he didn't want to be chief of staff in name only and suggested it was important for all involved to understand who was responsible for what.

Baker's public reputation in recent years has been that of a master political strategist, but one of his admirers may have characterized him more accurately when he said, "Baker didn't know all that much about conventional grass-roots politics. Hell, he wouldn't know a precinct captain from a bulldozer. His real strength was a keen appreciation of Republican protocol coupled with a real understanding of how Washington worked."

At no time was Baker's skill in those areas more evident than in the way he handled Meese. Even Spencer, the old pro, had told him there was no need to draw up a specific pact defining who did what. "I told him you're going to be the chief of staff and that's that," Spencer recalled. But that was not enough for the cautious Baker. During the initial meeting with Reagan, the President-elect had remarked that Meese had been very valuable to him through the years, the unspoken message being that even though Meese was not getting the top job, Reagan still looked on him as a vital player. Sensing this, Baker suggested that the whole idea of his being chief of staff might go down better if Meese had "Cabinet rank" and a nice title such as counselor to the President. (Years later Baker told a friend he had not given away anything: "I had been in the Ford administration long enough to know Cabinet rank meant nothing," the friend quoted Baker as saying.) Reagan thought Baker's suggestion was a fine idea, and the two parted so that Baker would have his "time to think." Meese, apparently, knew nothing of any of this when he met with the President-elect and Deaver later in the day for lunch. He had with him a detailed organization chart that had his own name penned in the chief of staff slot.

It was the presentation of the chart that gave the President-elect the opening to say that Meese would not be getting the top job, but would share responsibility for running the White House with Baker. To Deaver, Meese seemed stunned and obviously hurt, and in the hours that passed that afternoon, some around Reagan thought Meese might "walk," as one insider described it. But Meese decided to stay. Baker, meanwhile, had already begun to sketch out his own plan of who would be doing what in the Reagan White House. On a piece of standard typing paper, he wrote out his duties and those of Meese, dividing them into two columns. Here is a copy of that document.

*   *   *

MEESE   BAKER

Counselor to the President for   Chief of Staff
Policy (with cabinet rank)

Member Super Cabinet Executive   *as per*   Member Super Cabinet Executive
Committee (in absence of The   *published*   Committee
President preside over   *states*
meetings) *and V-P*

Participate as a principal in   Coordination and supervision of
all meetings of full Cabinet   White House Staff functions

Coordination and supervision   Hiring and firing authority over
of responsibilities of The   all elements of White House
Secretary to the Cabinet   Staff

Coordination and supervision   With Meese coordination and
of work of the Domestic   supervision of work of OMB,
Policy council and the   CEA, CEQ, Trade Rep and
National Security Council   S&T

With Baker coordination and   Participation as a principal
supervision of work of OMB,   in all policy group meetings
CEA, CEQ, Trade Rep and   *including full cabinet*
S&T

Participation as a principal   Coordination and control of
in all policy group meetings   all in and out paper flow
                                        to the President and of
attend any meeting   presidential schedule and
which Pres' attends – w/ his   appointments
consent
                                        Preside over meetings of
                                        White House Staff

1/17/80 *JAB II*
                                        Operate from office customarily
OK – [signature]   utilized by Chief of Staff
OK [signature]
                                        attend any meeting Pres.
                                        attends – w/ his consent.

It was a remarkable document. It was dated November 13, the day it was finally agreed upon, and the appointments of Baker and Meese were announced the next day. It had been one week since the President had offered the job to Baker. The two men initialed it again four days later, after adding a handwritten amendment that would allow both to attend all presidential meetings with the President's permission. The official announcement outlining responsibilities left the clear impression that Baker would be the administrator, the staff aide who "made the trains run on time," as one reporter wrote it. Meese would be the brains of the operation who decided where the trains went. It was easy to conclude at that point that Meese was the man in charge. At Baker's suggestion, the President had given him Cabinet rank while Baker had been left to carry the administrative load.

But if the document that Baker had euchred Meese into signing had been available for public scrutiny, those who know Washington would have understood that, in truth, Meese had wound up with a nice title and a beautiful office and little else. Baker had engineered a deal that placed him fully in control of the real levers of power in the White House. Although Meese had been given authority over the Domestic Council and the national security adviser would report to him, Baker had reserved for himself the power to determine what paperwork reached the Oval Office and who got in to see the President. Being in charge of the "staff functions," as the document outlined it, meant Baker had control of the White House press office, which determined what the public would be told about the administration; the White House speech writers, who would prepare the President's every utterance; the congressional liaison office, which would have responsibility for lobbying the President's programs on Capitol Hill; and the White House political office, which would shape the President's political agenda. Baker had seen to it that Meese was assigned Henry Kissinger's old corner office. He had taken the traditional chief of staff quarters, a much less attractive suite but the only staff quarters in the West Wing large enough for conducting meetings. (When the meeting is in your office in Washington, it's your meeting.)

What Baker understood and what Meese did not was that Meese had been given the assignment of developing policy but had been stripped of the necessary tools to make policy, to turn theory into reality. Meese may have known Sacramento, but Baker knew Washington. In Washington, the shortest distance between two points is never a straight line. A President cannot simply decide what is right and then expect others to implement it. Jimmy Carter tried that and failed miserably. In Washington, policy is made by managing the continual compromises that must be struck between the executive and legislative branches. Meese had Cabinet rank, but Baker had given himself the levers that are necessary to manage the compromises. More important to Baker, when Meese signed the document, he gave up his most precious asset: the right to see the President alone. In the opening months of the administration, Meese would appreciate more fully that his only real power to change policy depended on his longtime relationship with Reagan, and yet, in making his compact with Baker, Meese had given Baker "walk-in rights." He had agreed to let Baker join him anytime he went to the Oval Office unless Ronald Reagan objected. As Meese, of all people, should have known, Ronald Reagan found it extremely difficult to make such objections. Of course, Baker had been forced to give Meese the same rights, but with Baker's aides' monitoring who entered and left the Oval Office, Meese was never there without Baker's knowledge, yet it was easy for Baker to drop in without Meese's knowledge.

As surprising as it was to Washington, Baker's appointment would be seen in time as only part of a pattern that the Reagans often followed in naming top staffers. They had leaned heavily, as they so often did, on the advice of Stu Spencer, and they had gone to an outsider rather than one of the inner circle to handle a sensitive assignment. Richard Beal, a young staffer during the early days of Reagan's first term, once joked to insiders that the Reagans' hiring practices were similar to those of the Mafia. In the Mafia, the consigliere—the main adviser—is never a member of the family but always an outsider, for the simple reason that the top adviser must be expendable. Certainly the Reagans followed that practice in filling the chief of staff slot. At the end of the first term, Baker was succeeded by Secretary of the Treasury Donald Regan, who later confirmed just how much of an outsider he had been when he revealed that as Treasury secretary he had never met privately with the President to discuss economic policy. When he was fired, the job went to the "second Baker," Howard, a retired senator who was considered an alien by the California conservatives for many years, and finally, when Baker left in 1988, the chief of staff's job, by then largely a caretaker position, went to another outsider, Kenneth Duberstein, a longtime congressional lobbyist who had served under Baker. As debate continued throughout Reagan's years as to how much influence Nancy Reagan exerted, one aide summed it up this way: "Remember, Nancy always hired the consigliere—and fired him."

After his victory over Goldwater in 1964, Lyndon Johnson warned his legislative aides that they had no time to waste. "You've got just one year when Congress treats you right," he said. "Then they start worrying about themselves." LBJ spoke with rare authority. No man ever ascended to the presidency with as shrewd an understanding of how Capitol Hill worked as Lyndon Baines Johnson, who had wielded enormous power from the other end of Pennsylvania Avenue when he served as Senate majority leader during the Eisenhower years. By way of contrast, both Jimmy Carter and Ronald Reagan entered the White House with little or no knowledge of how to deal with Congress. But whereas Carter relied heavily on the counsel of fellow Georgians, who had as little experience in these matters as he did, the man in charge of achieving Reagan's legislative goals was James A. Baker III, who had been in Washington long enough to understand that the best way to get Congress to act is to move swiftly and decisively.

Baker knew that Reagan's best chance to get his program through Congress would be during his first months in office, the honeymoon period that follows a landslide election. He also knew that the first step in that process would be to develop a plan for those first months. So, in the weeks after the election, Baker moved quickly to solidify his own power and to lay the basic groundwork for turning Reagan's campaign promises into law.

During those early weeks of the transition when most attention was focused on the President's search for a Cabinet and Meese's daily pronouncements as head of the transition office, Baker quietly assembled a group to chart the course. In public, spokesmen for the President-elect were emphasizing the need for locating qualified conservatives to serve in the new administration, but the people whom Baker assembled were notable not so much for their ideology as for their Washington experience. As he would throughout his years in the White House, Meese leaned heavily on fellow Californians and those with strong conservative credentials during the transition, whereas Baker surrounded himself with those experienced in the ways of the Washington bureaucracy. Baker's key move was convincing Richard Darman to join the team. Darman was a Grand Old Party member of rare credentials: one of that tiny band known as liberal Republicans, a wing of the party exemplified by Elliot Richardson, the attorney general who had been fired by Richard Nixon because he refused to carry out Nixon's order to fire the special prosecutor investigating Watergate. Darman had been an aide to Richardson at one point, and eventually he and Baker would form one of the most powerful alliances of the Reagan era.

They had met by chance only a few years earlier when they had been minor players in a Cabinet shake-up initiated by Gerald Ford. Ford had ordered the reshuffling in an effort to stop the interoffice feuding among his staff and because, with an election approaching, he wanted to put his own stamp on the administration he had inherited from Nixon. At the time, Baker was just beginning to settle into his new job as deputy secretary of commerce, the post that had been secured through his close friendship with Bush. As part of the reshuffle, Ford named Bush to head the Central Intelligence Agency, replacing William Colby, with whom Ford had little rapport; Ford's chief of staff at the White House, Donald Rumsfeld, was named to head the Pentagon, replacing James Schlesinger, whom Ford despised.

Ford and his advisers did not want it to appear that the moves were ordered to settle personal scores, so in order to round out the package, Richardson (already rehabilitated by Ford and serving as ambassador to Great Britain) was called home to become Baker's boss as secretary of commerce. There was one hitch: the outgoing commerce secretary, Rogers Morton, needed a few additional months on the federal payroll to qualify for an increase in pension benefits. To accommodate Morton, who was having health problems, Richardson's starting date at Commerce was allowed to slide for a few months. In the interim, Richardson asked Darman to go to Commerce to supervise the transition. Morton was seldom seen at the department in those months, and Darman and Baker soon found themselves running the place. In the process, each gained respect for the talents of the other. Thus, it was only natural that when Reagan named Baker chief of staff, Darman was one of the first people to whom Baker turned for help.

Once Reagan was sworn in, Baker put Darman in one of the most sensitive White House posts: deciding what paperwork went into and out of the Oval Office and monitoring who saw the President personally. He reported directly to Baker.

Other members of Baker's team during the transition included David Gergen, a communications expert and speech writer who had worked in the Nixon White House; Richard Williamson, the Chicago lawyer and Republican strategist who had close ties to Reagan's friend Paul Laxalt; and Richard Beal, who had worked for Reagan's pollster Richard Wirthlin. Consulting with Wirthlin and relying heavily on his polling data, they concluded that Reagan could push through a massive tax cut during his first year, as well as a big increase in defense spending. Those two points would form the heart of their legislative agenda.

The strategy was as simple as the agenda was short. They would keep Congress focused on those issues and those issues alone. The rest of the campaign promises would be put on hold, and nothing would be allowed to interfere with the twin goals: build up defense; cut taxes. "If we can do that," Baker told his people at the time, "the rest will take care of itself." Jimmy Carter had beaten Jim Baker's candidate in 1976, but if Baker had learned one thing during the time he was out of power it was that no President can get everything he wants. Carter's legislative team had bombarded the Capitol with bills, programs, and proposals. Carter had wanted so much that Congress was never able to sort out what he really considered important. Baker was determined that that would not happen during Reagan's first year, and the way to prevent it was to keep the agenda simple. Give Congress no more than it could digest, and lobby it until Congress got it done.

In the first weeks of the administration, the plan was launched: Working with Howard Baker, the new majority leader in the Senate, the White House strategists persuaded Reagan to put aside the volatile social issues, such as school prayer and antiabortion legislation. The new secretary of state, Alexander Haig, was told that except for building up defense, major initiatives in foreign policy would have to wait until the economic goals had been achieved. In the end Baker and his people got what they wanted: the tax cut coupled with an increase in defense spending.

Except for Wirthlin and, with the later addition of Mike Deaver, the group that hammered out the plan for the "First 100

Days," as they called it (borrowing the phrase from the New Deal triumphs at the start of FDR's presidency) became the nucleus of the Baker wing of the White House, a group that conservatives derisively referred to in later years as "the pragmatists."

Laurence I. Barrett of *Time* magazine, who closely followed the early years of the Reagan presidency, concluded in his book, *Gambling with History*, that the decision to focus on so narrow an agenda may well have been one of the most important of the administration, in that Baker, Wirthlin, Gergen, and Darman had correctly read the mood of the country, sensed what was possible, and realized there would be only a limited time in which to take advantage of it. In retrospect, what seems equally important to Reagan's early legislative success is that Baker and those around him also correctly read the mood and the mind of the man they served.

It was during those first weeks of the transition that Baker's people realized that Reagan himself could not always be counted on to provide guidance for his administration. Reagan did espouse strongly held conservative views, but it would often be their responsibility not only to determine how to translate those views into policy but to determine as well *which* views were to be acted upon. It was an insight that proved as valuable to the Reagan team's early successes as the carefully thought-out planning documents that held the blueprints for the first three months in office.

University of Pittsburgh political scientist Bert A. Rockman has written that the problem for Reagan's staff was to develop a system of management for a "committed presidency" headed by a "detached President." In blunter terms, the Baker people learned that they were working for a President whose abilities lay in the field of salesmanship, a President who had little interest in plotting the strategy behind that salesmanship. In a sense, Reagan's people came to see him more as an abstract idea than as a flesh-and-blood leader, someone who represented a certain philosophy, to be sure, but as his budget director, David Stockman, would later conclude, "His conservative vision was only a vision. He had a sense of ultimate values and a feel for long-term directions, but he had no blueprint for radical governance." When Stockman published that assessment in his memoir, *The Triumph of Politics*, it shocked Washington, but among the points that stick most vividly in our memory of those years is just how widely shared that view was among the people who ran the Reagan White House,

and how at variance it was with the perception of those who saw
Reagan from afar.

Voters saw Reagan as a warm, friendly figure who might get
a little confused about details from time to time but had no doubt
about where he wanted to lead the country. In contrast, those
who worked closely with Reagan often viewed him as aloof, indifferent to those around him, and, at times, uninformed about
and uninterested in his own programs. In a variety of ways, Reagan's disengaged style would come to be recognized as the most
striking characteristic of his presidency.

But it had been there all along. For example, reporters who
traveled with him in 1980 said that when visitors were taken
aboard Reagan's campaign plane to meet him, they often remarked on his seeming lethargy. Eight years later Larry Speakes
recalled that Reagan sometimes took months to remember the
names of aides who worked closely with him. On more than one
occasion, he was noticed nodding off during briefings on legislation. Reports of Reagan's unscheduled naps became widespread
during the early months of the administration, to such an extent
that Reagan himself once joked that someday there would be a
chair marked, "RONALD REAGAN SLEPT HERE." To some, Reagan
was simply lazy. Others who knew him better explained it in a
different way: Reagan at heart was a contented man who raised
few questions as long as things were running smoothly; the sooner
you understood that, the easier it was to deal with him and work
for him.

"Ronald Reagan is not a stupid person," said one of the people
who helped draw up the planning document for the first hundred
days, "but he was the least curious person that I ever met."

Baker, himself, has never commented on that assessment, but
several of his people reached that conclusion when they briefed
Reagan on the hundred-day plan. It was, after all, a fairly controversial document. A small group of men who had hardly known
the President before the election were presuming to tell him how
to spend his first three months in office. No presentation could
have been more carefully planned. They plotted every word of
what they would say to him. They tried to anticipate what questions he would ask. They worked on back-up answers in the event
Reagan pressed them on a particular point. They would tell each
other such things as "Now if he raises this point, our answer should
be this," and so on. Finally, the day of the briefing came. Reagan

ushered them in and put them at ease with some old show-business stories. Then they outlined their plan, concluding with, "Any questions, sir?" The response? "Sounds great," said the man who would soon become the fortieth President of the United States. "Go to it." To the briefers' astonishment, Reagan did not ask a single question.

Reagan had evoked a similar response that week from outgoing President Carter during a meeting in the Oval Office. Carter aide Jody Powell recalled that Carter had spent several hours compiling a list of problems that only a President can deal with— matters of extreme sensitivity ranging from command and control of the nuclear forces to confidential assessments of various world leaders. "The boss really thought it was important for Reagan to know this stuff before he was sworn in," Powell said, "and as he ran through it he couldn't believe that Reagan wasn't asking any questions. He thought maybe Reagan wasn't taking any notes because he didn't have a pad and pencil and finally offered him one, but Reagan said, no thanks; he could remember it. It was just the damnedest thing." Carter was also so struck by Reagan's seeming lack of interest that he mentioned the session in his White House memoir, *Keeping Faith*. He reported that Reagan made only one substantive comment. When the talk turned to the situation in South Korea, Carter said Reagan expressed some envy for the kind of authority South Korean officials were able to exert to put down campus unrest.

Four years later, after he became White House chief of staff, Donald Regan was equally astonished when he presented Reagan a detailed set of goals for the second term and Reagan approved the plan without making a single change in it or asking any questions about it. To those in the White House, Reagan's apparent indifference would become known as Reagan's Way.

The passivity that so puzzled those around Reagan throughout his White House years had a far different effect on the public. Voters liked Reagan's laid-back management style. There was something reassuring, even soothing, about a chief executive who took events in stride. After the turmoil and confusion of the seventies, it was good to know that the man in charge saw no reason for concern. But to those on the inside, it was another matter. Reagan's desire to delegate placed an enormous burden on his staff. Because they were long on Washington experience, Baker's men were fairly successful in that first year at understanding what Reagan wanted, or at least in identifying programs that deserved top priority. Later, when men of far less experience found themselves with the same leeway, they were not nearly so successful in discerning what was in the best interest of Reagan or their country.

Marine Lieutenant Colonel Oliver North would later argue that he *thought* he was carrying out the President's wishes during the arms dealings with Iran, and National Security Adviser John Poindexter mistakenly concluded that responsibility stopped at his desk, not the Oval Office. Even an experienced operator like Reagan's one time spokesman Larry Speakes would concede, finally, that he had manufactured quotes and released them in the President's name because he assumed he knew what the President wanted to say.

Speakes had already left the White House and was serving as a corporate officer at a Wall Street brokerage house when he disclosed the practice in his book *Speaking Out,* but there was such an adverse reaction, especially from the press, that within a week, Speakes was forced to resign his high-paying post. To visitors and old friends, Speakes seemed generally stunned and surprised by the outcry. As he explained it to us, manufacturing quotes had become so routine that it was given little thought. "Mike Deaver did it all the time for me," Speakes said. "I would call him (during a news event or when there was a pending question from a reporter) and say, 'Okay, Deaver what's the one for this one?' and he would say, 'What can we say . . . how about this?' "

Deaver later confirmed this in an interview with the authors but said he did it only when the situation involved trivial matters such as what the President said when he opened a birthday gift.

"It was just a way to save the President's time," he said, ""and I always told him later what quote I had attributed to him. I would never have quoted him on substantive matters."

After some months in office, people in the Reagan White House were presuming to know what the President wanted with such regularity that it became easy to forget who was supposed to be in charge. In olden times, pagan priests claimed that only they knew what pleased the gods because only they could speak with them, but in the Reagan White House there was not even that pretension. Staffers seldom found it necessary to say that the President had instructed them to carry out an action; they simply presumed that if they acted within certain parameters, Reagan would not object. Reagan was not the kind of manager who asked for progress reports. Perhaps it was only natural that as the staff became more and more adept at reading Reagan's mind, they ascribed to it supernatural powers that were almost omniscient. For the sake of expediency, there evolved the prevailing view that nothing escaped the notice of the all-knowing chief executive.

"We had a rule," Speakes told us, "that the President is aware of everything. We would be asked, 'Is the President aware of what Congressman So and So said?' And the answer always was, 'well, yes he is,' " said Speakes. "It was such a doggone common practice, but nobody can afford to say so. The President is like the Good Lord: he's just aware of everything."

After Reagan was shot in the spring of 1981, it became apparent that the White House was not being run by Ed Meese as Washington had believed in the beginning, but by what came to be known as a troika: the team of Meese, Baker, and Deaver. It was Meese, Baker, and Deaver who were seen entering the hospital each morning. It was Meese, Baker, and Deaver who emerged later with the orders of the day. It was an unusual blending of talents that had not been on anyone's organization chart in the beginning, but it had evolved into a structure that seemed to work. Concerns about Meese's administrative abilities had proved well founded, but Meese did know the President's mind. All those years back in California when he had compressed staff suggestions into a paragraph or two that Reagan could understand had not been wasted; he did know Reagan's likes and dislikes, and when it came to anticipating Reagan's reactions on policy issues, he was the unparalleled expert. Deaver brought an even more specialized skill to the table: he knew how to handle Nancy, the bane of the staff as Donald Regan would later learn to his sorrow.

Deaver was often credited in those days with being a public relations genius, a master of images who had a knack for knowing just what photograph, just what setting, just what quotation (real or imagined) would best illustrate the point that Reagan wanted to make; as Reagan's reputation as the "Great Communicator" grew, Deaver was seen as the great packager. To those on the inside, however, those skills were not nearly so valuable as Deaver's ability to take care of Mrs. Reagan. He was her sounding board, errand boy, confidential adviser, and, in some cases, even her communications link to her husband. Pat Buchanan and others might sneer that Deaver was nothing more than "Lord of the Chamber Pot," but more discerning members of the White House staff appreciated the enormous load that Deaver was carrying. Every minute that Mrs. Reagan was on the phone to Deaver was a minute that she was not on the phone to other staff members. Like Deaver, she had a good sense of what reflected well on her husband and what didn't, and her advice often proved valuable, but "taking care of Nancy" was a taxing full-time job. Baker understood that from the beginning. His replacement, Regan, didn't understand even at the end, and that misunderstanding more than anything else was finally his undoing.

Reagan had never been one to spend a lot of time in the office, and as he was recovering from his wounds he was seen even less frequently. He would go to the office for a few hours each morning and then depart around noon to rest in the White House living quarters. By the time he arrived, Meese, Baker, and Deaver would have already met over breakfast in Baker's office and planned the strategy for the day. Once that had been decided, there would be a larger meeting with the staff to hand out assignments. Reagan would receive a general outline before he returned to the living quarters to rest. Just what part Reagan himself played in charting his administration's course during those months often depended on the viewpoint of the staff member who dealt with him. One man who saw Reagan often in those days said that if Reagan was presented with a proposal and told that the staff agreed that it was the right course of action, he seldom challenged it. As John Sears had discovered back in the campaign of 1976, Reagan just did not seem to delve deeply into any issue, but he did seem to possess an uncanny ability during discussion to read body language and to sense concerns among staff members even when they were unspoken.

"The important thing," said one staffer, "was to get him engaged. He often had good ideas but he had to be drawn out. He just wasn't the kind of person who volunteered things." It was a trait that had been noticed by people who had known Reagan in his youth. In college, he had been a rather indifferent student, but one whose memory allowed him to scan textbooks on the night before the quiz and retain enough to make a passable grade. Reagan, apparently, was able to absorb huge amounts of information, but as one person who knew him in college said, he seldom questioned the information or wondered about it. White House aides discovered that when Reagan was creative, it was most often when he had a pencil in his hand. "I never understood it," said one.

You could talk to him about options and he might or might not get interested. But if you gave him a pencil and said these are the options but maybe we're missing something, he would start doodling around, marking out words, and the first thing you knew he had taken a little of option one, and a little of option two, and added something of his own and you had a whole new option. Maybe it was all those years of editing his speeches, but somehow or other, that's when he was at his best.

What continually amazed the staff was how seldom Reagan felt the need to become involved. To Reagan, hiring the right people to offer advice was the key to decision making. "He really did believe that you hired people you could trust," Speakes said later, "and then you let them do their job." If Reagan trusted a staffer, he seldom questioned his recommendations. The problem was that once he placed his faith in someone, he seemed unable to revise his judgment about him. Once a good man, always a good man, seemed to be Reagan's view. "What resulted was a very undisciplined White House," said Edward J. Rollins, who ran the White House political office in Reagan's first term and later helped to run Reagan's 1984 campaign. "Reagan just couldn't bring himself to fire anyone. If he had fired some of the people who created some of the early problems, we wouldn't have had a lot of the others that came along later."

When Congress passed the big tax cut in the summer of 1981 and the President signed a budget that included a huge increase for the Pentagon later in the year, Jeff Fishel, professor of government at American University, called it a legislative achievement "virtually unparalleled" in the history of the modern presidency. That was not an isolated view. Even some of Reagan's former critics praised the President, who not only had set a new upbeat tone in Washington but could also point to concrete accomplishments. Columnist David Broder, who just months before had reported that questions were being raised as to whether Reagan were equipped to meet the challenge he faced, now wrote that

Reagan's first year had produced "one of the most remarkable demonstrations of Presidential leadership in modern history." It had been even more remarkable when one paused to consider that in the early months of that year, America's oldest President had been shot, but he had recovered rapidly and now appeared to be in better health than ever. So, as 1981 drew to a close, the mood of euphoria that permeated the Reagan White House was justified.

Yet even as they basked in all the praise that came their way, some of Reagan's more alert advisers realized that the overall picture was not so sanguine as it appeared to be. There were signs that the country was sliding into a recession, and that wasn't the only economic worry. The popular tax cut had been the cornerstone of Reagan's supply-side economic policy, but in an embarrassing public disclosure that fall, the administration's budget director, David Stockman, projected huge deficits on a scale never before seen in Washington. If that forecast turned out to be accurate, it could raise unsettling questions about the wisdom of the tax cut and the supply-side philosophy that inspired it.

Nor was that all. Baker's decision to concentrate all the resources of the White House on the two legislative priorities, to the exclusion of everything else, proved to be a stunning success in the short run. But in long-range terms, there were serious drawbacks to that approach. It was one thing to downplay controversial social questions such as abortion and school prayer, for it could be argued that a posture of benign neglect was the best way to deal with such flash-point issues. Foreign policy, however, was another matter. The failure to establish a clear and coherent system of leadership in that vital area soon created a tangle of problems that could not properly be ignored. In time, those problems, festering and feeding upon themselves, produced a climate of chaos and frustration so pervasive that it prompted a few adventurous deputies to embark on a series of covert actions that, when finally exposed, would leave a lasting and ignominious stain on the Reagan administration. But, of course, none of that could have been foreseen in the heady days of 1981.

6

From the Groves of Academe

"The system is being emasculated."
—*White House staffer*

The office of national security adviser was destined to become the nemesis of Ronald Reagan's presidency, the center of the Iran-Contra imbroglio that erupted midway through his second term and altered the perception that millions of Americans had of Reagan and his leadership. There was irony in that. For what was largely forgotten during all the tumult was that in the early months of the Reagan administration, no post seemed less likely to become a trouble spot, a source of turmoil and controversy, than that of national security adviser. The first in a long line of officials who held that job under Reagan was Richard V. Allen, and at the time of his appointment he was told that unlike most of his predecessors, he would not be given a major role in the shaping of foreign policy. For his part, Allen did nothing to exceed those low expectations, and when he was replaced in January 1982, he departed under the cloud of a petty scandal that had tarnished an already dubious reputation. That was no surprise to Allen's many critics, who believed that, given his track record, he should never have had the job in the first place.

Dick Allen was no stranger to the White House basement, which was the special domain of the National Security Council. He had worked there briefly, under Kissinger, during the early months of the Nixon administration, and when he returned to the White House twelve years later as Reagan's national security adviser, Allen already had been a figure of controversy. There had been, for one thing, a curious mix-up about his academic credentials. When he first came to public attention as a member of the Nixon team in the late 1960s, he was commonly referred to as "Dr." Allen. But it turned out, on further examination, that he had not quite earned the right to that lofty title. Nor was that the only aspect of his past that raised troubling questions.

Like John Sears, Allen was a graduate of Notre Dame, a school for which Reagan has had a romantic affinity ever since he played the legendary George Gipp in the popular film *Knute Rockne—All American*. A political science major, he received his B.A. in 1957 and his master's degree the following year, and from Notre Dame he went on to study international economics at the universities of Freiburg and Munich in West Germany. Then, throughout the sixties, as he moved through various "think tanks" in the States (notably at Georgetown and the Hoover Institution at Stanford), Allen did little to clarify the prevailing assumption that he was a bona fide Ph.D. It wasn't until after he went to work for the Nixon administration that the truth came to light: Allen never received his doctorate because his professors at Munich had rejected his thesis. "Dr." Allen was, in reality, a mere mister, and by then he was also getting low marks from the professor he worked for in Washington: Dr. Kissinger.

Unlike Kissinger, whose previous allegiance had been to Nelson Rockefeller, Allen entered the White House as a staunch Nixon man. Even in the days of exile, he refused to believe that Nixon's political career had been destroyed by the costly electoral defeats in 1960 and 1962. Indeed, as early as 1963 he expressed that sentiment in a fan letter to Nixon, and that act, along with his growing reputation as a conservative scholar, moved Allen into Nixon's orbit. When it was time to launch the comeback, he joined the campaign as Nixon's chief foreign policy adviser, and during that period he was encouraged to assume that if Nixon won, he would become national security adviser. But instead, that post went to Kissinger, and Allen had to settle for serving as one of Kissinger's aides.

It wasn't long before he had to settle for even less than that. As Kissinger began laying the groundwork for his primary long-range goals—détente with China and the Soviet Union—he soon discovered that, in Dick Allen, he had a deputy who regarded such efforts as a betrayal of conservative doctrine. It wasn't just a matter of being a hard-liner (Kissinger himself, after all, was no softie in that area), but Allen was the kind of inflexible cold warrior who opposed almost any gesture or overture toward improving relations with the Communist bloc. In addition, Kissinger eventually grew to regard Allen as an intellectual lightweight, and he arrived at that judgment even before the embarrassing story of the rejected doctoral thesis was unveiled. Henry Kissinger was, then and later, a man who excelled at getting rid of subordinates who did not agree with him or measure up to his standards, and after a few unhappy months in the White House basement, Allen was eased out. He later resurfaced in another part of the Nixon White House as a deputy assistant to the President for international trade and economic policy.

Having a reputation as a rigid right-winger who had rebelled against Kissinger's plans for détente was a surefire way to win the trust and approval of Ronald Reagan. Thus, by 1980, Allen was back in the political big time, having secured a place on the Reagan team as the candidate's top foreign policy adviser. But then other shadows from his past emerged. In the summer and fall of 1980, various articles were published that accused Allen of misconduct during the period when he was Nixon's assistant for international trade and economic affairs. One charge against him was that he had relayed vital information from private government meetings to certain Japanese contacts, warning them of a rise in protectionist sentiment and urging them to employ a lobbyist in Washington to look out for their interests. Then, when Nissan responded to that advice by hiring a $120,000-a-year consultant, Allen demanded half of the fee on the ground that "your introductions to Japan were arranged by me." Another allegation claimed that Allen, after having used his White House position to pressure Japan to buy planes from the Grumman Corporation, then asked Grumman for a $1 million contribution to Nixon's 1972 reelection campaign.

Still other charges dealt with Allen's activities after he left the government and formed his own consulting firm, Potomac International. It was noted, for example, that just one day after he quit his job at the Nixon White House, he began doing work for the lawyer of Robert Vesco, the notorious stock swindler and fugitive from justice. News accounts at the time suggested that their association led to various schemes in which, once again, Allen seemed to be misusing his government connections to benefit himself. None of the investigative pieces went so far as to assert that Allen had broken any law, but, at the very least, they raised disburbing questions about his ethics and sense of propriety.

Allen's response to the allegations was to label them as so much "BS," which he defined as "Bolshevik storytelling." At first, others in the Reagan camp were also inclined to dismiss the charges, but when the negative press persisted well into the fall of 1980, they decided that Allen had become a campaign liability, and five days before the election, he was forced to resign from the Reagan team. But he did not have to endure the indignity of exile for very long; one of the first decisions Reagan made after his victory was to bring Allen back. When reporters inquired about this act of instant rehabilitation, the President-elect explained that his own people had probed into Allen's record and "we find absolutely no evidence of wrongdoing whatsoever."

This was an early whiff of the pervasive odor that would later be christened the "sleaze factor," and it was also a harbinger of the way Reagan and his spokesmen would often deal with charges leveled against members of their administration. Even on those occasions when the allegations were serious enough to warrant indictments—as in the Iran-Contra cases against Oliver North and John Poindexter—Reagan's response, more often than not, would be to proclaim his faith in the innocence of those whose actions had dishonored his presidency. The man Reagan assigned to investigate Allen's past transgressions, if that's what they were, was none other than Ed Meese, who, in the years ahead, would spend much of his career as attorney general defending his own actions and reputation when he was accused of legal and/or ethical violations.

Once Reagan had bestowed his approval, the next step was to name Allen to the post of national security adviser. More than anything else, that was a political appointment, a calculated sop to disgruntled conservatives, many of whom were outraged by the moderate cast of the Cabinet that had been so haphazardly assembled. It was a modest concession to make to the hard-line conservatives, for Reagan had made it clear that he intended to downgrade the office of national security adviser, to curtail the power and prestige that so many of its occupants had flaunted in recent years. This was an attempt to redress the historical balance: Reagan and his people wanted to reduce the scope of the office to what had been its original purpose and function.

The advisory post came into existence as an offshoot of the National Security Council, which was established under Harry Truman as part of a massive reorganization of the executive branch. At the time, the formation of the council was overshadowed by other, more significant aspects of that restructuring: the creation of both the Defense Department and the Central Intelligence Agency. Authorized by the National Security Act of 1947, these sweeping changes were designed to meet the escalating challenge of the cold war. The National Security Council was set up to serve as a coordinating apparatus; it was chaired by the President, and the only other officers then designated to be members of the council were the vice president, the secretaries of state and defense, the chairman of the joint chiefs of staff, and the director of the CIA. In the beginning and throughout the Truman years, the council membership did not include a special adviser from the White House staff. That position was created later, after Dwight Eisenhower became President.

Eisenhower was the kind of chief executive who strongly believes in the broad delegation of authority. This had been his basic approach to the challenge of command when he was a five-star general leading the Allied forces to victory in Europe in World War II and he saw no reason to change now that he was President. In the aftermath of the D day invasion of Normandy, some critics complained that Eisenhower was not up front when his troops hit the beaches. There's no doubt that if one of the more swashbuckling American generals of that war—Douglas MacArthur, say, or George S. Patton—had been in charge of that operation, he would have made sure he was on hand at the front. But this was not Ike's style; he preferred to direct the assault without fanfare from his headquarters in England. A few years later, when a reporter had the temerity to recall that criticism in an interview with Eisenhower, he bristled. "Look," he said, "I planned the goddam thing and assumed full responsibility for it. What else did they expect me to do? Help load a truck?"

The general went on to become a President who saw no need to become immersed in governmental details and procedures. Among the many chores that Ike decided to delegate was that of supervising the National Security Council. He set up a planning board to chart the council's course and appointed one of his subordinates to head it. Thus was born the post of national security adviser, although at the time and for many years thereafter, those who took on the job had to bear the cumbersome title of special assistant to the President for national security affairs.

The man Eisenhower picked to run the National Security Council was a Boston lawyer and banker named Robert Cutler. During World War II, Cutler had served in Washington as a special assistant to Secretary of War Henry Stimson and Army Chief of Staff General George C. Marshall. When Marshall promoted him to brigadier general, he chose to praise Cutler in rather colorful terms, calling him "a rose among cabbages."

But he was a rose who knew his place, and neither then nor later did he try to encroach on the authority of the cabbages who outranked him. As Eisenhower's national security adviser, Cutler operated within precise limits. His main job was to interact with the Cabinet officers and other members of the council and pass on their policy recommendations to the President. Unlike his successors, Cutler stayed within the bounds of his advisory role and did not initiate policies. Indeed, at the time, the entire scope of U.S. foreign policy was under the rigid control of Secretary of State John Foster Dulles, the ardent cold warrior and stern Presbyterian who often treated the art of diplomacy as if it were a subbranch of theology. (In those days, the enemy was not just communism, but *Godless* communism.) In line with his executive style, even Ike was inclined to defer to Dulles on most foreign policy issues. That, after all, was Dulles's department, and as long as Eisenhower continued to have confidence in him, Dulles was free to run it without interference from the White House.

What was so striking about Robert Cutler, as we view him three decades later, was his unrelenting obscurity. Again, in contrast to his successors, he had the "passion for anonymity" that once was regarded as a prerequisite for high-level aides to the President. Throughout his years in the White House, he was virtually unknown to the general public, and even in Washington, he rarely attracted much attention. In the words of one friend from those days, Cutler was "untouchable, unreachable and un-quotable." Yet those who were familiar with the Eisenhower administration were aware that he was an important figure whose quiet voice was listened to in the discussions that mattered. Certainly the President he served placed a high value on his judgment and opinions, and Cutler was not shy about speaking his mind when Eisenhower turned to him for advice.

To cite one telling example: When the French were routed at Dien Bien Phu in 1954, a formidable group of high-ranking officials that included Dulles, Vice President Nixon, and the joint chiefs of staff urged Eisenhower to send American troops to Vietnam to prevent an outright Communist victory there. Cutler opposed the intervention, at least in part because it was economically unsound, and after weighing all the options, Ike sided with his national security adviser. Thus, a major military blunder was averted until a few years later when other Presidents, Kennedy and Johnson, were heeding the counsel of advisers who, having graduated from a different school of thought, redefined the priorities.

Shrouded in obscurity during his years of service to Eisenhower, Cutler left no personal imprint on the national consciousness, and he soon lapsed into the mists and shadows of historical neglect. Yet in hindsight, he appears to have been a figure of some consequence. He was also sui generis: the first man to serve as national security adviser, he turned out to be the last of his breed. There would be no more frugal bankers appointed to that post, and the assertive academics who followed in his footsteps would have neither his passion for anonymity nor his sense of restraint in responding to international crises of one kind or another. Least of all would they be content, as Cutler had been, to work within the limitations of a purely advisory role.

On the surface, there were certain similarities between Cutler and the man John F. Kennedy picked to serve as his national security adviser. McGeorge Bundy was another Boston aristocrat whose patrician sense of duty led him to seek a career in public service. He also had come under the influence of Cutler's Washington mentor, Henry Stimson. His father, Harvey Bundy, had served as assistant secretary of state under Stimson in the Hoover admin-

istration, and as a young man, "Mac" Bundy helped Stimson research and write his autobiography. Finally, they were both
Harvard men, although that school tie defined Bundy a lot more
than it did Cutler and underscored one of the main differences
between them. Whereas Cutler's professional background was in
finance, Bundy was a scholar and academic. A professor in the
department of government at Harvard, where his specialty was
foreign policy, he also served as dean of the faculty, a prestigious
position that extended his influence well beyond Cambridge. Bundy's political roots were Republican and he had supported both
Dewey and Eisenhower in the four preceding presidential elections, but when the Republicans nominated Nixon in 1960, he
shifted his allegiance to Kennedy. His reward for making that
public gesture was the post of national security adviser.

Bundy was endowed with creative energy and a forceful intellect, and, as he had demonstrated at Harvard, he had an ap-
titude for power and leadership. He was not one to settle for an
obscure backseat role, and he soon began to enlarge the scope of
his office and extend his authority into all areas of foreign policy.
Bundy made those moves with the full blessing of Kennedy, whose
reliance on his national security adviser directly corresponded to
his growing disenchantment with the man he had chosen as his
secretary of state, Dean Rusk.

Rusk was able and experienced. He had served in both the
Pentagon and the State Department during the Truman admin-
istration, and in more recent years he had been president of the
Rockefeller Foundation. But his placid temperament and bureaucrat's mentality had an enervating effect on Kennedy. A firm
believer in the status quo, Rusk approached most issues conven-
tionally, and that was not the way to impress the young President.
In his quest for innovation, Kennedy turned more and more to
Bundy, who had all the dynamic qualities that Rusk lacked.
Spurred by that encouragement, Bundy eventually eclipsed Rusk
in power and influence and became, next to Kennedy himself,
the chief architect of foreign policy in the administration.

After the assassination, Bundy stayed on at the White House
for two and a half years, but he never developed the rapport with
Lyndon Johnson that he had enjoyed with Kennedy. Unable to
adjust to LBJ's expansive personality and browbeating style, he
left in 1966 to accept a job as head of the Ford Foundation.

Replacing Bundy as national security adviser was another Kennedy import from the groves of academe: Walt Rostow, an MIT professor who had hooked up with Kennedy in the early stages of his run for the presidency. In fact, Rostow was credited with coining the term "New Frontier" and coming up with the slogan that became Kennedy's favorite battle cry: "LET'S GET THIS COUNTRY MOVING AGAIN." But Rostow's ambition was made of more than a mere flair for rhetoric.

Bundy and Rostow were just two of the professors who worked in the White House in the early 1960s. Their arrival marked the greatest infusion of academic clout to hit Washington since the days of Roosevelt's Brain Trust, and like all the other New Frontiersmen Kennedy had gathered around him, they prided themselves on their mental toughness. That concept, and all that it implied, had a special meaning for Bundy and Rostow and the others who had made the jump from the classroom.

During the Eisenhower years, intellectuals were generally in disrepute. They shared the stigma of the "egghead" label that had been pinned on Adlai Stevenson, the candidate who had been the hero of the liberal elite. To counteract that image, the professors who went to work for Kennedy set out to prove that they were a tougher breed: active and vigorous shirt-sleeved intellectuals who had no qualms about meeting the threat of communism with force. Thus, when faced with *their* moment of truth in Vietnam, they recommended military escalation—and that was their most enduring legacy.

The trend that began with Bundy and continued with Rostow accelerated when Henry Kissinger moved into the White House as Richard Nixon's national security adviser. Here was yet another strong-willed professor who had been recruited from the faculty at Harvard. In both academic circles and as a special adviser to New York governor Nelson Rockefeller, Kissinger had built a formidable reputation as an expert on Realpolitik in the cold war era, and he relished the opportunity to put his balance-of-power theories into practice. Although Bundy and Rostow did not shun publicity as Robert Cutler had in the fifties, they were introverts compared to Kissinger, who imbued in the post of national security adviser a high sense of theater. His penchant for shuttle diplomacy and clandestine missions to foreign capitals thrust him into the center of world affairs. In 1971, his secret trip to Peking, which for years had been the "forbidden city" in Washington's constrictive view of the world, set up the dramatic high point of Nixon's presidency: the diplomatic breakthrough with China.

To his admirers, Henry Kissinger was the star in the Nixon administration. But one inevitable side effect of his domineering presence was to further diminish the office of the secretary of state. The slights and decline in influence that Dean Rusk had to endure during the Kennedy years were little compared to the humiliation that was inflicted on Nixon's man at State, William Rogers, a seasoned Washington veteran who had served as attorney general under Eisenhower. Kissinger was not content merely to encroach on the traditional authority of the State Department; instead, he seized control of the entire apparatus of foreign policy. And as "Super K" strode across the world stage, drawing attention to himself and all his works, Rogers was reduced to the role of a ceremonial cipher.

Of course, all that changed in the spring of 1973, when Kissinger replaced Rogers as secretary of state, a move that enabled him to assume formally all the power he had been wielding as a "mere" adviser. Yet even then, he did not quit his day job. Having worked so hard to expand his White House operation into a department that not only dominated foreign affairs but military policy as well, he did not want to give it up, and for the next two years Kissinger was both secretary of state *and* national security adviser. When Gerald Ford became President, he chose to retain Kissinger as his secretary of state, but eventually coaxed him into relinquishing the national security post to his chief deputy on the White House staff, Lieutenant General Brent Scowcroft.

General Scowcroft was an able and respected official who went about his duties in a quiet and self-effacing manner that was reminiscent of that of Robert Cutler. He, too, saw his role as strictly that of an adviser and coordinator, and not an architect of foreign policy. (Also, as a Kissinger protégé, Scowcroft knew that his mentor would not countenance any challenge to his authority as secretary of state.) Hence, for a brief period, a sense of proportion was restored to the post of national security adviser. But nevertheless Bundy, Rostow, and especially Kissinger had established an unsettling precedent, one that, in certain circumstances, could provoke a bitter struggle for power within an administration. And that is precisely what happened when the next crowd came to town.

* * *

Although Jimmy Carter campaigned as an outsider and a critic of the established order, his major appointments in the sphere of foreign policy were entirely orthodox and consistent with the recent pattern. Like Kennedy and Nixon, he chose a veteran of the Washington bureaucracy as his secretary of state and recruited an imperious academic to serve as his national security adviser. The Cabinet post went to Cyrus Vance, who had served in the Pentagon during the Kennedy-Johnson years, first as secretary of the army and then as deputy secretary of defense; and the White House job was given to Zbigniew Brzezinski, another Ivy League scholar who had made his mark as a student at Harvard and, later, as a professor of government at Columbia.

It was not a good mix. Frictions developed between Vance and Brzezinski, at least in part because of philosophical differences. Vance was an avid supporter of the efforts toward détente with the Soviet Union, which had been the aim of Kissinger's foreign policy under both Nixon and Ford. On the other hand, Brzezinski, who rejoiced in being described as a militant anti-Communist, took a more hard-line view of the Russians and their motives. Their disagreement over how to approach the fundamental question of East-West relations was certainly part of the problem. But more than that, it was the historical or institutional legacy they inherited that made them natural enemies.

From Brzezinski's point of view, Kissinger's virtuoso performance during his tenure as national security adviser was the model to be emulated. What's more, he identified with Kissinger in other ways as well. The brilliant success of the Jewish immigrant, whose family fled Hitler's Germany when he was just a youngster, struck a responsive chord in Brzezinski, the son of a Polish diplomat. (He was born in Warsaw five years after Kissinger's birth in Fürth.) Then as young émigrés, they had excelled in their studies at Harvard, and, of course, they both went on to achieve distinction as professors of government. So, to Brzezinski, it was only logical that the next step would be the one that was now within his grasp. He, too, would become a larger-than-life national security adviser; he, too, would use that post to chart the course of U.S. foreign policy in such a way that he, too, would affect history.

But "Zbig" never came close to matching Kissinger's stature. Some of the ingredients were there, but not the whole package. He was knowledgeable, of course, and hardworking, but he did not have Kissinger's subtlety or grace. One of Kissinger's strengths was his charm, and he used it masterfully when it suited his purpose, a gift that helped to temper his less attractive qualities. Brzezinski had a more abrasive personality. Often he even alienated those who should have been his natural allies. Barry Goldwater, the dean of hard-liners who was then still an influential voice in the Senate, once griped to a reporter that he was getting "fed up" with Brzezinski's overbearing attitude. "He's a very arrogant, self-opinionated man," said Goldwater. "And he's a hawk. His advice is much more in line with mine than Cy Vance's. He should be my kind of guy. But he is arrogance with a capital A." And from Kissinger himself came this terse but pointed assessment: "Smart, but not wise."

But if Brzezinski was determined to become Carter's Kissinger, Vance was just as determined not to become the latest secretary of state to be reduced to a subservient role. Unlike Rusk and Rogers, Vance fought back and did everything he could to retain the traditional powers and prerogatives of his cabinet post. He was aware that Brzezinski's office in the White House, which put him in direct, day-to-day contact with the President, gave him a certain edge. (In fact, that proximity was one reason that other national security advisers had been able to gain the upper hand.) But Vance was able to combat that with resources of his own. One of his ploys was to sit down every night and write a short memo of events directly to the President. The next morning, Vance's memo would be near the top of the President's "in" file, and if Carter gave his concurrence (anything from a check mark to a brief note of approval), the State Department would promptly proceed with the announcement before Brzezinski had a chance to go through the memoranda and raise an objection.

Yet despite all the flanking maneuvers and internecine bickering, Vance and Brzezinski managed to find enough time to make solid contributions to Carter's foreign policy, which—lest we forget—had its moments of triumph. Two achievements, in particular, are worth noting: (1) the complete restoration of formal relations with China, the final step in the diplomatic revision that began with Kissinger's secret mission to Peking, and (2) the Camp David Accords that provided the framework for an official peace treaty between Egypt and Israel. But these accomplishments of the Carter administration were all but obliterated from the national memory when the country found itself in the grip of the hostage crisis in Iran. The White House never recovered from the frustration of that ordeal, and it was within the context of that savage affront to American pride and power that Vance and Brzezinski waged their final struggle for control of U.S. foreign policy.

In the early months of the crisis, Carter sided with Vance, who counseled a course of restraint and negotiation. It was his belief that a combination of economic pressure and the rule of reason would eventually move the Iranians to compliance. But the Islamic fundamentalist fanatics who had seized power in Tehran were beyond the reach of such conventional measures, and as time went on, the reality of what the United States was up against began to sink in at the White House. What helped to fuel the mood of desperation in Washington was the dynamic of a presidential election year. Carter did not need his pollsters or other political advisers to tell him that if he failed to resolve the crisis, the American electorate would take out *its* frustration on him. By the early spring of 1980, as the hostages began their sixth month in captivity, Carter was losing patience with Vance's cautious approach, and it was then that Brzezinski gained the upper hand.

From the beginning, Brzezinski had pushed for some kind of military response. His advice was to strike fast and strike hard, for that was the only way, he argued, that the lives of the hostages could be saved and the national honor restored. Although Carter seemed to reject that counsel in favor of Vance's diplomatic initiatives at the United Nations and other forums, he privately authorized Brzezinski to meet regularly with Pentagon officials and explore the various military options. Vance, in the meantime, had no idea such an alternative approach was even being considered, much less discussed in high-level meetings from which he was excluded. The climax came in early April when Vance, exhausted by his futile efforts to negotiate a solution, flew to Florida for a four-day weekend, his first rest since the hostages were seized the previous November. While he was gone, Carter convened a meeting of the National Security Council at which it was decided to launch a helicopter raid from the Persian Gulf into Tehran in an attempt to rescue the hostages by force.

When he returned to Washington, Vance was appalled, not only because a decision of that magnitude had been made in his absence and without his counsel, but more because he thought the proposed raid was reckless to the point of lunacy. In private conversations with Carter, he urged that the mission be aborted. It simply would not work, he insisted, and even if it did, some of the hostages would surely be killed or severely wounded. Even if, through some miracle, all the hostages were safely rescued, other Americans in Iran would then be seized and the whole ordeal would enter a new and no doubt even uglier phase. But Carter's mind was made up. He was, by this time, desperate for some kind of action, some show of force. That being the case, Vance said, he had no choice but to resign: in protest and in principle. And although he stipulated, in his letter of resignation, that it not be released until after the mission occurred, he made it clear that his decision was final. Whether the raid succeeded or failed, it was not the kind of action that he, in conscience, could support.

The mission was, of course, a failure. The helicopters, hampered by mechanical deficiencies, never even made it to Tehran, and eight members of the rescue team were killed when one of the choppers crashed in the Iranian desert. In the aftermath, Carter appeared even weaker and more ineffectual than before. What's more, the military blunder destroyed whatever slim hope had existed for an early resolution to the crisis through the process of negotiation. The Iranian zealots were now more determined than ever to punish Carter by keeping the hostages in captivity until after the November election, which meant that his chances of winning a second term were now doomed.

In a world where ambition dictates that behavior be governed by expediency and accommodation, Cyrus Vance's resignation was a rare occurrence. Not since the eve of World War II, when Britain's foreign secretary, Anthony Eden, resigned in protest of Neville Chamberlain's appeasement policies, had a government official of such stature quit his Cabinet post over a clear and unequivocal question of principle. But the circumstances that led to Vance's resignation underscored the all but inevitable problems that arise when a President permits two headstrong adversaries within his high command to compete for the power to direct the course of foreign affairs.

The mess that Carter made of his foreign policy apparatus was observed with more than routine interest by Ronald Reagan, who vowed that his presidency would not fall into a similar trap. In a speech two weeks before the election, Reagan promised to make "structural changes" to ensure that the secretary of state would be his "principal spokesman and adviser," and that his national security adviser would be obliged to accept a subordinate role as "team player and coordinator." That message, with all its implications, was not lost on Dick Allen. Shortly after he was named to succeed Brzezinski, Allen made it clear that it was his intention to play the good soldier in that effort. "My concept of the National Security team is that it should not be a policy-making center," he averred. In that respect, Reagan got what he wanted.

Agreeing to maintain a low profile was one thing, but Allen soon found he was being cropped out of the picture altogether. This was not entirely his fault. The structural arrangement devised by Jim Baker and Ed Meese put the National Security Council under Meese's command, which meant that Allen was denied direct and regular access to the President. Moreover, on those infrequent occasions when he could sit down face-to-face with Reagan, Allen's briefings were likely to be overly academic, and Reagan, never known for his rapt attention to detail, eventually passed the word that his national security adviser should report to him through Meese. But Meese, overburdened by other concerns, also tended to give Allen little attention, and the result was that the national-security operation floundered in a state of neglect and disarray. In his determination to eschew the power-grabbing style of Kissinger and Brzezinski, Allen went too far in the other direction, and it wasn't long before he became known as the "invisible man" in Ronald Reagan's White House. Just two months into the new administration, a former member of the National Security Council warned that "the system is being emasculated. Allen isn't going to be able to coordinate policy. He's too busy getting out of everyone's way."

Yet none of that seemed to matter much during those early months when Allen's superiors in the White House were focusing all their attention on the key legislative priorities, and Baker was instructing all those who had other agendas to "cool it" until the tax and spending bills were passed. Nor did urgent foreign-policy problems arise to distract them from their primary mission. To a remarkable degree, the world's trouble spots, normally indifferent to a change of government in Washington, seemed only too willing to join in the observance of the Reagan honeymoon. Even the terrorists in Iran had picked the day of Reagan's inauguration as the moment to end the hostages' captivity, which meant that one of Reagan's first public acts as President was to welcome the hostages home from Tehran triumphantly. That joyous event produced an upbeat mood, at home and abroad, that prevailed over the next several months, well into the summer of 1981.

What a glorious summer that was for the Reagan administration. By then, all the hard work that had gone into the new legislation had been completed, and the revolutionary economic measures were sailing through Congress. But Reagan was succeeding on other fronts as well. The tough stand he took against the striking air traffic controllers was popular with most Americans, many of whom were not only disenchanted with labor unrest in general but found it difficult to sympathize with the demands of a union whose members had incomes well above the national average. Even feminists, who regarded Reagan as their enemy because of his opposition to abortion and the Equal Rights Amendment, were pleased when the President appointed Sandra Day O'Connor, the first woman ever to be accorded the honor, to the Supreme Court. Throughout these weeks of presidential triumph, the news from abroad remained relatively calm and uneventful. In fact, the biggest story overseas that summer was the royal marriage of Prince Charles and Lady Diana Spencer in London, a pageant that required no official response from the U.S. government other than a suitable wedding gift. But of course, like all honeymoons, even Reagan's couldn't last forever.

On the night of August 19, when the President was in California on vacation, the Reagans were hosting a party in their suite at the Century Plaza Hotel in Los Angeles. Meanwhile, on the other side of the world, sixty miles from the coast of Libya, two U.S. Navy F-14 fighters were attacked by two Soviet-built Libyan jets. The F-14s retaliated and shot down both Libyan planes. When news of the incident came into the White House basement and was passed on to Allen, he followed the chain-of-command procedure that had been set up and informed Meese. Allen had no authority to contact the President directly. By then, it was 11:00 P.M., California time; the party at the hotel suite was over and the Reagans had retired for the night. Meese notified Vice President Bush and other members of the National Security Council, but he did not call the President until four-thirty the next morning. Reagan took in the news and then promptly went back to sleep. He later defended Meese's delayed communication on the grounds that the military action, by then a fait accompli, required no urgent presidential decision. But when Baker and Deaver learned that Meese had not awakened the President immediately, they were furious. They feared that once the story was discovered by the press, Reagan would be portrayed as a President who was not in command of a tense situation that easily could have escalated into a crisis.

They were right. In light of subsequent events that were far more notorious, it's worth noting that as early as 1981, when Reagan generally was being praised as a President who could do no wrong, he was criticized in the press for not being attentive in the vital area of national security. In the aftermath of the Libyan incident, *Newsweek* suggested that he was "laid back" to the point of laziness and drew a wry comparison between him and his predecessor: "Jimmy Carter gave hard work and attention to detail a bad name. Ronald Reagan will not make that mistake." Columnist Art Buchwald was even more derisive. Simulating the voice of Reagan as he recalled what he did on vacation that summer, Buchwald wrote: "We had a lot of fun. I cut brush, cleared out trees, hiked with my best girl Nancy, and shot down two Libyan planes. I was sleeping when we shot them down and my best friend Ed Meese didn't wake me up in time. But it was fun hearing about it."

Even before that blunder, Baker and Deaver were regretting the decision that placed the national security adviser and his operation under the smothering supervision of Meese. Meese had no background in foreign policy and no real sense of what should be the priorities in that sensitive area. Besides, even if that were not the case, he had too many other things to oversee, and therefore did not have the time to give national-security matters the attention they deserved. As a result, the vital information that should have been flowing from Allen and his cadre in the White House basement directly into the Oval Office was getting snarled up in the bottleneck of Ed Meese's deliberate and often disorganized style of management.

Disagreement over the way the national-security office was being run caused the first open rift in the otherwise harmonious Baker-Meese-Deaver troika that had taken shape in the early weeks of the Reagan administration. Meese naturally took the position that everything was just fine. Dick Allen was doing his job, regularly turning in his reports and recommendations, and Meese was dutifully passing them on to the President. But Baker and Deaver, convinced that Reagan was not getting the kind of incisive advice on national-security problems that he needed, began to push hard for major changes, nothing less than a dismantling of the cumbersome structure that had been erected. Their lobbying efforts were not confined to private conversations inside the White House. By the fall of 1981, some of Baker's subordinates were openly telling reporters that Meese had taken on too many responsibilities and was in so far over his head that he was losing control.

The one man who should have been in a position to take full advantage of this disarray and internal squabbling was Secretary of State Alexander Haig. Haig, after all, had been led to believe that he, and he alone, would be the voice and driving force behind Reagan's foreign policy, and no man could have been more eager to flaunt his presence. But it was up to Reagan to allow him to exercise that kind of sweeping authority, and Haig had his own problems getting through to the President, for he, too, soon discovered how difficult it was to penetrate the power structure that had formed like a shield around the Oval Office. Yet as far as the White House troika was concerned, the mercurial Haig had only himself to blame for that. Whatever differences had arisen between the Meese group and the Baker-Deaver faction on other matters, when it came to dealing with Al Haig, they were in complete agreement.

7

Alexander the Great

"I am in control here."
—Alexander Haig

Toward the end of Haig's stormy stint as secretary of state, long after disenchantment had set in and members of Reagan's inner circle had come to regard him as a chronic irritant, some of the people he antagonized would look to the past and focus their discontent on his two celebrated mentors, Henry Kissinger and Richard Nixon. They would grumble among themselves that if it had not been for Kissinger and Nixon, no one ever would have heard of Alexander Haig; therefore, he never would have been in a position to become such a disruptive presence in their midst. There was, to be sure, some truth in that observation. It was indeed during his years of service in the Nixon administration that Haig rose to prominence as an influential deputy who had earned the special trust of the two most powerful men in Washington. But Kissinger and Nixon could have pointed out that Haig was not entirely their creation, that he had come to them from the ranks of their political enemies. For it was the Democrats who first took

---

Al Haig under their wing and encouraged him to expand his energies beyond the narrow limits of a military career.

The year was 1963, and Major Haig was an obscure staff officer working in the Pentagon when he caught the eye of a young lawyer named Joseph Califano. Califano, then in the early stages of his own considerable pursuits in government (he would go on to become a leading member of Jimmy Carter's Cabinet), was general counsel of the Army, and he recommended Haig to his boss, Secretary of the Army Cyrus Vance. Vance took Haig on as his military assistant, and thus began Haig's "second" career as an aide-de-camp to high-ranking civilians. He worked for Vance until 1966, when he was assigned to a six-month tour of duty as a battalion commander in Vietnam, and upon his return to the States he was appointed commander of a regimental corps at West Point. But he had not been forgotten by his Democratic friends in Washington. When Nixon was elected and appointed Kissinger, the new national security adviser began shopping around for deputies, and once again it was Califano who recommended Haig, calling him "one of the new breed of sophisticated Army officers." Kissinger liked the sound of that and brought Haig into the White House basement as his military assistant.

After more than two decades of Army regimentation, the forty-five-year-old Haig was accustomed to serving coercive superiors, and so he was one of the few Kissinger aides who did not chafe under the professor's demanding and often abusive style of command. The more paperwork Kissinger piled on his desk, the more Haig labored into the night to get it done; yet he never failed to show up on time the next morning with a clear head and a spit-and-polish eagerness to plunge into another marathon workday. For his part, Kissinger appreciated not only Haig's industry but his orderly attention to detail. "He disciplined my anarchic tendencies," Kissinger later wrote, "and established coherence and procedures in an NSC staff of talented prima donnas."

Haig's devotion to duty and bureaucratic skills were duly rewarded. He eventually became Kissinger's most trusted deputy and his point man on a number of sensitive diplomatic missions. He also carried out the more nefarious assignments that Kissinger found distasteful, such as processing orders to the FBI to wiretap certain government officials in the name of national security, then sifting through the transcripts the tapes produced and, as he later put it, "passing on to Henry those that were significant." In the words of one former colleague, Haig played the role of "Stalin to Henry's Lenin."

But throughout his years of service in the White House basement, Haig remained unknown, obscured by Kissinger's shadow, for not even the most loyal of deputies was invited to share in the limelight. Nevertheless, Haig's dedication and Spartan work habits did not escape the notice of Kissinger's boss, Richard Nixon, who once remarked to an aide that "Haig's always down there while Henry's off having dinner in Georgetown." Thus, in the spring of 1973, when Nixon found himself embroiled in the Watergate scandal, he chose Haig to replace the fallen H. R. Haldeman as White House chief of staff, and it was then that he first became known to the general public. More than anyone else, it was Haig who nursed Nixon through the siege and torment of his last year as President, and it was Haig who orchestrated the delicate maneuvers that, in the end, persuaded Nixon that he had no choice but to resign. Haig emerged from that ordeal relatively unscathed, although for a long time afterward he was beset by rumors that one of his last acts as chief of staff was to cut a deal with Gerald Ford to procure the infamous Nixon pardon, a charge that Haig has steadfastly denied.

Whatever the merits of that allegation, Ford was quick to use Haig's talents. During the Nixon years, he had received several promotions, and when Haig resigned from the Army to take over as White House chief of staff, he had attained the rank of four-star general. (At the time, he joked that he was "the first general who had to retire from military service to enter combat.") Shortly after Ford became President, he recalled Haig to active duty and awarded him the two most prestigious overseas posts available to an American officer: Supreme Allied Commander, Europe, and Commander in Chief of U.S. Forces in Europe. After years of serving as a high-level aide to other strong-willed leaders, Haig finally had a domain of his own to rule, and he made the most of it. During his five years as head of NATO, a job that required shrewd political as well as military judgment, he did all he could to cultivate a reputation as an outstanding soldier-statesman in the Eisenhower tradition. In fact, by the time he resigned the NATO post in 1979, Haig was entertaining the idea of becoming the first general since Ike to be elected commander in chief. When the offer came to serve as Reagan's secretary of state, he naturally viewed that as a move toward his ultimate goal.

In bestowing that position on Haig, Reagan had to reject the pleas of two members of his inner circle, Caspar Weinberger and William Casey, both of whom had openly lobbied for the State portfolio. Left to his own resources, Haig probably could not have triumphed over rivals who had such strong inside connections going for them, but he did have a powerful advocate working on his behalf. In private conversations with Reagan, Nixon pressed the case for Haig, and his arguments carried considerable weight with the President-elect, who placed a high value on Nixon's judgment and expertise in foreign affairs.

Still, within the Reagan camp, opposition to Haig was not confined to those who wanted the job themselves. Some insiders viewed Haig as damaged goods precisely because of his intimate involvement with Nixon during the dark days of disgrace and impeachment hearings that preceded his resignation. Nor were they keen on having a secretary of state who was so closely associated with Kissinger's pursuit of détente, a policy that Reagan had clearly repudiated in the recent campaign. Yet another deficit was Haig's all-too-transparent ambition, which led many to suspect that his main goal was to further the cause of his own presidential aspirations rather than serve the interests of Ronald Reagan. Even after Reagan made the decision and appointed Haig, most of his top advisers accepted the general grudgingly. The way they saw it, Haig would have to demonstrate that he was joining the Reagan administration as a loyal subordinate. Unfortunately for all concerned, that was the last thing Al Haig had in mind.

He had developed, by this time, an ego that was every bit as large as his ambition. Thus, instead of taking steps to ingratiate himself to Reagan's inner circle—as another outsider, Jim Baker, had done so adroitly—Haig seemed to go out of his way to flaunt his interloper status. He portrayed himself as the solid professional, the savvy Washington veteran who, for the good of the country, had joined forces with a group of amateurs from California who had been suddenly thrust into power. He implied that he had been willing to take on that burden only because they, the amateurs, had agreed that he, General Haig—former commander of NATO and onetime confidant of the Washington elite—would be the one in charge of foreign policy.

During the transition, Haig proclaimed that he had been

anointed the "vicar" of foreign affairs, by which he meant that he had been granted unprecedented powers to preside over a vast range of policies, even including economic matters, trade agreements, and defense commitments, that normally would be within the jurisdiction of other departments or agencies. As Richard Allen later wrote, "This unusual view was so broad in scope that virtually every policy matter extending beyond the three-mile territorial limit would automatically come under the aegis of the Secretary of State." Two weeks before the inauguration, Haig presented Reagan with his grandiose plan and he left that meeting convinced that the President-elect had, in effect, "subcontracted" the entire responsibility for foreign policy to him. Although White House insiders later insisted that Reagan had done no such thing, Haig promptly set out to translate his scheme into concrete policies. But before the "vicar" had a chance to instruct his flock, he fell from grace.

It was Al Haig's misfortune that the most vivid and enduring memory of his tour of duty in the Reagan administration was the bizarre performance he gave on the afternoon of March 30, 1981, the day the President fell victim to an assassination attempt. In the moments of confusion after Reagan had been rushed to the hospital and was about to undergo surgery, Haig barged into the White House press room in a state of high agitation, even though the purpose of his visit was to assure reporters that there was no crisis and that all the levers of government were running in a smooth and orderly manner. That prompted one reporter to ask, "Well, who is making the decisions for the government right now?" Haig did not hesitate, and his overwrought response revealed both his ignorance and his arrogance:

> Constitutionally, gentlemen, you have the President, the Vice-President and the Secretary of State in that order and should the President decide that he wants to transfer the helm to the Vice-President, he will do so. He has not done that. As of now, *I am in control here*, in the White House, pending return of the Vice-President, and in close touch with him.

Haig had somehow managed to compress three serious blunders into one concise statement. To begin with, in the event of death or removal from office, the line of succession runs to the vice president, then to the speaker of the House, then to the president pro tempore of the Senate, and only after that does it extend to the Cabinet, starting with the secretary of state. Haig's suggesting otherwise indicated that he didn't understand the Constitution. Beyond that, he seemed to raise the sensitive question of the Twenty-fifth Amendment, which decrees that if a President is so disabled that he cannot discharge the powers and duties of his office, then the vice president is authorized to take over as acting President. Reagan had been seriously wounded, but his doctors already had indicated that there would be no need to invoke the Twenty-fifth Amendment. Finally, the clause "I am in control here" had the shrill undertones of a military coup. (*Calm down, everybody. General Haig has taken over and is "in control." Law and order will soon be restored.*)

Haig never fully recovered from that episode. The man who prided himself on being a solid professional who was always cool under pressure had behaved, in a tense moment of national anxiety, like a man on the verge of panic. Washington can be merciless in its treatment of the pompous who lapse into folly, and for a long time afterward Haig had to endure snickering allusions to his performance that day. He brushed off the sneers with bravado, taking the position that most of his critics were either political enemies or rivals within the administration who were envious of his status and power. That was one of Haig's obsessions. He saw himself as surrounded by adversaries of one kind or another who, in a variety of ways, were trying to undermine his efforts to direct Reagan's foreign policy. With his flair for melodrama, Haig no doubt made too much of that, but nonetheless there was truth in his complaint.

Some Democrats in Congress, for example, certainly had doubts about his integrity and judgment. True to their vow expressed during the transition, Senate Minority Leader Robert Byrd and other prominent Democrats gave Haig a hard time at his confirmation hearings. They grilled him about his activities at the Nixon White House during the Watergate crisis, focusing much of their fire on the suspicion that he had helped to engineer the Nixon pardon. Although they made no serious attempt to stymie his appointment, the Democrats warned Haig that they would be watching him vigilantly, and throughout his brief reign at State he had to endure a certain amount of sniping from liberals in Congress.

The irony there was that Haig saw himself as a moderate in a nest of hard-line conservatives, and he had a point. He believed in most of Kissinger's tenets, and those convictions were reinforced during his years as head of the NATO command. Most of the European leaders he had contact with were strong advocates of détente, and Haig was influenced by what he regarded as their sophisticated view of East-West relations.

But détente, at that time, was a dirty word to Reagan and other members of his foreign-policy team. They were, for the most part, unreconstructed cold warriors who looked upon Russia as an "evil empire," as the President himself described the Soviet system in one of his more memorable speeches. A case in point was Jeane Kirkpatrick, the Georgetown University professor who was named ambassador to the United Nations. A nominal Democrat who, like Reagan before her, deserted that party to embrace the conservative cause, Kirkpatrick brought a convert's zeal to her new faith. Her appointment was another move Reagan made to placate the right-wingers who felt betrayed by so many of his Cabinet choices, and although the UN job was, at best, a midlevel post, Reagan agreed to upgrade it to Cabinet rank to give it— and her—a little more stature. Kirkpatrick herself took it from there.

The hard-line stands she espoused in speeches at the United Nations and other forums soon made her a heroine to the true believers. She became so popular that for a time she reigned as the embodiment of conservative chic. This was a source of irritation to Haig, who frequently accused Kirkpatrick of trying to upstage him. Once, in a moment of pique, he tried to put the UN ambassador in her place by dismissing her as a mere "company commander." But she took it with grace, and the brusque putdown reflected more discredit on Haig than it did on his target. In the eyes of her many admirers, she was an ideal spokeswoman, and throughout the early years of the Reagan administration, the Kirkpatrick cult continued to flourish.

One rival who openly tried to upstage Haig was Secretary of Defense Caspar Weinberger. Weinberger had two advantages that gave him a decisive edge over Haig. One, he was a Reagan intimate who had worked closely with the President since the years in Sacramento when he served as state finance director. And two, the decision by the White House strategists to make a huge increase in the defense budget one of their top priorities put Weinberger and his department at the center of the action during the early months of the Reagan presidency.

Part of Haig's elaborate plan had been to include some of the major defense issues within his jurisdiction. As Haig saw it, defense was his natural domain. He, after all, was the man with the military experience, the four-star general, the former commander of NATO. Instead, here was Weinberger wielding more power than he. During the first year of the Reagan administration, Weinberger made frequent trips to foreign capitals, where he conferred with high-level civilian as well as military officials. Why, the way he was strutting around one would think *he* had been appointed vicar of "every policy matter extending beyond the three-mile territorial limit." What Haig failed to understand was how much Weinberger had wanted the State job in the first place. Having been denied it, he did the next best thing: he accepted the Defense post and proceeded to act as if diplomacy and other affairs of state were an integral part of his mission to build up America's military arsenal.

But Haig's biggest problem was not his detractors in Congress, or the mileage Jeane Kirkpatrick was getting from her ardent courtship of Reagan conservatives, or even the impressive strides Cap Weinberger seemed to be making at his expense. Neither was it a question of his having neglected to put together a strong agenda of his own. Convinced that he had been given permission to forge ahead on a variety of fronts, Haig came up with plans to adopt a more aggressive military posture in Central America, to renew efforts toward resolving the Arab-Israeli conflict, to take steps to strengthen the bond with our European allies, and—above all— to work boldly toward achieving arms-control agreements with the Soviets. His real problem was persuading Reagan to approve these proposals; or, to be more precise, getting through the wall of advisers who were blocking his access to the President. At a time when many observers were praising the smooth efficiency of the troika, the secretary of state was loudly complaining about chaos and disorder and indecision. In his resentful memoir, *Caveat*, Haig deplored what he called "schoolboy scuffles for personal advantage in the corridors of the White House."

One schoolboy he knew he couldn't trust was Dick Allen. In 1969, they both worked for Kissinger, and Haig remembered that

Allen, the rigid right-winger, had opposed Kissinger's intricate balance-of-power moves to play China off against the Soviet Union and vice versa, the evolving policy that later came to be called détente. What struck him at the time was Allen's naïveté in thinking that he could challenge Kissinger's intellect and authority. Recalling that, Haig was convinced that now, twelve years later, Allen was trying to undercut him, and he was right.

At the time of his appointment, when Allen was asked whether he and Haig would be able to avoid the kind of internecine battles that had characterized the Vance-Brzezinski relationship, Allen gave his assurance that they would get along, and then slyly added: "I've known Al since he was a colonel." It was his cryptic way of saying that he had not been all that impressed by Haig's rapid rise to the rank of four-star general, and that he remembered him well from the days when "Colonel" Haig was little more than a glorified clerk.

Allen had not forgotten his sharp philosophical differences with Kissinger, and, from time to time, they resurfaced in his dealings with Haig. For example, Allen believed that in its pursuit of détente, America had all but abandoned Taiwan, and he advocated sending more fighter planes to that loyal ally, regardless of what reaction such a move might provoke in Peking. Haig, who knew that Reagan had high regard for Taiwan, resourcefully countered with an argument that would also appeal to the President's ideological bias. Shifting the debate into the military context that was his strength, Haig pointed out that Chinese troops were pinning down one-fourth of the Soviet Union's divisions on the Sino-Soviet border, and for that reason, if no other, it made no sense to impair relations with the People's Republic of China. He then acidly informed Allen that the United States had readjusted its priorities in Asia. It's a new era, he explained, and Allen should make the effort to bring himself up-to-date. Yet despite these occasional clashes, Haig realized that he didn't have to spend much time worrying about Allen. Allen may have been national security adviser, but Haig knew he had no real power or influence and never would as long as he was boxed in by the structural agreement that put him firmly under the control of Ed Meese.

But Meese didn't exactly inspire Haig's respect, either. Much of the time when Haig went to the White House for meetings that he had assumed would be chaired by the President, they were led by Meese. Meese would frame the issues, lead the discussions, and occasionally exchange handwritten notes with Jim Baker and/or Mike Deaver, thereby reinforcing the impression that the troika was in full command. When the time came for Haig to present his agenda, Meese would nod attentively, then summarize the key points and give his assurance that they would be promptly called to the President's attention. But to Haig there never seemed to be any follow-through, any clear-cut decisions as to how they should proceed. Attendance at a few of those meetings was enough to convince Haig that Meese was just a provincial plodder who may have been a power in Sacramento, but was out of his depth in Washington.

Jim Baker, however, was another story. As one who had been White House chief of staff during a period of incomparable stress and turmoil, Al Haig had a connoisseur's appreciation of the office and its functions, and he admired the skill and finesse that Baker was giving to that demanding job. Haig was all the more impressed because, like him, Baker had joined the administration as an outsider, one who, in fact, had been closely associated with Reagan's two chief rivals within the Republican party, Gerald Ford and George Bush. Yet in a remarkably short time, Baker had managed to win the confidence of Reagan and his top California deputies, Meese and Deaver. Haig sensed that Baker was shrewdly using Meese and Deaver to run interference for himself, so that he and his staff would be free to shape the issues that would define the Reagan administration. The secretary of state grudgingly agreed with those who were applauding the Baker team's success in selling the President's program on Capitol Hill.

But it was precisely those legislative priorities, and Baker's insistence that no other agenda should be allowed to distract attention from them, that lay at the heart of Haig's frustration. Foreign policy was not something to be overlooked, and he found it puzzling that Baker didn't seem to understand that. As far as Haig was concerned, of all the people in the Reagan White House, Baker should have been his natural ally: they were both moderates whose appointments had infuriated the conservatives. Yet Baker was doing as much as—or more than—the other insiders to thwart the foreign-policy mission that Reagan had entrusted to him.

Haig no doubt would have been less puzzled if he had understood that Baker had political reasons for being wary of the secretary of state. Although Baker's first priority was to serve the President with honor and distinction, he remained deeply loyal to his old friend from Texas, George Bush. And even in those early days, he knew that seven years hence, if everything went according to plan, Bush would inherit the presidency. Nothing must transpire in the interim to jeopardize that right of succession; yet it was clear to Baker, as it was to others, that Haig had presidential ambitions, and that was a candidacy Baker had no interest in promoting. Beyond the question of politics, the cautious Baker thought that Haig had a reckless streak that, if indulged, would only cause the administration problems it didn't need. One White House staffer later recalled hearing Baker say that "if we give Al Haig his way, the next thing we know, we'll be carpet-bombing Central America."

Thus, Baker was no ally, and the more frustrated Haig became, the more he rebelled against the yoke the White House had imposed on him. By the fall of 1981, Haig was taking his complaints to the press. In one of his intemperate interviews, he charged that he was unable to take on the vital role Reagan clearly had intended for him because of "a guerrilla campaign" that was being waged against him from inside the White House.

The mounting discord between Haig and the White House staff, which eventually led to his resignation, would have exploded even earlier had it not been for the patient and conciliatory efforts of Haig's number-two man, Deputy Secretary of State William Clark. The fact that Clark found himself in the role of Haig's trusted aide was an anomaly, for he was a member of the California clique Reagan had taken to Washington. Indeed, when Haig learned who his chief deputy was going to be, he assumed, correctly, that the President's inner circle had sent Clark over to the State Department to make sure that he pursued the best interests of Ronald Reagan rather than the best interests of Alexander Haig, which were not necessarily identical. Haig naturally thought he was capable of carrying out his duties without a chaperon, and his first inclination was to treat his top deputy with cool suspicion.

But to the surprise of just about everyone, including themselves, Haig and Clark soon discovered that they worked well together and even grew to like one another. In the sense that opposites attract, their personalities complemented each other.

Clark, the soft-spoken introvert, was the perfect antidote to the volatile Haig, who was never more than a few minutes away from his next emotional outburst.

Each of them also had professional strengths that the other lacked. Clark had no background in foreign policy (at his Senate confirmation hearings, he revealed so many gaps in his knowledge of world affairs that his ignorance touched off a minor fuss during the transition), and he quickly learned to respect Haig's solid grasp of the issues and his dedication to the goals he hoped to accomplish. On the other hand, Clark knew, from his own experience, how to deal with Reagan and other members of the team he had worked with in Sacramento, and Haig appreciated the value of that knowledge. "You can't crowd Ronald Reagan," Clark warned Haig on one occasion when the secretary was on the verge of forcing a showdown over some slight or betrayal, and Haig was wise enough to heed that counsel. Finally, Haig, who beneath all the bluster was a sensitive man, was genuinely touched by Clark's loyalty to him, which he had not expected. And it was true that Clark often went out of his way to defend the secretary and his cause in conversations with Deaver and the other Californians who worked in the White House.

Clark's friends, in turn, were sympathetic to him, for they understood that working for Haig was not easy. They knew he had to listen to tirades about Jeane Kirkpatrick or Cap Weinberger or the "guerrillas" in the White House who were lying in ambush at every turn. They just hoped Haig realized how lucky he was to have at his side Bill Clark, a patient man gifted in the soothing arts of intercession and damage control. Haig did realize it, but in that respect his luck was about to run out. In the late fall of 1981, the decision was made to pull Clark out of the State Department so that he could take on a higher calling in the White House basement.

Throughout the early weeks of their first autumn in the White House, Baker and Deaver stepped up their campaign to streamline the national security operation by moving it out of Meese's supervision. Meese continued to resist that effort, in part because he didn't want to give up any of his prerogatives, but he especially didn't want to lose that one. He knew that as long as Dick Allen had to report through him, he would continue to have an active part in forming foreign policy. Besides, he argued, the existing chain of command was precisely what the President had requested, and it was up to the White House staff to give Ronald Reagan what he wanted.

So Baker and Deaver decided the time had come to take their case to the President, who had been stung by the criticism that on the night the Navy planes had their skirmish with the Libyan jets, every high-ranking official in the government had been awakened except the commander in chief. Citing that as well as other problems that had arisen, Baker and Deaver contended that the change had to be made, that the President simply wasn't getting all the information he needed to stay on top of the decision-making process. At Baker's request, Deaver also enlisted the support of Nancy, as he often did at such critical moments, and Reagan finally agreed, with some reluctance, to go along with the restructuring. But he was determined to make sure that it would not be interpreted as a setback for Meese. In a subsequent talk with Meese, he gently urged his longtime deputy to concentrate on the role that brought out his best talents—that of White House counselor—and relinquish some of the managerial responsibilities that were weighing him down. At that point, Meese knew that Baker and Deaver had bested him, and that he had no choice but to acquiesce. But, to make certain that he did not lose face, it was decided that he would announce the change as his idea. Soon thereafter, Meese told the press that he had recommended upgrading the office of national security adviser so that he would have direct access to the President. For Jim Baker, it was another in a series of small internal victories that steadily strengthened his position as the most powerful member of the White House troika.

The other part of that decision was to replace Dick Allen. Allen had his good points: no one questioned his commitment and loyalty to Reagan, and his conservative views were certainly in tune with the President's philosophy. But in personal terms, he had failed to win the President's confidence. Allen's earnest and academic approach did not jibe with Reagan's relaxed, anecdotal style, and their relationship was strained. He had been appointed national security adviser only because, in the original conception, it was to be a subordinate role with none of the power that would flow from day-to-day contact with the President. Now that the job was being upgraded, Allen would have to leave, and in October 1981, it was decided to recruit Bill Clark as his replacement.

But the change would not be made right away, and there was a fascinating motive behind that decision. At the time, everyone in Washington knew that Haig and Allen were feuding. In fact, Haig by then was treating Allen and his staff with such contempt that one of his deputies at State informed a reporter that "we've been told not to worry about anything they ask for. We treat their requests like junk mail." (It was widely assumed that Allen was the "guerrilla" Haig had in mind when he griped about interference from the White House; although the national security adviser was high on Haig's list of saboteurs, he understood that Allen himself would be powerless to thwart him without the support of his three superiors who made up the troika.) Hence, there was some concern that the decision to get rid of Allen would be perceived as a victory for Haig, especially because Allen was to be replaced by Haig's top deputy at State. The White House staff did not want to see that particular "spin" put on their machinations, and so they chose to postpone the move until after the first of the year in the hope that by then, tensions would have calmed. This was bad news for Allen. He had played such a minor role that had he been eased out in October, his departure would have been viewed as a routine and orderly change, one that would have provoked little comment. But instead, he was destined to end his brief stint in the Reagan administration with widespread negative attention.

In November, Allen became embroiled in another petty scandal reminiscent of the ethical violations he had been accused of in the past. It was reported that the previous January, he had accepted three expensive watches as personal gifts from Japanese friends who were high-level government consultants. (These were the same Japanese friends he had warned about trade protectionism back in 1972 when he was working in the Nixon White House.) In exchange, Allen had agreed to help a Japanese magazine get an interview with Nancy Reagan. When the interview took place on January 21, the day after the inauguration, the visiting journalists gave Allen an envelope containing $1,000 in cash. The gratuity, a common practice among Japanese journalists, was intended for Mrs. Reagan. Accepting the money on her behalf, Allen handed the envelope over to his secretary and told her to put it in a safe. He then promptly forgot about it, a lapse that he later attributed to "carelessness."

So once again, Allen became the target of an investigation, this time under the direction of the Department of Justice. While the probe was in progress, he went on administrative leave, but it was understood at the White House that regardless of the outcome, he would not be coming back. Allen eventually was cleared of any wrongdoing, but when he was replaced by Clark in January 1982, there was a lingering suspicion that there had been more to the case than had been made public. Allen himself knew that his departure had nothing to do with the scandal that had erupted, but he had trouble convincing skeptics, many of whom noted that this was not the first time he had been investigated. It was an unseemly end to a government career that once had seemed promising. Dick Allen had managed to work his way into the inner circle of two powerful Republicans, Richard Nixon and Ronald Reagan, but he had bungled both opportunities, and he had little reward for all the time and energy he had expended to gain the privilege of serving in the high councils of government.

Senate hearings to confirm nominees to sub-Cabinet posts tend to be routine and perfunctory proceedings that elicit little public attention. But that was hardly the case when Bill Clark appeared before the Senate Foreign Relations Committee to answer questions about his appointment as deputy secretary of state. The senators were stunned when they discovered that Clark could not identify the prime ministers of South Africa and Zimbabwe. All right, perhaps Africa was not one of his better subjects and, fair to say, P. W. Botha and Robert Mugabe were not all that familiar to many Americans. But when the focus shifted to Europe, Clark could not name the two NATO countries that opposed having nuclear missiles based on their soil, even though the objections of both Belgium and the Netherlands had been in the news recently. Sensing that he was not making a good impression, Clark suggested that he be allowed to discuss foreign policy in broad general terms, and not be quizzed so thoroughly on the "specifics," which, he conceded, were not his strength.

Most of the senators were appalled by Clark's inept performance. All but one of the Democrats on the committee voted to reject his nomination, and if that party had still been in control of the Senate, he almost certainly would not have been confirmed. In the meantime, the press, at home and abroad, was enjoying itself. An influential daily in Amsterdam, where the nuclear-missile debate was a vital issue, called Clark a "nitwit," and another foreign newspaper dubbed him the "Don't Know Man." Perhaps the most sardonic touch was the headline that observed that he would bring to his new job "A TRULY OPEN MIND."

Clark's critics would have had even more fun with the story if they had known about his experience many years earlier in California. After two years at Stanford University, to which he had been admitted on an athletic scholarship, he was forced to drop out because of low grades. He then flunked out of Loyola Law School and, after studying privately to obtain his law degree, failed his first attempt at the bar exam. From that unpromising start, Clark went on to build a modest reputation as a trial lawyer in the southern California town of Oxnard. But he had no experience in politics when, in 1966, he became Reagan's campaign manager for Ventura County. That appointment, at the age of thirty-four, dramatically changed his life. When Reagan was elected governor, Clark was appointed cabinet secretary, and he soon moved up to the post of executive secretary, which made him the second most powerful member of the Reagan team in Sacramento. His most enduring contribution in the California years had been his decree that all policy proposals be confined to one-page minimemos. Even then, apparently, he had no desire to get bogged down in tedious "specifics."

One of Reagan's more earnest promises in his first guber-natorial campaign was a vow to "take the cronyism out of judicial appointments." Critics took delight in reminding him of that pledge in 1969 when he appointed Clark to the Superior Court in San Luis Obispo County. Other judicial assignments followed. In 1971, Clark was promoted to the California Court of Appeals, and two years after that, Reagan appointed him to the state's highest court. "This was Governor Reagan's idea at all three levels," Clark told a San Francisco reporter in 1977. "It never crossed my mind that I would be a judge." It clearly never crossed the minds of California's legal scholars, either. Aware of Clark's poor academic record and undistinguished career as a lawyer, they opposed his nomination to the state supreme court. Leading the protest was a man with whom he would have to serve on that bench, Chief Justice Robert Wright, who asserted that Clark was "not qualified by education, training or experience to be confirmed."

But he was confirmed, and, as would be the case later on in Washington, Clark proceeded to surprise his critics. Although he certainly did not become a jurist of distinction, his overall performance was deemed to be adequate. "We thought he would fall flat on his face but he didn't," recalled Ephraim Margolin, past president of the California Attorneys for Criminal Justice. "He was a more competent justice than we expected, although that's still not saying much." Nevertheless, to be rated as "competent" on that level was high praise for a law-school dropout, and Clark was understandably proud of the status he had attained. He knew he had achieved much, and he had no desire to leave the court. But when he was summoned to serve as Al Haig's deputy, he felt he had no choice. After all, Clark owed his entire career to Ronald Reagan, and if the President-elect wanted him in Washington, then that's where he had to be. However, he did take his California title with him. Aides who answered his phone at the State Department greeted callers with "Judge Clark's office."

The unexpected rapport he developed with Haig was the main reason for the decision to move "Judge Clark's office" into the White House basement. It was hoped that as the new national security adviser, he could foster a more harmonious relationship between Haig and the White House, as well as smooth over some of the frictions between the secretary of state and his chief rival for power in the Cabinet, Cap Weinberger. Clark knew he was taking on a difficult assignment. "I want to be an honest broker," he said at the time of his appointment, but he made it clear that to succeed, he would need the cooperation of his colleagues on the White House staff; that meant that the announcement of the upgrading of the role of national security adviser had to be genuine.

It did not take Clark long to establish his presence in the new job. On his first day at the White House, Meese motioned him to a chair at his morning management meeting and asked him to review the National Security Council briefing. Clark demurred. "I'll be reviewing that with the President," he said.

Meese immediately backed down. Perhaps he suddenly remembered that Bill Clark had been his boss during the early years in Sacramento. In any event, the days of conducting all national-security business through Ed Meese were over. Clark would make his reports and recommendations directly to the President.

In the following weeks, Clark did the best he could to serve as a constructive liaison between the Oval Office and the different factions in the Cabinet. As a result, Reagan finally was getting the flow of information he needed and, more and more during the early months of 1982, he shifted his attention to foreign policy. Guiding a new President through such a broad complex of issues takes time, especially when the President has had no prior experience in foreign affairs and his day-to-day tutor has come into that arena with "a truly open mind." (Clark did his homework during his on-the-job training course at the State Department, but he was still no McGeorge Bundy or Henry Kissinger.) But at least and at last, they were making a start—and just in time. For in the spring of 1982, international concerns, which had been relatively dormant since Reagan took the oath of office, suddenly required urgent attention.

On April 2, the first shots were fired in an improbable war. The Falkland Islands are bleak, barely habitable specks of treeless turf in the South Atlantic, so remote from civilization that, prior to 1982, even those rare few who were aware of their existence had no clear idea where they were located. (In point of fact, the Falklands are situated off the coast of Argentina three hundred miles due east of the Straits of Magellan.) The dispute over the sovereign rights to the islands can be traced back to the eighteenth century, when Britain and Spain were competing for supremacy in the Western Hemisphere. Since 1833, however, most of the few hundred inhabitants have been descendants of British colonists, and the British have always insisted the Falklands belong to them. But Argentina, asserting that it had inherited the right to the islands from Spain, refused to accept Britain's claim. For more than a century, none of this mattered much because the desolate islands were of no strategic value and, in terms of real estate, had nothing to offer except grim isolation and a vile mixture of cold and rainy weather.

In the mid-1960s, Argentina began pressing its claim to the Falklands—to which it had given the Spanish name Las Malvinas—and that led to several years of fruitless diplomatic bickering between London and Buenos Aires. In February 1982, the military regime in Argentina broke off the negotiations and in early April dispatched troops to the Falklands and seized them by force. Britain responded with ships and planes of its own, and all of a sudden there was a war being waged in the South Atlantic.

As wars go, it was a rather modest, even frivolous enterprise. Yet it was a real war, with real casualties, and it inspired demonstrations of bellicose patriotism in both countries, which only hardened the military resolve of their respective governments. For the first time since 1945, Western powers were fighting over territory, and that posed a dilemma for the Reagan administration inasmuch as both countries were allies. Britain, of course, was our closest and most traditional ally, and those who viewed the Anglo-American alliance as the bedrock of U.S. foreign policy clearly sided with the British. On the other hand, Argentina could point to strong hemispheric ties that date back to the Monroe Doctrine. Hence, it was in Washington's best interests to end the bizarre conflict as quickly as possible. In the days before the British forces arrived in the South Atlantic and the war began in earnest, Secretary of State Haig—at Reagan's request—took on the role of mediator in an effort to resolve the crisis.

In recent months, Haig had been on his best behavior. Regardless of what the motive of the White House staff might have been, Haig viewed the dismissal of Richard Allen as a vindication. Moreover, the fact that Allen had been replaced by his own deputy further buoyed his spirits; there now was a key player in the White House who had demonstrated loyalty to *him*. He still believed that Reagan had designated him to be vicar of foreign policy, and he continued to chafe with impatience as he waited for permission to implement his ideas. But in the meantime, Haig made a real effort to restrain his tendency to issue demands and ultimatums, and he even held back the disparaging remarks he was wont to make about rivals within the administration. Recalling Clark's sound advice, he went out of his way not to "crowd Ronald Reagan."

The Falklands dispute, and the mission he had been given to end it, galvanized Haig. If 1981 was the year of the sweeping economic legislation—the tax cut and spending bill—then 1982 would be known as the year of decisive action in foreign affairs, and he, Al Haig, would emerge from that drama as the great peacemaker. During the years he worked for Kissinger, Haig had been impressed not only by his mentor's intellectual strength and firm grasp of the issues but also by his style and the high sense of theater he gave to his endeavors. That flair was never more in evidence than during the critical phase of the Yom Kippur War in 1973 when Kissinger flew back and forth between Cairo and Jerusalem in an unceasing quest for peace that an admiring press christened "shuttle diplomacy." So now, as Haig prepared to embark on similar negotiations between London and Buenos Aires, he would have his chance to emulate the Master.

It might have been helpful, however, if someone had directed Haig's attention to the relevant maps. Cairo is only about four hundred miles from Jerusalem, not much more than the distance between Washington and New York. But London and Buenos Aires are separated by eight thousand miles of Atlantic Ocean— a long shuttle, as Haig discovered when he began making the flights between the two capitals. There remains in our memory a vivid picture of how pale and frazzled Haig looked one day when he arrived in Buenos Aires on one of those trips from London. He had his health problems; he had been a chain smoker, and about a year before he became secretary of state, he had undergone triple-bypass heart surgery. Nevertheless, he normally appeared to be in robust condition, with his trim waistline and erect military posture. But that day in Buenos Aires, he didn't project even the appearance of stamina.

The chronic fatigue may also have impaired his performance, for Haig's mission was not a success. His goal had been to negotiate a cease-fire, then urge the two countries to resume diplomatic talks toward a permanent resolution of the conflict. But instead, the hostilities escalated into a full-scale air and sea war that continued into the late spring. In the end it was not Haig's skills as a mediator but Britain's superior military strength, bolstered by U.S. aid, that prevailed. One positive side effect of the otherwise pointless war was that Britain's decisive victory left Argentina's ruling military junta in such a state of turmoil and disgrace that soon thereafter the generals were overthrown and democratic government was restored in that country.

The White House was not critical of Haig's performance as a negotiator. Reagan and his staff knew that achieving an early cease-fire would have been nearly impossible and that the secretary of state had tried his best. But they were unhappy about other aspects of his behavior. For it was during the Falklands War that

Haig resumed his griping about lack of support and ominous conspiracies to undermine his mission and reputation.

Some of his complaints seemed to be petty. During the first week of the crisis, *The New York Times* reported that Haig had delayed taking off on a trip to London for half a day because he insisted on flying in an Air Force plane that had windows instead of one that was windowless. It was a throwaway item that ran in an inside page of the paper, and the smart move would have been to ignore it. Instead, Haig denounced the report, claiming that the reason he had chosen to wait for the second plane was not because it had windows but because it had superior communications equipment. Going further, his aides charged that Jim Baker or a member of his staff had "planted" the story to make Haig look pompous. One of his top advisers was quoted as saying, "This is typical of the sniping the Secretary has had to endure from the beginning of this administration." A White House spokesman dismissed the Baker connection as "ludicrous," but regardless of who planted the item, Haig's overheated reaction drew far more attention to the incident.

Besides, when it came to sniping, Haig himself had few equals. In the weeks ahead, as the war continued and Haig became frustrated with the failure of his mission, he renewed his attacks on other favorite targets. At one point, he lashed out at Weinberger for the secretary of defense's constant references to the long-standing military agreements the United States had with Britain. Haig argued that such pro-British statements made it difficult for him to present himself in Buenos Aires as an honest and impartial mediator; at the same time, in the eyes of the British, he appeared to be a lukewarm supporter of their cause, at least when compared to Weinberger. Haig may have had a legitimate grievance on that point, but he also had to know that Weinberger was only stating the facts as they existed—there *were* long-standing military ties with the British—and that his remarks were completely in line with what had become, by then, administration policy. As the war entered its second month, Reagan gave up all pretense of neutrality and pledged to support Britain. He ruled out direct U.S. military involvement but promised logistical support.

On June 3, the President, accompanied by Haig and other high-ranking officials, began a nine-day trip to Paris and other European capitals. Three days later, another war broke out, this time in the Middle East, where Israeli troops swept into southern

Lebanon, ostensibly to wipe out PLO bases there, although the assault quickly escalated into a full-scale invasion as Israeli forces encircled Beirut, the Lebanese capital. Now, all of a sudden, the Reagan administration had to cope with wars involving key allies in two hemispheres; it was a time for calm and responsible leadership. Yet the deepening crisis brought out the worst in Haig.

He quarreled with almost everyone during that European trip. There was a spirited argument with Jeane Kirkpatrick over a UN resolution calling for a cease-fire in the Falklands. When Haig made a last-minute decision to change the U.S. vote from a veto to an abstention, he not only failed to clear the switch with the President, who was sleeping at the time, but sent his instructions through bureaucratic channels in Washington instead of calling Kirkpatrick directly. It was in response to a question about why he chose that circuitous route that he belittled Kirkpatrick's status: "You don't talk to a company commander," he explained, "when you have a corps and a division in between." White House staffers reacted to that with indignation, not only because they knew Reagan had a high regard for Kirkpatrick, but even more so because of the way Haig boasted about having made the decision on his own, clearly implying that the President's opinion was irrelevant.

He also fought with Weinberger and his "former" ally, Bill Clark, over the war in the Middle East. Haig wanted to adopt a soft line toward Israel's invasion of Lebanon, but Weinberger and Clark argued that given the aggressive nature of the assault, that was not an appropriate position. Again acting unilaterally, Haig announced plans to fly to Jerusalem, but Clark and others persuaded Reagan to order him to cancel the trip. This demonstration of presidential authority was leaked to the press, which by now was fascinated by all the open turmoil within Reagan's high command.

Nor were Haig's battles confined to issues and matters of policy. He railed against certain protocol arrangements that, he claimed, were part of a systematic campaign to diminish his stature and humiliate him. He complained about being relegated to a secondary helicopter while White House aides shared a helicopter ride with the President. He demanded to be given more prominent positions on receiving lines at formal gatherings and insisted that he should be the one to sit next to Queen Elizabeth at a state dinner in London. Finally, on the flight back to Washington, Haig told all who would listen, "I'm either going to run foreign policy or quit."

It was not the first time that he had threatened to quit. One of Haig's favorite ploys over the past year of dissension was to announce, at the end of a stormy encounter, that if he didn't get his way, he would resign. Many members of the White House staff now wished he would make good his threat. By this time, Haig's detractors included the one insider whose support he could least afford to lose. In the course of all the turbulent events that spring, Clark had come to realize that the criticisms of Haig were on target: he *was* a disruptive force in their midst, and with his volatile temperament, he never would be able to settle down and become a team player. Clark had turned on Haig for good during the European trip. Once that happened, it was only a matter of time— or timing—until Haig would be forced out.

At first, Baker and the others hoped to put off getting rid of Haig until after the midterm election that fall. The dismissal of Allen was a recent and unsettling memory, especially in light of the confusing circumstances surrounding his departure, and the ouster of Haig so soon after that would give the impression that Reagan still did not have a solid grip on his foreign policy apparatus. On the other hand, they had to ask, Who was kidding whom? Haig's unruly behavior in Europe, so much of which spilled over into press accounts of the trip, had made it impossible to present even the veneer of harmony. The constant clamor and feuding had to end, and in the days that followed their return from Europe, it was decided that they no longer had the luxury of waiting until after the election.

Haig, in the meantime, continued to bluster. Over Haig's strong objections, the President accepted Weinberger's recommendation to tighten sanctions on a Soviet pipeline that carried natural gas into Western Europe. Haig considered that an unnecessary provocation that would not only antagonize the Russians but be resented by several European allies, and in a more personal sense, he regarded Reagan's decision as yet another betrayal. Moreover, he still was at odds with Weinberger and Clark over what position the United States should take toward Israel's invasion of Lebanon. That, in fact, was the dispute that propelled the prolonged struggle for power to its abrupt climax. On June 18, Haig met in New York with Israel's prime minister, Menachem Begin, and a few days later, Begin flew to Washington for a meeting with Reagan. When Larry Speakes subsequently announced that the President had extracted from Begin a promise that Israeli troops would not enter Beirut, Haig was furious. That had not been the gist of his discussion with Begin, and he could only conclude that, in the interim, Weinberger and/or Clark had induced Reagan to take a tougher stand against Israel. Once again, Haig felt he had been sabotaged, and once again his response was to submit his resignation.

This was the moment that Baker and Clark had been waiting for. They already had decided that the next time Haig ended one of his tantrums with a threat to resign, they would urge the President to accept it. They had no trouble selling that decision to Reagan, who, by now, had lost patience with Haig. He still had respect for Haig's experience and knowledge of foreign affairs, but all the carping and ultimatums finally had begun to grate even on his genial nature. On June 25, the day after Haig's latest outburst, Reagan called the secretary of state into his office and informed him that his resignation had been accepted.

Haig was stunned. Despite all the contrary evidence, he still clung to the belief that Reagan needed his wise counsel and that, when it came to a real showdown, the President would side with him rather than the bunch of "amateurs" who did not understand foreign policy. Combative to the end, Haig proceeded to issue a statement of resignation that made no attempt to paper over the differences; in fact, it all but accused Reagan of reneging on his original promise:

"Your accession to office," he wrote to the President,

> brought an opportunity for a new and forward-looking foreign policy resting on the cornerstone of strength and compassion. . . . It was in this spirit that I undertook to serve you as Secretary of State. In recent months, it has become clear to me that the foreign policy on which we embarked together was shifting from that careful course which we had laid out. Under these circumstances, I feel it necessary to request that you accept my resignation.

It can be argued that Al Haig was his own worst enemy from the beginning. He entered the Reagan administration as an outsider with no personal or professional ties to the new President or to members of his inner circle. Yet instead of making the effort to gain their confidence and establish a working rapport with other key advisers, he went out of his way to exacerbate the tensions among them and to flaunt his own ego and ambition. On the other hand, Haig's failure to assert the necessary leadership in foreign affairs was not entirely his fault. It's one thing to dismiss his claim that he was the "vicar" of foreign policy as so much pretentiousness, but Haig can hardly be blamed for having taken Reagan at his word when he declared that the secretary of state would be his "principal spokesman and adviser" in that vital sphere. Presumably, Reagan had meant what he said then, yet in the months that followed, the President permitted others, including some of his closest deputies, to stymie Haig's efforts to carry out that assignment. Given all the interference he had put up with, Haig's growing frustration was inevitable.

It also must be said that never before in recent history had a secretary of state, the most prestigious of Cabinet officers, fallen into disrepute so quickly and so decisively. Even Dean Rusk and William Rogers, both of whom had to endure the indignity of being overshadowed by more powerful men inside the White House, managed to maintain a bureaucratic stability and continuity that helped to keep the government in harmony. But Haig's early and sudden departure, following so soon after Allen's ouster, shook Washington's foreign policy structure. Haig's successor, George Shultz, would embark on the formidable task of trying to put Humpty-Dumpty back together again, but it would take him months, even years, to gain control over all the damaging forces that had been unleashed during those early months of turmoil.

Even more unsettling was the chronic instability in the White House basement that turned the post of national security adviser into a travesty. In time, Bill Clark would encounter frustrations in that job and abandon it to serve the administration in a less troubled haven. In the course of Reagan's presidency, six men would pass through that office, and two of them, Robert McFarlane and John Poindexter, would achieve notoriety as key participants in a scandal that dishonored the President they served in a most unseemly fashion: by exposing him as—at best—an uninformed figurehead whose only defense was the claim that he had no clear idea what was going on a few doors away from his own office or what disreputable deals were being made with shady foreign operatives in his name.

But the Iran-Contra affair was not an isolated aberration. It, or something like it, was inevitable, given the disorder that characterized Reagan's approach to foreign policy almost from the time he took the oath of office. Instead of setting up a clear and coherent structure to guide him, the new President followed his passive inclination to let things slide, creating an enduring climate of drift and neglect. Viewed as a joint failure, the swift downfall of Richard Allen and Alexander Haig was an early signal that the gears of government were not meshing properly in Ronald Reagan's Washington.

8

Content-Free

"We always dreaded Mondays."
—*White House staffer*

The early signs of disarray in the Reagan White House were not confined to foreign policy. In the late fall of 1981, even as Reagan himself continued to enjoy the extended honeymoon of his first year in office, his budget director, David Stockman, made an alarming confession: that the President's vaunted "supply-side economic program" was not only based on questionable premises but wouldn't work. It was no more than the old theory of "trickle-down economics" dressed up in new clothes, a theory that held that cutting the taxes of the rich would improve the climate for business, and, as a result, benefits would accrue to those in lower economic brackets.

Stockman's allegations appeared in an article by William Greider, one of *The Washington Post*'s senior editors, which had been published in the *Atlantic Monthly* magazine and was stunning in its candor. Stockman had used the expression "Trojan horse" to describe parts of the program. During the early months of the administration while the President was predicting good times ahead if his economic program were adopted, Stockman revealed that he and other economic advisers had already seen alarming projections that showed just the opposite: huge deficits ranging from $82 billion dollars in 1982 to $116 billion by 1984. Direct quotations from Stockman were devastating. "None of us really understands what's going on with all these numbers," he said. At another point, he explained that he and his staff had more or less "cooked the books" when computer forecasts on the economy did not provide the answers they wanted. During the first weeks of the administration, as Greider related the story, Stockman and his aides fed data into the Office of Management and Budget computer to determine what would happen if the President were able to carry out his plan to increase defense spending at the same time he cut taxes. The answer was so startling that even Stockman "blinked." Instead of economic growth, the computer predicted deficits larger than anything the country had ever experienced in peacetime. Stockman knew that if such projections were included in the President's first budget message to Congress, the interest rates the administration wanted to lower would instead rise even higher, and with them the possibility of panic in the financial markets. Stockman's solution was a simple one. He fed a new set of numbers into the computer. Projections of falling prices, for example, were substituted for earlier projections that showed continued double-digit inflation. Stockman justified the substitutions by reasoning that economic forecasts were generally wrong anyway.

As shocking as the disclosures were, Stockman later claimed that the White House was not all that concerned when Greider's story first appeared. He said that some of the President's top people, members of both the Baker and Meese wings of the White House, had given him an autographed copy of the article, which they jokingly called "the best cover story by a White House official in *Atlantic* magazine." Within days, however, the disclosures had become a sensation. The networks picked up the story and newspapers printed excerpts. Soon there were reports quoting unnamed White House officials who reported that the President's top command was in a fury. Most definitely, the sources had it, the President had been betrayed and Stockman was in danger of losing his job.

The stories were accurate as far as they went. As the furor

built, Deaver had indeed argued that Stockman should be fired, and for once the people in the Meese wing of the White House sided with him. Deaver's argument was that Stockman had never been a team player and that under no circumstances should he be allowed to get away with such disloyalty. It was not a difficult line to sell. A newcomer to the Reagan team, Stockman was a brash two-term Republican congressman when the President picked him to head the Office of Management and Budget (OMB). Reagan had not known him until the thirty-four-year-old congressman helped prepare him for the campaign debates against Jimmy Carter and John Anderson. During the preparation, Stockman served as a stand-in for both Carter and Anderson, the Illinois Republican who ran in 1980 as an independent candidate. Reagan had originally wanted Weinberger for OMB, but when Weinberger said no, Reagan had turned to Stockman on the advice of New York Congressman Jack Kemp. Kemp had become the leader of a group of young, ultraconservative economists who called themselves supply-siders. Their aim was to discredit, once and for all, the so-called Keynesian theory of economics, which had been the dominant economic theory in the Western democracies for half a century.

John Maynard Keynes, who fashioned the theory in the 1930s, believed the way to make the economy grow and keep inflation under control was to manipulate consumer demand through government spending and tax programs. When unemployment is high and the economy is sluggish, Keynes argued, government can increase consumer demand by cutting taxes and increasing public spending. On the other hand, when the economy overheats, taxes should be raised and public spending slowed. The supply-siders took an opposite tack. They said the way to get a sluggish economy moving was not by stimulating demand, but by stimulating production by cutting business taxes. Inflation could be controlled by budget cuts and tight money policy. Cutting taxes down the line would encourage more production because it would encourage people to work harder. It was an economic theory made to order for a President who had often told friends that back in the 1950s, when he first started making big money, he found himself in the 90 percent income tax bracket. Reagan readily understood how cutting taxes encouraged more production because in those "big money" days he remembered how many

Hollywood stars limited themselves to only four pictures a year. They knew that if they made any more their earnings would just be paid out to the government in taxes.

The other part of the supply-side philosophy—heavy cuts in spending—was just as important to Reagan, and spurred on by the President's support, Stockman went about his task of cutting with zeal. Among his chief targets were the social welfare programs that had been inherited from the Great Society legislation of the 1960s. Stockman asserted that they had transformed the federal budget into "a coast-to-coast soup line," and he wielded his knife on those and other programs with so much vigor that he quickly became the most unpopular man in Washington. In fact, at one point the President quipped, "We won't leave you out there alone, Dave. We'll all come to the hanging." But nobody laughed when Stockman turned his attention to Social Security and other entitlement programs. His proposal to make large cuts in that area infuriated lobbying groups that represented the elderly and stirred an otherwise docile Congress into a mood of defiance. The ensuing uproar was so strong that, even in the midst of the honeymoon period, the Reagan White House had to retreat: Stockman's ax would not be allowed to fall on Social Security.

But that isolated setback in the spring of 1981 did not dampen his enthusiasm for making deep cuts in other programs, and his ruthless measures antagonized most members of Reagan's Cabinet. Except for Cap Weinberger, who presided over Defense— the one department that had been promised a sharp increase in spending—the Cabinet officers began to realize that they were at Stockman's mercy. They soon viewed Cabinet meetings as ambush sites where Stockman would overwhelm them with statistics and arguments to cut programs they had not been aware were at risk or even on the agenda for discussion. They were often surprised, embarrassed, and defenseless as Stockman whittled away at their turf. No one found Stockman's brashness more difficult to digest than Secretary of the Treasury Donald Regan. By the fall of 1981, Regan was becoming more and more disenchanted with the way economic policy was being formulated, for he had yet to have a private meeting with the President to discuss the economy. (Indeed, he never did have one.) Regan not only resented being overshadowed by Stockman but increasingly felt that the young financial whiz was ignoring him.

Nor did Stockman endear himself to other high-ranking

members of the White House staff. He considered Deaver an intellectual inferior and made no effort to conceal his disdain; he looked upon most members of Baker's team as little more than glorified campaign workers who knew nothing about policy; and he managed to irritate Meese and the coterie of Reaganites who worked for him. Thus, by that fall when Greider's article was published in the *Atlantic*, few in the White House would have protested if Reagan had decided to fire Stockman. As one White House staffer later put it, "There were any number of people around Reagan who would have been happy to buy Stockman an airplane ticket for any destination he chose."

Stockman no doubt would have been fired had it not been for his one protector, Jim Baker. Baker was as angry as the others, but a friend said he recognized two things: First, firing Stockman would only give credibility to the charges raised in the article; his dismissal would only give him an opportunity to go into more detail in what were certain to be additional confessions. Second, and more important, Baker knew that it would be a lot harder to run the government without Stockman. On the White House organizational charts, domestic policy was Ed Meese's bailiwick because the Domestic Council staff, which was charged with shaping all domestic policy, reported to Meese. In reality, the diagrams on the organizational chart meant nothing. David Stockman was Jim Baker's "Domestic Council," and it was at the daily meetings with Stockman in Baker's office that domestic policy was really being shaped.

Baker needed Stockman, so he came up with another plan. The President would meet with Stockman over lunch to see what the young man had to say for himself. It was after that meeting that a chastened Stockman went before an assembly of reporters to announce that the President had taken him "to the woodshed." He had been publicly reprimanded in a way that government officials seldom are in Washington, and the controversy over the "Atlantic affair" soon dissipated.

It had been a remarkable episode in a city where straight talk was generally passed over for euphemism, where underlings and their bosses seldom criticized each other in public, and where administration officials—Democrat or Republican—almost never spoke of their programs and proposals in anything but the most favorable terms. Even more remarkable than the episode itself was the way in which Baker's tactic of sending Stockman to the woodshed had resulted in shifting attention from the disclosures in the *Atlantic*. Instead, the attention was focused on questions about Stockman's loyalty and motivations. And as was often the case in Reagan's White House, Stockman's "woodshedding" had been as much a public relations maneuver as a reprimand. As Stockman later revealed in his memoir, the President had not chastised him at all. That had been done by Baker, who had given him a private dressing-down that would have done credit to a Marine drill sergeant. Baker had ended the meeting by ordering Stockman to meet the President for lunch. The menu, Baker explained, would be "humble pie," and, Baker said, he expected to see Stockman's "sorry ass dragging the carpet" as he left the Oval Office.

During the meeting with the President later that day, Stockman said Reagan expressed disappointment but advanced the notion that the budget director had been a victim of a hostile press, that his quotations had been taken out of context, and that he hoped Stockman would stay on. As he was leaving the President's office, Stockman said, Reagan told him that the staff thought he should go before reporters to explain what had happened. Thus, it was Stockman himself who concocted the woodshed story.

Real or not, the story had worked. It had been a case study of public relations damage control. Startling disclosures about the health of the economy were all but overshadowed by the human story of a kindly old President who had been embarrassed by a young aide but was too big a man to fire him. Instead, the youngster had been harshly reprimanded and was now better and wiser for the experience. The ruse allowed Stockman to remain in the administration on into Reagan's second term, but his standing within the White House was never the same after that. He never again enjoyed the full confidence of the inner circle, even of Baker, who had salvaged his job. When he finally left early in the second term, he wrote a book that was even more critical of Reagan and his team than the *Atlantic* article, but it had little impact in Washington. White House officials were again able to shift attention away from Stockman's dire assertions and direct the debate to questions concerning his loyalty. Even so, as the years passed, the enormous deficits that Stockman had predicted materialized. The deficit became the most glaring flaw in the policy known as

"Reaganomics," and the administration's public relations specialists had to work hard to prevent it from becoming a destructive political issue.

For all the talk about the need for Cabinet government, it never became a working reality. Reagan's utopian idea had envisioned a group of high-minded men and women of good judgment who would gather at the same table and make policy by thrashing out differences in good-natured give-and-take. Unfortunately, Cap Weinberger and Al Haig represented such differing points of view they could hardly sit at the same table, let alone settle arguments there, and the rapport between Weinberger and Haig's successor, George Shultz, was no better. Within weeks after Schultz had taken over at State insiders realized that the two men were barely able to resolve even the most minor disagreements.

In the meantime, the Cabinet officers on the domestic side were finding that the White House did not want them to be policymakers at all. Rather, they were encouraged to become a sales force for policy developed by the White House staff. In Reagan's Washington, as had so often been the case during the terms of other modern Presidents, major policy was shaped by aides who worked in the White House, not appointees in the outlying bureaucracy. It was the White House staffers who were closest in proximity to the President, who were generally his most trusted advisers, and who controlled his schedule. Thus, it was the team around him that had the best opportunities to get his signature on programs and, conversely, to block from his view programs that did not meet with their approval. Since the coming of television, most Washington news coverage has centered on the presidency. Presidents encouraged the trend, and in the Reagan White House it was honed to a fine art, but it was the nature of television that was a major factor in the shift in focus.

Once news conferences began to be televised affairs, the demeanor of the news maker sometimes received as much attention as what he or she said. John Kennedy's mastery of news conferences was not so much grounded in the substance of his answers as in the cool, witty, and self-assured way he gave them. It was only natural, then, that as television came to dominate news coverage, more and more of the attention centered on the White House and on the President. A plan to give block financial grants to the states, for example, quickly became "the President's plan to give block grants" because pictures of a President explaining or defending his programs were always more interesting than statistics about the program itself. As Presidents and their aides came to understand this, they also realized that to ensure the most favorable coverage, there had to be a constant effort to find ways to tie the administration's accomplishments directly to the President. Above all else, the White House had to become the focal point for administration successes, the place where good news happened and bad news never did. It was in the far reaches of the bureaucracy that the mistakes were always made.

Melvin R. Laird, who had been Richard Nixon's first secretary of defense, learned all this during the days when the country found itself bogged down in Vietnam. Having been sent out to announce yet another dismal development, Laird had wondered aloud to an aide why there was never any good news to proclaim. Then the answer occurred to him. "I suppose if there were good news," he sighed a moment later, "the President would announce it." Television encouraged the star system, and no group of people appreciated the significance of that more than Reagan's inner circle.

At the daily early morning breakfast attended by Baker, Deaver, and Meese, the story line of the day—the policy or personnel development to be highlighted—would be chosen. Then White House Press Officer Speakes would hold a conference call with information officers in the various Cabinet departments. The standing orders were to inform the White House of pending events that might reflect well on the President. Events occurring within the various departments that had the potential for pushing "the story of the day" at the White House off the network news broadcasts were discouraged. A reporter making his normal rounds during those years would often be told by various departmental press officers, "We have a story today but the White House is announcing it."

In such an atmosphere, it is easy for even a Cabinet officer to be overlooked. Except for the President's old friend Weinberger, who clearly enjoyed the publicity, most of the Reagan Cabinet was seldom heard from on substantive issues. Shultz did become a formidable presence within the top command, but he was a quiet man by nature and, unlike Weinberger, seldom flaunted his

power. Regan at Treasury was continually overshadowed by Stockman, so much so that by the second term he was eager to trade
his Cabinet slot for the job of White House chief of staff. Such a
swap would have been unheard-of in earlier days. At Justice,
changes were taking place—Reagan appointees had a much more
relaxed attitude toward enforcement of antitrust and civil rights
laws—but the personable attorney general, William French Smith,
left most controversial decisions to underlings and maintained a
low profile during business hours. (He did, however, develop
something of an after-dark reputation as the administration's ambassador to Washington society. Seldom was a charity ball held
that did not include the dapper Smith and his attractive wife.)

A few members of the Cabinet became so disenchanted with
this state of affairs that they left their posts well before the first
term came to an end. Energy Secretary James Edwards, the South
Carolina dentist, did little on the job to justify his appointment,
and in November 1982 he quietly resigned; he was replaced by
Donald Hodel, who had been the number-two man at Interior.
(A few years earlier, when Edwards returned to his private practice after serving one term as governor of South Carolina, he
rejoiced, "It's so satisfying to have my hands in the saliva again,"
and we can only assume that he experienced a similarly blissful
reunion after he left the Reagan administration.) Transportation's
Drew Lewis won acclaim for his handling of the air traffic controllers' strike, but then he faded into the shadows, and in December 1982 he decided to return to his successful career as a
businessman in Pennsylvania.

Another early casualty was Richard Schweiker, who had been
picked to preside over Health and Human Services. Schweiker
was one of the few marquee names appointed to the Cabinet, but
he soon discovered that running the department that oversees
welfare programs was a miserable job in the Reagan administration. Except for the role he played in the attempt to cut Social
Security benefits and another embarrassing episode in which he
found himself pictured in white tie and tails on the cover of a
Washington magazine just as a new round of welfare cuts was
being proposed, Schweiker, too, was seldom heard from, and he
stepped down in January 1983. He was replaced by Margaret
Heckler, an eight-term congresswoman from Massachusetts, who
had been defeated in the 1982 election, and another woman,

Elizabeth Dole, was chosen to succeed Lewis at Transportation. Dole, in particular, went on to become a forceful presence in the Cabinet, yet another indication of Reagan's knack for naming outstanding women to high-level posts.

Then there was the troubling case of Secretary of Labor Raymond Donovan, who had come into the administration under a cloud of suspicion. Even as he took over his Cabinet post, Donovan was being investigated for alleged ties to union corruption and organized crime during the years when he was running a construction company in New Jersey. Although the questions about his past associations made his presence in the Cabinet a continuing embarrassment, Reagan stoutly defended Donovan until the time came when his legal problems could no longer be ignored. In early 1985, Donovan was formally charged with defrauding the New York City Transit Authority of $7.4 million. The distinction of becoming the first sitting Cabinet officer ever to be indicted forced Donovan to resign, and he was replaced by U.S. Trade Representative William Brock III. When Brock left the post later in the second term to manage Bob Dole's presidential campaign, he was succeeded at Labor by yet another woman, Ann McLaughlin. As for Donovan, he eventually was acquitted of the charges against him, but the jury's verdict did little restore his reputation.

Of all the Cabinet officers who presided over domestic programs during the first term, the one who attracted the most attention was James Watt, the secretary of the interior. Most of the publicity about Watt, however, was unfavorable. The most ideologically motivated of all the Cabinet appointees, Watt was the kind of antiestablishment hard-liner whom the true believers had expected Reagan to appoint to most key government posts. Yet as Reagan put together the kind of moderate, business-oriented Cabinet that Dwight Eisenhower might have formed, it was Watt who became the administration's most acute embarrassment. Two Westerners with much broader credentials, Wyoming's former senator Clifford Hansen and Arizona's longtime congressman John Rhodes, had been leading contenders for the post, but Hansen didn't want it and Reagan intimate Paul Laxalt didn't like Rhodes. So, Watt got the appointment at the urging of Joseph Coors, the wealthy Colorado brewer, a longtime financial supporter of Reagan and sponsor of many conservative causes. Although he was Reagan's third choice, Watt was a conservative's dream. A born-again Christian whose children attended the fundamentalist Bob Jones University, he had no tolerance for anyone who disagreed with him and once declared there were two kinds of people in the country, "liberals and Americans." Of all the people in Ronald Reagan's Washington, no one saw his mission with more clarity that James Gaius Watt.

Watt knew his way around the Washington bureaucracy. He had first gone to the Capitol in 1962 as an aide to Wyoming's new Republican senator, Millard Simpson. It was during this period as a diligent young Capitol Hill staffer that Watt reached a turning point in his life: shortly after attending his first gospel service he became a born-again Christian, a commitment that would become the moral center of his life. Connections at the Senate also led to a post with a U.S. Chamber of Commerce advisory panel on natural resources. By 1968, Watt's "prodevelopment" environmental stance had caught the attention of aides to Richard Nixon, and when Nixon won the presidency, Watt was invited to join the team. He was asked to coordinate the confirmation strategy for Walter Hickel, another "prodevelopment" advocate whom Nixon had picked to be his interior secretary.

That was no small assignment. Hickel was an outspoken former Alaska governor who had been a builder. Early on, he had enraged environmentalists by disclosing that he saw no point in "conservation for conservation's sake." As a builder, Hickel had buldozed his share of the environment and at one point had announced, "A tree just looking at a tree really doesn't do anything." As might be expected, the Senate Interior Committee gave Hickel a rough going-over, and he was the last member of the Nixon Cabinet to be confirmed.

Once in office, however, Hickel quickly became a convert to the conservation cause, a commitment that led to his eventual undoing. His new association with ecology groups had put him in touch with many college students, and he became concerned about a deepening resentment of Nixon administration policies in Vietnam that seemed to be building on college campuses. Unable to set up a meeting with Nixon to discuss the problem, he wrote the President a letter in which he accused the administration of consciously trying to alienate the young; he further suggested that the problem was due in part to the President's own isolation. A staffer leaked the letter to the press and Nixon's palace guard was enraged. Hickel eventually was summoned to the Oval Office and told to resign. The next day, White House aide Fred Malek, who sometimes handled unsavory assignments for the administration (at Nixon's request he once compiled a list of Jews who worked for the Bureau of Labor Statistics), was dispatched to Interior, where he told six of Hickel's staffers: "We want you out of the building by five o'clock." Watt survived the purge. Unlike Hickel, he had not become a convert to the cause of "conservation for conservation's sake," nor did he evince any sympathy for the growing antiwar protests.

By 1975, Watt had moved on to the Federal Power Commission through the largess of Gerald Ford and was becoming increasingly known as one government official who believed industrial and commercial concerns were at least as important as environmental interests. When Joe Coors decided to form a nonprofit legal foundation to fight the growing power of environmental groups in 1977, Watt put together the ideal résumé to get the $70,000-a-year top job. (That was big money to Watt. Unlike many in the Reagan administration, he was not a wealthy man, and at his confirmation hearings, he listed his net worth at less than $100,000.)

Over the next three and a half years that he headed the foundation, Watt and a corps of lawyers and legal assistants filed more than forty lawsuits, thirteen of them against the Department of the Interior, on behalf of oil, power, and mining interests. The suits challenged government policy on issues ranging from grazing rights on public lands to air pollution standards and stripmining regulations. At one point Watt's lawyers tried to overturn a Colorado law that required public utilities to give the poor, the disabled, and the elderly lower rates. A twenty-minute interview was all Ronald Reagan needed to be convinced that Watt was the kind of interior secretary he wanted, and he was offered the job despite widespread opposition from many conservation groups. As had been the case when he coordinated Hickel's confirmation activities for the Nixon administration, Watt found considerable hostility when he arrived at the Capitol for his own hearings. His penchant for outlandish comments did not help his cause. He confirmed during the hearings that he had once observed that "as a white man I will be very hesitant to allow a black doctor to operate on me because I will always have the feeling that he may have been carried by the quota system." There was also uneasiness about his declaration that he had to "follow the scriptures which call upon us to occupy the land until Jesus returns." Did that mean that Watt thought he had been given divine sanction to do as he pleased with the land? Such remarks touched off vociferous environmentalist protest, but as opposition to Watt grew stronger, Reagan lobbyists pressed the senators harder and Watt was confirmed in time to take office when Reagan was sworn in.

To anyone even slightly familiar with his background, Watt's policy proposals to develop public resources as a way of stimulating the economy should have come as no surprise. Even so, his comments continued to amaze. In March of that first year, he told a *Washington Post* reporter that he had "an accounting to the President, to the American people and to God and I take it seriously." One of the newspaper's columnists, Colman McCarthy, responded, "Watt can doubtlessly leap to the altar with favorite 'subdue the earth texts' that make it seem as if God created the earth just for Mobil Oil."

Watt moved quickly to reorganize Interior. Democrats and those who disagreed with his policies were rooted out and fired. Early in his tenure, he showed that he was not afraid to stir controversy when he proposed to offer 200,000 offshore acres for oil and gas drilling. Watt's idea was to let the oil companies, rather than the Department of the Interior, decide which tracts should be placed at auction. When he decided to offer tracts off Big Sur along the California coast, there was such a bipartisan outcry from conservationists, that the proposal was postponed. By the fall of 1981, the Sierra Club had obtained one million signatures on a petition calling for Watt's ouster.

But the White House continued to give Watt strong backing in its public statements, and, despite all the controversy, he remained personally popular with the President and conservatives in the West. As he began to speak out for his policies, the President's advisers discovered that Watt had skills they had been unaware he possessed. He could be mesmerizing when the audience was conservative, and as a result, he became one of the leading fund-raisers for the Republican party as well as one of the President's biggest boosters. When the right wing complained that White House "pragmatists" were reining in the President, it was Watt who coined the slogan "Let Reagan be Reagan." But Watt would prove as much a liability as an asset as the months wore on, and there was a feeling among Reagan's inner circle—especially those in the Baker wing—that Watt would eventually have to be dismissed.

During the summer of 1982, Watt provoked a diplomatic incident with the potential for serious political repercussions. The episode came about when he wrote a letter to the Israeli ambassador in Washington, warning him that Jewish Americans who were opposing the administration's energy policy "could weaken America's ability to be a good friend to Israel." American Jewish leaders were outraged, as were many members of Congress, and Watt eventually apologized. He also managed to get on Nancy Reagan's bad side during a celebrated incident in which he blocked an appearance by the Beach Boys, a rock-and-roll group that had been scheduled to entertain at a Washington Fourth of July celebration. Watt considered Wayne Newton, a Las Vegas entertainer, to be more appropriate for a patriotic celebration, failing to understand that the Beach Boys were personal favorites of the First Lady. As a result, she now added her voice to the growing anti-Watt faction inside the White House.

Watt's attempt at humor in the fall of 1983 finally led to his undoing. Commenting on the balance he had given to a coal mining advisory committee, he remarked that the panel was composed of "a black, a woman, two Jews, and a cripple." Even many who had stood by him through earlier gaffes now realized that Watt had to go. Reagan himself had always gone to Watt's defense in the past, but he separated himself quickly from that one, and with all signs indicating the Senate would soon pass a resolution calling for Watt's removal, the interior secretary decided he had done enough to embarrass the administration. He declared in his letter of resignation that Reagan would be best served by a different type of leadership.

By then, Watt's departure had been expected, but the President's choice to replace him was a surprise even to many of the insiders. In a twist on Watt's celebrated "Let Reagan be Reagan" line, the President had decided to "let Clark be Watt." The Clark in question was Bill Clark, the national security adviser. In a move that caught even many on Clark's staff by surprise, he was leaving a powerful White House job for what many in Washington considered a minor Cabinet post. Yet, as was so often the case

during the Reagan years, Clark's appointment at Interior had
more to do with backstage infighting than either the appointee's
aspirations or the desires of the President he served.

Clark had been brought to the White House to restore order at
the National Security Council, which had all but disintegrated
under Richard Allen. Instead, his arrival provoked the most acrimonious period at the White House during Reagan's first term.
For all practical purposes, it destroyed the balance that had
evolved within the Baker-Meese-Deaver troika of the early and
most successful months of the Reagan administration. After the
assassination attempt on the President's life, the newsmagazines
and newscasts were filled with stories about the unique arrangement that seemed to be holding the White House together.

What was often misunderstood was that no one had envisioned such an arrangement in the beginning. When Spencer and
Deaver conspired to prevent Meese from becoming White House
chief of staff by getting the job for Baker, it was never intended—
even by Deaver himself—that he would become a part of the
White House high command. Deaver at that point had planned
to remain in private business and concentrate on building up his
list of public relations clients. Even after Deaver agreed to work
for the White House, he was never considered on equal status
with either Baker or Meese, and organization charts at the time
listed him simply as Baker's assistant. "No one thought the three
were anything remotely resembling equals," said one member of
Baker's group. "If you had tried to sell that, you wouldn't have
been able to. The President at that point did not think of Deaver
as a whole lot more than a bag carrier."

What Reagan and Meese had envisioned in the beginning was
a White House where Meese designed policy and Baker implemented it. Baker, of course, had maneuvered himself into a policy-
making position by convincing Meese to give him control of the
key members of the White House staff. What Deaver soon realized, however, was that Baker and Meese often differed over
policy direction. Thus, with his connections to Mrs. Reagan,
Deaver found it relatively simple to arrange to be in position as
"the third and deciding vote" when Baker and Meese were split.
Deaver's status as an equal partner in the management of the
White House was further enhanced, at least in the public's mind,

during the period when Reagan was recovering from the assassination attempt. It was Meese, Baker, and Deaver who were seen day after day entering and leaving the hospital where Reagan was recuperating. Then Deaver made other moves to entrench himself. Just as Baker had used his bureaucratic skills to maneuver into a position of equal status with Meese, so it was that the status of the Reagans' favorite image maker had been enhanced by the kind of "visual" that Deaver so often planned to show Reagan's accomplishments. In Washington, where perception is often as important as reality, the fact that people were coming to believe that Deaver was powerful only added to his power. And, as one of those who had conspired to prevent Meese from becoming chief of staff in the beginning, it was not surprising that he usually sided with Baker.

To Baker aide Richard Darman, decision making in those days sometimes took on the aspects of appellate court proceedings. The President, in effect, had four votes, Darman told us one morning over breakfast; the troika of Meese, Baker and Deaver each had one. Second-echelon aides such as Darman, then–Cabinet secretary Craig Fuller, budget director Stockman, and others would function as friends of the court, in effect filing briefs with their superiors and arguing among themselves. "If Meese and Baker were split," Darman said, "then the President would often be undecided in his own mind because he tended to see both sides." It was a polite way of saying that the President sometimes seemed to have no view of his own but was always eager for his aides to agree upon a plan of action that he could then endorse. Reagan, as insiders so often described him, wanted "solutions not problems," and in such an atmosphere Deaver could exercise significant influence when he chose. (More often than not he would make his argument to Mrs. Reagan, who would then pass it on to the President, who would then come down on Baker's side.)

The arrival of Clark changed all that. Now there were four men of equal stature in the top command. Although Deaver had been one of those who wanted to bring Clark into the White House, he failed to understand that Clark still looked on him as no more than the errand boy who had handled menial tasks for Clark back in the days when they all worked together in Sacramento. Clark had been in charge of the governor's office back then, and now, after he had been in the White House only a few hours, he let Baker, Meese, and Deaver know that he intended to deal with his old friend Ronald Reagan directly and not through any of them. Like Meese, Clark was close to Reagan, and that was his greatest strength. Unlike Meese, whose poor administrative ability and sloppy work habits usually made it possible for Baker to outmaneuver him, Clark was an able administrator and sensitive boss who seemed to get the most out of his staff. Clark's weakness was not work habits, but a lack of background for the job he had been chosen to fill. His experience in foreign policy consisted solely of the months he had spent at the State Department, where his main responsibilities had been to serve as a bridge to the White House for the egocentric Haig and to assure conservatives that Haig would never deviate very far from the hard-line foreign policy they demanded. To Clark's credit, he never pretended to be a foreign policy expert. Although he insisted on dealing with the President directly, he always took with him a specialist to brief him when a complicated matter arose. Such sessions proved to be great morale boosters for those obscure aides who were flattered to have a chance to meet the President. Because the President seldom asked questions, the specialists could leave the sessions feeling that their expertise and conclusions had carried the day. As Baker and Deaver had hoped, Clark did bring some order to the National Security Council staff. Clark was even finding new ways to persuade Reagan to focus on foreign policy matters. Beyond his strong anti-Communist views, foreign policy had never held much attraction for Reagan, and aides often found it difficult to induce him to concentrate on policy papers dealing with foreign affairs. During Clark's tenure, however, a new briefing method was developed: movie shorts, what amounted to training films on foreign policy.

Early in the administration, White House insiders had come to understand that "visuals" often made more of an impression on the President than printed materials and that his favorite source of news was television. "We always dreaded Mondays," one person who held the title of assistant to the President told us,

because Reagan always watched "60 Minutes" religiously and he would come in Monday morning wanting to check out something or other that he had seen on the program. Most of us had nothing against Mike Wallace, but we were putting in twelve- and fourteen-hour days in that period and the last thing we wanted to do on Sundays was watch "60 Minutes" in order to be ready for the President's questions. It was the one evening we could spend with our families.

It was such stories, however, that led to development of the "training films" as supplements to the thick briefing books on policy prepared for the President. For example, when Reagan was planning to travel overseas, a movie that included scenes of all the places the President would go and the people he would meet would be made.

"The movies were generally very good," said Press Officer Speakes.

They took a lot of pride in them. And they were very well done. The narrator would say for example, "You will arrive on Air Force One at Joe Blow Airport and then take a 15 minute ride to the ancient palace where you will meet Prime Minister So and So." And, then there would be a still photo from the CIA or somewhere and [the narrator would say] "he's known for right wing policy or he's having trouble with the parliament" . . . that kind of stuff.

Speakes stressed that Reagan still received the customary briefing books, although, he said, he had no way of knowing whether they were ever read.

Baker had been content to let Clark brief the President in any way he chose on routine matters, but as the months passed he became concerned about secret end runs that Clark often attempted on foreign policy matters. Clark was so unsure of himself in some foreign policy areas that he often felt it necessary to depend on specialists to brief the President, yet he seemed to have no hesitation about launching foreign policy initiatives without notifying the secretary of state. Baker uncovered instances in which Clark had brought UN Ambassador Jeane Kirkpatrick into the Oval Office and discussed plans to send her on secret missions into Central America without the secretary of state's knowledge. On other occasions, Baker discovered that Clark had tried to open secret lines of communication to Moscow through the Soviet ambassador in Washington, again without George Schultz's knowledge or approval.

Deaver discovered another instance when Clark had given Reagan papers authorizing ambassadorial appointments that had not been cleared by the State Department. To Baker's people, Clark's schemes seemed so unsophisticated and uninformed that they began referring to him as the one adviser who was "content-free." The constant battles over spheres of authority that were now being waged brought with them deepening personal animosity among the top men. It became so bad at one point that Deaver arranged for the President to call Meese, Baker, and Clark into the Oval Office. At Deaver's prompting, the President urged the three to try to get along in a civil fashion. When that produced only grunts and low murmuring, Deaver tried a new approach. He invited the three to late afternoon cocktails at Blair House, the residence for presidential guests across the street from the White House. Deaver thought a setting away from their offices would be conducive to making peace. That didn't work either. Meese and Baker finally shook hands, but Clark refused, and the meeting degenerated into another round of name calling. Understandably, the White House was filled with rumors that Baker was trying to force Clark out and Clark knew it and that Clark had countered by presenting the President a plan that called for eliminating Baker's job. That particular plan had been squashed when Deaver overheard Clark as he presented it to Reagan on *Air Force One*. When Deaver told the President he couldn't operate under such an arrangement and would have to leave, the idea was soon dropped.

Baker and George Shultz had never been particularly close, but they shared the concern that Clark's secretive ways might lead the administration into a foreign policy disaster. Baker's people were already busy keeping track of CIA Director William Casey. Baker felt that Casey had a rare ability to play to Reagan's "dark side," and at Baker's direction Darman had set up an elaborate system to make sure that Casey did not see the President without Baker's knowledge. (Relations between Baker and Casey had never been good after the two had called each other liars during a controversy over how one of Jimmy Carter's briefing books had wound up at Reagan headquarters during the 1980 campaign.)

What worried Baker's people during this period was Reagan's penchant for doing whatever had been suggested by the last person who had talked to him. To Reagan, a large part of decision

making was simply picking people you trusted and then doing
what they recommended. Baker always had "walk-in" rights to
the Oval Office when Meese was there, but he enjoyed no such
privileges when it came to Casey, and now there was Clark to
contend with as well. Baker tried to deal with Clark in the same
way he had dealt with Casey. Once he learned that either man
had been to the Oval Office, either he or Deaver would drop in
and casually debrief the President. If they concluded that Reagan
had been asked to do something unwise, they would say, "Mr.
President, don't you think it would be better to . . ." and invariably
the President would respond, "Oh, certainly." But even though
they had instituted an elaborate system to monitor visitors to the
Oval Office (Darman had even worked out procedures that alerted
them if messages were sent to the President's upstairs residence),
Baker and his staff continually worried that Clark or Casey might
slip in quietly one day and God only knew what might happen
then.

They all remembered the time Clark had convinced the President to go along with a plan to track down news leaks that would
have required everyone in the administration, including the vice
president, to submit to lie detector tests. Under Clark's plan those
who refused would be asked to resign. A letter to the attorney
general that authorized the plan had been prepared by Clark and
Reagan had signed it. Baker had been en route to the Madison
Hotel for lunch when he learned of the plan on his car phone.
He ordered his driver to reverse course immediately and return
to the White House. The President was having lunch with Secretary of State Shultz and the vice president, but Baker did not
hesitate to break in. He went right to the point, telling the President that the letter he had signed gave the White House chief of
staff authority to demand that the vice president take a lie detector
test and to ask for his resignation if he refused, a course of action
that was clearly unconstitutional. According to a person who was
in the room, Baker said, "Do you really want the vice president
polygraphed?" Shultz and Vice President Bush both objected,
Shultz vociferously. Reagan then responded, "Well, Bill [Clark]
shouldn't have done that." At Baker's urging he then picked up
the phone and told the attorney general to disregard the order.
As had happened so often when Reagan backed off a controversial
position, he seemed to accept no blame for it himself. It had been
something "Bill" had done. Baker had no problem with that, but

as much as anything else, the incident convinced him that Clark's presence in the White House was becoming a problem that had to be resolved.

With relations between Baker and Clark worse than ever, the forced resignation of Watt provided a way for both to save face. Clark was as exhausted by the constant fighting as Baker and decided that replacing Watt would suit him just fine. As a rancher and outdoorsman, he had a real interest in programs that fell under the authority of the secretary of the interior, and it was the perfect way to get out of "the living hell" the White House had become for him. For once, Deaver and Baker agreed with Clark. They didn't care where he went, as long as it was out of the White House. If he was willing to go to Interior, then so be it.

As was usual during backstage maneuvering at the Reagan White House, Baker and Deaver were motivated by more than making it easy for Clark to have a more peaceful life. His departure opened up all sorts of interesting possibilities. Until now, Baker had focused almost all of his attention on domestic policy, and he wanted to get involved in the foreign side. ("It was the one thing we just couldn't seem to get right," he told us later.) The job of national security adviser was just the place for Baker to move into foreign policy, and by taking on that post, he would clear the way for Deaver to realize *his* ambition, which was to replace Baker as chief of staff.

As both men had calculated in advance, they had no trouble selling the plan to Reagan, and Deaver drew up a press release announcing the changes: Baker to replace the departing Clark as national security adviser and Deaver to take over as chief of staff. They knew that Clark would probably oppose them, so they wanted the decision announced before Clark had a chance to argue the President out of the idea. But unfortunately for Baker and Deaver, Reagan ran into Clark in a White House hallway as he headed to a previously scheduled meeting of his top defense and national security advisers. The chance encounter gave Clark an opportunity to direct a parting shot at the two men who had made his life so difficult for nearly two years. As the advisers gathered, he slipped notes to Meese, Weinberger, and Casey, telling them of the President's intentions. Before the afternoon was over, they had convinced Reagan not to go through with it. As Reagan later explained to Baker and Deaver, "I had no idea the

fellas would be so adamant." Of all "the fellas," no one opposed
the plan more fervently than Meese. For him, as well as Clark, it
was a moment of revenge, a way to retaliate for the steps Baker
and Deaver had taken back in 1980 to prevent him from becoming
chief of staff.

All that took place on a Friday, and by the next Monday, the
hard-liners, led by Clark, had come up with a plan to give the
national security adviser post to Jeane Kirkpatrick. That proposed
move set off another spirited battle, with Baker, Deaver, and Secretary of State Shultz opposing Kirkpatrick's supporters, Clark,
Meese, and Weinberger. They eventually resolved the dispute by
settling on a compromise candidate, Robert C. "Bud" McFarlane,
a seasoned bureaucrat who had originally moved over from the
State Department to serve as Clark's deputy in the White House.

The appointment of Bud McFarlane seemed a good idea at
the time. Although Clark had been an improvement over the
ineffectual Dick Allen, he, too, had failed to achieve full control
of the national security operation. Having entered Washington
with "a truly open mind" in foreign policy, Clark found that his
lack of knowledge and experience eventually caught up with him.
Clark's major asset—the trust Reagan had in him because of their
longtime relationship—enabled him to succeed over the short run.
But as time went on, his provincial conservative outlook led him
into partisan squabbles for which he was not equipped, and that
steadily weakened his influence. In the end, Bill Clark was no
match for the savvy men aligned against him.

McFarlane brought no such defects to the post. Having served
in the National Security Council during both the Nixon and Ford
administrations, the retired Marine colonel had a firsthand familiarity with the job, the kind of experience that Clark so sorely
lacked. Although he did not have the academic background of a
Henry Kissinger or Zbigniew Brzezinski, he was a solid staff man
and he was no ideologue. He had a reputation for working
smoothly with both conservatives and moderates that made him
acceptable to all sides. Just as Deaver had been willing to accept
Baker as chief of staff in order to keep Meese out of the job, now
Meese was willing to accept McFarlane as national security adviser
in order to block Baker. McFarlane was sold to the White House
troika as an impartial mediator in the mold of his onetime mentor
Brent Scowcroft, and his appointment was welcomed by both bu-
reaucrats and Reagan insiders as a move that was long overdue.

They were further encouraged by some of the early steps Mc-Farlane took to strengthen the operation. He picked a hardworking staff man, Admiral John Poindexter, to serve as his chief deputy and upgraded the role of another military assistant, a promising and zealous Marine colonel named Oliver North. Thus, by the autumn of 1983, the sensitive apparatus in the White House basement finally appeared to be in the hands of capable professionals.

9

The Acting President

"Give the public what it wants."
—Harry Cohn

As 1983 drew to a close, questions of policy and key changes in personnel were no longer the only major items on the White House agenda. Time now had to be set aside for politics and mapping plans for the next presidential campaign. Reagan and his top advisers were confident that, barring some unforeseen calamity, he would win reelection, and by a comfortable margin. The President also viewed the forthcoming challenge as a personal milestone. He knew that win or lose, the 1984 campaign would be his last, his final run as an active candidate, and he was determined to make the race a crowning achievement.

On one occasion, when the inner circle gathered in the Oval Office to discuss campaign strategy, a member of the group noted that if Reagan did win and went on to complete another four years in the White House, he would become only the fourth President in this century to serve two full terms, an achievement that would place him alongside Woodrow Wilson, Franklin D. Roosevelt, and Dwight Eisenhower. One of the aides who attended the meeting later remembered that for a moment Reagan seemed stunned by that, as though he were suddenly struck by how far he had come in a second, late-blooming career that had begun less than two decades earlier. Lapsing into a reflective mood, he talked about the anxieties he felt back in the mid-sixties when he first made the decision to run for public office. "My God," he recalled thinking at the time, "what am I doing in politics? The kinds of things I've done so far are far away from this." But he quickly added that as time went on, he realized "a substantial part of the political thing is acting and role-playing, and I know how to do that." Then, after a pause, he broke into his smile and said, "So I used to worry about that, but I don't anymore." Indeed, the roots of Ronald Reagan's extraordinary success at what he called "the political thing" can be found in the skills and personality he first unveiled to the public as a professional actor.

The twenty-six-year-old Reagan who arrived in Hollywood in 1937 came equipped with the values and many of the virtues of the rural Midwest as it existed during his formative years, a period that extended, roughly, from the start of World War I to the end of the 1920s. His identity was shaped in that world of strong family ties, homespun morality, and Fourth of July patriotism. Growing up in the small Illinois town of Dixon was not entirely an idyllic experience; his father's alcoholism, for one thing, was a persistent source of family shame and anxiety. But overall, Reagan says he had a happy childhood, and it was followed by good times at Eureka College, where he played on the football team and, with an eye toward the future, joined the student dramatic society.

That, in turn, was followed by his early success as a radio sports announcer in Iowa, where, among other things, he mastered a form of harmless deception that was a standard operating procedure in those days. In broadcasting Chicago Cub baseball games to fans in Iowa, Reagan had to re-create the action from the terse pitch-by-pitch reports that came in over the telegraph wire, and he became adept at inventing colorful details to flesh out the skimpy information at his disposal. It was a gift that carried over into later life when, drawing from his trove of anecdotes, he often would embroider a story with fanciful incidents to buttress the point he was trying to make.

The Ronald Reagan who left the heartland to try his luck in Hollywood brought to that adventure a genial disposition, an earnest belief in his own worth and the values that had shaped him, and an open, Candide-like optimism. Those traits formed the basis of the persona that soon began appearing on motion picture screens throughout the country.

Hollywood then was firmly under the control of the big studios, and the foundation of the movies they churned out with fervent regularity was the star system. Actors were not encouraged to take on a wide variety of demanding roles that would enable them to expand and fulfill their talents. Instead, they were repeatedly cast in roles tailored to fit their own personalities. So it was with Reagan. He rarely played villains; that was the specialty of others, like James Cagney and Edward G. Robinson. Nor did his studio, Warner Brothers, try to build him into a larger-than-life hero, à la John Wayne or Gary Cooper. And although he had his share of romantic roles, he was no threat to Clark Gable or Cary Grant. In the late 1930s and early 1940s, Reagan invariably played characters who were affable, easygoing, and idealistic, all qualities that were ingrained in his own personality.

Reagan was given enough meaty roles to establish his presence and gain recognition (notably as Drake McHugh in *King's Row* and George Gipp in *Knute Rockne—All-American*), and his marriage to the young actress Jane Wyman was the kind of glamorous Hollywood romance that attracted the attention of gossip columnists and movie magazines. But he never evolved into a solid leading man, the kind of star who could be counted on to draw people to the box office. Most of the time, he was cast as the second male lead in someone else's film. Even his most celebrated role, the ill-fated Gipper, was tucked into a larger story: the biography of Rockne, the legendary Notre Dame coach, who was played by Pat O'Brien. The perception of Reagan as a second lead was so enduring that years later his entry into politics inspired a famous utterance by his former studio boss, Jack Warner. When he was told that Reagan was running for governor of California, Warner, always quick to recognize a casting blunder, protested, "No, no! Jimmy Stewart for governor, Ronald Reagan for best friend."

Yet on a more profound level, Warner inadvertently hit upon the secret of Reagan's political success. He came across to voters not as a lofty star beyond their reach, but as an old friend, a man of warmth who could be trusted, and that was a large part of his appeal.

* * *

The years in Hollywood helped to shape him in other ways as well. Once he left the Midwest, Reagan's movie career became the beacon that led him to everything else that followed, and when he ventured into a political career, a part of him remained firmly anchored to his Hollywood past. It provided him with a secure frame of reference in the insecure world he now found himself in, and it was the prime source of the anecdotes he was so prone to relate. He told those yarns from his movie days not only to entertain his listeners—although, for an actor, that was certainly part of it—but to draw analogies between his past and the present that, much of the time, were not altogether apt.

A few weeks after he became governor, Reagan chaired a cabinet meeting that was convened to consider budget cuts in state mental hospitals. It was a tedious discussion, laden with statistics about the problems of mental health, the kind of enervating details that generally taxed his attention span. At one point, in an apparent effort to enliven the conversation, the new governor interjected a personal reminiscence: "Do you know how hard it is to mispronounce 'psychiatric' once you know how to do it right? I had to do it in *King's Row* and at first I couldn't do it. It's like deliberately singing a flat note." Reagan's cabinet officers responded to this digression with appreciative chuckles, then returned to the business at hand.

Even after he had gone on to the White House, Reagan continued to draw on material from his Hollywood reservoir. During the period when Lebanon was in turmoil and terrorist attacks were an almost daily occurrence in Beirut, the Lebanese foreign minister visited Washington and, in a meeting with Reagan, tried to explain the intricate political factions that were rending his country. It was a complex subject, one that even the most well-informed President might have found difficult to grasp. Even so, the foreign minister was somewhat taken aback when, after he finished his briefing, Reagan cheerfully remarked. "You know, your nose looks just like Danny Thomas."

Tip O'Neill, the former Speaker of the House, has his own favorite anecdote. On Inauguration Day in 1981, Reagan went to O'Neill's office to change clothes after the swearing-in ceremony on the steps of the Capitol. While there, he couldn't help but notice a huge and ornate oak desk that seemed to take up nearly half the room, and he told the Speaker how much he admired it.

O'Neill thanked the President and acknowledged that it was one of his most prized possessions. He then went on to say that the desk had quite a history because it once belonged to Grover Cleveland when he was President. To which Reagan replied: "That's very interesting. You know, I once played Grover Cleveland in the movies."

O'Neill politely corrected his visitor. "No, Mr. President, you're thinking of Grover Cleveland *Alexander*, the ball player." Reagan had indeed played the old Hall of Fame pitcher in a film called *The Winning Season* and, as fate would have it, O'Neill had recently seen it on television. As might be expected, the Speaker couldn't resist dining out on that story, and when one of his colleagues in the House heard it, he quipped that perhaps Reagan was under the impression that Grover Cleveland's schedule in the White House had been as light as his own, and that he spent his idle afternoons pitching for the old Washington Senators.

The congressman was referring to the laid-back management style that soon became Reagan's trademark, and that, too, can be traced to his Hollywood training. Under the system established by the major studios, movie stars—even those in the second echelon—were a pampered breed who had almost everything done for them. Their scripts were provided by writers. The glamour was furnished by the makeup staff and the wardrobe department. The lighting and sets and camera angles were the handiwork of the technical crews. Above them all was the supreme commander of the enterprise, the director, who made all the critical decisions and told the actors when to move and how to recite their lines. It was a fairly mechanical process, and some actors, accustomed to the more liberating atmosphere of the stage, found movie work frustrating to their own creativity.

Yet Ronald Reagan thrived in that stifling milieu. He had no real background in the theater and no professional training to speak of, and so he welcomed a process in which all he had to do was follow directions. There was, of course, a bit more to it than that—lines had to be memorized, proper emotions expressed—yet the actors knew that the director and his cohorts behind the cameras were united in an effort to make them look good when they appeared on the screen. This reliance on the guidance of co-workers, whose job it was to make the stars shine, carried over into Reagan's political career and helps to explain his remarkable passivity and the broad delegation of authority that puzzled so many Washington observers when he became President.

The major studios in those days turned out movies with assembly-line efficiency. Reagan, for example, made eight films in 1938 and eight more the following year. That kind of pace kept an actor bouncing from one project to the next. During the four to six weeks necessary to shoot a picture, tentative friendships would form; working so closely together under a demanding schedule, people did get to know each other. But more often than not, the friendships were fleeting and soon languished once the movie was completed and the actors moved on, in separate directions, to their next roles, perhaps never to work together again. (There were, of course, exceptions, and they were not confined to mere friendship. Reagan met Jane Wyman on the set of a movie they were filming, *Brother Rat.* They began dating and, with the gossip columnists cheering them on, married in January 1940.) But the general pattern for the Hollywood actor—and here Reagan was no exception—was a few weeks of camaraderie, then on to the next role and a new group of casual friends to replace the ones he had left. This, too, was a pattern repeated in Reagan's political life.

Michael Deaver, who was closer to Reagan than any of his other political aides, wrote in his memoir that his longtime boss was often described as "an amiable loner, friendly to all but intimate friend to very few." Deaver implied that it was an accurate observation. Others who worked for Reagan over the years would agree. Members of the White House staff often marveled at the President's demeanor: all genial smiles on the surface, yet always maintaining a certain distance and avoiding any real intimacy. Nor was he one to play favorites. He was just as likely to stop and banter with an obscure member of the Secret Service detail as he would with a high-level adviser.

Yet just as the star on a movie set would tend to be oblivious of members of the crew who did not directly interact with him or his performance, Reagan evinced almost no curiosity about officials on his team who were not among his inner circle. Beneath the friendly façade was a relentless indifference. From time to time, some of the White House people who were in a position to see the President with some regularity would speculate about his reaction if one of them suddenly left the staff. Would he inquire why so-and-so had quit? Or would he even notice that the person was no longer there? They felt that the only ones he would be sure to miss were the old California hands, like Meese and Deaver, and they may even have been wrong about that.

Deaver and Donald Regan were two of Reagan's closest advisers during his years in the White House, and they both made the mistake of assuming they had a special relationship with him. Yet when Regan fell out of favor and Deaver found himself in legal trouble, they discovered that Reagan was something less than a friend in need, and they both later confessed how hurt they were because the President never called to offer words of solace or wish them well. It might be accurate to suggest that yes, they had been key players, but their part of the film was now finished.

Finally, there was the triumph of craft, the fine points of acting technique, that Reagan brought into politics. Back in 1937, when he made the screen test that landed him the contract with Warner Brothers, his new employers were impressed by Reagan's natural assets: his good looks, his pleasant personality, and his resonant, expressive voice. But beyond that, the young actor had a great deal to learn.

While working on one of his first movies, a veteran cameraman, James Van Tree, taught Reagan a few basic techniques: how to react to the camera during close-ups and how to be conscious of posture and balance so that he would look as good in profile or from the rear as he did when he was directly facing the lens. Reagan later recalled the value of those early instructions in *Where's the Rest of Me?*, his 1965 prepolitical autobiography. "Very few of us," he wrote, "ever see ourselves except as we look directly at ourselves in a mirror. Thus we don't know how we look from behind, from the side, walking, standing, moving normally through a room. It's quite a jolt." But he soon learned to conquer the jolt, to be aware of how he looked at all times and from all camera angles. In recent years, several photographers noted how remarkable it was that Reagan never seemed to have been caught off guard when his picture was being taken. Even though he often appeared to be unaware that he was being photographed, there was never a slouch, an awkward gesture, an unflattering scowl, or any of the other unconscious defects that show up in candid shots of conventional politicians. The reason seems simple enough: the trained actor is always "on" when he appears before his public.

* * *

In writing about the Great Communicator and the television persona that earned him that sobriquet, Garry Wills described Reagan's basic technique as the "choreography of candor." But this raises an intriguing question: How much of it was choreography and how much candor? One way to define acting is as the art of deception. Triumph for an actor is to give such a convincing performance that it persuades viewers that the illusion they saw was, in fact, the real thing. Thus, accusing a professional actor of blurring the lines between illusion and reality is like accusing a banker of charging interest. That is what he's trained to do. But when an actor becomes a politician and projects illusions about his life and character that distort or gloss over the less attractive realities, that's cause for concern, and in certain vital areas, Reagan and his image makers did precisely that.

No political party in recent memory did so much to portray itself as the staunch guardian and advocate of traditional family values as the Republican party during the Reagan years. At their conventions and in campaign speeches across the country, they hammered away at the message that the most sacred of institutions, the American family, would somehow be undermined if the Democrats returned to power. Implicit in all this moralizing was that the First Family—Ron and Nancy and their kids—was the embodiment of the stern and stable values being espoused. That was the myth. The reality was otherwise.

First of all, Reagan himself was the first divorced man to be elected President. There was, to be sure, no shame in that. But there was a time not that long ago when divorce was a stigma that worked heavily against a man who aspired to the presidency. Adlai Stevenson was divorced when he ran against Eisenhower in the fifties, and the campaign against him whispered that a man who could not keep his family together had no business living in the White House. Then a few years later, when Nelson Rockefeller divorced his first wife to marry another woman, there was such an outcry that it effectively killed the hopes he once had of becoming President. Both men, it's true, had to cope with problems that did not afflict Reagan. Stevenson, who never remarried, campaigned as a divorcé, and that status only drew attention to his marital shortcomings. As for Rockefeller, the popular perception that he "deserted" his wife of thirty-one years for a younger woman made him a target for moral condemnation.

Reagan, by contrast, was happily settled into his second marriage by the time he entered politics. By then, the breakup of his marriage to Jane Wyman back in 1948 was a dimly remembered episode from his Hollywood past. Yet at the time it created quite a stir. What began as a model Hollywood romance cheered on by the gossip columninsts came crashing to an end in the glare of raucous publicity. The doyenne of the columnists, Louella Parsons, who felt a special affinity to Reagan because she, too, was a native of Dixon, Illinois, professed that she was "genuinely shocked" to learn that "Ronnie" and "Jane" were dissolving a love match that she, Louella, had done so much to champion.

Some observers blamed the divorce on professional tensions, noting that Wyman's movie career was flourishing (she won an Oscar in 1948 for her role as the deaf-mute in *Johnny Belinda*) while Reagan's was clearly in decline. Closer to the mark were those who attributed the problem to Reagan's growing obsession with the political passions that were then raging in Hollywood. This was the period when the movie colony was in the grip of cold war hysteria, and Reagan, as president of the Screen Actors Guild, was leading the crusade to rid the industry of all Communists, real and imagined. Parsons, in fact, quoted Reagan as saying, "Perhaps I should have let someone else save the world and saved my own home instead."

That was the crux of Wyman's complaint when she sued for divorce. In the court proceeding that followed, she asserted that inasmuch as she did not share Reagan's all-consuming interest in the Screen Actors Guild and related matters, she felt increasingly spurned and neglected. In the years since then, as Reagan moved on to his second marriage and his soaring political career, Wyman has been admirably reticent on the subject of why their relationship went sour. But from time to time, she has confided to friends that it was indeed Reagan's preoccupation with politics that alienated her. One such confidant related a conversation he had with Wyman in 1973, in which she recalled how "boring and exasperating it was to awake in the middle of the night, prepare for work, and have someone at the breakfast table, newspaper in hand, expounding on the far right, far left, the conservative right, the conservative left, the middle of the road." (Years later, when Reagan was running for President, some disgruntled Democrats wore campaign buttons that proclaimed, "Jane Wyman was right!")

As for Reagan, he has portrayed himself over the years as

the all-but-blameless victim of the breakup. On more than one occasion, he has described himself as a divorced man only "in the sense that the decision was made by somebody else." Adopting that posture no doubt helped to diminish the social stigma on a man who, then and later, claimed to be so dedicated to the preservation of traditional family values. Yet Reagan also had to realize that he was not the only victim.

The children of that first marriage, their daughter, Maureen, and adopted son, Michael, primarily lived with their mother after the divorce, a home they shared for a brief time with musical director Freddie Karger, whom Wyman married in 1952 and divorced two years later. Reagan had his allotted time with the children in accordance with the usual custody arrangements; but as they grew older, he saw less of them, especially after he married Nancy Davis and they began raising a family of their own. From all accounts, Maureen adjusted more easily to those circumstances; she remained fairly close to both parents and later became a highly visible presence in her father's political campaigns. Yet even then, they sharply disagreed on certain key issues, such as his opposition to the Equal Rights Amendment, and when the thrice-married Maureen decided to seek a Senate seat in California, her father declined to support her.

As for Michael, he clearly did not have a happy childhood, and some of his resentments from those years left scars. A free spirit who spent much of his adult life selling gasohol and racing speedboats, Michael wrote a plaintive book in 1987 in which he revealed that he had been sexually abused as a child but had never been able to tell his parents. He also recalled that when he was a quarterback on his high school football team, his father never saw him play, a snub that was all the more cutting because (as Michael well knew) Reagan had played football himself in school and has been a lifelong fan of the game. The neglect carried over into his adult life. Michael informed his readers that when his father and stepmother invited him, his wife, and their two children to join them for Easter and his daughter's fourth birthday, it marked the first time the four of them had ever been alone with the Reagans as a family.

Nancy Davis, who married Reagan in 1952, has never complained that her husband's obsession with politics was "boring and exasperating." On the contrary, she has been an ideal helpmate, his most loyal supporter, and friends and foes alike would agree that their marriage has been an unusually happy union. When she first accompanied him on his political campaigns, many reporters were struck by the look of devotion she bestowed on Reagan when he was making a speech or fielding questions at a news conference. (Lou Cannon once described this beatific gaze as "a kind of transfixed adoration more appropriate to a witness of the Virgin Birth.") Nor have the Reagans ever suggested they were anything but doting parents who cared deeply about their own two children, Ron and Patti. Yet even within the context of that second marriage, the Reagans' relationship with their kids made them something less than a close-knit, traditional family.

Both Ron and Patti were college dropouts (so, too, were Maureen and Michael), and like so many other children raised in the sixties, they adopted life-styles that rubbed against the grain of their parents' wishes and basic values. Ron, the family pet, quit school to pursue his dream to become a ballet dancer, which put him in an ethereal world that had a subterranean culture of its own; at one point, he lived with a woman to whom he was not yet married, an act of moral defiance that infuriated his parents, especially Nancy.

Patti was, if anything, even less tractable; her rebellious spirit swept her into the rock culture of the sixties. A singer and composer, she first became estranged from her parents when she entered into a romantic liaison with a member of the Eagles rock group. Patti also once admitted in a television interview that her political and social views were closer to those of her friend Jane Fonda than to those of her father. Like Michael, she poured out her grievances in a book, in her case a novel obviously based on her own life in which she was critical of characters closely resembling her parents. Then later, when her mother underwent surgery for breast cancer, a White House spokesman confirmed that Mrs. Reagan had received no phone calls from her only daughter. Other stories about the Reagans' estrangement from their children surfaced from time to time during the presidential years, but at Mrs. Reagan's insistence, the staff did its best to suppress them. In his White House memoir, former chief of staff Donald Regan related one incident when the First Lady became upset about press reports that Reagan had not talked to any of his children after his cancer operation in 1985. Ordering Regan to correct that impression, she explained that it had been impossible for her husband to talk to anyone but her because he had tubes in his mouth and nose.

The Reagans, to be sure, were not the only conservative American parents who had to cope with the generation gap of the 1960s, a point that they themselves emphasized on those rare occasions when they discussed the family in public forums. "Look, in the sixties it was a very difficult time for children and for parents," Nancy acknowledged in a 1980 interview with Mike Wallace on "60 Minutes." "They all went through periods of rebellion to one degree or another." Fair enough, but elsewhere in that interview, Wallace noted, "When you and your husband talk so often about simple virtues and a wholesome family life and morality and a breakdown in values in the United States, you don't talk about any of that as it relates to your own family."

Starting with his first campaign for governor and on through the years when he ran for President, Reagan repeatedly lashed out at the "permissiveness" of parents who, having failed to uphold the standards of morality and patriotism, were largely to blame for the political and social disorders that characterized the generation of youthful protest. In taking that righteous stand, Reagan clearly implied that as one who had gone through the experience of being a father in those troubled times, he had kept his own house in order. That was the image or illusion. The reality was otherwise.

Reagan's habit over the years of making erroneous statements and palming them off as facts baffled many observers. Much of the fascination came from trying to decide whether Reagan's gaffes were deliberate distortions, conscious acts of deception, or simply evidence of ignorance of the subject. Tip O'Neill adhered to the latter view. Reagan made a striking early impression on O'Neill when he confused Grover Cleveland the President with Grover Cleveland Alexander the baseball player, and the more the Speaker of the House saw of him, the more convinced he became that Reagan often didn't know what he was talking about. "He knows less than any President I've ever known," O'Neill once said, more in sorrow than in criticism. But others took the more cynical position that Reagan purposely skewed the truth to bolster points he was trying to make. According to this view, the old actor looked upon facts in a speech much as he had lines in a movie script:

that is, it was perfectly all right to make changes as long as the revisions improved a scene or strengthened the overall performance.

In the autumn of 1979, shortly after he announced that he was running for President, Reagan appeared on the "Today" show where he was forced to confront the sensitive issue of his age. When Tom Brokaw, then the host on "Today," noted that at sixty-nine, Reagan would be the oldest man ever elected to the presidency, the candidate countered with the smiling assertion, "I would be younger than all the heads of state I would have to deal with except Margaret Thatcher." A puzzled Brokaw promptly pointed out that "Giscard d' Estaing of France is younger than you."

"Who?" said Reagan, giving the impression that he had never heard of the man. Aides later insisted that Reagan did indeed know who the president of France was but that he had not heard the question from Brokaw, who was sitting just a few feet away. Whatever the case, the fifty-three-year-old Giscard d'Estaing was not the only leader Brokaw could have cited. Helmut Schmidt of West Germany and Anwar el-Sadat of Egypt were sixty. Menachem Begin of Israel was sixty-six and the new prime minister of Canada, Joe Clark, only forty. And there were others, too. As a head of state who was younger than Reagan, Margaret Thatcher, it turned out, had plenty of company.

Later, when he was President, historical distortion became one of Reagan's specialties. In a speech he delivered in the spring of 1982, he informed his listeners, "Justice Oliver Wendell Holmes once said, 'Keep the government poor and remain free.' " A member of the White House speech-writing team later revealed that the President "came up with that one himself. Holmes never said anything point-blank exactly like that." When consulted, Holmes scholars maintained that the late jurist never said anything *remotely* like that.

In another speech earlier that year, Reagan quoted Winston Churchill as having said: "The idea that a nation can tax itself into prosperity is one of the crudest delusions which has ever befuddled the human mind." He then added, "Now I don't know how that quote happened to catch my eye." Neither did anyone else. This time the White House speech writers acknowledged that they had no idea "where he got that one from." One human mind that was befuddled by Reagan's allusion was that of the British historian at the Library of Congress, who told reporters that there was no such passage in the library's voluminous collection of Churchill quotations.

Some of Reagan's historical misstatements didn't even have to be checked out with scholars; they simply defied common sense. In 1983, when the President and Secretary of the Interior James Watt were being attacked by conservationists for their environmental policies, Reagan sought to ease their concern by pointing out, "There is today in the United States as much forest as there was when Washington was at Valley Forge." Taking that remark at face value, one would have to conclude that the Indians, who then inhabited most of the continent, must have been living in condominiums and driving to work every day on freeways. For the record, the U.S. Forest Service calculated that only about 30 percent of the forest land that existed in 1775 was still preserved in 1983.

On another occasion, in chastising other governments that had threatened to use nuclear arms to resolve their disputes, Reagan averred, "When the United States was the only country in the world possessing these awesome weapons, we did not blackmail others with threats to use them." That show of restraint would have been news to those Japanese citizens who had the misfortune of being in Hiroshima or Nagasaki in August 1945. Beyond that, both Truman and Eisenhower later threatened to use nuclear weapons during critical moments of the Korean War, at a time when, although the absolute monopoly had recently come to an end, the United States still had an effective monopoly of long-range delivery systems. In each instance, the threat may well have been justified, but it was sanctimonious to pretend that American Presidents never flaunted superior military power when it was at their disposal.

Criticism of U.S. relations with South Africa prompted another historical miscue. In an effort to justify his decision to support that government in spite of its apartheid policies, Reagan posed this question in the spring of 1981: "Can we abandon this country that has stood beside us in every war we've ever fought?" In point of fact, South Africa's current ruling party, the Afrikaners, opposed their country's entry into both world wars but were overruled by the pro-British majority, which then controlled the government. Moreover, every South African prime minister since 1948, except one, was imprisoned during World War II for pro-Nazi sympathies.

At other times, instead of glossing over the shortcomings of governments he supported, Reagan exaggerated the flaws in a political system that did not meet with his approval. "I'm no linguist," he said in the fall of 1985, "but I have been told that in the Russian language there isn't even a word for freedom." In fact, the Russian word for freedom is *svoboda*. And, it might be added, the Russian word for gaffe is *ogovorka*.

In the early 1980s, an adult toy called Rubik's Cube became such a hit that the man who created it made a fortune. Citing that success at a meeting in the White House, Reagan praised the invention of Rubik's Cube as yet another fine example of American free enterprise. The President then had to be told that the inventor, Erno Rubik, was a Hungarian professor who lived in Budapest under Communist rule.

Reagan had a special knack for telling stories about American war heroes. The following yarn is one he told on several occasions, including one a few days before Christmas in 1983: "The young ball-turret gunner was wounded, and they couldn't get him out of the B-17 turret there while flying. . . .The last man to leave saw the commander sit down on the floor. He took the boy's hand and said, 'Never mind, son, we'll ride it down together.' Congressional Medal of Honor, posthumously awarded."

A reporter for the *New York Daily News*, Lars-Erik Nelson, combed through the citations for all 434 Medals of Honor awarded in World War II and could not find that particular story. He did, however, come up with a possible source for Reagan's stirring account of heroism: a 1944 movie called *Wing and a Prayer*, starring Dana Andrews. When he saw that film, that scene must have made such an indelible impression on Reagan that he filed it away in his memory. Then at some point over the years, he came to believe that it was a real event in the real war. That, at least, is one way of looking at it.

There also were times when he was equally misleading about his own experience in World War II. "I know all the bad things that happened in that war," Reagan told a group of foreign journalists in the spring of 1985. "I was in uniform four years myself." That was true, but his personal knowledge of "all the bad things that happened" did not include combat. Reagan was disqualified from serving in combat because of his nearsightedness. Instead, he was assigned to the First Motion Picture Unit of the Army Air Corps, and he spent the entire war acting in training films.

On one memorable occasion, Reagan even tried to dramatize that assignment. In November 1983, he met with a delegation of Israelis, a group that included Prime Minister Yitzhak Shamir, and assured them that he sympathized with their historic mission because he had seen for himself the devastation of the Holocaust while filming the liberation of the concentration camps. "From then on," the President was quoted as saying, "I was concerned for the Jewish people." Without questioning the sincerity of his concern, the truth is that Reagan never left the United States during World War II. The film unit to which he was assigned worked out of the Hal Roach studios in Burbank. This enabled Reagan to live at home, and his day-to-day regimen did not differ that much from what it had been before he joined the war effort. When reporters asked about this discrepancy, a White House spokesman explained that what the President meant to say was that he had seen Army films of the liberation and had been "deeply moved" by the experience.

Reagan's gift for gaffes did not go unnoticed by his critics, and two of them, Mark Green and Gail MacColl, tracked down about three hundred misstatements of one kind or another, ranging over his entire political career, and assembled them in a mischievous little book called *There He Goes Again: Ronald Reagan's Reign of Error*. In the book, published in 1983, the President wasn't the only target of the authors' exasperation. They also took reporters to task for failing to tell the American people how inept and/or deceitful Reagan was. The authors cited an article by Robert Parry of *Newsweek* in which he observed that the press "seemed a little fearful that if it wrote stories that were perceived as tough on this President, the public would not like them."

Yet it would be a mistake to make too much of that. For Reagan's frequent gaffes *were* dutifully reported, both in print and on television. In accusing the media of being lenient on the President, Green and MacColl glossed over the fact that all the examples they compiled had been gleaned from press accounts of what Reagan had said at one time or other. Without the press, they would have had little to put in their book. But the larger point is that reporters have no right to play jury. Their job is only to gather and present the evidence, and it is up to the public to deliver the verdict.

To cite a celebrated example: Although Richard Nixon and his coconspirators often complained about the hostile media, it was not the press coverage of the Watergate crimes that brought his presidency to its end. What is often forgotten is that during the early months of the scandal, the Nixon White House was quite successful in defending itself against the charges that were being aired and published. (Just ask George McGovern, whose strident attempts to make Watergate a hot campaign issue did not stave off the landslide defeat he suffered at the hands of Nixon in the 1972 election.) But as time went on, the public mood shifted from mild concern to a sense of betrayal and outrage, and it was the wave of protest from ordinary citizens that prodded a reluctant Congress to initiate the process of impeachment. Reporters can exhort and fulminate all they want, but if their readers and viewers do not respond, then the press, for all its presumed influence, is powerless to make them respond.

In the case of Reagan's gaffes and distortions, the public generally chose to shrug them off. Reagan had a formidable weapon going for him, an impregnable shield that came to be known in Washington as the "Teflon phenomenon." All the reports of flaws in his character or judgment, which would have been severely damaging to the reputation of an ordinary politician, made no lasting impact on the popular perception of this President. The public had made up its mind about Ronald Reagan, and no matter what was written or said about him, the majority of Americans continued to like and support him.

Reagan's advisers, especially those who had been with him a long time, were aware of his casual approach to the truth, and they did all they could to program his various activities. Speeches and other public appearances were tightly structured, and the effort was made to keep the President to his script. This attempt to exercise control even extended to meetings with other government officials within the privacy of the White House. Congressional leaders and Cabinet officers were struck by the fact that when they sat down with the President, he invariably made his comments from notes on three-by-five index cards, a practice that dated back to his first run for governor, when such cards were prepared for him by Philip Battaglia, the young lawyer who had managed that 1966 campaign. Yet even those precautions did not always prove to be fail-safe.

In November 1983, a few days before Reagan left on a trip to Japan, the heads of the big three auto companies were invited to the White House for a talk with the President. The main purpose of the meeting was to discuss trade policies, a subject of vital concern to the carmakers, who were feeling the competition from Japanese imports. Hence, they were puzzled when the President began the discussion with remarks that had nothing to do with that or any other relevant subject. But it did not take the auto executives long to figure out what had happened: Reagan had taken the wrong set of index cards to the meeting. One of the participants later recalled that no one had the heart to call the mistake to his attention. Instead, as the President talked on, the visitors stared at the floor in embarrassment until Reagan himself finally realized he was reading from the wrong notes.

But most members of the White House staff came to realize that such lapses really didn't matter. They, too, were aware of the Teflon phenomenon. The public didn't seem to be bothered by any of his blunders, so why should they care? Thus, as time went on, White House spokesmen became almost brazen in their dismissal of questions from reporters who wanted to know why the President had said such-and-such when the facts were otherwise. Once, when asked why the President had "cited" a nonexistent British law in order to discredit arguments for gun control, Larry Speakes breezily responded: "It made the point, didn't it?" By then, Speakes had learned what Reagan had known intuitively for years: that it was the punchy line and performance that "made the point," not substance or accuracy.

By the fall of 1983, as Reagan's advisers began to shift their attention to the next Presidential campaign, they were fully confident that the power of illusion would see them through that battle. Their most potent weapon would be the candidate himself—the Acting President.

No one understood that better than Jim Baker, and he was the one who would be in charge of the 1984 campaign. The departure of Bill Clark from the post of national security adviser brought a temporary end to the infighting that had such a disruptive effect on the White House during most of 1983. Baker emerged from those struggles in an even stronger positon than before; now, more than ever, he reigned as the most powerful member of the White House troika. One of the many areas under his command was political strategy. It was, after all, as a campaign strategist—first for Gerald Ford in 1976 and then for George Bush in the 1980 primaries—that Baker had caught the attention of the Reagan insiders, and once he solidified his own status in the inner circle, there was never any doubt that he would be the man in charge of the reelection effort in 1984. Baker's two top deputies in the political sphere were Edward J. Rollins, a onetime protégé of Lyn Nofziger, and Lee Atwater, a young political scientist from South Carolina. Together, they constructed the basic plan for the 1984 campaign.

Atwater's off-duty pastimes included playing blues on his guitar and telling ribald stories in the down-home manner of his native region. But that posture concealed a shrewd and incisive mind. Atwater learned his politics under the old master from his home state, J. Strom Thurmond, and he went on to serve as Reagan's Southern regional coordinator during the 1980 campaign. It was his belief that the South and the West—the so-called Sunbelt with its 266 electoral votes, just 4 fewer than the number needed to win—would hold the key to Republican victories for the rest of the century, and perhaps beyond. Baker agreed with Atwater's thesis: the Sunbelt would form the power base on which the Reagan reelection bid would be built. In the fall of 1983, he told Rollins and Atwater to set up a campaign headquarters and begin to implement that strategy. (Replacing them in the White House political office was Margaret Tutwiler, a long-time Baker aide, who, in the months ahead, would serve as their key link to Baker.) Rollins and Atwater understood that their assignment was merely to carry out the basic groundwork. The real campaign chief would be Baker and the real campaign headquarters would be his office in the White House.

Stuart Spencer, the old pro from California who had advised Reagan on every one of his campaigns except 1976 when he worked with Baker on Ford's team, was brought in to help plan the overall strategy. Deaver was assigned to handle the delicate and important tasks that had long been his specialty: taking Mrs. Reagan's phone calls and seeing to it that Reagan himself was kept on a schedule that did not overtax him. Richard Wirthlin, who had been Reagan's pollster in 1980, would remain in that role, work that would eventually earn him $1 million dollars a year from the Republican National Committee. Baker utilized Wirthlin's data but did not always agree with his analysis, so Robert Teeter, a Detroit pollster who also had worked with Baker on the Ford campaign, was hired on as a consultant. Richard Darman, who had emerged within the White House structure as Baker's strong number-two man, served as the conduit for programs and proposals that could be exploited for political gain. Whenever the campaign team saw the need for action by the administration, it was Darman who knew how to get the government machinery moving. He was the one aide who "knew where everything was," Spencer was fond of telling reporters.

Thus there were talent and experience at every position. One would probably not find a more solid group of campaign specialists in any election. And they had a candidate who seldom, if ever, questioned their decisions. In that respect, Reagan was a campaign manager's dream. ("Whatever we told him to do," one adviser said, "he did.") The only real hitch the campaign team had to deal with during those weeks of planning in the fall of 1983 was a conflict over when the President should formally declare his candidacy. Atwater, in particular, wanted it done right away, but he was repeatedly told that Mrs. Reagan did not feel the time for that announcement was "propitious." That baffled him, and when he continued to press for an explanation, Deaver finally took him aside and disclosed that Nancy's reluctance was based on an astrologer's warning.

The First Lady's dependence on astrology caused a brief sensation when it was first revealed in Donald Regan's memoirs in 1988, but to a few it had been known for years. One Californian, whose friendship with the Reagans went back to the days before they lived in the governor's mansion, said Mrs. Reagan had consulted astrologers even then. For a long time, the only senior member of the White House staff who was fully aware of Nancy's fascination was Deaver, but he felt that her reliance on the advice of astrologers did not become a serious problem until after the assassination attempt on the President. An astrologer apparently had warned Mrs. Reagan prior to the shooting that her husband was in some kind of danger, and after that—at her insistence—the signs of the zodiac became a major influence in planning the President's schedule, especially travel arrangements. On more than one occasion, events had to be rescheduled at the last minute because the First Lady had been told by an astrologer that the outlook was not promising. And so it was that in the fall of 1983, the reelection announcement was put off until she was assured that the stars and planets were in proper harmony. For his part, Reagan has always maintained that he never based any governmental or political decision on astrology; if that's true, then he was unaware that his own reelection announcement was dictated by shifts in the cosmos.

In any event, as the early months of 1984 rolled by, all the signs here on earth pointed to a Reagan sweep in November. As Walter Mondale struggled through an unexpectedly tough primary fight with Gary Hart, the President remained calmly in the White House, and by the time the Democrats concluded their convention in San Francisco, the Reagan top command was in a state of euphoria. Once Mondale announced that Geraldine Ferraro would be his running mate and that if elected, he would raise taxes, Reagan's strategists were convinced they could not lose. Atwater was passing the word to intimates that "barring a catastrophe," the only remaining question was how large the Reagan margin would be. To Atwater, the selection of Ferraro had doomed Democratic chances, not because she was a woman but because she, like Mondale, was a Northern liberal. A ticket whose candidates both came from the "snow belt," as Atwater labeled it, just wouldn't sell in the South and West. Some members of Reagan's team were already predicting that the President might carry every state but Mondale's native Minnesota, a forecast that turned out to be as accurate as it was devastating to the Democrats.

The Republican convention in Dallas, a joyous celebration of patriotism and the traditional values that Reagan espoused so effectively, set the tone and theme for the GOP campaign. All the emphasis would be on the upbeat message that it was "morning in America," and voters all across the country, regardless of party, should feel grateful that Ronald Reagan was their President. The strategy called for the reelection campaign to differ sharply from the one Reagan had waged four years earlier. The 1980 campaign, designed to play on voter dissatisfaction with Carter, was built around serious issues: rebuilding defense, restoring national pride, and reducing the taxes that Reagan said were too high.

Reagan had made good on many of his 1980 promises, even thought his economic achievements had come at enormous cost: the huge deficits that Stockman had projected were now a reality.

But Reagan's strategists concluded that 1984 was not a year when voters were likely to be concerned about the deficit. Had Reagan been the challenger in 1984 instead of the incumbent, one can imagine the language he would have used to deplore an economy that was running over with red ink, but his advisers were confident that the Democrats would not be able to make much headway with that complex issue—and they were right. They also understood that Reagan's soothing style of leadership had played well in communitites throughout the country. After all the turbulence of the decades that had preceded his arrival in the White House, he now presided over an electorate that, for the most part, was enjoying a tranquil interlude. Americans seemed content in 1984 and they were willing to give Reagan much of the credit for that.

Reagan and his campaign team were also helped by the kind of good luck that had characterized so much of his political career. There were no major problems, at home or abroad, to disturb the voters in 1984, nothing that even remotely resembled the hostage crisis that undermined Carter's reelection bid four years earlier. In addition, the Olympic Games in Los Angeles produced a spate of gold medals for U.S. athletes, and that played dramatically into the exuberant mood that the United States was a better and happier country than it had been in many years. Reagan's advisers recognized that an image-oriented President could only benefit from all the television pictures of sturdy young champions being honored on the victory platform to the refrain of the "Star Spangled Banner."

The euphoric mood of that summer carried over into the fall campaign, but it came to an end on the evening of October 7, when Reagan and Mondale confronted each other in the first of their two scheduled debates. Reagan was at his worst that night. He fumbled repeatedly with statistics and at one point said he was "confused" by the format. The man who had so often presented himself as the personification of the strong and wise leader came across to many as a befuddled old man. The gifted performer had flopped. "I was just awful," Reagan conceded shortly after the debate ended. It was an assessment that went unchallenged.

Reagan's top advisers, of course, had long been aware that the President never paid much attention to details, but never before had his deficiencies been so transparent in front of such a large audience. Moreover, the Reagan team was certain that the

President's stumbling effort would be blamed on his age and that the "age issue" would become a major factor in the campaign. Indeed, within a week, the three networks aired reports on the age factor, as did *The Wall Street Journal*; similar stories soon appeared in newspapers around the country. Nancy Reagan was furious, and the President's close friend, Paul Laxalt, who had been given the largely ceremonial title of campaign chairman, called a news conference at which he acknowledged that Reagan had performed poorly. But it had nothing to do with age, he insisted. The President simply had been overbriefed. Zealous aides had bombarded him with too much information, said Laxalt, and no human being could have absorbed all the data they had tried to force on Reagan. The poor man had been "brutalized by a process that made no sense."

The news conference was stopgap measure, needed to give reporters something to write about until a top-to-bottom review of the overall strategy was completed by Baker and his aides. A less experienced campaign team might have panicked, but the Reagan strategists kept cool. They realized the campaign now had a serious problem, but Baker concluded that the overall plan was still sound. It would be fine-tuned but not overhauled. There would be no major change in direction.

From the beginning, the strategy had been built around Reagan's personality and his skills as a performer. Now, having made the decision to stick to that strategy instead of shifting to one based more on hard issues, the immediate challenge they faced was to get the Great Communicator back communicating. Baker saw to it that Reagan would not be "overbriefed" for the second debate. Mike Deaver, who was closest to Reagan, was given a major role in preparing the President for the return match. Instead of loading Reagan down with statistics, Deaver coached him, encouraged him, and praised him, all part of a program to rebuild his confidence.

While Reagan and Deaver concentrated on those preparations, other members of the team took steps to refine the overall objectives of the campaign. It was not only going to be more of the same, but a lot more of the same. Reagan's message would remain upbeat while Atwater and the others went about the task of stressing Mondale's "negatives" in the minds of voters. Specifics on the issues facing the country would be kept to a minimum. The thematic "feel good" television commercials, featuring quiet pastoral scenes and laughing children, would be continued, but they would now be supplemented by another pitch they called "the Bear commercial," an advertisement that showed a huge bear lumbering through the woods as an announcer intoned: "There is a bear in the woods. For some people the bear is easy to see. Others don't see it at all. Some people say the bear is tame. Others say it's vicious and dangerous. Since we can never really be sure who's right, isn't it smart to be as strong as the bear—if there is a bear?" The commercial never said what the bear represented or identified the "others" who were not concerned about it. But there was no need to explain. Ronald Reagan was the man who was on guard against the Russian bear, and the commercial reinforced that visceral feeling.

But bear or no bear, the Reagan team still had to clear the formidable hurdle of the second debate, and despite the drastic changes in preparation, there was still the possibility that he would repeat his dismal performance. Therefore, in the week before the rematch with Mondale, the President's advisers drew up a contingency plan that would go into effect if Reagan floundered again. "We didn't really think it would be needed," Atwater later told us, "but we all felt better having something written down just in case things did go wrong again."

If Reagan failed to meet the test of the second debate, the plan called for the launching of a full-scale effort to obscure the results of both encounters with Mondale. His advisers were certain that if Reagan turned in another poor performance, it would be attributed to his age. In that event, the campaign would then have to move away from Reagan himself. The strategists would have to convince voters they were faced with the choice between Reagan and Bush and their administration, and Mondale and Ferraro and all the liberal, soft-on-communism, big-government people they were certain to bring back to Washington. Baker and his team would flood the media with foreign policy experts from the Reagan administration and even some who had served in previous Republican administrations, who would stress the need for the Republicans to stay in power. Former President Ford would be enlisted to remind voters of Mondale's "Carter connection," and Senate Republican Leader Robert Dole would point out Mondale's cushy life as a Washington lobbyist during the very years when Reagan was giving tireless service to the nation.

Documents formulating that alternative strategy were discovered by political columnists Jack Germond and Jules Witcover after the election, and they published them in their campaign memoir, *Wake Us When It's Over*. In one of the documents, Atwater actually listed detailed excuses that Reagan's defenders could put into play if the second debate went badly. Included among the "talking points" Atwater recommended: stress that the whole debate process was degrading, that no national leader should be subjected to it; that debates often did not reflect which candidate had the better grasp of the issues under discussion; that national security considerations always prevented the President from revealing everything he knew. Finally, Atwater urged Reagan's defenders to blame the press. "Everyone knows the Big Media, especially the networks, have been out to get Ronald Reagan since day one," Atwater wrote.

The contingency plan proved to be unnecessary and was never followed. As he had so often at critical junctures in his career, Reagan found his own escape route at just the moment when he seemed to be at his greatest peril. The actor was a hard man to upstage in the clutch, as he demonstrated once again on the night of the second debate in Kansas City.

Before a television audience estimated at 100 million, almost half the country's population, Mondale and Reagan squared off on foreign policy. As before, Mondale got off to a fast start, hitting Reagan hard for his apparent unfamiliarity with basic facts. At one point, Reagan was pressed to explain why he once had indicated that he thought missiles fired from submarines could be recalled. But just when it seemed as if the President were losing his grip again, one of the panelists, Henry Trewhitt, a reporter for the *Baltimore Sun*, brought up the age issue. Noting that Reagan was the oldest chief executive in the nation's history and that the previous debate had seemed to tire him, Trewhitt observed that John Kennedy had been forced to go for days on end without sleep during the Cuban missile crisis. He then asked the President: "Is there any doubt in your mind that you would be able to function in such circumstances?"

"Not at all," Reagan said, "and I want you to know that I also will not make age an issue in this campaign. I am not going to exploit, for political purposes, my opponent's youth and inexperience." The quip was a big hit in Kansas City as it must have been in millions of homes where the debate was being viewed on television. The studio audience erupted into spontaneous laughter and prolonged applause. Germond and Witcover would later argue that the election was decided, once and for all, at that moment, and the evidence supports that view. Surveys later revealed that once most voters had been reassured that Reagan hadn't drifted toward senility, they were happy to stick with him. Because Reagan's people understood this, they saw no reason to take the campaign beyond the imagery and generalities that had been the heart of their strategy. They were repeatedly criticized for ignoring the issues, but the campaign team ignored those complaints as studiously as they did the issues themselves. As one adviser bluntly put it: "We are not here to educate America. We are here to re-elect Ronald Reagan."

Mondale believed that the only chance he had of beating Reagan was to persuade voters that the economic picture was not nearly so rosy as Reagan had painted it. But he could not persuade the public. In his effort to make the deficit an issue, he came across to many Americans as simply a bearer of bad news, the latest example of what Jeane Kirkpatrick had branded the "Blame America First Crowd." That was only part of Mondale's problem. His candidacy was done in by the nature of television as much as it was by the natural human aversion to bad news. Television gives voters the opportunity to make instant judgments about whether they "like" or "dislike" someone, and there was no doubt that in 1984 the vast majority of Americans liked Reagan, even if they didn't always agree with him on certain issues. Because of the affection they felt, they were willing to forgive him his faults in much the same way they would have overlooked the shortcomings of a favorite relative. Reagan himself understood that Americans liked him, and so while others compiled lists of his mistakes and snickered over his gaffes, he remained serene, knowing that in the minds of most voters, his blunders really didn't matter. As for Mondale, he eventually came to realize that he was up against a rare force in politics, a candidate who was all but impervious to conventional attacks on the issues. Four years later, at the Democratic convention in Atlanta, he reminisced about his doomed campaign in 1984. "I tried to get specific and Reagan patted dogs," he said in a wistful tone. "I should have patted more dogs."

Reagan had gone before the electorate in 1980 with promises of change, but he and his people recognized that 1984 was a year when the voters wanted to be left alone. Critics could harp all they wanted about a campaign that failed to address the issues, but the

Acting President and his supporting cast knew precisely what they were doing. Harry Cohn, a Hollywood studio boss in the days when Reagan was acting in the movies, liked to sum up his basic philosophy with a phrase that became his trademark. "Give the public what it wants," Cohn would counsel his producers, and Ronald Reagan understood, as did few others, that the formula for success in Hollywood could serve equally well in Washington. Thus, when the curtain came down on Reagan's first term, he was given the equivalent of a standing ovation, a landslide victory. The extravagant prediction that had been made in the privacy of the Reagan camp several months earlier was correct: Reagan did carry every state except Minnesota.

10

Trading Places

"It's good, Don, really good."
—President Reagan

The reelection landslide overshadowed the fierce infighting that characterized the White House throughout the first term but did not alleviate it. If anything, the factionalism grew worse in the weeks after the election. Fueled by ideological differences, the professional jealousies that had arisen in the first months had degenerated into feelings of deep animosity.

The hard-core conservatives saw the start of the second term as an opportunity finally to rid the White House of Baker and the so-called pragmatists, a desire that also fit into the career plans of Bill Clark. Clark's move to the Department of the Interior during the first term had proved to be an exile. He had accepted the reassignment quietly, but friends said he still saw himself as the keeper of the conservative flame that Ronald Reagan had carried from California and, they said, he still coveted Baker's role as the White House chief of staff. Within days after the election, Clark went to two of the hard-liners who shared his dislike for Baker, CIA Director William Casey and Defense Secretary

Caspar Weinberger. Together, they made one more attempt to oust the man who had given Clark so much grief. But this time, Reagan said no, and this time it was Nancy Reagan, not Baker or one of the other pragmatists, who had played the major role in blocking the move. Despite his long association with Reagan, Clark had never dealt easily with Mrs. Reagan, and once again, he misread her. He had launched his new bid to get Baker's job unaware that his standing with the President's wife was already so low that there was virtually no chance the plan could succeed.

Clark's Nancy problem grew out of an episode during his tenure as national security adviser when he had proposed that Reagan go to the Philippines in an effort to shore up the crumbling regime of president Ferdinand Marcos. Nancy considered such a trip dangerous and never forgave Clark for proposing it, remarking to friends that he seemed more interested in national security than her husband's welfare. "Usually, Deaver would be the one who would draw her into personnel matters," said an aide who worked closely with the First Lady in those days, "but in this case, it was Nancy's doing all the way. She just never got over that he wanted Reagan to go to the Philippines during that turmoil, and after that she wanted nothing to do with Clark."

To be sure, Deaver had no use for Clark either, and neither he nor anyone else in Baker's wing of the White House grieved when Clark finally gave up his quest and announced he would soon be resigning his Cabinet post and returning to California. Clark's pending departure cleared the way for one of the strangest job swaps in Washington history, a maneuver that could have happened only under Ronald Reagan's "bring me solutions not problems" management style.

As Clark's power diminished, those on the inside could see signs that Baker, too, was growing restless. The infighting had fatigued him as well, reaching what Deaver later called "horrible levels." Baker was exhausted and had become so dispirited that he seriously considered accepting an offer to become commissioner of baseball. Among those who became aware of his frustration was Secretary of the Treasury Donald Regan. As early as the summer of 1984, he had sensed that Baker might want to move on after the election. By this time Regan knew the real action was at the White House. He was increasingly frustrated at having to defer on economic policy to the much younger David Stockman, and he and Baker had actually discussed swapping jobs a year earlier at the end of an angry exchange over news leaks.

During that episode, Regan had lectured the President and other members of the Cabinet on the need for discipline when dealing with the press. He had stressed that strong disciplinary measures should always be taken against White House staffers who gave unauthorized information to reporters. Almost as if to taunt him, his confidential economic report to the Cabinet was promptly leaked to a *Washington Post* reporter and appeared in the *Post* the following day. Regan exploded. He called Baker and told him to go to hell, then wrote a letter of resignation to the President. Reagan refused to accept it, and when Regan finally cooled down, he tried to patch things up with Baker. At the end of their conversation, Regan observed that Baker seemed "tired" and said half in jest that maybe the two should swap jobs. The wry impression was that Baker would be able to get plenty of rest at the Department of the Treasury. Baker told us later that he responded, "Watch out, I might just take you up on that."

Thus, Regan was not surprised when Baker called several weeks after the election and asked whether he had been serious about the swap. Regan assured Baker that he was, and the two thrashed the idea out over lunch and by mid-December had decided that trading places would be a good move for both of them. At Baker's insistence, Deaver, who had already concluded he had no chance to become chief of staff and, in fact, was planning to leave the White House, was also briefed on the swap. The three met at Baker's house to map out a plan of operation. Baker and Regan had agreed to the plan in principle, but there were still details to be worked out. For one thing, there was the small matter of informing the President of the United States as well as the delicate mission of convincing his wife that it was a good idea. Deaver agreed to help on both fronts. Still unfamiliar with Reagan's mode of making decisions at that point, Regan wanted to tell the President immediately. He reasoned that Reagan would want time to mull over the idea during his Christmas vacation in Palm Springs. Baker knew that would be unnecessary. There would be plenty of time, he said, after the first of the year.

Reagan finally got the news on January 7 and signed off on the plan in one brief meeting. Even though Regan was getting what he wanted, he felt that Reagan ought to have taken more time before making a decision that carried with it such ramifications. Had he faced such a choice, Regan later wrote, he would have asked many questions: How will you be different from Jim Baker? What will be your approach to Congress? What members of the staff will you keep? Whom should we get rid of? What are your views on foreign policy and press relations? And so on. If such questions begged answers in Regan's mind, in Reagan's they did not. He seemed satisfied that Regan and Baker had worked out a good move, and even when they told him there was no need to make a decision immediately, he said simply that he saw no reason for not going ahead. It had become "a done deal," in Baker's phrase, in less than an hour.

Coupled with Clark's departure, the swap set off a chain of Cabinet-level changes as Reagan prepared for his second term. Attorney General William French Smith had already declared his intention to resign, and the President planned to replace him with Ed Meese. (That nomination had been put on hold as investigators looked into matters involving Meese's personal finances.) To replace Clark, Reagan shifted Donald Hodel from Energy to Interior. John Herrington, who had headed the White House personnel office, got the Energy portfolio. In another unrelated move, the President replaced retiring Secretary of Education Terrel Bell with William Bennett, an articulate conservative who had been serving as chairman of the National Endowment for the Humanities.

Over the years, Cabinet changes have been the rule rather than the exception when Presidents have begun their second terms, but Washington had never seen anything like the Baker-Regan swap. The right wing loved it because it meant that at long last, Baker, the despised "pragmatist," would be leaving the White House, even if he were getting the second-ranking Cabinet post. Conservatives had opposed the selection of Regan for the Treasury post in 1980, considering him too middle-of-the-road, but this time it was a different story. Conservative fund-raiser Richard Viguerie spoke for many on the Right when he said, "Regan's main qualification to be Chief of Staff is that he is not Jim Baker."

Others viewed the switch with less enthusiasm. In a city that had become accustomed to chief executives who allowed no detail to escape their notice, the reaction to the casual way that Reagan had allowed two key aides to trade jobs bordered on disbelief. "Can you imagine what Lyndon Johnson would have done if two of his people had proposed something like that?" was a typical remark overheard during those first weeks in January. It was said that Johnson kept such a close eye on his aides that he did not allow them to lock their desks when they left the office each night, and those who had worked for Johnson during his days on Capitol Hill swore that they had actually seen him going through the desks of underlings who had departed for the day. As Washington came to understand, however, the change had been no more complicated than the explanation that Baker and Regan had given: both men wanted the change and Reagan said fine. Even so, the swap did trigger a new round of speculation about Reagan's leadership—or lack of it.

When the subsequent Cabinet changes were eventually made public, a White House reporter jokingly asked whether Reagan had been informed. "That's a loaded question," White House Spokesman Larry Speakes responded. By this time, *Newsweek* was referring to Reagan's management style as a sort of "you guys work it out" technique, but the magazine went on to conclude that however Reagan chose to manage the White House, it seemed to be working. In short, Reagan was still getting media approval for his "hands-off approach" to the presidency.

As Mike Deaver later told the story, he had cleared the way for the sixty-five-year-old Regan's takeover as chief of staff by telling the President, "I've brought you a playmate your own age." Deaver had also brought the President a much different kind of manager from any who had ever served him before, and Regan saw no reason to gloss over the differences. "I'm not like some of these other guys," the new chief of staff told Reagan early on. "I have fuck you money." Regan's point was a coarse put-down of Meese and Deaver, who had devoted their professional lives to Reagan and had little to show for it. Regan apparently felt it important to let them and the President know that he had come to the White House to serve not only at the President's pleasure but at his own as well. He didn't need the salary. If things didn't go his way, he could leave.

Regan *was* different. For most of his life Ronald Reagan had depended on people whose lives had revolved around his own, men of unquestioned loyalty such as Deaver, Meese, and Clark, or in other cases, men who had been hired for their expertise, such as Baker. Baker was as financially secure as Regan, but he had been hired because of his intimate knowledge of the inner workings of Washington, not his independence. In Regan, the President would have a chief of staff who was secure enough financially to maintain a certain independence and who was also brash enough to flaunt it. What Reagan needed, however, was an expert in the ways of Washington or, failing that, an expert in the ways of Ronald Reagan. Unfortunately, Don Regan was neither.

Donald T. Regan had been a highly visible, if not a universally admired, figure in the financial community during the days when he had been chairman of Merrill Lynch, the huge Wall Street brokerage firm. One financier said derisively that Regan had been known as head of the "largest brokerage firm, not necessarily the best one," but whatever his reputation on Wall Street, he was barely known to Reagan when he was named Treasury secretary. Even though their names were similar and despite the fact that Regan had arranged several fund-raising dinners for him during the campaign, candidate Reagan had trouble remembering booster Regan's name during their early acquaintanceship.

Nor was there much chance for the relationship to bloom once Regan went to Washington. Regan had joined the administration believing he would be responsible for shaping economic policy but soon discovered he was expected to do little more than be a spokesman who explained policies that had been developed by others—Baker, his assistant Richard Darman, and David Stockman. Regan had a particular dislike for Stockman because of the way the aide had paraded his status in Cabinet meetings. He was even more galled by never seeing the President alone and never having his views solicited—let alone accepted—in a serious way. The situation might have been less of a blow to Regan's considerable ego had he known that Reagan seldom met privately with anyone, but there was little chance he could have known that because only those few on the inside were aware of Reagan's work habits.

Regan would find Reagan's management style as perplexing as he had found Reagan's quick acceptance of the job swap that he and Baker had arranged. Even so, Regan saw no reason to move cautiously. Reagan might be laid back, but Regan was not. He would run the White House in the same hard-charging way that he had risen to the top job at Merrill Lynch. Don Regan had not come into wealth because he had inherited it as Jim Baker had. He was Harvard, yes, but he was a scholarship kid, the tough Irish son of a Boston cop who knew that you had to work for everything you got and sometimes you had to proceed brutally to get it. Baker was smooth, adept at placating those egos up on Capitol Hill, but Regan was a former Marine who knew you could also get what you wanted by just forging ahead, and that's what he planned to do. Being diplomatic with Congress was a job for his congressional liaison officer, just as handling the press was a job for his press officer. That's how he had done it in business, and that's how Don Regan intended to run the White House: the way you would run any big enterprise. The idea was to set goals and then kick people in the butt until they achieved them, to set up a chain of command and make sure nobody got around it.

In Regan's view, Reagan was the chairman of the board, and he was the chief executive officer, who saw to it that the boss's orders were carried out. The boss would issue orders to only one person: the CEO. But Regan's plan had one flaw: his basic assumption was wrong. The government is too large and complex to be managed. It must be led. Nor is it in any way like a business because no business must have its budget and its plans approved by 535 members of Congress who represent widely disparate constituencies. For Ronald Reagan, his new chief of staff's flawed assumption would create chaos, and the timing could not have been worse. In his second term, Reagan would face the most serious political crisis of his life, but the retainers who had guided him so carefully over the years were leaving his side. Some were going home or into business; others like Meese would be close by in Cabinet posts, as would some of the newer people, such as Baker. But, for the first time since those early days in Sacramento, the aides closest to Ronald Reagan would be people he hardly knew.

Reagan's second term began in such bitter cold that most of the inaugural events were cancelled, but the weather was only the first of the problems he would face. Reagan's fast start in 1981 had been due in large part to the detailed plan for the first hundred days that had been made by Baker and his aides in the weeks before Reagan was sworn in. In contrast, it would be August 1985 before the new chief of staff was able to put together a similar plan for the second term.

There was another reason for the drift that characterized the beginning of the second term. It had nothing to do with Regan but was rooted in the nature of the President's victory. Reagan's "feel good" campaign themes had produced the largest landslide ever, but the decision by Reagan's political handlers to make it a campaign that was void of any real issues made it difficult for the administration to convince Congress that Reagan had received a mandate to work for any specific program. "When Reagan got to town in 1981 he had run on a program and everybody knew that program was the economy and defense," said Larry Speakes. "That's why the Southern Democrats went along with Reagan and why the others did. "In '84, we ran on 'Morning in America,'—make no waves, offend no constituency. We got there in '85, and we had no new ideas, no new programs. The people had only voted for a popular president; they hadn't voted for any programs." That made it more difficult to plan any kind of realistic legislative strategy. And for most of Reagan's second term, there was none.

Once Regan finally drew up his blueprint for the second term, he was proud of it. It may have been late in coming, but it was his, and he beamed like a new father when he gave it to the President for his consideration. To Regan, this was how management worked. An executive laid out his goals and then decided how to go about accomplishing them. He gave the plan to Reagan that August, as the President was departing for California and a few days' rest. When Reagan came back, however, the chief of staff was stunned to discover that the plan had been returned to him without comment. Only when he pressed the President, he later wrote in his memoir, did he discover that Reagan wanted him to implement the plan. Only then did the President reveal what he thought of it and his assessment was so brief it was almost an insult. All he said was, "It's good, Don, really good."

Regan had poured countless hours into that plan and all the President could say was "really good"? Reagan had approved a detailed program that had been prepared by someone else and had not asked for a single change. Nor had he asked a single question. Regan was dumbstruck, but he should not have been. The episode mirrored the way Reagan had reacted when he had been briefed on Baker's plan for the first hundred days. Baker's people had been dumbfounded too, but they eventually came to the same understanding that Regan would later reach: Reagan didn't get very excited about complicated long-range proposals.

Overhauling the White House staff and the decision-making process came about more quickly, and easily, for the new chief of staff than charting policy. Purging the inner circle of Baker and Meese loyalists had been fairly easy because many of them were moving on, anyway. Deaver planned to leave in the spring to launch his own public relations business. Darman went with Baker to Treasury, as did Baker's chief political aide, Margaret Tutwiler. Craig Fuller, who had served as Meese's chief aide (and as some told it, Baker's mole in the Meese camp), took up new responsibilities as Vice President Bush's chief of staff. Looking to protect his right, Regan brought in columnist Patrick Buchanan, the ultraconservative onetime aide to Richard Nixon, to serve as the new communications chief. His responsibilities would include overseeing the President's speech writing staff. For the most part, however, Regan hired people who had worked for him at Treasury, people who were little known to the public but could be counted on to give absolute loyalty to the man who had brought them to the White House. Regan demanded such loyalty from his subordinates and generally got it, but the group that he assembled possessed neither the Washington expertise that characterized the Baker wing of the White House nor the familiarity with Reagan and his ways that had been the most valuable assets of Meese, Deaver, and the other Californians.

The White House during the first term had been torn by factional infighting, and Regan thought he could end that by tightening the reins on the staff and gathering as much power as possible for himself. This did result in a more peaceful atmosphere for Reagan, but the White House became a two-level world where conflict went on at a layer the President never saw. But as Baker's people had come to understand, an executive of Reagan's work habits *needed* to see ideas being thrashed out because he was too passive to explore issues on his own. "Ronald Reagan's mind is a lot like a dog sleeping in the sun," said one of the President's admirers. "Dogs can sleep all day and then all of a sudden something can happen and a dog turns into a wolf and you wonder how that can be. When left undisturbed, Ronald Reagan's mind just doesn't do much but when challenged he's very good . . . when he becomes engaged."

Regan's new chain of command not only made it more difficult for Reagan to learn of the conflicts that were developing over policy but also made it more difficult for his chief of staff to understand whether or not the President was pleased with the direction his administration was taking. Unfortunately the management system that Regan installed played directly to Reagan's weakness, rather than his strength. A President who had never shown any interest in detail now had been left all the more isolated from the problems of his presidency. The decision making had been more free-form during the first term, and as Richard Darman, a key member of the team in those early days, later said, "Seeing the interplay between us, a lot of things happened. First of all, Ronald Reagan learned much more about reality."

For Don Regan and his new White House crew, learning about reality began in mid-February and the lesson was that the Reagan administration was going to have a mess on its hands with Congress. It had been more than a year since the President had nominated Ed Meese to replace William French Smith as attorney general, and the nomination still had not been brought to a vote. Smith wanted to go home to California and people kept having farewell parties for him, but Meese's confirmation hearings just continued to drag on. At one gathering, Smith jokingly said he wanted everyone to know that the movie *The Long Goodbye* was not a documentary produced by the Justice Department. Congress had spent months preparing for and then holding acrimonious hearings on Meese's nomination. Then the hearings had been suspended while a special prosecutor delved into Meese's tangled personal finances, and now there was something else: as if to put the President on notice that nothing would be easy in the second term, a group of farm state senators had decided to make voting on the Meese nomination contingent on government relief for hard-pressed midwestern farmers. A filibuster had droned on for five days as the rebellious senators refused to allow Meese's nomination to come to a vote. There would be no vote on Meese, they vowed, until the administration authorized emergency credit measures for their constituents.

The Senate had been in session only a few days, and already tempers were boiling. "The Republicans are willing to let the farmers go to hell," stormed the Democratic leader in the Senate, Robert Byrd. It was Rhode Island's Republican senator John Chafee who better characterized what was really happening when he said, "This has nothing to do with the farmers . . . nothing to do

with Mr. Meese. It has to do with who is going to run the show."
Reagan had won his landslide, but Congress already understood
that he had no particular mandate from the public as he had in
1980. Public opinion was no longer Reagan's monopoly. Congress
already knew that and holding up Meese's nomination was just
one way to let the White House know it, too.

After five days of wrangling, the farm state senators extracted
the necessary promises from the White House, and Meese's nomination was finally approved during a rare Saturday session. Meese
was going to realize his lifelong ambition. But he would not be
going to Justice with what could be called a rousing send-off: the
final Senate tally had shown sixty-three senators voting for Meese
and thirty-one against him, the largest number of votes in opposition to a nominee for attorney general since 1923, when Calvin
Coolidge's candidate, Charles B. Warren, was rejected forty-one
to thirty-nine. Never one to dwell on the negative, Meese told
reporters that it was still a victory margin of two to one.

By March when he was finally sworn in, Meese could already
lay claim to being the most investigated attorney general in the
nation's history. In the twelve months between his nomination
and his confirmation the onetime prosecutor from Oakland had
been the subject of eleven separate investigations by Special Prosecutor Jacob Stein, who had probed charges ranging from financial dealings Meese had conducted with people who later got
federal jobs to irregularities in the financial disclosure reports that
those who hold high government positions are required to file.
Stein said there was no basis for prosecuting Meese, and the director of the Office of Government Ethics—despite a contrary
preliminary conclusion by his staff—ruled that Meese had committed no ethical violations. The letter of the law had not been
violated. Yet, neither investigator was willing to state whether or
not Meese had obeyed the spirit of the law; nor would either
unequivocally endorse Meese's conduct. The special prosecutor
stated that it was not within his jurisdiction to make a judgment
about ethical violations, and the report from the ethics office concluded that some of Meese's dealings had the "appearance" of
impropriety.

That had been the trouble with Meese since his first days in
Washington. Even some of his oldest acquaintances conceded that
once he got to the White House, it was as if he had been cursed
with bad luck, and worse, bad judgment. No matter what he

touched, it never seemed to come out quite right. Even the most insignificant things had a way of looking not quite right. The tireless executive who had served Ronald Reagan so efficiently in Sacramento just kept falling into one trap after another once he reached the White House. His friends pointed with some bewilderment at the mess Meese had gotten into over a promotion in the Army Reserve. It seemed impossible he could not have known that he was being given preferential treatment when he had been promoted to colonel. After the promotion, Meese had called Secretary of Defense Weinberger to praise the general who approved the promotion and to support the general's own reappointment. It just didn't make sense, to even his friends, that anyone would open himself up to severe criticism over something as minor as a promotion in the Army Reserve.

The mess that investigators had uncovered in Meese's personal finances caused him continual trouble. Meese was not a wealthy man; he had spent most of his life working in government. Although he did not have an extravagant life-style, once he reached Washington, Meese and his wife traveled in the same circles as Reagan's other appointees, maintaining the social contacts that are expected of any ranking Washington official. For a person of Meese's financial resources, it apparently was a strain on the budget. Investigators discovered that Meese's financial underpinnings were debt-laden. Meese had been in a precarious financial position from the day he arrived in Washington, apparently able to keep his balance only because of repeated and unorthodox loans from strangers and friends.

Moving a family usually causes some financial hardship, but thousands of others have managed it. For Meese, however, even an act as mundane as selling the house in California involved tangled financial maneuvering that raised questions about his sense of propriety. Maine's Democratic senator George Mitchell went to the Senate floor one day to lay out in detail how Meese was aided in selling his home by a man named Thomas Barrack. According to Mitchell, Barrack advanced the seller a $70,000 loan to consummate the deal, then paid the mortgage for a period of time, and finally absorbed an $83,000 loss on the transaction. Within a week after arranging the sale, Barrack met with Meese. He was subsequently appointed to two federal positions. Both he and Meese told investigators they had never met previous to the real estate transaction. Meese denied any connection between it and the efforts to get Barrack a federal post. Meese testified before Congress that he had moved to Washington at his own expense. Shortly thereafter, it was revealed that Meese had accepted a $10,000 check marked "MOVING EXPENSES" from the Presidential Transition Trust Fund set up after the 1980 election. (After advice that the payment for moving expenses was probably illegal, the notation concerning "moving expenses" on the check was marked out. Meese kept the money, billing the transition office for consulting fees.)

It was also confirmed that Meese had obtained $60,000 in unsecured loans from John McKean, his tax counselor. Meese paid no interest on the loans until their existence was revealed in a news story twenty-six months later. In the meantime, McKean had twice been appointed to the Postal Board of Governors and was serving as its chairman when the Meese confirmation finally reached the Senate floor for a vote. In his opposition to Meese's confirmation, Mitchell pointed out that Meese had personally cleared McKean for the federal appointments.

The loans that the Meese family obtained from friends did not go to Meese alone. Meese's immediate subordinate at the White House, Edwin Thomas, had once lent Meese's wife $15,000, interest-free. Meese told investigators he saw no reason to include the loan in the financial disclosure statements that ranking government officials are required to file. Thomas was later appointed a regional director of the General Services Administration. In yet another convoluted transaction, Meese obtained a series of mortgage loans, bridge loans, and rescheduled loans totaling $420,000 from a bank. He fell behind on repaying some of the loans for as long as fifteen months. Although Meese maintained that there was no connection, four of the bank officers were later appointed to federal positions after Meese reviewed their nominations.

At no point throughout the hearings did Reagan's support for his old friend ever waver, nor was there ever a time when Meese showed signs of giving up the fight for confirmation. To friends, he claimed the charges were grounded in politics, an attempt to turn public opinion against the President by attacking one of the people closest to him. But to his many critics, Meese remained the most visible symbol of the questionable deals that shadowed the Reagan administration, a long string of ethical or illegal transgressions that came to be known as the "sleaze factor."

Regan and his people had hoped that Meese's Senate confirmation would finally get Meese and his troubles off the front pages
and for a time it did. Unfortunately for the new White House
team, Meese and his troubles were pushed aside by a fiasco of
Reagan's own making: his decision to visit what was soon to become the most famous graveyard in all of Europe, a small cemetery
called Bitburg.

If God is found in the details, so too are the demons on occasion,
and Bitburg was one of those occasions. Poor staff work by Reagan's usually reliable advancemen, missteps by the West German
government, and a series of errors by Reagan himself resulted in
the most embarrassing episode—up to that point—in Reagan's
presidency. What had been planned as a quick trip to Bitburg
became the "Bitburg mess." For days it consumed Washington.

Washington's cherry blossom trees had produced their first
buds on schedule, but to Regan's beleagured staff it seemed that
was the only thing that had gone right that spring. Everything
else had been overwhelmed by the controversy that flared over
Bitburg, which brought a crisis atmosphere to the Reagan White
House. All programs were delayed while everyone searched for
some way to extricate the President from the mess.

The idea of Bitburg had seemed so uncomplicated in the
beginning. It had started when West German Chancellor Helmut
Kohl had visited Washington the previous November. He told the
President he wanted to organize a small ceremony to pay tribute
to the dead of World War II and proposed to do it by having
Reagan join him for a visit at a German military cemetery. Reagan's White House retainers saw no harm in that, nor did experts
at the State Department, so Reagan agreed to do it. It seemed
such a minor matter that no one gave it much thought. Besides,
as the State Department people saw it, the proposal had a real
value: staffers on State's German desk were reporting that Kohl
was irked because he had not been included in the ceremony
earlier in the year marking the fortieth anniversary of the Normandy invasion. Reagan had gone to Normandy Beach to join
British Prime Minister Margaret Thatcher and French President
François Mitterrand for that ceremony, and it had received a lot
of favorable press coverage. Kohl, the State Department specialists
reported, felt that he had been snubbed. If a little ceremony

in a German cemetery would put Kohl in a better humor, the people at State reasoned, then why not?

Reagan was already scheduled to go to Bonn in the spring for an economic summit, and the ceremony could easily be folded into that itinerary. Kohl had reminded the President when he proposed the stop that the timing was ideal. The economic conference was scheduled to take place just days before the anniversary of VE Day. Kohl said that he and French President François Mitterrand had recently clasped hands at a similar ceremony in Verdun and it had gone off especially well, because both German and American soldiers from World War I were buried there. The Bitburg ceremony would be a wonderful way, Kohl said, to show the strong bonds that now existed between two World War II adversaries. It would underline as well to the Warsaw Pact countries just how strong the ties were between NATO's two most important partners. It could all take place as a sort of prelude to the economic summit, Kohl said, and Bitburg was the best site because it was close by.

Kohl had also mentioned that Reagan might wish to visit one of the Nazi death camps, but that idea was quickly rejected. Too depressing, Mrs. Reagan thought, and Deaver agreed. Deaver knew his man and what he had learned early on was that Reagan neither enjoyed depressing settings nor handled them well. The President did well in hopeful, cheery settings and he was even better when he could combine those visits with a touch of nostalgia. So there would be no visit to a death camp. As for the rest of the trip, however, all was agreed and Deaver left for Europe in February to lay the groundwork.

The trip came at a bad time for Deaver and an awkward time for the White House. Regan had been on the job for only a matter of weeks and the staff was still in transition. With Meese gone to Justice, a lot of his people had left and replacements had not yet arrived. It was a time when many on the White House staff were either leaving or trying to find new patrons in order to stay. Deaver himself was recovering from a kidney ailment that had been complicated by an allergic reaction to his medicine. But handling the advance work for Ronald Reagan was what Deaver had been doing all his life, and even though he had his mind on his own pending departure from the White House, this was not a particularly difficult trip to plan. Deaver's main concern was

to be sure Reagan's schedule was not loaded down with too
many events. On a previous trip to Europe, Reagan had made
so many stops that by the time he was ushered in for an audience
with the Pope he fell asleep. What had made it all the worse
was that the snooze had taken place in full view of television
cameras.

By March, word had leaked that Reagan would take part in
some kind of ceremony with Kohl, and American Jewish leaders
were upset when they learned that the White House had already
vetoed a visit to a death camp. Asked why, Reagan said that he
simply wished to look forward, not backward. "I feel very
strongly," he had said, "that in commemorating the end of that
great war, that instead of rewakening the memories and so forth
and passions of the time, that maybe we would observe this day
as the day when forty years ago, peace and friendship began."

The statement did little to pacify American Jews, and when
it was officially announced on April 11 that the ceremony would
take place in a military cemetery, the expressions of concern grew
even sharper. "A calculated insult," said one Holocaust survivor.
The outcries of April 11, however, were only a prelude to the
explosion of outrage the next day. European newspapers reported
there were no Americans buried in the cemetery as the White
House had first believed. All American dead had been taken home
after World War II or were buried in the huge U.S. cemetery
overlooking Omaha Beach in Normandy. But, the news agencies
reported, the cemetery held the bodies of forty-seven members
of Hitler's notorious Waffen SS, a collection of murderers who
had eventually become part of Hitler's elite guard. They had been
buried there among other German soldiers from the regular army.
"How in hell," new Chief of Staff Regan demanded to know, "did
we get into this?"

It was Deaver who had to take the blame, and he knew it. He
lamely explained that it had been snowing when he visited Bitburg, and it was impossible to tell who was buried there. He did
point out that the German government had given every assurance
that the ceremony would produce "nothing embarrassing." Regan
was furious but he couldn't say much. After all, he had approved
the trip in those first days after he had switched jobs with Baker
and his rage was mild compared to what was happening on Capitol
Hill. "The White House has gone bonkers," said New York con-

gressman Bill Green. Fifty-three senators, Republicans as well as Democrats, signed a letter urging the President to cancel the visit. Cornered by a group of reporters, Regan brushed them off by saying, "I'm not ready to talk about it."

Everyone else was. Every time reporters confronted the President, they wanted to know about little but Bitburg. Unfortunately every time Reagan tried to explain it, the situation got worse. The trip not only appeared to have been ill thought out, but Reagan's explanations produced what seemed to be glaring gaps in his knowledge of World War II. In their initial meeting, Kohl had told the President that 60 percent of the German population had been born since World War II. That was true, but the information apparently confused Reagan, who took it to mean that most Germans were unaware of what had happened during the war. He told a news conference, "Very few Germans are alive that even remember the war, and certainly none of them who were adults and participated in any way." To a group of out-of-town editors, the President tried to explain who had actually been buried at Bitburg. He conceded that the SS officers buried there had been the ones "that conducted the persecutions and all" but added, "the other German soldiers there, these were young teenagers that were conscripted, forced into military service in the closing days of the Third Reich when they were short of manpower." As reporters checked out Reagan's story the next day, they discovered it had either been simply made up or based on a misunderstanding of the facts. Reagan compounded that blunder by asserting that the young soldiers were also victims of nazism because they had been drafted "to carry out the hateful wishes of the Nazis." That conclusion further angered the already outraged Jewish leaders. To them, drawing parallels between German soldiers who may or may not have been drafted against their wills and the atrocities carried out against the inmates of the death camps was intolerable. Rabbi Alexander M. Schindler, the president of the American Hebrew Congregations, called the President's remark "a perversion of the language." The controversy now extended far beyond the American Jewish community. "Somehow," said a White House aide, "we have accomplished the impossible, we have even got the American Legion to criticize Ronald Reagan."

A previously scheduled ceremony in the Capitol Rotunda honoring the American Army units that had liberated the death

camps now became a televised forum for criticism of the President
and the decision to go to Bitburg. Elie Wiesel, who had survived
the death camps and devoted his life to writing about the Nazi
savagery, urged Secretary of State Shultz, the main speaker at the
Rotunda ceremony, to explain to the President how deeply Jewish
outrage was running. The stoic Shultz almost never deviated from
a prepared speech text, but on this occasion he did. He appeared
deeply moved as he told Wiesel that even in a spirit of reconcil-
iation, there was no place for understanding for those who were
responsible for the horrors of the death camps. By coincidence,
Wiesel was being honored the following day at the White House,
where he was to receive the Congressional Gold Medal of Achievement for his writings about the death camps. The ceremony produced one of the most remarkable scenes of the Reagan
presidency. The President had made a moving statement as he
presented the medal to Wiesel. He promised that Americans
would never allow what had happened in the death camps to be
forgotten. The ceremony was being televised and Jewish leaders
from across the country, congressmen and senators, and White
House aides had crowded into the Roosevelt Room to see it. But
as moving as the President's words had been, there was an overriding question: What would Wiesel say? Would he mention
Bitburg? Would he confront the President face-to-face? Regan
would later claim Wiesel had promised in advance not to raise the
subject, but only a few seconds after Wiesel had been given the
medal, he gave it to his son, turned to the President, and said
quietly, "Mr. President, I would not be the man that I am if I did
not tell you of the sadness in my heart for what happened during
the last week." It was a stunning moment. Almost never is an
American President lectured in public, but that was precisely what
was happening. Except for Wiesel's voice no sound could be heard
in the room.

Looking directly at the President, Wiesel said,

> I am convinced that you were not aware of the presence
> of the SS graves in the Bitburg cemetery. Of course you didn't
> know, but now we are all aware. May I, Mr. President, if it's
> possible at all, implore you to do something else, to find an-
> other way, another side. That place, Mr. President, is not
> your place. Your place is with the victims of the SS. Oh, we
> all know there are political and strategic reasons. But this

issue, as are all issues related to that awesome event, transcends politics and diplomacy. The issue here is not politics, but good and evil. That place, Mr. President, is not your place. Your place is with the victims of the SS. I have seen the SS at work and I have seen their victims.

Reagan sat silently. He applauded but did not respond. While he seemed perplexed and hurt, Mrs. Reagan was in a fury, and the episode became the worst time of Deaver's public life. The First Lady demanded that the trip be cancelled and railed that Deaver's poor advance work had not only ruined her husband's presidency but perhaps his life as well. Others in the White House were just as adamant in taking the opposite side. While Deaver was trying to mount some kind of damage control, Pat Buchanan was arguing for an even harder line, anything that would suggest the President was not bending to the Jewish lobby. Pressure from outside the White House was equally intense. While everyone from rabbis to American Legionnaires was demanding that Reagan cancel the trip, Kohl was on the overseas line pleading that a cancellation would be taken in Germany as an insult and do him serious personal harm. Henry Kissinger and Richard Nixon called in to say Reagan should not back down. Reagan reluctantly agreed that he had to go. He couldn't be in the position, he told those around him, of being seen as a person like Jimmy Carter, someone who always vacillated in tough situations.

Deaver found himself for the first time on opposite sides with Nancy Reagan, but it couldn't be helped. Now that Reagan had decided to go, it was Deaver's job to salvage what he could out of the mess. Despite the earlier objections, Deaver concluded that a death camp visit would be necessary after all. It was the only way to gain something positive from the trip. The Reagans might not be comfortable in depressing settings, but they would just have to tough it out this once. Deaver chose Bergen-Belsen for Reagan to visit. It was the place where Anne Frank had died. If the trip were to be saved, it would require one of Reagan's most eloquent speeches. Ken Khachigian, the onetime writer for Reagan who had crafted some of his best, was brought back to fashion some appropriate remarks. Reagan would speak at the camp, not the cemetery. The Bergen-Belsen stop would be scheduled first. That way, with a little luck the White House people thought, what Reagan said at the death camp would be the news of the day and

it would overshadow the brief cemetery stop. It did not. But Deaver's effort did staunch the flood of bad publicity. The speech
that Reagan finally delivered at Bergen-Belsen was one of the
most moving of his presidency. "Rising above all this cruelty, out
of this tragic and nightmarish time, beyond the anguish, the pain
and the suffering for all time," Reagan said, "we can and must
pledge: Never Again." The speech took some of the edge off the
controversy, and the entire episode was eventually overtaken by
other events. But the Bitburg mess would be remembered as the
first major blunder of the post-Baker White House. It set the tone
for the far more serious fiascos in foreign policy that cast such a
pall over the second term of Ronald Reagan's presidency.

11

FOR THE PRESIDENT

"Let's do them all!"
—President Reagan

When George Shultz returned to Washington in the early summer of 1982 to replace Alexander Haig as secretary of state, he brought with him a reputation as a quiet and pragmatic leader who was adept at steering conflict into consensus. Low-key and methodical, he was, by temperament, the antithesis of Haig, and partly for this reason he was judged to be suited for the task of restoring stability to the post. For his part, Shultz recognized that need. He had watched with dismay Haig's erratic performance, and he agreed with those who felt that Haig had brought most of his troubles on himself. Yet in one vital area—Haig's frequent complaint that Secretary of Defense Caspar Weinberger had set out to undercut and usurp his authority—Shultz guessed that his predecessor's grievances were legitimate. Shultz did not need Al Haig to tell him how difficult Weinberger could be, for he knew that from his own experience. He, too, had clashed with Weinberger over the exercise of power, and the frictions in their re-

---

lationship went back to the days when they both were working in
the Nixon administration.

Fourteen years earlier, when George Shultz first went to
Washington to serve in a Cabinet post, he was scarcely known
outside academic circles. A professor whose special field was industrial economics, he became dean of the University of Chicago's
business school in 1962, and that was the job he left in late 1968
when Nixon appointed him secretary of labor. He endured in the
Nixon administration longer than any other member of the original Cabinet, and Labor was just one of his three portfolios. He
went on from that post to serve as budget director, and from there
to Treasury secretary. By the time he finally left Washington in
the spring of 1974, Shultz had established himself as a major
figure, one who, next to Kissinger, was regarded as the most
valued member of the Nixon team; and the fact that he was untainted by the Watergate scandal only added to his reputation as
a man of principle and integrity. (The celebrated incident in which
Nixon belittled him as a "candy ass" grew out of Shultz's refusal
to take part in the pernicious plot to harass people on the White
House enemies list.)

When the Office of Management and Budget was created in
the spring of 1970, Shultz was named to head it and Weinberger
was picked to serve as his top deputy. Almost from the very start,
the two men clashed. Shultz was the boss, of course, and in his
quiet way he could sometimes be imperious in his treatment of
subordinates. (His renowned skills as a mediator were more likely
to come into play when he was dealing with peers or superiors.)
Weinberger, who had been a litigator before he went into politics,
had a feisty and assertive manner that annoyed Shultz, and what's
more, he was unaccustomed to being anyone's number-two man.
In California, he served as state finance director under Reagan,
and his first job in the Nixon administration had been as chairman
of the Federal Trade Commission. At OMB, Weinberger felt that
Shultz was intentionally acting superior, and he resented it. Joseph
Laitin, who worked in the budget office in those days, later recalled, "Cap became so frustrated with his lack of clear authority
that he finally insisted that George sign a memorandum desig-
nating him as the acting director when George was out of town."
Another colleague from those years remembered budget meetings
at which Shultz would tell the assembled officials, many of whom
were apprehensive about impending cuts in their departments,

that he was "turning you over to Cap, whose mercies are tender."
The line usually provoked a laugh from everyone except Weinberger, who did not appreciate being set up as the scapegoat, the
dreaded "Cap the Knife."

The edge in their relationship rarely erupted into open quarrels, but the tension was there and it persisted through the two
years they worked togther at OMB. In 1972, Shultz moved on to
the Department of the Treasury, and Weinberger was promoted
to a Cabinet post of his own, secretary of HEW. That put them
on separate tracks, with each man pursuing his own agenda, but
it wasn't long before they were once again competing with each
other, this time in the private sector.

After leaving the Nixon administration, Shultz became president of the Bechtel Corporation, a giant construction company
based in San Francisco, and soon thereafter, the firm hired Weinberger as its general counsel. Once again, Weinberger chafed in
the role of subordinate to Shultz; at Bechtel the disparity in stature
and authority was even greater than it had been in Washington.
But power would eventually tip toward Weinberger, for he was
the one who had close ties to Ronald Reagan. When Reagan was
elected, Weinberger lobbied to become secretary of state, but other
members of the inner circle blocked that move and he had to
settle for the Department of Defense. Yet before that decision
was made, Shultz was on the short list of candidates for the State
portfolio. But once Weinberger was given Defense, Reagan's advisers realized it would not be proper to appoint two executives
from the same company to such high-level Cabinet posts, and
among those who argued that point most effectively was Weinberger himself. As far as the powerful Israel lobby was concerned,
an executive from Bechtel should not have been given either State
or Defense. Because it has major interests in the Arab world,
Bechtel had exercised its influence to get Senate approval for the
sale of AWACS surveillance planes to Saudi Arabia, and Shultz,
in particular, was suspected of harboring a pro-Arab bias.

It was against this background that George Shultz commenced his
mission to give some sense of direction and coherence to U.S.
foreign policy, and it did not take him long to discover that his
hunch had been correct: Haig's complaints about Weinberger had
been justified. Yet now, for the first time in their discordant relationship, it was Weinberger who was the more powerful. Al-

though Shultz had the more important Cabinet post (and even that was debatable), he was the outsider who had to compete with Weinberger's close association with the President. For his part, Weinberger had no intention of curtailing his efforts to treat certain aspects of foreign policy as his domain at the Pentagon. His was the most-favored department in the Reagan administraiton, the one that kept getting budget increases while cuts were being inflicted on all other programs, and that made him privileged in the Cabinet.

Shultz's initial response was to concentrate on building up his own working relationship with the President before making any definitive moves against Weinberger. He had been through all this before and, as he had demonstrated during the Nixon years, he knew how to accumulate power and establish authority. Above all, he knew how to persevere. In that respect, his deliberate and courtly manner was deceptive, for Shultz was highly skilled and tenacious in the art of bureaucratic combat. So, in his first few months on the job, he patiently gathered his resources, preparing for the inevitable conflict over who had command of foreign policy.

Shultz made his first overt move in early 1983 when he came up with evidence that Weinberger—with the help of Bill Clark, who was still natiohnal security adviser— had been making decisions that clearly intruded on his jurisdiction. This was exactly the kind of thing that had so often driven Haig into a rage, but Shultz, more adept at these games, did not just gripe to aides and reporters. He went directly to the Oval Office and confronted Reagan in person, telling him, "You don't need a guy like me for Secretary of State if this is the way things are going to be done." Reagan, as was customary, professed ignorance of any back-channel ventures and assured Shultz, as he had previously assured Haig, that he was his chief foreign policy man. But Shultz also extracted from Reagan a promise that from then on, he would have walk-in privileges to the Oval Office, a freedom of access that would increase his own leverage with the President. Shultz left that meeting satisfied, but his power struggles with Weinberger were not over.

One of their most bitter battles was over the presence of U.S. Marines in Lebanon. The Marines had been sent there in the late summer of 1982 as part of a multinational peacekeeping force, and their original mission had been a modest one: to help maintain order in that divided country while the various factions tried to resolve the differences that had plunged them into civil war and, more recently, had prompted Israel to invade Lebanon. But the Marines soon found themselves involved in a far more ambitious undertaking. Shultz, who had just recently taken over as secretary of state, viewed the U.S. military presence as an opportunity to pry Lebanon away from the influence of its powerful neighbor Syria. Accordingly, the Marines were ordered to support Lebanon's government, which was engaged in the formidable task of trying to control the warring factions. This no doubt was a worthy objective, but the fragile government in Beirut was dominated by Christians, and the factions opposing it were Muslims. By taking sides in that complex and violent struggle, the U.S. Marines assumed a new role, changing from a peacekeeping mission to partisan intervention.

A critical point was crossed in September 1983 when Muslim forces launched a heavy attack on the government's army just three miles from the presidential palace. The U.S. envoy in Beirut warned Washington that the government was in imminent danger of falling, and if that happened the way would be clear for Syria to move in. He urged that U.S. Navy ships off the coast of Lebanon be ordered into action with artillery and air assaults on the Muslim strongholds. Shultz supported that proposal, and he sold the idea to Reagan, who later explained that he had been under the impression that the purpose of the Navy attack was to defend the land-based Marines in Lebanon. But the Lebanese Muslims viewed the shelling of their villages as clear proof that the United States had changed its policy and was now intervening on the side of their enemies. And they vowed to take revenge on the U.S. "peacekeeping" troops.

When the retaliation came, it was devastating. On October 23, a driver rammed a truck full of explosives into the main Marine barracks at the Beirut airport, and the explosion it set off killed 241 American servicemen. That tragedy, the worst to befall the U.S. military since Vietnam, was a severe setback for Shultz's policy, a point that Weinberger emphatically noted in the postmortems that followed. Though on the defensive, Shultz still insisted that the Marines should remain in Beirut; to retreat now, he argued, would only send a message that the United States could be intimidated by such terrorist attacks. But Weinberger pushed just as hard for withdrawal, and he had both the joint chiefs and public opinion on his side. Thus, in early 1984, what was left of the U.S. peacekeeping force was pulled out of Beirut, and Reagan and his advisers did their best to downplay the lamentable misadventure.

But that was not the end of the story, far from it. The Muslim terrorists continued their war against the United States; one of their tactics was to abduct American citizens and hold them hostage in Lebanon. Thus began the long and melancholy ordeal that, among other things, helped to trigger the Iran-Contra affair. Long before that became an issue, however, Shultz and Weinberger clashed angrily over the question of how to deal with terrorism. Shultz, still pressing the hard line, advocated military strikes against suspected terrorist hideouts, even at the risk of killing a few innocent civilians. Weinberger countered that *his* armed forces would not take part in military actions that did not have the support of Congress and the American people, and those kinds of attacks clearly did not. At one stormy meeting at the White House, Shultz all but accused Weinberger of being too weak. "If you're unwilling to use force," he snapped, "maybe we should cut your budget." To which Weinberger replied that he, not Shultz, was the one who had known Reagan over the years and therefore understood what the President wanted.

Their disputes were not confined to terrorism and the Middle East. They quarreled over arms control and the overall question of relations with the Soviet Union, and in this area it was Weinberger who adopted the hard-line stance. He was the kind of Reagan conservative who had an almost morbid suspicion of any deal that might be struck with the Russians. His basic position was to meet what he perceived to be a perilous threat with ever-increasing military strength. Keep building up the arsenal; that was the only language the Soviets understood. But Shultz, who had been influenced by the Nixon-Kissinger policies of détente, argued for a more flexible approach. Here, too, their differences often led to heated exchanges. One arms-control expert was so appalled by a Shultz-Weinberger confrontation he had witnessed that he later told a member of the White House staff: "They were fighting like a couple of kids in there."

In their dealings with other officials, both Shultz and Weinberger were, for the most part, civil and decorous, even when there was disagreement on the issues. But their own relationship was fueled by a deep and personal animus, and by the end of 1984 George Shultz decided to force the issue. He was aware that he had lost or was losing most of his major policy arguments with Weinberger, and so he urged the President to choose between them. A few weeks after the reelection landslide, at one of his regular meetings with Reagan, Shultz bluntly put it to him: "Mr. President," he said,

> I think you will do better in the second term if you build your strategy around Cap or around me, but the two of us together will only lead to paralysis. I have strong views, and I think mine are correct. But I think you would do better even if you adopted Cap's views and not mine. The two of us are unable to work congenially, and so you should take one or the other.

Fending off the ultimatum, Reagan resorted to the reassuring charm that was his preferred way of dealing with awkward situations. "George," he said, "I definitely want you on my team. Make no mistake about that."

Shultz felt he had gone as far as he dared, and faced with the President's amiable indecision, he chose not to press the point. He agreed to stay on but made it clear that he was not happy with the arrangement, and in the weeks ahead he continued to brood about it.

That Oval Office conversation was later recounted in *Landslide*, the thorough book on the Iran-Contra affair by Jane Mayer and Doyle McManus. The authors noted that the meeting was also attended by Robert McFarlane and he, too, was dismayed—though not surprised—by Reagan's reaction. A little more than a year had passed since he replaced Bill Clark as national security adviser, and more than anyone else, McFarlane had become the man in the middle of the feud between the two Cabinet officers. That was a thankless position, and a couple of times he had tentatively suggested to the President that something should be done to break the stalemate in the Shultz-Weinberger rivalry. Reagan's response on those occaisons had been no more promising than the answer he had just given Shultz. Yet McFarlane realized that this was no way to run foreign policy, and the more he thought about that, the more he felt the pressure building up inside him. For by the end of 1984, he was moving toward the reluctant conclusion that if the President continued to refuse to break the logjam and set a decisive course of action in foreign affairs, then he, McFarlane, would have to seize the initiative himself.

Bud McFarlane was a complex man whose crisp, buttoned-down manner concealed a tangle of anxieties and contradictions. He gave to the post of national security adviser a Marine's devotion to duty and a strong sense of mission that reflected a mixture of old-fashioned patriotism and personal ambition. Yet there were times when he was plagued by feelings of insecurity, fears that the job he had inherited was too great a challenge. That was how he felt on his bad days. On his good days, McFarlane's mood swung to the other extreme and he entertained visions of crafting diplomatic achievements so impressive that they would leave as firm an imprint as Henry Kissinger's initiatives had when he was national security adviser in the early 1970s. The Kissinger model was altogether apt, for the adroit and self-assured professor had been one of McFarlane's early mentors.

The son of a Texas congressman, a New Deal Democrat, McFarlane was eight months old when his mother died, and that brought him even more under the influence of his domineering father, from whom he inherited his commitment to government service. The other strong presence in his early life was the family's Calvinist housekeeper, and her values also made an enduring impact. So much so that in McFarlane's junior year at the U.S. Naval Academy, he considered forsaking a military career to study for the ministry (shades of the young Mike Deaver), but instead remained at Annapolis and obtained his commission in the Marine Corps. He served two tours of duty in Vietnam and that experience also left its mark. Like so many other young officers of his generation, he went to Vietnam in a spirit of high optimism, convinced that American ideals and military strength would prevail. Then later, when things collapsed, McFarlane succumbed to anguish and disillusion, and for years afterward he was haunted by what he once described as a "profound sense of very intolerable failure."

A White House fellowship in 1971 put him into the Nixon administration, and he eventually was drawn into Kissinger's orbit. As an obscure young military aide working in the White House basement, McFarlane was awed by the imposing presence of Kissinger, who was then at the height of his "Super K" reputation.

A more realistic mentor for him at that stage of his career was Kissinger's chief deputy, General Brent Scowcroft. Scowcroft was a military career man whose scholarly pursuits in political science and international relations gave him credentials in another dimension, and his was the example McFarlane set out to emulate. By 1975, after Kissinger had become secretary of state and Scowcroft had replaced him as national security adviser, the general had taken the Marine major into his confidence, and the two men had become quite attached. Scowcroft was impressed by McFarlane's earnest dedication, his eagerness to succeed, and his industry; even in those days, he was known as a workaholic. Other colleagues, however, were a little put off by his reticence. Although generally cordial and correct in his dealings with associates, McFarlane prided himself on his cool and unflappable manner and his ability to keep his personal feelings hidden behind a solid veil of reserve.

There was one moment in particular that captured McFarlane's tight-lipped demeanor. One of the foreign policy crises Gerald Ford had to confront during his brief tenure as President was the *Mayaguez* incident. A U.S. merchant ship, the *Mayaguez*, was seized by Cambodian patrol boats in the Gulf of Siam in May 1975. Denouncing the seizure as an "act of piracy," the Ford administration responded with military strikes, sinking three Cambodian gunboats. Faced with that show of force, the Cambodians released the *Mayaguez* and its thirty-nine crew members. But in Washington, tension had been building during the two days it took to resolve the crisis, and Ford had his top foreign policy advisers gathered around him in the Oval Office the night they received the word that the ship's crew had been freed and was unharmed. A White House photographer was also present, and he snapped a picture at the precise moment they heard the good news. The photo showed Ford, Kissinger, and Scowcroft reacting with exuberance, their faces bursting into broad smiles of relief. And there, in the midst of all that unrestrained glee, was Bud McFarlane, his jaws locked in their customary clench with just the suggestion of a smile visible at the corners of his mouth. The contrast revealed in that picture came rushing back to mind twelve years later when, under the mounting pressure of the Iran-Contra scandal, McFarlane's pent-up emotions finally snapped and he tried to commit suicide.

McFarlane's first stint at the White House came to an end

when Jimmy Carter was elected. He returned to active military duty but resigned from the Marine Corps in 1979 with the rank of lieutenant colonel and joined the staff of the Senate Armed Services Committee, where he came under the tutelage of another shrewd mentor, that committee's chairman, John Tower. Over the next two years, he continued to hone his skills as a bureaucrat, and Reagan's election presented him with another opportunity to serve in the executive branch. One of his colleagues from the days when he worked in Kissinger's domain was Alexander Haig, and when Haig was named secretary of state, he took McFarlane to the State Department. There he soon developed a close relationship with Bill Clark, who was eagerly reaching out to people like McFarlane for expertise on foreign affairs, and in 1982 when Clark was moved into the White House to replace Dick Allen as national security adviser, McFarlane went along as his top deputy. The following year, Clark sent him to Lebanon to inform Clark about the peacekeeping mission that was rapidly evolving into something more. McFarlane, in fact, was the envoy who, convinced that the Lebanese government was on the verge of being overrun by its enemies, cabled the urgent proposal that the Navy open fire on the Muslim camps. Some Middle East experts at both the State Department and the National Security Council thought McFarlane's anxiety was overheated and unjustified, and they disdainfully referred to his dire warning as the "sky-is-falling" cable. But he won the support of Shultz, who then persuaded the President to approve the action, and the fateful decision was made.

Even as U.S. forces in Lebanon were launching the attacks that provoked a terrible retaliation, the power struggles inside the White House were edging toward upheaval. The infighting was so severe that Clark felt he could no longer cope with the turmoil, and began to look for a graceful way to leave the White House. Thus, when Secretary of the Interior James Watt embarrassed himself—and the administration—one time too many, Clark hastily latched onto that post, which, as we have seen, led to the choice of McFarlane as national security adviser. So Bud McFarlane, the taciturn bureaucrat and loyal deputy, was suddenly thrust into the kind of leadership position he had coveted for years, and he promptly found himself embroiled in crises, including the one that he had helped to ignite.

* * *

In his first nine days on the job, the Marines were blown up at the airport in Beirut and U.S. forces invaded Grenada. Although the action in Grenada touched off some loud but minor criticism, McFarlane stoutly defended that operation. He viewed the invasion as a message that Communist takeovers in the Western Hemisphere would not be tolerated by the Reagan administration, and it was a message that had been delivered with a minimum of risk. In contrast, the tragedy in Lebanon revealed just how severe were the risks, and consequences, of the decision to intervene in that country's bitter civil war. In the postmortems that followed the disaster, McFarlane sided with Shultz's argument that the Marines should stay in Beirut to demonstrate that the United States would not be intimidated by terrorists. But in private, McFarlane's confidence in his own judgment had been shaken by the terrorist attack; he agonized over the killing of all those Marines and the role he had played in creating the conditions that triggered the reprisal. It was not exactly an ideal frame of mind for assuming the challenge of the job as national security adviser, and this mood of self-doubt and insecurity lasted, off and on, for several weeks. At one point, he confided to a friend: "This job is way beyond me. They should have gotten somebody better, like Kissinger."

Part of the problem was that McFarlane barely knew Reagan, and he felt this put him at a distinct disadvantage. At first, Jim Baker, in particular, encouraged him to think that. Still smarting from the power play that had prevented him from replacing Clark, Baker was determined to keep the new national security adviser under his authority. But Baker soon realized that he had no need to be concerned about that. This was the first time McFarlane had ever been in a position where he reported directly to the President, and he was awed by both the man and the office. In fact, as time went on, Baker and Mike Deaver began to worry that he wasn't being assertive *enough*. On one occasion, McFarlane went to Deaver and said the President was on the verge of giving his okay to a course of action that, in his view, was doomed to fail. Deaver, who had long been accustomed to speaking frankly to Reagan, urged McFarlane to warn the President that such a move would be a mistake. Taken aback, the former military man protested, "You can't talk to the Commander in Chief like that." Deaver replied, "Yeah, but you're not a soldier anymore. He hired you to give him the best advice."

In another effort to bolster McFarlane's relationship with the President, Deaver arranged for McFarlane and his wife, Jonda, to get together socially with the Reagans. In the more casual and relaxed atmosphere of small, private dinners at the White House, McFarlane felt more comfortable about expounding on foreign affairs and related matters. The social gatherings were a success, primarily because McFarlane made a favorable impression on the First Lady; ironically, it was his very diffidence that won her over. Mrs. Reagan decided that the courteous and unassuming McFarlane was one of the few top-level White House aides who was not trying to exploit his privileged position to build up his own reputation. She became one of his main supporters, and, as Deaver himself had discovered many years earlier in Sacramento, being in Nancy's good graces was a surefire way to win her husband's approval.

Yet even as he became more secure in his relationship with Reagan, McFarlane still had frustrations to contend with, not the least of which was being caught in the quarrels between Shultz and Weinberger. During his first few months on the job, he did his best to serve as an impartial mediator because he did not want to alienate either of the strong-willed Cabinet officers. Like Bill Clark before him, he tried to be an honest broker, but for him to be effective in that role, there had to be a President who was willing to resolve the disputes by taking decisive action himself, and it did not take McFarlane long to discover that Ronald Reagan was not that kind of President. In an effort to persuade himself that there was hope of a resolution, McFarlane eventually decided that it was a temporary problem, one that had been dictated by the political calendar. After all, his first year as national security adviser coincided with the 1984 campaign, and even a President who was less passive than Reagan might have preferred to avoid controversial foreign policy moves in the heat of an election year. So, except for urgent matters that required immediate attention, 1984 adhered to the pattern of the previous three years: major foreign policy issues were relegated to the back burner.

Once McFarlane reconciled himself to that state of paralysis, he began to look forward to the second term as the time to engineer new foreign policy initiatives. It was his hope that Reagan, with another large electoral victory behind him, would be inspired to take action in foreign affairs as forcefully as he had in economic issues in the early months of his first term. McFarlane, of course, had no way of knowing that the legislative triumphs of Reagan's first year in office had been hammered together by Jim Baker and his deputies, and that the President had done little more than give his sanction to the goals and strategy that his staff had conceived for him.

A few days after the election, McFarlane presented Reagan with an elaborate list of major foreign policy objectives that could be pursued in the second term. The options were ambitious in scope, ranging from summit meetings with the Soviets, to the creation of a common market in Asia. He felt that a breakthrough in any one of those areas would be an impressive diplomatic achievement, but the key question was which one should be given top priority. What McFarlane wanted from the President was a firm choice, a clear sense of direction. But, to his dismay, he found that Reagan was still unfocused. After looking over the list, the President suggested: "Let's do them all!" It was a response that made about as much sense as ordering every entrée on the menu at a four-star restaurant. McFarlane was disheartened, and his spirits sank even lower a few weeks later when he sat in on the Shultz-Reagan meeting at which the secretary of state all but demanded that the President make a choice: get rid of him or Weinberger. Reagan's lame response to that ultimatum only reinforced McFarlane's growing belief that the President had no intention of asserting his leadership in foreign policy. Thus, as 1984 drew to a close, he faced a daunting realization: If the stalemate in foreign policy were ever going to be broken, then he, Bud McFarlane, would have to break it himself.

This was an extraordinary decision for a man who, just a year earlier, had been so stricken with self-doubt that he seriously questioned whether he were equipped to handle the job of national security adviser. But a year in the post had recharged his confidence, and McFarlane was further emboldened by the changes in key personnel that were taking place inside the White House. Baker was moving on to the Treasury Department, Ed Meese's nomination as attorney general was finally on the verge of being confirmed by the Senate, and Deaver was scheduled to leave in the spring to put his influence to work as a Washington lobbyist. One side effect of Meese's departure was that it enabled McFarlane to obtain a highly coveted perquisite. Back in the days following the 1980 election, when Baker put together his adroit memo for Meese, one of the frills bestowed on the Californian was the corner office that had acquired a sublime cachet because it once had been occupied by Henry Kissinger. Now that Meese was leaving, that office was given to McFarlane, yet another indication that he was rapidly moving up in status. In short, the breakup of the troika was creating a power vacuum in the White House, and McFarlane had convinced himself that he was the man to fill it.

In reviewing the list of options he had prepared for Reagan, McFarlane decided that the number-one priority in foreign policy should be arms control negotiations, eventually leading to a U.S.-Soviet summit meeting, and on that issue, he came down on the side of George Shultz. In his dealings with the two Cabinet officers, McFarlane began to veer away from his cautious stance of impartiality, and he also became more direct and forceful in his private talks with the President. Reagan seemed to welcome his more assertive approach, and gradually, through the early months of 1985, the President who once had denounced the Soviet Union as an "evil empire" was moved closer and closer to Shultz's more flexible position. It was a delicate process, but it was given an immense boost in March when the death of another Soviet premier, the third in fewer than three years, put Mikhail Gorbachev into power. Gorbachev quickly demonstrated that he was a new type of Russian leader, and from his side of the cold war, he, too, began to push vigorously for improved relations between the two nations. All of a sudden, the long-rejected spirit of détente was once again in vogue in both Moscow and Washington.

By the spring of 1985, there were signs of definite progress: the arms control talks had resumed in Geneva and plans were being formulated for a Reagan-Gorbachev summit in the fall. So, at least on that one vital issue, there had been a break in the stalemate, and McFarlane's patient prodding had had a large part in precipitating it. There were, to be sure, other influential voices that came into play. In his last few months in the White House, Deaver solidly supported the Shultz-McFarlane line, and—lending even more weight to the argument—Nancy Reagan began to urge her husband to adopt a more conciliatory attitude toward the Soviets. They were further aided in their efforts by the fact that two of Weinberger's hard-line allies were no longer around to take part in the debate. Clark had been out of power ever since he left the White House, and having recently resigned his post at Interior, he was now back in California. Jeane Kirkpatrick also was gone. When she was thwarted in her attempt to replace Clark as national security adviser, it was a clear signal that her influence was waning, and in December 1984, she resigned her post as ambassador to the UN. But all these factors notwithstanding, it was McFarlane who played a decisive role. In the official day-to-day briefings, he was the man in the pivotal position, and he deserves much of the credit for steering the foreign policy of the Reagan administration in a promising new direction.

McFarlane was exercising his authority in other ways as well. He had begun to make himself more accessible to the press, and by spring 1985, he was emerging as the administration's chief spokesman on foreign policy and national security issues. Nor was he content merely to upstage Shultz and Weinberger; on some occasions, he even had the audacity to criticize or present his revision of positions held by one Cabinet officer or the other. And in taking those steps, he clearly implied that he had Reagan's personal approval. It was also around this time that directives from the White House began to appear with the startling signature "FOR THE PRESIDENT: Robert C. McFarlane." Such a presumption was not without precedent; there were times when Bill Clark had signed documents in a similar way. But that symbolic gesture revealed how confident McFarlane had become in the exercise of authority. "Power," as Kissinger once observed, "is the greatest aphrodisiac," and now that he had Reagan's first summit meeting firmly on track, McFarlane was eager to take on new challenges. There were other fields needing his initiatives, which he could implement into action simply by signing his name—FOR THE PRESIDENT.

12

Comrades in Arms Sales

"That was the President's own idea!"
—White House advance man

As a man who had spent so much of his life viewing the world optimistically, Ronald Reagan seldom allowed himself to be drawn into somber moods of introspection. There was little room in his genial nature for the dark tones of angst or what Herman Melville described as a "damp, drizzly November in my soul." Yet on occasion even Reagan found it difficult to maintain his cheerful outlook, and one of those times was the spring and early summer of 1985 when he lapsed into stretches of melancholy brooding over the plight of the seven American citizens who were being held hostage by Muslim terrorists in Lebanon. Outside pressures helped to nudge the President into such an atypical state of mind. This was the period when relatives of the hostages were taking their grievances to the media, and there was rising criticism of the Reagan administration's failure to resolve the ordeal, through negotiation or some kind of military action. At one point, Reagan himself met with the families of the captives, but that only served to deepen his own emotional involvement in the issue. Though

---

less dramatic, the situation was becoming hauntingly similar to the dilemma Jimmy Carter faced during his last year in office when he struggled to cope with the hostage crisis in Iran.

In his public posture, Reagan still adhered to the hard-line rhetoric he had been affirming since he moved into the White House: under no circumstances, he asserted, would the United States yield to terrorist demands. But in his meetings with Mc-Farlane and other foreign policy advisers, he gave vent to his growing frustration and anguish, almost pleading, on occasion, that something had to be done to help those "poor people." Aides were struck by Reagan's urgent tone of compassion, which was such a contrast to his customary mien of passive amiability. McFarlane, in particular, was moved by the President's concern, and more than that, because he now was convinced that he had been delegated the role of leadership in shaping foreign policy, he felt it was up to him to work out a solution.

But how? The years of violence in Beirut had reduced that once-elegant city to a ravaged and chaotic battle zone, where the Muslim terrorists operated deep within their underground network, and intelligence efforts had failed to locate where the hostages were being held. A military attempt to rescue them had little or no chance of success. As for obtaining their freedom through peaceful means, their captors had made impossible demands (such as the release of Iranian terrorists from a prison in Kuwait), and even to consider acceding to them would be a clear violation of Reagan's policy. By the early summer of 1985, McFarlane shared the President's yearning for an end to the hostage ordeal, and it was then that he endorsed a proposal that, in time, would draw him and the administration he served into a major scandal.

On the afternoon of July 3, a delegation of visitors from Israel met secretly with McFarlane in his office at the White House. The leader of the group was David Kimche, a specialist in espionage and other covert operations who had risen to a high-level post in Israel's foreign ministry. McFarlane, of course, was well aware that when it came to combating terrorism in the Middle East, no country had a more impressive record than Israel, and he listened attentively when Kimche told him he had a daring plan to get the American hostages released. The plan, he confided, had been brought to the Israeli government by an Iranian named Manucher Ghorbanifar.

Ghorbanifar was a devious character who was well known in

the clandestine world of international arms merchants. Describing himself as an Iranian patriot, he claimed to represent moderates burrowed within the despotic regime of Ruhollah Khomeini, who were deeply concerned about their country's future after the eighty-five-year-old ayatollah died. The time would soon come, they knew, when Iran would have to deal with the world's hostile reaction to the excesses that had been committed in the name of Khomeini's Islamic revolution, and toward that end, they were seeking to establish discreet contacts with the ayatollah's number-one enemy, the United States. To demonstrate their goodwill, Ghorbanifar's friends in Tehran were prepared to exert their influence on their fellow Shiite Muslims in Beirut to secure the release of the American hostages. All they wanted in return, as a corresponding gesture of goodwill, were a few hundred U.S. anti-tank missiles to help them in their protracted war with Iraq.

Ghorbanifar seemed to have the credentials to back up his dramatic offer. Because of his close association with the shah's regime, Ghorbanifar had been obliged to leave Iran shortly after Khomeini came to power. But in the years since then, he had won the trust of some high-ranking officials in the revolutionary government by serving as their political and commercial agent in the outside world. His chief value to them was as a procurer of arms; through his contacts in the international arms market, he was able to buy sorely needed weapons for Khomeini's army. Ghorbanifar was a shrewd merchant, and although he lived in Europe and adopted the mannerisms of the West, his methods were rooted in the tradition of the Persian bazaar. "People betray me, I betray them," he later told an American reporter. "People are honest with me, I give them everything. If not, I cut their throat."

By 1985, Iran's need for sophisticated weapons had become so acute that the Khomeini government authorized Ghorbanifar to use his influence to purchase arms from the Great Satan itself. At first, he tried to make direct overtures to Washington, but he soon discovered there was no way he could penetrate the resistance created by the Reagan administration's strong antipathy to the Khomeini regime. What he needed was an effective broker, a reliable go-between, and through his contacts, he established communication with officials of the Israeli government, who, at first, were unresponsive. But their attitude changed once they verified Ghorbanifar's claim that his signature, along with those of three ayatollahs, was on a $100 million Swiss bank account.

After working out a preliminary deal to sell Israeli mortar shells to Iran, Ghorbanifar moved on to his primary mission: to purchase U.S. antitank missiles that Israel had in its possession. In presenting his offer, he adroitly played his two gambits: hostage release and the presence of pragmatic moderates in the Khomeini government. That was the plan David Kimche and his compatriots presented to McFarlane's office in the Reagan White House.

Unlike the Reagan administration's eventual decision to sell arms to the Ayatollah Khomeini—which *was* an aberration—Israel's willingness to ship weapons to Iran was not a deviation from its fundamental policy. For unlike the United States, which had sided with Iraq in the Persian Gulf war, the Israelis viewed the Khomeini regime as the lesser of two threats. Although the Iranians were Muslims, they were not Arabs, and Israel had a history, dating back to the early days of the shah's reign, of courting Iran as a potential ally against its Arab enemies; or, failing that, at least a neutral country with which it could do business. The Islamic revolution threatened that arrangement, for Israel soon became a target of Khomeini's demonic wrath. Even so, Israeli arms dealers were able to keep in touch with their contacts in Tehran, and when Iraq invaded Iran in 1980, they quietly began selling their own weapons to Iran as well as airplane parts they had procured from the United States. Their motive was not strictly political. The Israelis felt they had to sell arms to help keep their own shaky economy afloat, and in making deals with a shifty man like Ghorbanifar, they were under no illusion that he was a person of high principle and character. "Sure he is a liar," an Israeli arms salesman later told *The Washington Post*, "but what do you expect to find in this business? Sons of rabbis?"

Israel's transactions with Iran were a source of great irritation in Washington. Back in November 1979, when the fifty-two Americans were seized at the U.S. Embassy in Tehran, one of Jimmy Carter's first reactions was to impose an embargo on arms shipments to Iran, and it remained in effect during the early Reagan years, long after those hostages had been released. One of the main reasons Reagan won the election in 1980 was that his strong campaign rhetoric gave him the reputation of being tougher on Khomeini than Carter had been, and throughout his first term at least, he worked at maintaining that image. For their part, the Israelis knew that their arms deals with Tehran ran counter to the Reagan administration's objectives, but they believed they had as much right to sell weapons to Khomeini's government as the United States did to sell AWACS to one of *their* enemies, Saudi Arabia. But eventually pressure from Washington induced Israel to modify its position and tactics. In December 1983, Secretary of State Shultz announced the formation of "Operation Staunch," a policy admonishing all U.S. allies to stop selling American arms to Iran. That was followed, one month later, by a U.S. government directive officially citing the Khomeini regime as a sponsor of international terrorism. The Israelis understood and they stopped transferring U.S. military parts to Iran but still retained the option to sell their own arms.

Bud McFarlane, of course, was aware of all this on the afternoon of July 3 when the visiting Israelis told him what they had in mind. He also knew that in a few days, Reagan would be delivering a harsh speech before the American Bar Association in which, once again, he would denounce Iran and other "outlaw states." As it turned out, that speech was the most bellicose indictment of terrorism Ronald Reagan ever made during his presidency. "Let me make it plain to the assassins in Beirut and their accomplices that America will never make concessions to terrorists," he told the assembled lawyers on July 8, 1985. Then, citing Iran and Libya, among others, Reagan said: "The American people are not going to tolerate . . . these acts from outlaw states run by the strangest collection of misfits, Looney Tunes, and squalid criminals since the advent of the Third Reich."

It was within this official climate of public vituperation that McFarlane sat in his office at the White House and listened to a proposal that called precisely for "concessions to terrorists" in the form of selling U.S. arms to the Khomeini government in Tehran. So why, then, did he respond favorably to the plan?

The hostages provided the emotional bait, the visceral motive, but what McFarlane found more engrossing was the prospect of building a relationship with those moderates who were said to be operating within the Khomeini government in Tehran. That challenge fed directly into his personal ambition to achieve a diplomatic triumph of Kissingerian stature and significance. As an obscure military aide on the staff of the National Security Council, McFarlane had watched the initiative into China that transformed Henry Kissinger into a hero. Now, fourteen years later, he saw an opportunity to achieve a similar coup with Iran and thereby become a hero, too: the Super K of the Reagan era. Never mind that in his covert negotiations, Kissinger had moved through reliable diplomatic channels that put him in direct contact with the head of the Chinese government. And never mind that in his negotiations with Chou En-lai, the geopolitical stakes—a major shift in the cold war balance of power—were high enough to justify the risk. McFarlane overlooked those critical differences; in his enthusiasm to make the gamble, he did not give sufficient consideration to the pitfalls and contradictions inherent in the proposal.

A couple of days after his talk with the Israelis, he met privately with Reagan and mentioned the plan, including the condition that would so clearly violate the administration's policy: the sale of U.S. arms to Iran. Yet, according to McFarlane, the President was so excited by the quid pro quo, the release of the hostages, that his initial response was positive, even enthusiastic. But before McFarlane had a chance to pursue the matter any further, he and other members of the White House staff had to focus their attention on a more personal presidential problem.

That was the summer Reagan underwent surgery to remove a malignant growth from his intestines, and he spent much of July convalescing from that operation. The cancer diagnosis and treatment brought out Reagan's tendency to put a happy face on unpleasant realities. The man who liked to imply that he had never really been divorced because the end of his marriage to Jane Wyman had not been his idea now asserted, in the aftermath of his surgery, that he had not been afflicted with cancer, as such. "I didn't have cancer," he told reporter Lou Cannon. "I had something inside of me that had cancer in it and it was removed." That was a rather novel approach to medical science, and when the President's comment appeared in *The Washington Post*, it provoked more derision and was added to the ever-growing list of Reagan gaffes. In a more serious vein, one explanation for the fiasco that followed was that Reagan's escapist mentality enabled him to embrace the notion that swapping arms for hostages was not a betrayal of his avowed policy to "never make concessions to terrorists."

As Reagan was recuperating from the malignancy that was not really cancer, McFarlane conferred with him in his hospital room, and one of the subjects he called to the President's attention was the proposed arms sale. Once again, Reagan's instinctive reaction was positive; cheered by the prospect of getting the hostages out of Lebanon, he approved the plan in principle. But according to McFarlane, he and the President were not unmindful of the political repercussions, and in anticipation of that potential problem, they worked out a modified version of the project that, they hoped, would help to conceal the U.S. role. It was decided that Reagan would not give his approval to the sale of U.S. weapons directly to Iran, but would authorize Israel to sell missiles it had obtained from the United States. When that message was passed on to the Israelis, their response was that they could not go ahead with their end of the bargain until they received explicit assurance that the President authorized the sale and agreed to replace the missiles Israel would be relinquishing.

It wasn't until after Reagan returned to work in the White House that a meeting was arranged to bring other key officials into the picture. Among those who attended that August 6 meeting were the President, McFarlane, Secretary of State Shultz, Secretary of Defense Weinberger, and Vice President George Bush, who later claimed he never took part in any meeting at which Shultz and Weinberger voiced objections to the arms sale. But the other participants insist that Bush was there, and if he was and failed to hear the protests raised by Shultz and Weinberger, then he couldn't have been listening very carefully. When the two Cabinet officers learned about the proposal, they were appalled; it was one of the few times that Shultz and Weinberger found themselves in agreement on a major question of policy. The two men were not convinced by McFarlane's argument that the deal offered a dramatic opportunity to make contact with the presumed faction of moderates in Tehran, and they were scornful of the notion that by using Israel as a go-between the Reagan administration could later disavow any direct responsibility. Instead, Shultz and Weinberger protested that no matter how McFarlane tried to camouflage it, the plan was nothing more than a transparent arms-for-hostages deal, and as such, it would undermine everything the United States was trying to accomplish in its battle against terrorism.

Reagan was noncommittal at that critical meeting, and everyone later agreed that it ended without a formal decision. Yet each of the participants was inclined to interpret the President's passivity as a subtle sign of concurrence. Both Shultz and Weinberger left convinced that they had effectively vetoed the deal. Mc-

Farlane, on the other hand, was just as convinced that Reagan had merely given the Cabinet officers a polite hearing, and that he still wanted to pursue the project. Whatever the case, McFarlane later testified that "a day or so" after the August 6 meeting, Reagan telephoned him at home and gave him unequivocal approval to tell the Israelis that he had authorized the plan. That was the decisive moment, yet the circumstances remain mysterious and confusing.

For one thing, Reagan later insisted that he could not remember when or how he had given his approval and that he had no recollection of the telephone call to McFarlane. In addition, McFarlane said that when he received the call ordering him to proceed, he assured the President that he would inform Shultz and Weinberger, and that he did, in fact, notify them, but neither Cabinet officer could remember being told of the President's decision at that time. Finally, there was no formal record of this momentous decision—not even a note about the telephone call—and that was unusual because McFarlane, as a rule, was meticulous in such matters. The Tower Commission and congressional investigators later chose to believe McFarlane's story, and in a 1988 interview with us, he reiterated it was true. But some insiders remain convinced that he took it upon himself to interpret Reagan's general inclinations and tentative comments as a license to pursue an initiative he personally favored.

As it eventually took shape, the first arms deal called for Israel to deliver five hundred U.S. antitank missiles to Iran in two shipments and, in exchange, for the American hostages to be released. But on September 14, within hours after Iran had received the second shipment, David Kimche telephoned McFarlane with some bad news: instead of getting all seven hostages out of Lebanon, Ghorbanifar's contacts in Tehran could secure the release of only one, and it was up to McFarlane to choose which one. McFarlane was shocked. Not only had the Iranians failed to live up to their promise, but now he was being asked to make the appalling decision of which one of the hostages should be freed, or, to put a darker slant on it, which six would have to remain in captivity.

Faced with that unhappy choice, he had no trouble deciding. The hostage whose fate aroused the most concern and anxiety in Washington was William Buckley, who had been the CIA station chief in Beirut. Because of the sensitive nature of his mission,

Buckley was in an especially vulnerable position, and intelligence reports indicated that he had been cruelly tortured by his Muslim captors. But when McFarlane asked for the CIA man, Ghorbanifar sent word that Buckley was "too ill" to be moved, and before McFarlane had a chance to respond to that, a report came in from Beirut that one of the hostages, a Presbyterian minister named Benjamin Weir, had been released. Someone on the other side, apparently, had taken it upon himself to decide. (Several months passed before the White House found out the grim truth about Buckley. The victim of his torturers, he had died in captivity in early June 1985. In other words, Buckley already had been dead for three months when Ghorbanifar cynically suggested that he was "too ill" to be moved.)

At the time of the first transaction with Iran, McFarlane had no way of knowing the extent of Ghorbanifar's duplicity, but he already had ample reason to distrust the arms dealer. For by then it was obvious, to put it bluntly, that Ghorbanifar had used his Israeli connections to swindle the Reagan administration. Yet incredibly, McFarlane, with Reagan's blessing, decided to overlook the fact that they had just been "taken to the cleaners," as George Shultz later put it in his testimony to Congress. In what can only be described as an implausible act of faith, they chose to regard the release of Benjamin Weir as a positive first step and proceeded, through the early fall of 1985, to negotiate a second arms sale to Iran.

Ghorbanifar's next move was to demand still more. He said the antitank weapons delivered in September were fine as far as they went, but now his "moderate" friends in Iran needed more sophisticated weaponry: antiaircraft missiles capable of shooting down the high-altitude bombers that were attacking Tehran with increasing regularity. In response, McFarlane countered with a strong condition of his own: Iran could purchase the antiaircraft missiles (again via Israel), but not one of them would be delivered until after the rest of the hostages had been freed.

Unfortunately, the negotiations for this second arms sale carried over into the early weeks of November when McFarlane was working nonstop to prepare Reagan for his first summit meeting with Mikhail Gorbachev. So instead of overseeing the transaction himself, McFarlane entrusted the assignment to one of his deputies, Oliver North, who, guided by his own zeal for success, allowed the weapons to be delivered without insisting on his boss's stipulation. Even so, this time it was the Iranians who claimed they were swindled. A furious Ghorbanifar protested that the missiles flown into Iran were an obsolete model that did not have the firepower to reach high-altitude planes. Even worse, many of them had clear Israeli markings. How could the Iranian Army be expected to go into battle with missiles bearing the Star of David? Ghorbanifar accused the Reagan administration of "cheating us" and said his friends in Tehran were "very angry." As for the hostages, the Americans could forget about them. They would continue to rot in captivity.

Thus the second arms deal was even more of a fiasco than the first one had been, and it came at a time when McFarlane was growing disheartened in other ways as well. In terms of his public reputation, he was now at the height of his prestige, for it was generally recognized that he had been instrumental in getting Reagan to the summit meeting in Geneva. And although that first summit was little more than a cosmetic success, a bland triumph of mutual public relations, the mere fact that Reagan and Gorbachev had met face-to-face was considered a positive step, and it augured well for the future. The most encouraging development was an agreement to meet again the following year, and the long-range plan called for a Reagan visit to Moscow in 1987.

But even as he accepted congratulations for all he had done to prod Reagan toward the summit, McFarlane was privately discouraged by the lack of substantive progress in Geneva. He had hoped for something more than window dressing, some kind of opening that could lead, in time, to a concrete agreement on arms control, and toward that end, he had worked to deepen the President's understanding of that complex issue. But he was up against Reagan's chronic resistance to details, and the inattentive President simply was not prepared to discuss the problems on Gorbachev's level of sophistication. At one point during the talks in Geneva, Press Spokesman Larry Speakes became so concerned over the way Gorbachev seemed to be dominating the event that he decided to manufacture two quotes and claim they were comments Reagan had made to the Soviet leader: "There is much that divides us, but I believe that the world breathes easier because we are talking together. Our differences are serious, but so is our commitment to improving understanding." In pretending to the press that the words were Reagan's, Speakes clearly erred, but given his choice of phraseology, he could not be accused of putting dramatic words into the President's mouth.

On the other hand, Reagan did excel in the one area where he had so often excelled: image building. For instance, he made a point of not wearing an overcoat at his first outdoor meeting with Gorbachev, thereby projecting a ruddy and robust contrast to his Soviet counterpart, who, more sensibly, was dressed to ward off the chill November air. One of the White House advance men was so dazzled by that trivial bit of one-upmanship that nearly two years later he still had trouble containing his enthusiasm. "That was the President's own idea!" he gushed in an interview with reporters Jane Mayer and Doyle McManus. But McFarlane had hoped to have something more to celebrate. Of course, the day would come when Reagan and Gorbachev would indeed sign a history-making treaty at a summit meeting, but by then, Mc-Farlane, disgraced, would be out of government.

The public perception of McFarlane would have been much different if the press had known about his covert dealings with Iran, and when he returned to Washington in late November he had to confront the blunder of the second arms sale. The combination of disappointment in Geneva and failure in Iran had worn him down and made him more vulnerable than ever to the attacks being leveled against him by a formidable adversary within the White House. Throughout most of 1985, even as he strengthened his position as the main planner of Reagan's foreign policy, McFarlane had been engaged in an on-again, off-again battle with the new White House chief of staff, Donald Regan. In the early stages of that struggle for territory and power, he had been able to call on enough resources to stalemate the aggressive Regan. But now, as the year was drawing to a close, McFarlane was conceding to friends that he was on the verge of surrender.

During his first year as national security adviser, McFarlane was inclined to be deferential in his dealings with Jim Baker and other members of the White House troika. But by early 1985, after he had been on the job for more than a year, McFarlane had a much stronger view of himself and his place in the White House hierarchy. By then, he had won Reagan's trust and was becoming more assertive in his efforts to influence the President's judgments and decisions, and his success in those efforts inspired a corresponding rise in self-esteem. In addition, now that Baker and the other top-echelon veterans of the first term were leaving the White House, McFarlane could claim the edge in seniority over other high-ranking members of the staff. In short, Bud McFarlane saw no reason why he should not have the right to run his domain without any interference from others, including the man who was coming in to replace Baker as chief of staff.

Don Regan did not entirely disagree with that. The swift moves he had made to overhaul the command structure and consolidate his own power base were largely directed at the staffs he inherited from Baker and Meese; and he replaced numerous deputies with people he knew would be loyal to him. He made no attempt, however, to extend his direct control over the National Security Council. Regan was the first to admit he had no solid background in foreign policy, and, quite frankly, he did not want to get entangled in that snarl of complex and perilous issues. Nor did he have any desire to become embroiled in the long-running feud between Shultz and Weinberger. Regan was more than content to let McFarlane cope with those problems, while he concentrated on managing the operation and charting the legislative goals in economic and domestic affairs. In fact, as a gesture of his good faith, the new chief of staff passed the word that except for him, McFarlane was the only member of the staff who would be allowed unlimited access to the President.

But Regan's willingness to grant McFarlane a certain amount of latitude and autonomy did not indicate that he looked upon the national security adviser as his equal in rank, much less his superior. To Regan, the determining factor was not seniority but title and position, and he was the chief of staff. Because he viewed that post as the equivalent of a CEO in a large corporation, it meant that he outranked everyone else in the administration except the chairman of the board, Ronald Reagan. He expected McFarlane to acknowledge and respect his superior position, and when McFarlane failed to do so, Regan began to regard him as an unreliable subordinate.

The two men rarely quarreled over policy matters. That part of it did not concern Regan nearly as much as the *perception* of power, the perks and priorities he felt were his due. He had an almost visceral craving for being recognized as the man in charge. He instructed McFarlane to keep him informed of all developments in foreign affairs, but McFarlane was less than dutiful in that regard. Nothing infuriated Regan more than McFarlane's neglecting to tell him that he had called the President in the middle of the night with news of an international incident. He didn't appreciate meeting with Reagan the next morning and being asked his opinion about some blowup in the Middle East or Asia that he didn't even know had occurred. Don Regan did not like to be caught unprepared, especially in his conversations with the President. On one occasion, not long after Regan had taken over as chief of staff, Reagan himself inadvertently fueled the growing tension when, in Regan's presence, he told a group of reporters: "When I hear the phone ring in those early morning hours, I know that all I have to do is pick it up and say, 'Hi Bud,' and there he is on the other end." It was a casual remark, a bit of harmless banter, but Regan didn't take it that way. The last thing he wanted was for the press to form the impression that the one man who was so close to the President that he talked to him day and night was someone other than Donald Regan.

By the spring of 1985, Regan had begun to retaliate. In a variety of ways, he set out to show McFarlane who was boss. In his own briefings with reporters, Regan would sometimes make spontaneous comments on foreign policy, as if to demonstrate that as the chief spokesman for the administration, his authority extended into that sphere. (On more than one occasion, his observations were so mistaken that either McFarlane or Shultz hastily gave a counterbriefing to set the record straight.) Regan also made it clear that when it came to dealing with Congress, he was the one who determined strategy. One day, when McFarlane was preparing to go up to Capitol Hill to lobby for money to build more MX nuclear missiles, the chief of staff interceded. "I'll go," he told McFarlane. "They don't want to hear from you."

McFarlane's initial reaction to these power plays was to try to take them in stride. If Regan had made a serious effort to undermine the arguments McFarlane and Shultz were making on behalf of arms control, or had tried to impose his views on other questions of foreign policy, that would have been worrisome. But what seemed to matter most to the chief of staff was form, not substance. He merely wished to be perceived as the dominating presence, without having any real say in the formation of policy. As long as that was all the man wanted, McFarlane did not feel threatened in any tangible way. Regan's demands were a nuisance, a constant source of irritation, but if it was only a question of ego, McFarlane felt he could contend with that. Such was his early assessment of Regan's manner, but by the summer of 1985, McFarlane realized that the problem was more serious than he had thought.

One sign of trouble was evidence that Reagan was starting to get information on sensitive foreign policy matters that did not move through proper channels—that is, McFarlane's office. He sensed that he was losing control of the flow that dictated the agenda. When he investigated, McFarlane discovered that Cap Weinberger, CIA Director William Casey, and Regan's own point man, Patrick Buchanan, were making visits to the Oval Office without McFarlane's knowledge, much less his approval. All three men were opposed to the Shultz-McFarlane position on arms control, and they were now bypassing the national security adviser in hopes of persuading the President to harden his stance against the Russians. The hard-liners would have liked to sabotage the scheduled summit meeting that Shultz and McFarlane had worked so hard to arrange. McFarlane understood that there was only one way those men could have been ushered into the Oval Office without his knowing about it, and that was with Regan's blessing. What McFarlane found so galling was that Regan's main motive in arranging the back-channel visits was not an ideological concern—that, he could have respected—but a desire to undercut his authority.

Even worse, Regan began taking steps to block McFarlane's *own* access to the President. This was especially evident during the period in July when Reagan was in the hospital recuperating from his cancer surgery. During the first four days of the convalescence, Regan barred McFarlane from the hospital room and insisted that all vital national-security information be relayed to the President through him. Even when McFarlane finally did get in to see Reagan in person, the chief of staff made a point of being on hand to monitor the visit. Hence, Regan was there when McFarlane brought up the proposed arms-for-hostages deal, but he later claimed to have only a vague memory of that conversation and could recall nothing at all about arms shipments to Iran. (This was to be Regan's customary posture during the weeks after the scandal broke. He also was present at the critical August 6 meeting; yet Regan's most enduring memory of that discussion was that McFarlane kept mispronouncing the Latin words *bona fides*. One of Regan's claims to distinction was that he was "an old Latin scholar.")

McFarlane also had to contend with a distressing personal problem that summer: the persistent rumors that he was having an extramarital affair with a member of the White House Press Corps. He kept insisting to friends that there was no truth to the gossip, and indeed, given his stern Calvinist upbringing, he was deeply offended by the innuendo. But Regan did not hesitate to pounce on McFarlane's discomfort and exploit it to his own advantage. He would allude to the rumors in the presence of staff members, and he generally did so in a ribald, boys-will-be-boys manner. He and his sycophants began referring to McFarlane as "Loverboy." Another nickname they bestowed on him was "Henry Kissinger, Junior," an insult that was not altogether off the mark, for in fact—with his lofty visions of grand achievements in foreign policy—McFarlane had become somewhat pretentious. (Yet on that particular subject, McFarlane was capable of laughing at himself. On those rare occasions when he relaxed, he would entertain friends with a deft and mischievous imitation of his idol's famous accent that Kissinger himself found hilarious.)

Regan's campaign against McFarlane brought out all his latent insecurities and pushed him toward the edge of another crisis in self-confidence. Once again, he began to brood about the strains in his relationship with Reagan, especially compared to the easygoing rapport Regan enjoyed in his dealings with the President. McFarlane recognized that Regan had definite advantages over him in that important area. At sixty-five, Regan was much closer to the President's age than the forty-eight-year-old McFarlane, and the two men also had similar cultural backgrounds: both Reagan and Regan had grown up in hardworking Irish families and had emerged from those modest origins to achieve early and solid success in their respective spheres, Hollywood and Wall Street. Moreover, Regan's brash and outgoing personality appealed to the President. The chief of staff shared Reagan's zest for anecdotes and off-color jokes. Yet even when they shared a kind of locker-room camaraderie, Regan was shrewd and calculating. "I always let him tell his joke first," he once confided to a friend.

What McFarlane resented perhaps more than anything else

was that the President seemed to have a higher opinion of Regan simply because he was a millionaire, whereas McFarlane was not a man of means. McFarlane had discovered, as others did before him, that Reagan viewed men of wealth with a respect bordering on awe. This had been true since the California years when he dutifully followed the instructions set down by the coterie of millionaires who steered him into politics. For his part, McFarlane believed that service as an officer in the Marine Corps for more than twenty years and the career in government that followed gave him credentials worthy of respect, but it was apparent that, in Reagan's mind, they did not compare to those of a Wall Street man who had made a fortune as chairman of Merrill Lynch. Regan also recognized Reagan's bias, and he was adept at exploiting that advantage.

By the fall of 1985, McFarlane had become testy and abusive in his treatment of certain deputies. That had never been his style— and some of them were worried that he was on the verge of a nervous breakdown. One telltale sign of the turmoil he was going through was that he began smoking again, reverting to a habit he had broken several years earlier. Moreover, he had to endure the spectacle of Regan's unseemly behavior in Geneva.

Regan had done little to bring about Reagan's first encounter with a Soviet leader. Yet when the time came for the President's summit meeting, Regan went around Geneva with such an air of self-importance that one would have thought the effort to revive détente had been his idea. The most bizarre moment came on the final evening when, after signing the joint communiqué, the two leaders positioned themselves on a sofa to have their picture taken together. As the photographers and cameramen prepared to record that historic occasion, other members of both the Soviet and the American teams moved discreetly into the background. All of them, that is, except Don Regan. The chief of staff leaned over from behind the sofa and struck a pose between Reagan and Gorbachev, a tableau that suggested that he had served as a vital link in the process that brought the two men together. It was a scene that captured the essence of a man whose values were focused on form and appearance. From their vantage point outside camera range, Shultz and McFarlane, the two men who *had* done so much to make that first summit a reality, observed Regan's behavior with contempt.

Then came the news that the second arms sale to Iran had

turned into a calamity. Not only were there to be no hostages released, but the Iranians were furious because they thought they had been tricked, and relations between Washington and Tehran were now even more hostile. As McFarlane struggled to assess the damage, he was stricken with guilt and foreboding. He had a vivid appreciation of what the reaction would be if the story of this fiasco ever became public.

Even before McFarlane went to Geneva, rumors had been circulating around the White House that he was planning to resign at the end of the year, and in private conversations with his aides, he confirmed that he was considering that option. Now, in light of all that had happened, he almost felt that he had no choice in the matter. Disappointment and chagrin over events in Geneva and Iran, coupled with Regan's unrelenting harassment, had exhausted him. In early December, he met with the President and submitted his resignation. Friends of McFarlane later suggested that actually he had hoped Reagan would try to talk him out of it. If so, it was yet another indication that McFarlane did not understand the man he had tried to serve with such diligence. Reagan offered a few perfunctory remarks of regret and then accepted his resignation.

Bud McFarlane had plenty of regrets of his own, and they were not perfunctory. He later characterized his resignation as a "cop-out" and berated himself for allowing Regan's bullying tactics to get the best of him. "I never should have let that son of a bitch run me off," he said. McFarlane also said that if he had stayed on as national security adviser, "I'm sure I could have stopped things from getting worse." He was referring, of course, to the arms-for-hostages deal, and perhaps he could have exerted enough influence to shut down the operation. But the evidence suggests that by the time he stepped down, it already was too late. What McFarlane himself did not realize at the time of his resignation was that the transactions in Iran were starting to have a beneficial impact on another covert and potentially illegal enterprise that, for more than a year, had been proceeding along on a separate course. Not until several months after he left the White House was McFarlane finally told that the arms deal he had done so much to foster had become inextricably linked to the effort to raise money for the rebels who opposed the Sandinista regime in Nicaragua, a group that had come to be known as the Contras.

13

North Wind

"We have to box him in so there's only
one way he can go—the right way."
—Oliver North

Acrimonious disputes between Congress and the President are as
old as the Republic itself, and during the Reagan years it was a
foreign-policy issue, Nicaragua, that plunged the two branches
into a bitter conflict. Reagan had assumed office highly critical of
the Carter administration's toleration of the Sandinistas, the Marxist revolutionaries who had overthrown the oppressive regime of
Anastasio Somoza in 1979. As far as Reagan and other conservatives were concerned, the Sandinistas were turning Nicaragua
into "a second Cuba," thereby giving the Soviet Union another
base in Latin America perilously close to the U.S. border. It did
not take the new President long to back up his apprehension with
action. Early in his first term, Reagan signed an order authorizing
the CIA to fund a small band of rebels in Nicaragua.

Encouraged by the CIA's guidance and support, the ranks of
the Contras soon swelled, and the escalating guerrilla war provoked alarm on Capitol Hill. Convinced that the CIA had em-

barked on a reckless course that would lead, in time, to overt military action—in much the same way that U.S. forces had been drawn into Vietnam two decades earlier—Democrats in Congress mounted an effort to shut down funding for the Contras. But CIA Director William J. Casey was able to persuade influential members of the two intelligence committees (which were authorized to monitor all CIA activities) that his agency's goals and tactics were limited. The objective, he said, was not to drive the Sandinistas out of power, but merely to provide the rebels with enough strength that their demands for democratic reform would be heeded by the government in Managua. Taking Casey at his word, Congress reluctantly agreed to continue financing the CIA's support of the Contras, though it clearly stipulated that the funds could not be used "for the purpose of overthrowing the Government of Nicaragua."

As time went on, however, it became apparent that the CIA undertaking was far more ambitious than Casey had acknowledged. Yet even as the little war grew in scope and intensity, there were no victories on the battlefield to justify the U.S. commitment. The Sandinistas, bolstered by a corresponding increase in Soviet arms and matériel, had no trouble keeping the Contras in check and on the defensive. In its frustration, the CIA became more aggressive in its efforts on behalf of the Contras, and in Washington the debate grew more heated. Critics continued to warn of another Vietnam, while defenders of the policy argued that a Communist foothold in Central America was a serious threat to U.S. security.

A critical point came in early 1984 when Congress discovered that the CIA had planted mines in Nicaragua's harbors, a tactical move that was nothing less than an act of war. Now even Casey's supporters realized the extent to which he had lied to them, and they reacted with anger and dismay. ("I am pissed off!" the venerable Barry Goldwater fumed in a personal letter to Casey.) The mining disclosure gave the Democrats all the ammunition they needed to pass an amendment cutting off U.S. funds for the Contras. The architect of that resolution was Representative Edward P. Boland of Massachusetts, the chairman of the House Intelligence Committee, and the measure became known as the Boland Amendment. Even before it was passed, House Speaker Tip O'Neill triumphantly proclaimed that the Contra war was "dead," but in doing so he underestimated the will and cunning of the CIA director. For Bill Casey was a man on a mission, and he was not about to be deterred by a mere law passed by Congress.

Casey had been a member of Reagan's inner circle since February 1980, when, on the eve of the New Hampshire primary, he was hastily summoned to replace John Sears as campaign manager. But his role, in the months that followed, was largely ceremonial; the overall strategy had been carefully charted by Sears, and after the win over Bush in New Hampshire, all that really had to be done was ride the momentum through the rest of the primaries and on to victory in November. But even though he was little more than the titular head of the 1980 campaign, Casey expected to be rewarded with a high-level post in the Reagan administration, and the job he wanted was secretary of state. He was therefore not happy when that appointment went to Alexander Haig, a man he regarded as his intellectual inferior, and one whom he also distrusted on ideological grounds, primarily because of Haig's close association with Henry Kissinger and détente. But Ed Meese persuaded Casey to accept the CIA post as a sort of consolation prize, in much the same way that Cap Weinberger was talked into taking Defense after he, too, had been passed over for State.

CIA was the more logical slot for Casey, whose early background had been in intelligence. As a young man in World War II, he had been a top agent in the OSS, the forerunner of the CIA, and that experience shaped him. In the years since, Casey had become rich as a tax lawyer, had dabbled some in politics, and had served in the State Department and as chairman of the Securities and Exchange Commission during the Nixon administration. But his great passion remained the exploits he had directed and participated in during the war, especially those that related to espionage and other covert missions. Shortly after Casey's appointment as CIA director, a reporter asked him what he considered to be his most impressive achievement in a long and successful career. "Getting out alive," Casey replied with a chuckle. "After you've been shot down . . . I'd say the thrill is to still be here."

It was no idle boast, and his colleagues at the agency knew it. "Bill Casey was the last great buccaneer from OSS," said his deputy director for operations, Clair George. "He was dropping agents into Germany and France and saving lives when most of us were doing nothing." Now, as the first director of the CIA with cabinet rank, Casey was determined to use his power to revive that swashbuckling spirit in an agency that had been saddled with restraints since the mid-1970s, when Congress, in response to excesses that had been committed by the CIA over the years, imposed its watchdog authority over all intelligence activities. From Casey's point of view, the quarrel with Congress over CIA support of the Contras was merely the first test in a long-range battle "to restore the earlier, good days," and it was a battle he was resolved to win.

Casey's basic attitude toward the congressional watchdogs was contemptuous. He did not believe they understood the importance of clandestine operations and, therefore, could not be trusted to keep them secret. In private conversations with his deputies, he would refer to his adversaries as "those assholes on the Hill." Thus, Casey viewed the Boland Amendment as a challenge to his guile and resourcefulness, and he soon found a way to circumvent the new law.

Ed Boland and his allies in Congress distrusted Casey as much as he did them, and they were determined to make the wording of the amendment airtight; they were sure that if they left any loopholes, Casey would not hesitate to exploit them. Accordingly, the measure forbade the CIA or "any other agency or entity involved in intelligence activities" to spend money to aid the Contras, "directly or indirectly." When the law was drafted, Boland declared that it "clearly ends United States support for the war in Nicaragua. There are no exceptions to the prohibition." But Bill Casey discovered his loophole. In his interpretation of the amendment, it did not extend to the White House, and therefore Bud McFarlane and his cadre on the National Security Council could be pressed into duty on behalf of the Contras. Casey and McFarlane also agreed that the law did not prevent the Reagan administration from reaching out to other sources—that is, foreign governments—to obtain money for the rebels. That ploy came up for discussion at a White House meeting of top foreign policy officials in June 1984, and once again it was George Shultz who cut to the heart of the issue.

"You can't do indirectly what you can't do directly," Shultz averred, and he went on to warn that if the President were to become involved in a scheme to solicit money from other countries for that purpose, it could be "an impeachable offense." Those words should have had a disquieting effect on Casey, McFarlane, and especially Reagan, for all three men were aware—as Shultz was not—that such an overture already had been made, and that Saudi Arabia had agreed to fund the Contras. A few weeks earlier, McFarlane, at Casey's behest and with Reagan's blessing, had made the request in a secret meeting with the Saudi ambassador to Washington. He said Congress was on the verge of stopping U.S. support for the Contras, and that they needed at least $1 million a month to keep their war going. The request was relayed to King Fahd in Riyadh, and within a few days, word came back that he would provide the monthly stipend. For the oil-rich Saudis, that was a relatively painless way to win the gratitude of the Reagan administration, especially at a time when Fahd's government was in the middle of negotiations to purchase Stinger antiaircraft missiles from the United States.

Thus, by the time of the June meeting, the President already had approved a deal that, in Shultz's blunt phrase, could be construed as "an impeachable offense." McFarlane and the others left that discussion with a clear understanding that the secretary of state was not going to be an ally on this issue; and to prevent the unpleasantness of internal bickering over legalities, it was agreed that Shultz and others in the State Department should not be told about the agreement with the Saudis. Nor, in the months that followed, would they be informed of similar transactions that were even more dubious on legal grounds.

But raising money for the cause was just part of the solution. Now that the CIA was being forced to abandon its active role, someone other than Casey or one of his deputies at the agency would have to take over the operational burden of working directly with the Contras. Peering through the loophole he saw in the Boland Amendment, Casey's gaze came to rest on the White House. The new chief would have to come from there, from within McFarlane's domain, and when Casey took that request to the national security adviser, McFarlane had no trouble deciding who should be given the assignment. The man he picked to step in and run the Contra operation was a dedicated and hardworking young Marine officer on his staff named Oliver North.

North had been a member of the NSC staff since the early days of the Reagan administration, but his efforts to assert himself did not succeed until the fall of 1983, when McFarlane took over as national security adviser and, in his first few days on the job, had to resolve a major crisis: the upheaval in Grenada. That was North's territory. He had become, by then, a minor specialist in military strategy for Central America and its environs, and he worked closely with McFarlane in planning the invasion of Grenada, an exercise North later characterized, with customary flourish, as the only instance in history when democracy had triumphed over a Marxist regime. Whatever it was, the invasion was a success, and McFarlane appreciated the help he received from North.

Aware of that, North quickly set out to build on that advantage. He seized the opportunity to latch onto McFarlane as his personal patron. As a rule, middle-level aides such as North rarely dealt directly with the national security adviser; this was especially true of McFarlane, whose detached and reticent manner did not make him an easy man to approach. But that didn't stop North, who even exploited a quirky family connection to gain access. His secretary, Fawn Hall (who was destined to achieve a small slice of notoriety of her own because of her association with North), was the daughter of McFarlane's secretary, and through that link it was easy to find out when it was convenient to make an impromptu visit to McFarlane's office to seek his advice on some matter or other.

For his part, McFarlane encouraged North to look upon him as his mentor. He developed a strong sense of kinship toward the eager deputy, six years his junior. They were both, after all, graduates of Annapolis who had chosen to serve in the Marine Corps, and beyond that, they shared the bond of combat in Vietnam. Like McFarlane, North had fought with valor in that war and, like McFarlane, he was anguished and embittered by the eventual outcome. He fervently believed that the U.S. military and its allies on the battlefield were betrayed by political cowardice in Washington. "We didn't lose the war in Vietnam," he later declared in his testimony before Congress. "We lost the war right here in this city!"

That kind of rhetorical passion was not McFarlane's style, but opposites attract, and he admired North's brash self-assurance and exuberant personality. Later, in looking back on their working relationship, McFarlane conceded that North was "a romanticist" who sent him memos that, at times, were "rather lurid." But he quickly added: "I don't fault him for it. . . . I don't fault him for being an imaginative, aggressive, committed young officer." McFarlane's view of his protégé's impetuous manner might have been less indulgent if he had known that back in 1974 North had been hospitalized for "delayed battle stress" after a superior officer discovered him running around naked, screaming incoherently and brandishing a pistol. But that incident from his past was not known until much later, long after Oliver North had been exposed as a central figure in the Iran-Contra scandal.

McFarlane also might have been more wary of North if he had paid more attention to what other members of the NSC staff thought of the "romanticist." If they had talked with him, Mc-Farlane would have discovered that some of North's peers regarded him as a hustler who had a habit of bending the truth to enhance his own reputation. There was, for example, his version of the Grenada invasion. The way North told it, he had initiated the decision to send in the troops and had orchestrated the operation from beginning to end. He liked to boast that he was the one who actually got Reagan's signature on the order to invade; that was true, but he usually neglected to point out that he was a messenger who had been dispatched to the Oval Office by Mc-Farlane.

"Ollie was about 30 to 50 percent bullshit," one of his colleagues was later quoted as saying. "He was notorious for constantly exaggerating his role in things. He was always 'coming from a meeting with the vice president.' We checked once, and he hadn't been in to see the vice president at all." North also exaggerated his personal relationship with the President. When he appeared before pro-Reagan citizen groups, as part of his campaign to raise money for the Contras, North told them that he frequently met alone with the President. Later, when that assertion was aired by the media (some television reports even broadcast tapes of North making that claim), the White House issued a statement that although North had been present at various meetings with the President, he and Reagan had never met alone. But it certainly wasn't for lack of trying. North was never more zealous than in his efforts to get Reagan's attention and impress him with his proposals on how to defeat communism in Central America and elsewhere. When Michael Deaver was still controlling the schedule, he did everything he could to insulate the President from North's manic enthusiasm. "I used to keep Ollie out of Reagan's office because he was dangerous," Deaver recalled. "He scared me."

One colleague who should have been a natural ally of North

was Constantine Menges, who worked with North on the NSC staff. Both men were militant anti-Communists who were in fundamental agreement on Nicaragua and other key issues. Yet in his own White House memoir, *Inside the National Security Council*, Menges drew a savage portrait of North. Among many disturbing revelations, he wrote, "North once told me, complete with highlights of the conversation, about a dinner he'd had with then-ambassador Jeane Kirkpatrick. I later asked her if a certain subject had come up during that dinner. The ambassador looked blank. 'I've never had dinner with Oliver North,' she said."

Menges also recounted a story that another colleague, Jacqueline Tillman, had told him in the summer of 1984:

> A journalist friend of hers had described, in colorful detail, certain events that occurred during Secretary of State George Shultz's flight to Nicaragua in June 1984. In a casual office chat, she had related the events to Ollie. About two weeks later, Ollie told her the same stories and said that a journalist who had been on Shultz's plane had related this to him. Startled, Tillman reminded Ollie that she had originally told him this story. Yet Ollie insisted, for about twenty minutes, that this had been his rather than her experience.

As time went on, Tillman became increasingly alarmed about North's stability and character. Menges quotes her as saying: "I've concluded that not only is he a liar, but he's delusional, power-hungry, and a danger to the President and the country. He should not be working on the NSC staff."

Menges himself came to share that judgment. He recalled the time North told him, "We have to make the right things happen and make sure that the President goes the way we want." Menges protested, "We don't cause things to happen. The President is the one who decides what the government will do, and our job as his staff is to give him the facts and point out the alternatives so he can make an informed decision."

"No," North replied, "you're wrong. We have to box him in so there's only one way he can go—the right way."

Still another former colleague, Chris Lehman, offered his own assessment of North: "Ollie's like a chain saw. He can do constructive work if supervised, but let loose he can cut a tragic swath." And in the spring of 1984, when it became clear that

Congress was going to impose its restraints on the CIA, the chain saw was let loose to cut a swath through the barriers that stood in the way of direct U.S. support for the Contras. "Your mission," McFarlane told North, "is to hold the resistance together, body and soul."

North may have been chosen for that mission because he was McFarlane's favorite protégé, but he also had a legitimate claim to the assignment. Central America was his field of expertise, and for the past year or so, he had been the NSC's liaison to the CIA's operation in Nicaragua. The major difference was that now he would be serving as Bill Casey's secret surrogate, and that would bring him into the sphere of the CIA Director. Or to put it another way, he was moving into a larger orbit where he would come under the influence of a new and more powerful mentor. North was quick to recognize that he had been given another opportunity to advance his career and ambitions. So, just as he had curried favor with McFarlane, he now set out to ingratiate himself to the crusty cold warrior who presided over the CIA.

It was not difficult, for Casey soon discovered that Ollie North was his kind of man. Others might find him reckless and unstable, deceitful and power-hungry, even delusional and dangerous. But Casey, for the most part, saw only those qualities that were sure to impress him: the gung-ho Marine, the passionate anti-Communist, the bold innovator who was not afraid to take risks, and the crafty bureaucrat who had a zest for intrigue and high adventure. Those were the traits one found in a first-rate spy or undercover agent, and those were the traits Bill Casey admired in a man. In taking on North as his pupil, Casey seemed to recapture a part of his own youth when he was a daredevil with the OSS. There soon developed between them a kind of father-son relationship, not unlike the fraternal bond North previously had nurtured with McFarlane. "Bill loved Ollie very much," said one of Casey's top deputies at the agency. "He liked action people."

Nor was it merely a matter of calculation by North. The "romanticist" grew to revere the "the last great buccaneer from OSS," as he later acknowledged in testimony before Congress: "Bill Casey was, for me, a man of immense proportions . . . a philosophical mentor." Casey eventually took North into his confidence and told him that the apparatus being set up to help the Contras was merely the first step in his grand plan. Casey's long-range vision called for a broad network of covert missions to combat communism throughout the Third World, which would be funded entirely by foreign countries and other secret contributors. "It was always the intention to make this a self-sustaining operation," North later revealed in his testimony. "Director Casey said he wanted something you could pull off the shelf and use at a moment's notice." The director also implied that North, his chosen surrogate, would be at the center of all the action. This was exhilarating for the ambitious young Marine officer, and he was, as always, eager to demonstrate that he was worthy of the challenge.

Casey's patronage enabled North to embark on the frenetic crusade that would define his existence for more than two years, until the autumn of 1986, when the scandal broke and he was summarily fired. As was later said, not altogether in jest, this was the period when critical decisions were made by "the only lieutenant colonel in the U.S. military with five-star rank." Assuming personal command of the war against the Sandinista government, North advised the Contras on strategy, helped them sort out their requests for specific weapons, and furnished them with intelligence from the CIA and the Pentagon. In the words of John Poindexter, who was then McFarlane's chief deputy and would later succeed him as national security adviser, North was "the switching point that made the whole system work."

Nor were his efforts confined to overseeing the operational details, for North also took on the administrative task of raising funds for the cause. The $1 million a month from Saudi Arabia may have been enough to keep the war going, but the Contras' powerful friends in Washington soon realized that much more money would be needed to turn resistance into victory. At one point, the Saudis themselves were asked whether they could possibly be a little more generous. The response to that request was delivered at the highest level, from one head of state to another, when King Fahd visited Washington in February 1985. In a private meeting with the President—a conversation that deepened Reagan's personal involvement in the covert campaign to solicit funds from foreign governments—Fahd volunteered to donate another $24 million to the rebels in Nicaragua. North also reached out to other friendly countries. Later that year, for example, he had tea with a representative from Taiwan at the Hay-Adams Hotel and told him that Reagan "would be very grateful" if his government could see its way to make a contribution. Soon thereafter, Taiwan joined the list of secret donors. But North's boldest move came when he began encouraging wealthy American citizens who were known to be ardent supporters of Reagan to make donations to the cause. In his appeal to these groups, North would stress how much the Contras meant to the President, but would generally steer clear of the legal question that in raising money this way, the Reagan administration was defying a law passed by Congress.

North soon came to realize that running a secret war was too much for one man. So he began to recruit a team of unofficial aides and allies to help him carry out the mission. Among those was a retired Air Force major general, Richard V. Secord, whom Casey personally had recommended to North. Dick Secord was himself something of a buccaneer in the Casey tradition. Although he had flown combat missions in Vietnam and had served in high-level posts at the Pentagon, his chief distinction was in the sphere of covert operations. He had been a key figure in the CIA's secret war in Laos, and, before that, he had been in charge of the clandestine group that built the shah's air force in Iran. Like Casey, he believed that covert activities should be governed by their own rules, outside the normal process of checks and balances. Years earlier, in his master's thesis at the Naval War College, Secord had written, "The unconventional warfare instrument of national policy is so important that bureaucratic obstacles should be dismissed out of hand."

In addition to his military credentials, Secord had the right kind of business connections. Since his retirement from the Air Force in 1983, he and his partner, an Iranian exile named Albert Hakim, had been running a small equipment trading firm that specialized in selling military parts and security devices to Third World governments. Thus, in hiring Secord to help the Contras win their war, North tapped into the world of international arms merchants where Secord and Hakim had been conducting most of their business. Secord's initial assignment was simple and straightforward: to buy guns for the rebels and run the supply system into Nicaragua. But in the summer of 1985, as it became increasingly apparent that the Contras did not know how to organize their own rebellion, his role expanded to the point where he took over the supply and distribution of weapons and was also in charge of allocating the funds coming in from the Saudis and other sources. Secord became, in effect, the field marshal and chief finance officer of the enterprise that North had dubbed "Project Democracy."

The more North became immersed in that project, the more he began to shift his personal allegiance to Casey and drift away from McFarlane and his control. Some of this was nothing more than cynical careerism, the upscale gravitation toward a more powerful patron, but there was also a stronger, more compelling force at work. As early as the autumn of 1984, North and Casey began to suspect that McFarlane was losing his enthusiasm for the secret mission to help the Contras, and there was some truth to that assessment. McFarlane still believed in the overall purpose of the cause—to put unrelenting pressure on the Sandinista government—but the man whose introspective nature often led him into moods of agonizing reappraisal now began to question the efficacy of the U.S. effort and commitment. He was finding it difficult to ignore the mounting evidence that the Contras simply were not very good at guerrilla warfare. In a startling confession, McFarlane later told Congress, "Where I went wrong was not having the guts to stand up and tell the President that. To tell the truth, probably the reason I didn't is because if I'd done that, Bill Casey, Jeane Kirkpatrick and Cap Weinberger would have said I was some kind of commie."

By the summer of 1985, McFarlane had edged further and further away from personal involvement in the enterprise to aid the Contras; North and Secord were more or less running the mission on their own, with Casey in the background as the all-but-invisible mastermind. McFarlane, by then, was preoccupied with preparations for the forthcoming summit meeting in Geneva, and his new project, the arms-for-hostages negotiations with Iran. Although his relationship with North was not as close as it once had been, he still regarded him as one of his most trusted aides, and therefore North was among the few people told about the secret arms deal. North responded with typical ebullience; to borrow a phrase he would later employ in another context, he thought it was "a neat idea," and he couldn't wait to participate personally in the adroit scheme to score a diplomatic coup that would secure the release of the American hostages in Lebanon. Even though the problems created by the Contras' inept performance on the battlefield were taking up most of his time, North volunteered to help McFarlane on the Iran transactions in any way he could.

North, in fact, was the deputy McFarlane called on to oversee the second arms sale in November when he had to go to Geneva, and North badly bungled that assignment. Instead of insisting on McFarlane's condition that no weapons would be delivered until the rest of the hostages were freed, he allowed the missiles to be flown into Iran as a first step in the transaction; even worse, he then had to endure Ghorbanifar's angry accusations that the United States had swindled the Iranians by shipping them obsolete missiles instead of the ones they had requested. Yet that deal, a fiasco in every other respect, did produce one unexpected benefit that would have profound implications on the future course of events. As the details of the arrangement were being worked out, North persuaded one of the Israeli arms dealers, Al Schwimmer, to put up $1 million to cover *expenses,* a euphemism for potential bribes that might be necessary. That money was deposited in the Swiss bank account that Secord had opened when he assumed control of the funds that were being donated to help the rebels in Nicaragua. Yet for some reason, when the arms sale boomeranged, Schwimmer did not ask for his money back, and because relatively little of it had been spent, $850,000 still remained in Secord's special account. So he and North decided to keep it there, as an addition to the assets they were accumulating to finance Project Democracy. Secord was not known for his sense of humor, but later, in recalling that mix-up, he offered a pun: "Mr. Schwimmer," he said, "made a contra-bution."

That was the first link in the chain that would bind the one covert operation to the other and provide the hyphen in the scandal that would later be christened "the Iran-Contra affair." The timing of that initial link is of some importance, for North later claimed that it was Ghorbanifar who came up with the proposal to divert funds from the Iranian arms sales to Nicaragua, and that he, North, first heard about it when he met with Ghorbanifar in London in January 1986. But the evidence does not support that assertion. Al Schwimmer's "contra-bution" was made in November, and an Israeli official later testified, in a government document submitted to the U.S. Congress, that in early December, North told him he intended to use the profits from the next arms sale to Iran to help the Contras. Whether the "neat idea," as North called it, originated with him or Ghorbanifar or even Secord remains a point of conjecture, because all three men have declined to claim credit. But there is no doubt that the idea was formed in the minds of North and Secord in November at the time of that first "contra-bution." It also is true that North did not get around to telling his boss about the diversion plan until January, and by then his boss was no longer McFarlane, but his successor, Vice Admiral John Poindexter.

14

The March of Folly

"You've had it, pal!"
　　　　　　　　—George Shultz

McFarlane's abrupt decision to resign surprised Reagan, but it also presented him with an opportunity to exert some leadership. Since the early days of his administration, the post of national security adviser had been the source of chronic problems and instability—Poindexter would become the fourth occupant in less than five years—and in view of that, one might have thought the President would have taken more interest in making sure that this time, at last, he would be getting the right man for the job. Yet, as he had in so many other major appointments, Reagan played no active role in the decision to elevate John Poindexter to that post.

It was McFarlane who recommended Poindexter, and because none of the top officials who would be working directly with him (Regan, Shultz, Weinberger, Casey) had any strong objections, a consensus quickly formed in his favor. One man who did express serious misgivings about the appointment was Mike Deaver, who by then had left the White House and was exploiting his special relationship with Reagan to promote the public relations firm he had set up in Washington. When he learned that Poindexter was about to be named national security adviser, he telephoned the one influential person in the White House he knew would listen to him: Nancy Reagan. "It's a big mistake," he warned the First Lady. "He's a classic number-two guy. He's too weak to mediate between Defense and State." Besides, Deaver added, "you shouldn't put a military guy in that post." Mrs. Reagan told him it was too late. The President already had decided to accept McFarlane's recommendation.

Deaver's concern was justified. It wasn't so much that Poindexter was "a military guy," but rather that he was nothing more than a military guy. The only other career officer who had served as national security adviser was General Brent Scowcroft during the Ford administration, but he came to the job equipped with graduate degrees in political science and related subjects and had taught courses at West Point; in many ways, his appointment had been in the academic tradition established by Bundy, Rostow, and Kissinger. McFarlane, it's true, also had a military background, but in the years following his retirement from the Marine Corps, he had worked on Capitol Hill and at the State Department, and those experiences had helped to broaden his perspective. But Poindexter had spent his entire career in the Navy and even within that sphere, his training had been narrow and technocratic.

His forte was science and mathematics, and he had exhibited in his various assignments an engineer's gift for precision and order. He had a reputation for being the kind of officer who operated in strict accordance with the rules. Even as a youngster growing up in rural Indiana, Poindexter was a stickler for regulations. One relative later revealed that he was the kind of kid who would always wear his trunks when the other boys went skinny-dipping. He also was a model student, the type who always turned in his homework on time and scored the highest mark on every test, a habit of excellence that carried over into his years at the Naval Academy. He breezed through Annapolis with straight A's and graduated first in his class. Yet for all his formidable intelligence, there was something missing; some of Poindexter's professors felt that his skills were too abstract and technical, that he lacked the special spark of creativity that stamps a superior student as a destined leader of men. "He didn't give me the impression he would be a great man in the future," one of them later told a reporter from the *Los Angeles Times*. "He just didn't strike me as a man who was outstanding in his overall judgment or perspective."

Poindexter's rise in the Navy was steady and methodical. Although he had his share of sea duty, he mainly made his mark as a staff officer who excelled at problem-solving desk jobs; he served as an administrative assistant to three secretaries of the Navy. In 1980, at the age of forty-four, he was promoted to rear admiral, and five years later, while working as McFarlane's chief deputy in the White House, he moved up another notch to vice admiral. At the time of McFarlane's resignation, Poindexter was in line to become the next commander of the Sixth Fleet in the Mediterranean, an excellent assignment that McFarlane noted, as a possible option, in his memo to the President suggesting that the admiral be named as his successor. In approving the appointment, Reagan couldn't resist a characteristic quip. With prophetic though unconscious irony, he expressed the hope that the decision to keep Poindexter in the White House would not "hurt his future career."

The bald, pipe-smoking Poindexter may or may not have been a "classic number-two guy," but those who worked with him had no doubt that he was a classic introvert. He was so drawn to solitude that some colleagues believed he actually preferred to communicate with them via computer rather than in person. He frequently ate all three meals in his office, and when an aide asked him why he had lunch at his desk but then moved to a corner table for dinner, Poindexter explained, "Variety is the spice of life." On those occasions when he did have to meet with others in the flesh, he projected an aura of such stoic reserve that his associates could never be sure what he was really thinking behind the opaque, unblinking eyes that stared out at them through trifocals. Compared to him, the taciturn McFarlane was downright jovial and exuberant.

The combination of Poindexter's reclusive personality and narrow military background made him ill-equipped to deal with the hurly-burly aspects of the democratic process that defines governmental life in Washington. He had no gift at all for politics or public relations. He regarded Congress and the press as, at best, intrusive irritants and, at worst, menaces to national security. "Poindexter," said Larry Speakes, who had to serve as his conduit to reporters, "thought the press was unpatriotic." Time and time

again, he deliberately misled reporters, members of Congress, and
even other officials in the Reagan administration, sometimes to
the point of outright lying, and he never seemed to grasp that in
doing so, he not only damaged his own credibility but undermined
the honor and integrity of the President he served. Every now
and then, some intrepid colleagues would try to persuade him to
forsake his us-versus-them hostility toward other power centers
in Washington, but those arguments always failed. "You couldn't
explain things to Poindexter," one of them later told a reporter.
"He had an engineer's mind." Another member of the NSC staff
described Poindexter's executive style as "secretiveness applied to
all issues. He changed the NSC routine from constant meetings
to one-on-one negotiations where only he saw all the cards." He
was, in short, a very tough man to know, but one who did manage
to penetrate his impassive façade was Oliver North.

For North, McFarlane's sudden resignation was a reprieve, for if
McFarlane had stayed on as national security adviser, the zealous
Marine would probably have found himself banished from the
White House. Frictions in their once-fraternal relationship had
been building for some time, and when McFarlane discovered
that North had mishandled the second arms sale, he was furious.
In disregarding his specific instructions to withhold the shipment
of any weapons to Iran until after the hostages were released,
North had sacrificed the leverage needed to keep the Iranians
honest. That irresponsible act confirmed McFarlane's suspicion
that Ollie North had to be carefully supervised, and, in retrospect,
McFarlane realized it had been a mistake to give North such a
sensitive assignment. Following that thread of hindsight over the
past several months, he even had second thoughts about his decision to put North in charge of the covert operation to help the
Contras. There, too, he had seen signs of reckless behavior.
    A large part of the problem, McFarlane concluded, was that
his aide had become the victim of his own zeal, and he now was
buckling under the strain of taking on too many ambitious projects. Because McFarlane was going through a similar case of bureaucratic fatigue, he sympathized with North's condition. Thus,
he tried to impose on North the same remedy he had prescribed
for himself: a retreat from all the pressure. In one of his last
moves as national security adviser, McFarlane recommended that
North be transferred out of the White House because he was

becoming "too emotionally strung out." But when McFarlane resigned in early December 1985, that decision, along with so many
others, was passed on to his successor.

North, of course, would have ridiculed the notion that he was
"too emotionally strung out." As usual, he was full of zip and he
promptly went to work on Poindexter in much the same way that
he previously had made McFarlane and Casey targets of his bold
ideas and voluble enthusiasms. In terms of temperament, no two
men could have been less alike, and yet Poindexter also succumbed
to North's calculating charm. The quiet man of caution was dazzled by the blustering man of action.

North certainly didn't waste any time. The day Poindexter's
promotion was announced, he received a long memo from North
proposing a third arms sale to Iran. North built his case around
the in-for-a-dime, in-for-a-dollar argument. "We are now so far
down the road that stopping what has been started could have
even more serious repercussions," North wrote. He then raised a
point that was clearly designed to address the President's primary
concern: that if they bailed out now, the hostages might be killed
as a form of reprisal. But he neglected to mention the other, more
personal reason he had for wanting to keep the deal alive: that
profits from another arms sale could be siphoned off to help the
Contras. North concluded his memo with a request for permission
to fly to London to meet with Ghorbanifar and the Israeli middlemen. That, too, was part of his power play; now that McFarlane
was leaving, there was an opening for him to establish himself as
the officer in charge of the arms-for-hostages operation.

Given the circumstances, one might have thought that a man
as deliberate in his habits as Poindexter would have put off a
decision on so momentous a proposal until he was more settled
as national security adviser. As McFarlane's top deputy, he had
been privy to the two previous arms sales and knew that they had
not gone well; he also was aware that McFarlane now had serious
reservations about pursuing the enterprise any further. Then, too,
there was the question of North's stability and McFarlane's assessment that he should be removed from the pressure he had
been working under for the past several months. Finally, if only
to protect himself, it would have been more prudent for Poindexter to hold off until he had a chance to discuss the matter with
the President and other key advisers. Yet Poindexter chose to
ignore all those warning signals. Instead of transferring North

out of the White House, he gave him permission to fly to London and resume negotiations with Ghorbanifar. That in itself did not constitute an official commitment, but it clearly indicated the direction in which the admiral was leaning. One day on the new job and he already was giving the dubious arms deal his preliminary approval.

Two days later, McFarlane, in a parting gesture, chaired a top-level meeting, the purpose of which was to review and discuss the secret policy of selling arms to Iran. Other high-ranking officials at that December 7 meeting were Shultz, Weinberger, Regan, Poindexter, and the President. (One man not there was Vice President Bush, who had made a prior commitment to attend the Army-Navy football game and later made much of the fact that he was "out of the loop" that day.) It was the first full-scale meeting on the subject since the contentious session in early August, and the mood at this one was no less divisive. McFarlane began with a brief progress report, but he omitted a few key developments. For example, there was no mention of the second arms sale in November, the one that had provoked such an angry reaction from Ghorbanifar, and Shultz and Weinberger were not even aware that it had taken place. Yet for the sake of amity, it was probably just as well that McFarlane did not tell the whole story, for the partial version he did present was more than enough to get the two Cabinet officers angry again.

With force and passion, Shultz and Weinberger reiterated the objections they had raised at the August meeting: that swapping arms for hostages was an unequivocal violation of U.S. policy, which forbade making any deals with terrorists. Shultz stressed the point that he and others in the State Department had been urging reluctant allies in Europe to support that policy, and he shuddered to think what their reaction would be if they found out "we were helping Iran in spite of our protestations to the contrary." And even more than before, both men ridiculed the notion that reliable "moderates" were lurking within Khomeini's regime. Regan, who had been noncommittal at the earlier meeting, joined in this time on the side of the opposition. Accustomed to the vagaries of Wall Street, with all its chaotic ebbs and flows, he said that he knew a sour deal when he smelled one and advised the President to "cut your losses." But Reagan kept steering the conversation back to the hostages. He apparently had been told about North's concern that their lives were now in greater danger than before, and with the Christmas holidays coming up, their plight was troubling him even more than usual. One participant quoted him as saying, "The American people will never forgive me if I fail to get these hostages out."

In the aftermath of that meeting, McFarlane decided on one more act before he turned the problem over to Poindexter and the others. He would fly to London to join North in the discussions with Ghorbanifar. Until then, McFarlane had never met Ghorbanifar, and he was resolved to take his measure and decide whether it made any sense to continue doing business with him. On arrival in London, he tried, rather naïvely, to persuade Ghorbanifar that in the interest of international harmony, Iran's next move should be to arrange for the release of all the hostages without receiving any weapons in return. Then, once Iran had made that demonstration of goodwill, the two sides could proceed down further avenues of cooperation, including the sale of more arms. But Ghorbanifar, who was entirely a creature of deals and profits, had no interest in discussing lofty diplomatic goals, and his response was to laugh in McFarlane's face.

"What the hell is *this?*" he said. "You just left a mess behind and you want something else? Better you cut off, and don't put the blame on us." Ghorbanifar then launched into a long and abusive tirade about the perfidy of the Reagan administration and how it had "cheated" him and his people by shipping the wrong missiles in November. After listening to a few minutes of that, McFarlane lost his temper. "Go pound sand!" he shouted back and stormed out of the room. He was still livid when he returned to Washington and sat down to brief the President, Poindexter, Weinberger, and Regan about his encounter with the arms dealer. McFarlane was now determined to scuttle the operation. He described Ghorbanifar as "a borderline moron . . . the most despicable character I've ever met."

Had he left it at that, he might have achieved his objective. But when Reagan asked about the hostages, McFarlane conceded that the point North had made in his memo may well have been on target: Ghorbanifar and his clients were so volatile that there was some need to worry about reprisals against the hostages. As soon as he said it, McFarlane realized he had made a mistake. Now, once again, all the focus was back on the hostages. Reagan, dismissing the alleged flaws in Ghorbanifar's character, indicated that he wanted to continue pursuing every effort to secure their release, and he didn't particularly care to be told how difficult that would be. As McFarlane understood better than most, the President was a man who wanted his advisers to give him solutions, not problems.

That was McFarlane's last meeting as an official member of the Reagan administration, and as he left the White House, he had a sense of foreboding that the project he had done so much to initiate—and now had tried, in vain, to terminate—would continue to lurch forward on a hazardous course toward a conclusion they would all live to regret.

For his part, North had no qualms about doing business with the "borderline moron," and he quickly moved to bring the Iranian initiative firmly under his personal control. The major snag, he argued, was having to go through the Israeli middlemen, and in another memo to Poindexter, he proposed folding the arms-for-hostages effort into his other covert operation, Project Democracy. The apparatus that he and Secord had set up could take on the responsibility of selling the weapons and delivering them to Iran. Of course, the whole point of using the Israelis in the first place was to provide a legal and diplomatic cover, flimsy though it was, which was why Reagan and McFarlane had insisted on that condition back in July when they first considered the proposal. But like a man who chooses to ride a motorcycle without a helmet, North considered that layer of protection an unnecessary encumbrance.

North's plan called for the limited cooperation of the CIA and the Pentagon, and therefore it could not go forward unless the President signed a special order, or *finding*, authorizing the action. Actually, Reagan already had signed a similar finding after the fact. As part of North's clumsy handling of the second arms sale in November, he and Secord had used an airline owned by the CIA to help ship the missiles to Iran, and when the agency's deputy director, John McMahon, found out about that, he demanded a retroactive finding to cover the flight. One of John Poindexter's first official acts as national security adviser was to persuade Reagan to sign that finding. This was in marked contrast to the first arms sale, when there was no written record of Reagan's approval, nothing more than McFarlane's assurance that he had been given verbal sanction to pursue the mission. Still, that first finding was signed retroactively, and if the matter ever came to light, it could always be argued that the President had no prior knowledge of the deal and had signed the order merely as a legal formality, a punctilious gesture to keep everything in line.

But now, under North's plan, the President would have to make an official commitment in advance, and he would never be able to plead ignorance or lapse of memory subsequently. In spite of the perils implicit in North's proposal, Poindexter gave it his approval, and a draft of the new finding was drawn up. Yet for all his own insouciance, Poindexter was startled when he took the document into the Oval Office one morning in early January and Reagan signed it immediately. Poindexter had assumed the President would want to discuss the issue, weigh the various pros and cons, before he made such a critical commitment, but then the admiral was still new to Reagan's casual approach and aversion to details. Yet it did not take Poindexter long to adjust to Reagan's executive style. This was the customary ritual in the months that followed: Poindexter would present various options to Reagan and, more often than not, the President's only response would be, "Where do I sign?"

The finding wasn't even mentioned the next day when Reagan assembled his top advisers for another discussion of the secret policy on Iran. Most of the men who attended the meeting McFarlane had chaired one month earlier were on hand: Shultz, Weinberger, Poindexter, and Regan. But this time, there were some new faces: Bill Casey, Ed Meese, and Vice President Bush. Even more than before, it was evident that Reagan wanted to pursue the arms-for-hostages scheme, and once again, Shultz and Weinberger went on the record with their opposition, advancing the arguments they had made in the past. At the meeting in early December, they were not alone; Regan had advised the President to "cut your losses," and even McFarlane, in the throes of his growing doubts about the project he had launched, had given vague indications he was shifting to the Shultz-Weinberger position. But McFarlane was now gone, and in the intervening month, Regan had completely reversed himself. He now realized, far more than he did before, how much the hostage issue was gnawing away at Reagan, and whatever private misgivings he might have had, he decided to support the President. After all, he had vowed, when he became chief of staff, to let Reagan be Reagan.

As for the new faces—Casey, Meese, and Bush—they all endorsed the plan with varying degrees of enthusiasm, although

Bush later claimed he would not have done so if he had clearly understood that it was an arms-for-hostages deal or realized that Shultz was so firmly against it. (For that assertion to have any credence, the vice president couldn't have been paying much attention at the key meetings he attended.) Shultz and Weinberger did the best they could, but by now they knew they were isolated on the opposite side of a consensus that had formed in favor of the operation. Stunned by the realization that he and Weinberger were alone in defending a clear-cut and fundamental public policy of the Reagan administration, Shultz later described that January meeting as "almost unreal." This was the last time he and Weinberger made a determined effort to reverse the decision to sell arms to Iran, with the result that Reagan would never again be exposed to a thorough and spirited debate on the issue until the scandal broke ten months later.

There were several reasons that Shultz and Weinberger chose, at that point, to retreat. First, they had already, on at least three occasions, voiced their objections as forcefully as they dared, and both men had important agendas to pursue in their respective domains. If they continued to rail against an enterprise the President clearly favored, they would only squander the leverage they needed to exert influence on other issues. At the same time, they felt a pressing need to put distance between themselves and a course of action they regarded as not only a violation of principle and public policy but also one likely, in time, to bring some of their colleagues to ruination. Both Shultz and Weinberger had weathered a similar crisis more than a decade earlier when they were serving as Cabinet officers in the Nixon administration. At that time, both men managed to steer clear of the Watergate storm that engulfed Nixon's presidency, and they emerged from the wreckage of that scandal with their reputations unscathed.

Shultz's position was especially vulnerable. As the reigning moderate in the Reagan administration, he knew he was out of step with such influential conservatives as Casey, Weinberger, Regan, and now Poindexter, all of whom would have been happy to see him lose Reagan's confidence and be forced to resign. He had witnessed, from a distance, the successful campaign against McFarlane, whose moderate views on arms control and other issues had coincided with his own. And there's no doubt the hardliners were mistrustful of Shultz; among other things, they suspected him of being a prime source of leaks to the press. Shultz knew of this mistrust, which was another reason he told Poindexter he did not want to know any of the details of the arms-for-hostages project. Taking himself out of the picture was a form of self-protection, for he could hardly be accused of leaking information that had not been imparted to him.

There was, of course, another option. Shultz could have elected to take a defiant stand on principle and accept the consequences. Six years earlier, another secretary of state, Cyrus Vance, had resigned in protest over the Carter-Brzezinski decision to launch a helicopter raid to rescue the U.S. hostages being held in Tehran. Faced with a similar crisis of conscience, Shultz chose caution over courage, survival over principle, and in doing so, this fundamentally decent and able man gave up a small part of the moral resource that meant so much to him: his honor. So did Weinberger, for even though he was in a less vulnerable position, he, too, made the discreet choice to remain silent.

At the time of the last full-scale debate on the subject in early January 1986, the Contra link had not yet become part of the secret policy to sell arms to Iran. But later that month, North once again flew to London to resume negotiations with Ghorbanifar, and when he returned to Washington, he went to Poindexter and declared, "I think I have found a way we can provide some funds to the democratic resistance." North then attributed the "neat idea" to Ghorbanifar, but as we have seen, the evidence indicates that he and Secord had been enamored of the notion since November.

Poindexter had to realize that if the diversion plan were implemented, it would radically change the dynamics of both covert operations. In terms of the Iranian initiative, the administration would now have a motive to pursue the arms sales that would have nothing to do with the hostages or the quixotic diplomatic goal of establishing relations with the alleged moderates in Tehran. Far more perilous, the architects of Project Democracy would no longer be able to justify their actions on the grounds that all the funds they raised for the Contras had come from foreign governments or private citizens. The vast sums targeted for the rebels in Nicaragua would now include profits from the sale of weapons owned by the U.S. government, a clear and undeniable violation of the Boland Amendment. As Henry Kissinger later wrote: "On the formal level, the case is obvious. The executive branch cannot be allowed—on any claim of national security—to circumvent the Congressional prerogative over appropriations by raising its own funds through the sale of government property." Moreover, if the President were to be implicated in such a scheme, he could be subjected to impeachment.

This is why Poindexter's testimony was deemed to be so critical at the congressional hearings into the scandal. At those hearings, the admiral readily acknowledged that he gave North permission to go ahead with the diversion plan, but he insisted that he did not inform the President, thereby corroborating Reagan's repeated assertion that "they just didn't tell me what was going on." Poindexter's record did not inspire confidence in his veracity. He admitted that on other matters, he repeatedly had lied to Congress, the press, and even colleagues in the Cabinet. So why, many asked, should they believe he was not lying when he claimed that he never told Reagan—or anyone else—about the diversion plan? Given the fact that he had spent his entire career within the framework of the military chain of command and that he, in particular, was known as an officer who strictly adhered to rules and protocol, it seemed inconceivable that Poindexter would take that awesome burden on himself. Yet that was his story. "I made a deliberate decision not to ask the President, so that I could insulate him from the decision and provide some future deniability for the President if it ever leaked out," he told the investigating committees. His justification for that arbitrary act was a perversion of Harry Truman's famous dictum on the subject of presidential responsibility. "On this whole issue," Poindexter proclaimed, "the buck stops here with me."

His credibility was not helped by the fact that in the course of the hearings, he seemed to have lost his reputed powers of recollection. One of the qualities that had made him such an outstanding student was his exceptional memory, and that gift carried over into his naval career. In a fitness report on him in the 1970s, a superior officer had written: "Poindexter has a spectacular mental capacity . . . he retains fully, recalls accurately, and evaluates with a keen sense of what is important and what isn't." Yet in his testimony before Congress, there were long stretches in which his responses to questions were a steady drone of "I don't remember that . . . I don't recall . . . I am very fuzzy on that." And so forth.

Even so, Poindexter was treated with more respect than he probably deserved. For the most part, his congressional inquisitors confined their reactions to skeptical glances and polite demurrals. One exception to that pattern was Jack Brooks, a feisty Democratic congressman from Texas, who offered his blunt opinion that Poindexter was "a lying son of a bitch." Many of his colleagues privately agreed with Brooks, but without any concrete evidence to refute the admiral, they could only mount a limited challenge to his testimony. In their formal report, however, the majority refused to give Poindexter the benefit of the doubt. Their conclusion was that they were unable to determine whether or not Reagan knew about the diversion. And with that, they passed the critical question on to future historians.

With or without the President's knowledge, the diversion plan went into effect with North at the controls. Negotiations for the third arms sale led to a shipment of one thousand more U.S. missiles to Iran in February, and although the terms of the deal (as North and his cohorts understood them) called for the release of all the hostages, the result was predictable: not one of them was freed. The ignominy of yet another swindle prompted an angry Don Regan to inquire, "How many times do we put up with this rug merchant type of stuff?" But from North's point of view, the mission was not a complete failure. The Iranians paid $10 million for the weapons, and after deducting $4 million for the cost of the transaction, that left $6 million to add to the swelling bankroll for the Contras. The problem, however, was that the patrons of Project Democracy were not getting much of a return for their money. On the battlefields of Nicaragua, the rebels continued to flounder. According to one gloomy report from the scene, the leaders of the resistance spent more time bickering with each other than concentrating on their crusade to overthrow the Sandinistas.

In the meantime, the Reagan administration was planning a show of strength on another front. The most blatant advocate of terrorism was the leader of Libya, Colonel Muammar Qaddafi. An outlandish figure who allegedly had a private fetish for wearing women's clothes and makeup, Qaddafi preached the doctrine of hate, and his favorite target was the United States. He did more, however, than just preach. Libya was an active sponsor of terrorism, and there were times when Qaddafi was flagrantly indiscreet in his zeal to claim responsibility for such acts. From Washington's point of view, the temptation to teach him a lesson was difficult to resist, and in the spring of 1986, Libya provided a suitable provocation.

In early April, terrorists blew up a discothèque in West Berlin that was a popular hangout for U.S. servicemen. Two Americans and one Turkish woman were killed, and 230 others were injured. All the evidence pointed to Libya as the culprit, and later that month, U.S. bombers retaliated with raids on two Libyan cities, Tripoli and Benghazi. Because Qaddafi was the perfect enemy, almost a cartoon villain, the majority of Americans approved of the attacks, and no one was more gleeful than George Shultz. This was precisely the kind of aggressive action he had been urging for more than two years. In the aftermath of the raids on Libya, Shultz proclaimed that they were the start of a more militant policy toward terrorism. Resorting to the kind of pugnacious language seldom heard in diplomatic circles, he told an international press conference that the new American message to terrorists was "You've had it, pal!"

But the declaration concealed a troubled spirit. For Shultz had recently learned from one of his deputies that the Poindexter-North contingent was still pursuing the arms-for-hostages scheme. If there was one man the American public despised more than Qaddafi, it was the Ayatollah Khomeini, and if there was one country that was a more lethal sponsor of terrorism than Libya, it was Iran. Shultz realized that if his colleagues in the White House were still doing business with the Iranians, then his strong public statement was a sham. While U.S. forces were inflicting retaliation on Libya, others in the government were trying to persuade Khomeini's henchmen into another arms deal. How long, Shultz wondered with some disgust, would it take these people to recognize the senseless contradiction?

The situation was even more absurd than Shultz imagined. By the spring of 1986, Poindexter and North had finally become disillusioned with Ghorbanifar. Inasmuch as Ghorbanifar was their primary contact, the pivotal middleman, there was no way they could cut him out of the negotiations, but they could go over his head and deal directly with his clients. So it was decided to send North and his team to Tehran. But in order to give that mission a little more weight—North was, after all, still only a mid-level aide and lieutenant colonel—McFarlane was summoned out of retirement to head the delegation.

In the months since his resignation, McFarlane had kept in

touch with Poindexter and North. When he was told what happened with the third arms deal in February, it only deepened his
sense of regret for having failed to terminate the operation back
in December before he left the White House. McFarlane believed
that because he was the one who had launched the initiative, he
should have made a more strenuous effort to shut it down. At
the same time, he felt a certain responsibility to Poindexter and
North, his former comrades in arms sales, who, undaunted by all
the setbacks, were still trying to convert repeated failure into success. The proposed trip to Tehran struck him as just the kind of
bold stroke needed at this point; at last, there seemed to be a
promising move in the right direction. Hence, when he was asked
to lead the delegation, McFarlane welcomed the assignment. Once
again, North was dispatched to London to meet with Ghorbanifar
and arrange all the details for the forthcoming visit in May. Unfortunately, Ghorbanifar was still deceitful, and the American
team that went to Iran would once again be stung by his treachery.

The secret mission to Tehran was, in many ways, the ultimate
folly. All the delusions that had fueled the enterprise from the
beginning were in full play on that venture: the notion that there
were "moderates" in Khomeini's government who yearned for
improved relations with the United States, the belief that Iran had
the will and power to order the release of the American hostages
in Lebanon, and, even at this late date, the readiness to accept
Ghorbanifar's portrayal of himself as a trustworthy spokesman
for his Iranian clients. In their London talks, North and Ghorbanifar had agreed on the following sequence of events: The
United States would sell spare missile parts and other military
equipment to Iran, some of which would be transported on the
same plane that would be flying the American team into Tehran.
On their arrival, all the hostages would be released; then, and
only then, would the rest of the shipment, loaded on a plane
standing by in Tel Aviv, be delivered to Iran. Once all that had
been accomplished, McFarlane would meet with high-ranking Iranian officials and commence formal talks toward resolving the
serious differences between the two governments.

It was the last chip in the equation that especially appealed
to McFarlane and his sense of destiny. He once again found himself entertaining visions of a diplomatic masterstroke, worthy of
comparison to Kissinger's breakthrough visit to China in 1971.
After all, he reasoned, China at that time was a pariah, an outlaw

nation scorned by most of the Western world, and in that respect at least, Khomeini's Iran was no different.

On the morning of May 25, 1986, McFarlane and North arrived in Tehran, and that in itself was extraordinary. Six years earlier, during the long hostage crisis that destroyed Jimmy Carter's presidency, Khomeini's regime had all but declared war on the United States, and since then, a state of open hostility had existed between the two nations. There were no formal relations, no legitimate contact of any kind, between Washington and Tehran. Yet there, in the capital of an avowed and bitter enemy, were Bud McFarlane and Oliver North, two men who, as members of Reagan's National Security Council, were privy to the most sensitive foreign and military secrets of U.S. policy. But as they soon discovered, they had nothing to gain from having taken that high risk.

The only responsible official they met during their visit was a prominent member of the Iranian parliament who, though courteous and unthreatening, fully disabused them of the expectations they had brought to Tehran. No, he explained, McFarlane would not be able to have formal talks with Iranian leaders at this time. Instead, he extolled the virtue of patience, offering the hope that such a meeting might take place at some later date, after the Americans had done more to demonstrate their good intentions. No, he told McFarlane, the immediate release of the hostages was out of the question. But as a "humanitarian gesture," contacts had been established with their captors in Lebanon, and there was reason to believe that at some future point the result would be positive. Again, he counseled patience. The only subject that did not inspire a paean to patience was the arms shipment. When, the Iranian politely inquired, would the rest of the missile parts be delivered?

McFarlane, struggling to control his temper, protested that those were not the terms of the deal. He and his associates had been promised the immediate release of the hostages and official, high-level meetings with the Iranian government. That clearly seemed to surprise the man who had been designated to negotiate with the American visitors. He replied that he and his people were unaware of any such promises. McFarlane could only conclude that he was lying, or, more likely, that Ghorbanifar had been as brazenly deceitful in his relations with his own clients as he had with his Washington contacts. Striving to preserve whatever shred of honor he still had left, McFarlane stood firm: until the Iranians could arrange the release of all the hostages, they would receive no more U.S. weapons—not now, not ever.

With the mission in shambles, McFarlane left Iran in a state of dejection. He had just come face-to-face with the reality of his own folly. There now was no escaping the conclusion that from the very beginning, the enterprise had been a swindle. North, however, was more adept at the art of escaping reality. In a chipper mood on the flight out of Tehran, he professed to have seen glimmers of hope and progress in the discussions with the Iranian official, and he began to talk about a renewed effort to negotiate an arms deal that would be acceptable to both sides. McFarlane could hardly believe what he was hearing; even from North, this was preposterous. He started to protest, but North broke in with a startling disclosure. "Don't be too downhearted," he told McFarlane. "The one bright spot is that we're using part of the money in these transactions for Central America."

Although he was stunned by the revelation, McFarlane's response was curiously reticent. He did not press North for details, nor did he allude to that phase of the operation when he returned to Washington and met with the President, Bush, Regan, and Poindexter to give them his report on the futile trip to Iran. McFarlane later explained that he had no need-to-know basis for pursuing the question. He was no longer an official member of the Reagan administration, and therefore, the diversion plan was simply none of his business. He naturally assumed that before implementing such a momentous scheme, North had cleared it with Poindexter, and that he, in turn, had secured the approval of Reagan and his legal advisers. In truth, he was privately relieved that this, at least, was one aspect of the enterprise that had not occurred on his watch. For in the aftermath of the mission to Tehran, McFarlane was again seized by the mood of foreboding that had gripped him five months earlier when he stepped down as national security adviser. He knew that even the best-kept secrets in Washington could not be concealed forever, and the fact that the two covert operations had failed to meet their objectives only increased the risk of exposure. He could not shake the dread feeling that he and all the others who had been involved in those projects were sitting on a bomb that, sooner or later, would explode in their faces.

*   *   *

For the time being, however, that hidden peril posed no threat
to the serene and sunny surface of Ronald Reagan's presidency.
In terms of public perception, the summer of 1986 was the high
point of the second term, an upbeat season of success that rivaled
the long honeymoon of Reagan's first year in office. The administration was still being congratulated for its decision to bomb
Libya, and there were clear signs that Shultz's "you've-had-it-pal"
message had produced the desired effect. In the aftermath of the
raids, there was a notable decline in terrorist attacks on American
targets in Europe and elsewhere. On the Fourth of July, the President led a celebration at the kind of festive ceremony that always
brought out the best in him. The occasion was the one hundredth
birthday of the recently refurbished Statue of Liberty, and the
old actor, playing to the balconies, hit all the patriotic and senti-
mental grace notes about the generations of immigrants who had
come to these shores in search of freedom and whose many contributions helped to make America the greatest nation on earth.

But there was more than just ruffles and flourishes. Even
some of Reagan's critics joined in the chorus of "Hail to the Chief"
over his impressive string of victories in Congress. The President
had put his prestige on the line behind a sweeping tax reform
bill, which many skeptics had airily dismissed as unattainable. But
by that summer, the White House had nailed down enough votes
to pass the landmark legislation, and even with the compromises
that had to be made to win bipartisan support, it was a striking
achievement for the administration. On Wall Street, meanwhile,
stock prices continued to soar, reflecting the strong boom in the
economy that had begun four years earlier, and both inflation
and interest rates were under control. The White House naturally
claimed full credit for all of that.

The retirement of Chief Justice Warren Burger presented
Reagan with an opportunity to give the Supreme Court a sharp
nudge to the right, and again he made the most of it. To succeed
Burger, he nominated William Rehnquist, who already was serving as an associate justice. A Nixon appointee, Rehnquist was
regarded as the most rigid conservative on the Supreme Court,
and to fill the seat he would be vacating, the President chose
another stringent conservative, Antonin Scalia. The nomination
of Rehnquist, in particular, aroused the ire of liberal opponents,
and they fought hard to block his confirmation. But 1986 was not

their year, and the Senate eventually approved both appointments.

But the most gratifying victory of all was scored on the volatile issue of Nicaragua. After two years of being rebuffed every time it came up for a vote, the Reagan administration finally was able to command enough support to persuade Congress to renew military aid for the Contras. The turnaround vote came just ten days before the Fourth of July, and Reagan couldn't resist drawing a parallel. "As we approach the celebrations of our own Independence Day, we can be proud that we as a people have embraced the struggle of the freedom fighters of Nicaragua," he declared. "The cause is freedom, the cause is just, the cause will triumph." Neither the President nor any of his advisers bothered to mention that during the two years of prohibition, the cause had been financed by Iranian arms sales and other sources that were induced to circumvent the law. Of course, the ironic side effect of approving the administration's request was to make Project Democracy irrelevant. But the new authorization was not scheduled to go into effect until October, and until then, the Boland Amendment would still be binding. North and his colleagues would still have a few more months to flout the law they had been treating with such disdain over the past two years.

So, all in all, the summer of 1986 was a heady time for the Reagan White House. The tone of public adulation was expressed most vividly in a *Time* magazine cover story that summer. "Ronald Reagan has found the American sweet spot," *Time* observed.

> The 75-year-old man is hitting home runs. . . . Reagan inhabits his moment in America with a triumphant (some might say careless or even callous) ease that is astonishing and even mysterious. . . . He is a Prospero of American memories, a magician who carries a bright, ideal America like a holograph in his mind and projects its image in the air. . . .

With praise like that to sustain them, it's little wonder that other members of the Reagan team did not share Bud McFarlane's gloomy apprehensions about what might be in store for them.

15

Coming Apart

"We have some tidying up to do."
—John Poindexter

Even before the covert operations exploded into the public disgrace that became known as the Iran-Contra affair, the autumn of 1986 was a time of trouble for the Reagan White House. The President, who just a few months earlier had been hailed as "a Prospero," was rapidly losing his magic touch, and by the time that season passed into history, his style of leadership would invite comparisons to the bumbling antics of a less gifted sorcerer—the Wizard of Oz.

What had kept the illusion of mastery humming on such a smooth and steady course for so long was the skillful public-relations apparatus that had been in operation since the early days of the Reagan administration. But in the autumn of 1986, that apparatus began to veer out of control. One early sign of trouble was the uproar over a so-called disinformation plan that had been concocted within the White House. In early October, Bob Woodward reported in *The Washington Post* that White House spokesmen, with Reagan's approval, had deliberately misled the press with statements that Qaddafi was once again promoting terrorism in the Middle East and Europe and that the administration was not going to tolerate it. That raised the possibility of another U.S. attack on Libya, and stories to that effect were published in several newspapers. Woodward had discovered a memo exposing the scheme, and in response to his story, the White House had to admit that it had made a calculated effort to plant the exaggerated reports in the hope of upsetting Qaddafi. Indeed, Reagan's own reaction seemed to condone the disinformation ruse. "Our position has been one which we would just as soon have Mr. Qaddafi go to bed every night wondering what we might do," he explained.

Woodward's story touched off quite a stir, which came as a surprise to those who knew that for years the White House—and often Reagan himself—had made a practice of promulgating distortions of one kind or another. This, after all, was the President who had compared the corrupt and inept leaders of the Contra movement in Nicaragua to the Founding Fathers of the United States; who had described nuclear missiles as "peacekeepers" and tax hikes as "revenue enhancements"; and who had quoted a nonexistent British law to justify his opposition to gun control. It's true, however, that this latest attempt to misuse the press as an arm of its own propaganda was especially brazen, and for that reason, the disinformation scheme struck a nerve. It was almost as if reporters were saying that they finally had had their fill of the deceptions that had been emanating from the White House for the past six years.

Another embarrassing episode that fall was the administration's handling of the Nicholas Daniloff story. Daniloff, an American journalist in Moscow for *U.S. News & World Report*, was arrested in late August a few moments after a Soviet acquaintance had handed him certain classified documents. Shortly after he was taken into custody, Daniloff was accused of espionage. His arrest came just one week after FBI agents in New York had picked up Gennadi Zakharov, a Soviet diplomat assigned to the United Nations, and charged him with spying. The White House claimed that it had hard evidence that Zakharov was a real spy, whereas Daniloff had been framed in a cynical move to set up a trade of one man for the other. If that, in fact, was the case, then it must be said that the maneuver worked. In late September, Daniloff was released, and the very next day, Zakharov was given his freedom to return to Russia. The White House maintained that it was not an official swap, an act of reciprocity. The Washington press corps scoffed at that clumsy effort at "spin control" and reported the Daniloff-Zakharov story as a negotiated agreement to exchange one man's release for the freedom of the other.

One completely unexpected offshoot of those negotiations was the announcement of another Reagan-Gorbachev summit meeting, to take place in Reykjavík, Iceland, in mid-October. On any list of misguided undertakings that occurred during the Reagan years, the Reykjavík summit deserves a special place. The first Reagan-Gorbachev meeting, in Geneva the previous fall, had been preceded by months of careful planning and preparation. But this hastily scheduled second conference would occur in less than three weeks after the White House agreed to the Soviet proposal, which left almost no time to prepare Reagan's position on the complex issues of arms control. Administration officials insisted, however, that there was no need to worry. The October meeting was billed as little more than an aperitif, a kind of casual lounge act, the sole purpose of which was to set a clear agenda for a subsequent summit in the United States. But it came close to evolving into something much more than that. For a few breathtaking moments on an overcast Sunday in Iceland, Reagan's face-to-face encounter with Gorbachev hovered on the verge of a staggering breakthrough: a daring plan to eliminate all of the nuclear weapons in the arsenals of the two superpowers.

In the end, the dramatic negotiations collapsed into stalemate over the President's pet project: the Strategic Defense Initiative (SDI), or, as it's known colloquially, "Star Wars." Gorbachev was adamant in insisting that all work on SDI be confined to laboratory research; Reagan insisted on the U.S. right to develop and test the experimental system he believed would someday form an impregnable shield to protect the nation from nuclear attack. It should be noted that few experts, even those who favor some form of SDI, think it's possible to build a system that will guarantee 100 percent protection, but that was the President's dream, and to him, SDI was the key to arms control of the future. That dispute brought the encounter to an end on a discordant note. There was no discussion of plans for a future summit meeting, which had been the official reason for going to Reykjavík in the first place. Reagan was furious with Gorbachev and at one point said to him, "I don't think you really wanted an agreement."

There are many who believe the snag over Star Wars rescued the President from a monumental embarrassment. Had it not been for that, he would have gone along with Gorbachev's sweeping proposal; and had he done so, there would have been turmoil in Washington and other Western capitals. Such a treaty would have had to be ratified by the U.S. Senate, and there the opposition would have been led by Sam Nunn of Georgia, regarded by both Republicans and his fellow Democrats as the foremost defense expert in Congress. Nunn later said that if Reagan had closed the deal in Reykjavík, he would have committed the most serious arms control blunder of the nuclear age.

Like millions of other Americans that Sunday afternoon, Senator Nunn was at home watching a football game on television when the Reagan-Gorbachev talks came to an end. As the networks broke into their regular programming with a series of special reports on the summit, Nunn watched with growing uneasiness. He had not expected much in the way of substance from the meeting in Reykjavík, but what brought him to the edge of his seat was Secretary of State Shultz's description of the agreement the two leaders almost reached. Shultz seemed to be saying that before the negotiations ran aground over Star Wars, the two sides had agreed to get rid of all their "offensive strategic arms," the heart of the nuclear arsenal. As Shultz explained it, the agreement had called for a gradual reduction over ten years, with all strategic weapons to be eliminated by 1996.

Nunn was astounded. As the ranking Democrat on the Armed Services Committee, he was privy to the most sensitive secrets concerning arms control and defense matters, and he knew of no one in the government who had been contemplating such a sweeping proposal prior to the summit. There just had to be some mistake; no one would sign off on an agreement like that without at least having it reviewed by experts in the Pentagon. Yet a subsequent statement by Donald Regan made the deal sound even more ludicrous. He said later that evening that the agreement had called for the phasing out of not just strategic weapons but *all* nuclear arms, including tactical systems. Now, more than ever, Nunn was convinced that there had been some breakdown in communication. Before going to bed that night, the senator concluded that the U.S. officials in Iceland must be very tired.

But as Nunn soon learned, what he had heard was not the result of fatigue. Two days later, Shultz arranged a meeting at the White House to brief congressional leaders on the summit talks. There he heard Reagan describe how close he and Gorbachev had come to getting rid of all nuclear weapons. The President said "bombs and everything else" had been included in the agreement. The only thing that stood in the way was the falling out over Star Wars. Nunn was still finding all this hard to believe, and when the time came for discussion, he asked whether he understood correctly that the President had agreed to do away with all strategic arms. When Reagan nodded yes, Nunn raised the critical question: If the nation were prepared to eliminate its nuclear force, what did the administration intend to do to counter the overwhelming advantage the Soviets and their allies had in conventional arms? After all, everyone knew it was nuclear weapons that enabled the Western powers to maintain a military balance.

Reagan seemed to be taken aback by the question, and so Shultz intervened. The secretary of state conceded that it would be "a new world" without nuclear weapons, but he expressed confidence that the NATO countries would find the will to build up their conventional forces to match those of the Warsaw Pact nations. As the White House meeting broke up, Nunn approached Admiral Poindexter and said, "John, do you realize they're talking about doing away with all strategic weapons—bombers, subs, cruise missiles as well as ballistics?" According to another official who was at the meeting, Poindexter looked pale and somewhat shaken. But all he said was, "Well, we have some tidying up to do."

Later that week, Nunn voiced his concerns on the floor of the Senate. He urged the administration to withdraw whatever offers it had made in Iceland before the Soviets had a change of heart and accepted them. The kind of agreement that had almost been reached in Reykjavík, he warned, made war more likely, not less. Nunn noted that such an agreement would have elevated other nuclear nations, for example, Britain and France, to superpower status. He recalled that years earlier, the Kennedy administration had tried to convince Charles DeGaulle that France didn't need any nuclear weapons because the United States had at least a thousand in its arsenal. Now, he suggested, DeGaulle must be having quite a chuckle somewhere because the United States had proposed that by 1996, "France will have a thousand and we will have none." Turning to Asia, Nunn asked: "Do we really want China to be not only the country with the largest standing army in the world, but also one with more missiles than we have?"

In response to Nunn's remarks, Shultz delivered a speech of his own later that same day at the National Press Club. In it, he now claimed that there had been no agreement to phase out all strategic arms by 1996. What the U.S. negotiators had been prepared to accept, he said, was a plan to cut the strategic arsenal in half in the first five years. After that, the only weapons targeted for elimination would be long-range ballistic missiles. That meant the United States would have retained its missiles that could be fired from submarines, as well as its bombers and cruise missiles. But Shultz's speech contradicted the statements he had made earlier, both in Reykjavík and at the White House briefing for congressional leaders. By then, in fact, there were so many conflicting versions of what had been agreed to in Iceland that Washington officials, both inside and outside the administration, were thoroughly confused.

Then, as if to clarify matters once and for all, the next authoritative voice to be heard was Mikhail Gorbachev's. In a speech on the summit meeting, Gorbachev said that Reagan indeed had accepted his proposal to do away with all nuclear weapons, and not just the ballistic missiles. Moreover, a Soviet foreign ministry official later released a partial transcript of the negotiations between the two leaders in which Reagan was quoted as agreeing to the elimination of "all nuclear explosive devices." The Soviets also quoted the President as saying that a treaty to that effect could be signed when Gorbachev made his then-expected visit to the United States.

Much later, officials who were familiar with the proceedings in Iceland told us what actually happened: When Gorbachev proposed doing away with strategic weapons, Reagan left the negotiating table and went to the room where his arms control specialists were standing by. They told him that their aim was to eliminate "ballistic missiles," not all "strategic weapons" and that phasing out the missiles would be a meaningful accomplishment. But apparently, Reagan did not understand that "ballistic missiles" were a subset of "strategic weapons" and mistakenly concluded that his advisers were talking about two separate categories of firepower, one called "ballistic missiles" and the other "strategic weapons." Returning to the negotiating table, he asked Gorbachev

what he meant by "strategic weapons." When Gorbachev replied
that what he had in mind were missiles, bombs, and so on, the
Soviets quoted Reagan as saying, "Apparently, we misunderstood
you. If that's what you want, all right." Officials later speculated
that in his confusion, Reagan must have thought he was agreeing
to a ban on two separate but relatively equal categories—"ballistic
missiles" and "strategic weapons"—and not to the elimination of
all nuclear arms.

As for Sam Nunn, he later noted, with some relief,

> It was not an agreement that was irrevocable. It had not been
> put through even the most cursory review process and it
> would never have been approved by the Senate. But had it
> not fallen apart because of the stalemate over Star Wars, it
> would have been the most painfully embarrassing example
> of American ineptitude in this century, certainly since World
> War II.

To Nunn and a relatively few others who had a clear understanding of what the stakes had been in Reykjavík, the second
summit meeting revived the disturbing questions about Reagan's
ability to grasp complex issues. But because the issues were so
complex and because the ill-conceived agreement fell apart, the
White House was able to graft a positive face onto the President's
bewildered performance in Iceland. Don Regan and his people
launched a public relations blitz that portrayed Reagan as a tough
negotiator who had stood up to the Soviets and refused to bargain
away the right to develop his Star Wars defense system. The PR
campaign seemed to achieve the desired result; some surveys
showed that confidence in Reagan's ability to deal with the Russians actually went up after his weekend in Reykjavík. But that
brief sign of approval was fleeting. Later that fall, the White House
team had to absorb a much different kind of message, one that
had to make them wonder whether Reagan were losing his touch
with the group that had always been the greatest source of his
strength: the electorate.

It is customary in a midterm election for the party in power
to lose ground, yet some polls in 1986 indicated that the Republicans not only had a good chance of holding their own but even
of gaining a few seats in Congress. Encouraged, Reagan campaigned extensively for GOP candidates in several key Senate

races. But by 1986, Reagan's coat had lost the tails that had carried so many Republicans into office when he won the presidency six years earlier. The Democrats not only gained ground but recaptured the Senate. For the first time since the start of the Reagan era, the opposition would now control both houses of Congress, and from the President's point of view, the clear message that his power was waning could not have come at a worse time. For in the weeks to come, he would need friends on Capitol Hill in ways he never had needed them before.

From time to time over the past year, reporters in Washington had picked up hints of the covert operations that were being conducted by the Reagan administration. Even when pursued, however, the indistinct trails never led them to anything conclusive. But the administration's luck began to run out in early October when a supply plane on a mission for Project Democracy was shot down in Nicaragua. The only survivor was Eugene Hasenfus, a former CIA man who had been recruited by North and Secord to help them in their secret campaign on behalf of the Contras. Hasenfus readily admitted that he had been on a government mission (he claimed, in fact, that his flight had been supervised by the CIA), but officials in Washington indignantly denied that. Even so, the Sandinistas knew they had captured an important prize, and the fuss they raised galvanized the press into action. Two weeks after the crash, reporters from UPI and *Newsday* came up with damaging evidence: telephone records in San Salvador, where the air crew was based, linked Hasenfus to Oliver North's office in Washington. It was the first crack in what, until then, had been a solid wall of resistance.

In early November, one day before the midterm election, an obscure magazine in Beirut printed a story that, to the public, seemed preposterous. Acting on a tip from Iranian sources, the left-wing magazine *Al Shiraa* reported that a special envoy from the White House named Robert McFarlane had flown into Tehran on a secret mission to sell U.S. weapons to Khomeini's government. The story said that both the visit and the sale had been approved by President Reagan.

That faint spark from such a remote and unlikely source was enough to set off the explosion. Like an infection from a tiny cut in a toe or finger that quickly spreads through capillaries and arteries until it poisons the entire bloodstream, *Al Shiraa*'s disclosure rapidly wormed its way into the mainstream of American journalism. One day after the story hit the streets in Beirut, reporters covering the President began badgering Larry Speakes and other White House officials with questions about the bizarre report. Later that week, two of the most powerful newspapers in the country, *The Washington Post* and the *Los Angeles Times*, published the first detailed accounts of the arms deal, including a number of fresh revelations: that some of the sales had been made through Israel, that their purpose had been to secure the release of the American hostages in Lebanon, and that they had been carried out over the strong objections of two Cabinet officers, George Shultz and Caspar Weinberger. Democrats in Congress called for a full-scale investigation, to be capped by public hearings. By the end of that first week in November, the scandal had hit the Reagan administration with full force.

The initial reaction at the White House was to stonewall the reports, in the hope that the commotion would soon end quietly. But once it became clear that the President would have to make some kind of official response, the advisers who had the most to lose from a full disclosure advocated a sanitized version of the arms deal that would conceal its most damaging elements. During the Watergate crisis, that approach was defined, in the vivid language of the Nixon White House, as "the limited, modified hangout route." Yet as every student of the Watergate scandal knows, it was the elaborate cover-up, not the "third-rate burglary," that put Nixon on the road to impeachment, and now, fourteen years later, the Reagan team was edging dangerously toward a similar pitfall. One major difference was that the Watergate cover-up had been coherently orchestrated from the top, by Nixon and his chief of staff H. R. Haldeman, whereas the frantic efforts of the men around Reagan were marked by a lack of coherent direction.

Each of the principle players had his motives and therefore suggested a scenario that would best serve his own interest—and survival. Bill Casey's main concern was to keep Project Democracy alive, not so much as it pertained to the Contras, but in terms of its larger scope and vision: the independent, self-sustaining network of covert operations that could be pressed into action beyond the reach of any law passed by Congress. Poindexter and North shared that concern, but their primary goal was to protect the

Iranian initiative and keep *it* going. Incredibly, they were still deeply involved in that enterprise and, in fact, had been encouraged by recent developments. Since the ill-fated trip to Tehran in May, there had been two more arms sales to Iran, and this time the results were a little more promising: one hostage, Father Lawrence Jenco, was released in July, and another, David Jacobsen, was set free in early November, just before the scandal broke. (But as if to compensate for their release, the terrorists in Lebanon abducted two more American citizens in September.)

McFarlane was mainly driven by a desire to obscure the facts about the two arms sales he had arranged in 1985. He wanted the President to imply that the Israelis had acted on their own; or if the U.S. role had to be acknowledged, he wanted it clearly understood that he had Reagan's approval to pursue the project. But that ran counter to Don Regan's central objective, which was to put as much distance as possible between Reagan and the Iranian arms deal. He didn't particularly care how much of the story leaked out, just as long as others were blamed, not the President. Exploiting his contacts with the press, Regan spread the word that the entire scheme had originated with McFarlane. "Let's not forget whose idea this was," he told *The Washington Post*. "It was Bud's idea. When you give lousy advice, you get lousy results." Regan, by this time, was feeling the cumulative strain from all the mishaps that had beset the White House in recent weeks. In an interview with *The New York Times*, he reminisced about the problems he and his staff had to contend with that fall: the disinformation ruse, the Daniloff swap, and Reagan's performance in Iceland. "Some of us are like a shovel brigade that follows a parade down Main Street cleaning up," he said. "I don't say we'll be able to do it four times in a row. But here we go again, and we're trying."

On November 13, ten days after the story broke in Beirut, Reagan went on national television to present his version of the "limited, modified hang-out route." All the conflicting advice he had received from his warring deputies produced a speech that was a hodgepodge of disinformation. "The United States has not swapped boatloads or planeloads of American weapons for the return of American hostages," the President asserted. Although he admitted approving the sale of "small amounts of defensive weapons," he insisted that "these modest deliveries, taken together, could easily fit into a single cargo plane." Reagan then went on to say: "All appropriate Cabinet officers were fully consulted. . . . The actions I authorized were, and continue to be, in full compliance with federal law."

All these statements were false, in one way or another, and would later have to be retracted or revised. Reagan's speech was so full of distortions that by giving it, he only made matters worse. Even some of his supporters were now convinced the President was either covering up the truth or—in a more charitable interpretation—speaking out of ignorance. Among the skeptics was Reagan's political godfather, Barry Goldwater. Never one to mince words, Goldwater offered this pithy assessment: "Reagan has gotten his butt in a crack."

Six nights later, the President made another attempt to extricate himself when he faced a swarm of reporters at a televised press conference. Under the circumstances, the decision to subject him to that kind of grilling was ill advised. Even when there was no major controversy to explain, the spirited give-and-take of an open news conference was a forum that did not bring out the best in Reagan, and on this night he was overwhelmed by the trenchant questions that were hurled at him. Most of his answers were confused and inept. Indeed, one of his misstatements was so serious—an outright denial that the United States had condoned the shipment of arms by Israel—that as soon as the conference ended, the White House issued a correction.

Never before—not even during his lethargic performance in the first debate with Walter Mondale in 1984—had the American public seen Reagan so befuddled. To be a convincing liar, one must have command of the facts that are being omitted and distorted. On other matters where he was more sure of his ground, such as his devotion to family values and his military activities during World War II, Reagan had demonstrated that he could mislead convincingly. But on this night in November 1986, the more he said in response to the questions, the more he seemed to be talking himself into deeper and more perilous waters.

It was at this low point that George Shultz began an aggressive campaign to save the political soul of the Reagan administration, a bureaucratic struggle he later described as a "battle royal." The past few months had been a trying time for Shultz. He had to endure the humiliation of knowing that a secret policy he opposed had been put into operation. He also knew how out of step he was with the strong-willed conservatives who had formed a phalanx around the Oval Office. Finally, he sensed that he was falling out of favor with the President, losing the influence he once had been able to wield.

When the scandal broke, and all the sordid details began spilling out, Shultz was appalled to discover how much had gone on behind his back. He had not known about the findings Reagan signed authorizing the arms sales, or the extent of those transactions, or the ambitious undertaking that had been dubbed Project Democracy. Nor, of course, did he know about the diversion plan that provided the link between the two covert ventures. To a large extent, this was his own fault; he purposely had made clear that he did not want to know about actions he had opposed. But now, in November, all that would change. Using the resources of the State Department, Shultz set out to gather all the pertinent facts and details so that he could back up his arguments with the force of knowledge.

He waged his battle on two fronts. In private conversations with the President, he went to work on Reagan's perceptions in an effort to bring them more into line with reality. Shultz could not undo the damage that had already been done, but at least he could try to alter the course and direction of where to go from here. His twin goals were to put an end to the Iranian operation and to shut down Project Democracy, and in his meetings with Reagan he concentrated most of his fire on the Iranian question. One of their most confrontational sessions took place the day after Reagan's dismal news conference. "It was a long, tough discussion," Shultz later told Congress, "not the kind of discussion I ever thought I'd have with the President of the United States. . . . It was 'bark off' all the way." Hurt and angered by the criticism, Reagan continued to insist that the purpose of the arms sales had been to improve relations with Iran, and not to trade for the hostages. But by this time, Shultz had marshaled enough data to know better. "Mr. President," he replied, "no one looking at the record will agree with you."

The second front was to go public with a campaign to win support for his position. In interviews on television and with print journalists, Shultz confirmed reports that he had opposed the secret operations from the beginning, and he vowed they would not be allowed to continue if he, the nation's chief foreign policy officer, had anything to say about it. This went beyond discreet disagreement; if the administration had been a military vessel at sea, Shultz could have been tried for mutiny. His "public pouting," as Bill Casey characterized it, aroused the wrath of the "shovel brigade" and others who were still committed to the cover-up and wanted the discredited policies to continue. In a personal letter to the President, Casey urged him to fire the secretary of state. Other loyalists did not go that far, but some of them—notably, Regan, Poindexter, and Bush—grumbled among themselves that if Shultz couldn't support the President, he should resign. The First Lady also turned against Shultz, although her main concern, as usual, was not over policy per se, but perception and loyalty. Nancy Reagan was enraged because Shultz was not standing up for her Ronnie in his hour of trial.

But the secretary of state also had his share of allies. The press generally hailed him as a hero for taking a strong stand on principle, and Reagan's critics on Capitol Hill warned the President he would only make matters worse if he now turned against the man who had tried to prevent the tangled mess into which the administration had blundered. Even within the administration, there were many officials, especially in the second and third echelon, who sided with Shultz. They went on the offensive in their own background briefings with reporters, contending that Poindexter and North were dangerous men who, if not stopped— and stopped soon—would drag the vacillating President to the brink of impeachment. On the battlefield the Reaganites had always regarded as their natural turf, public relations, candor and criticism were scoring impressive victories over the forces of "spin control."

The other man who helped resolve the situation, almost in spite of himself, was Attorney General Edwin Meese. Meese was still being overshadowed by the performance of the other member of the original White House troika who had gone on to a Cabinet post. For James Baker was enjoying almost as much success as Treasury secretary as he had during the first term as chief of staff. There were, to be sure, some unconquered problems, such as the huge budget and trade deficits. But in general terms, the economy was still strong, and the malevolent forces that had plagued the

Carter administration—soaring inflation and interest rates—were under control. In addition, it was Baker and his people at Treasury who had formed the strategy and led the fight for the tax reform law, and in the fall of 1986, he was still savoring that triumph.

Ed Meese, on the other hand, was merely plodding along at the Justice Department. He was, in fact, lucky even to be there. The result of the long investigation into Meese's tangled financial affairs that preceded his confirmation was that he had stopped just short of violating any law, and enough senators were willing to give him the benefit of the doubt to vote to confirm his nomination. (Ironically, the new attorney general, who had such a heavy cloud of suspicion hovering over him, still prided himself on being a staunch law-and-order man. "You don't have many suspects who are innocent of a crime," he once asserted in a disturbing reversal of the time-honored view that one is innocent until proved guilty.) At Justice, Meese did little to justify his appointment. Shortly after taking office, he launched a much-ballyhooed campaign against pornography that, more than anything else, was an object of mirth and derision. Beyond that, he spent much of his time and energy in generally unsuccessful efforts to overturn Supreme Court decisions on civil rights and other social issues.

Now that Mike Deaver and Bill Clark had left the administration, Meese had the distinction of being Reagan's most loyal and enduring deputy, the only member of the team who had been serving the President since the earliest days in Sacramento. Because of their long-standing relationship, Meese was especially attuned to Reagan's shortcomings, which were so vividly on display at the November 19 news conference. It was obvious to Meese that the President had not been given a clear and coherent picture of the events that had taken place, and two days after the press had worked Reagan over, the attorney general went to him and volunteered to help. Meese proposed conducting a series of interviews with all the principal participants in an effort to bring cohesion to the facts. What he had in mind was not a formal inquiry, but just an attempt, as he put it, "to get our arms around the problem." Meese stressed that he would not be acting in his official capacity as attorney general, but merely as the President's personal troubleshooter, a role he had taken on many times in the past. Nor, of course, would he be an impartial investigator;

he had sat in on at least one critical discussion of the secret policy and had lent his support to those who advocated the arms sales to Iran.

In the months that followed, the Meese probe would be harshly criticized, and with good reason. The interviews he conducted were so casual that there was almost no written record of what was said in them. Moreover, according to some of the people he interrogated, Meese's questions were less than penetrating, and much of the time he neglected to make follow-up inquiries on salient points. His overall tone was friendly and sympathetic, even when confronting those who were reluctant to accept their just share of the blame. Nor was that the worst of it. Instead of imposing an immediate clamp on all the relevant documents, Meese gave North and Poindexter ample time and opportunity to destroy vital evidence—and destroy it they did. As soon as he found out about the Meese inquiry, North convened a massive "shredding party," as he called it, while Poindexter, the computer expert, went to work clearing all his memory banks of pertinent data. Months later, during the congressional hearings, Warren Rudman, the highest-ranking Republican on the Senate committee, delivered a blunt assessment of Meese's investigation in an interview with *The New York Times*. "I tend to believe it was a case of gross incompetence," said Rudman. "I guess it's better to be dumb than crooked."

Nevertheless, Meese's slipshod inquiry did somehow manage to stumble across the memo that revealed the diversion plan. That piece of legal dynamite was enough to alarm even Meese, who now realized that Reagan had no choice but to separate himself as cleanly as possible from the covert operations and the aides who had engineered them. When Meese took that evidence to the President, the old actor professed to be shocked and claimed he had no idea that funds from the Iranian sales had been used for that purpose. Yet he, too, now understood that the scandal could no longer be contained, and it was then that Reagan made the moves that were necessary to salvage his presidency. It was a vital point of recognition. Had Reagan not acted to reverse his course, he would have sunk deeper and deeper into the intricacies of the cover-up.

Prodded by an angry Don Regan, who now realized the burgeoning scandal was likely to harm *his* reputation, the President agreed that Poindexter would have to resign. Regan and Meese were dispatched to deliver the news, and when Poindexter walked into the Oval Office to submit his resignation, Reagan said that he hoped the admiral understood this was "in the tradition of the Navy . . . of the captain accepting responsibility." A noble sentiment, but Reagan seemed unable or unwilling to comprehend that in this particular context, *he* was the captain of the ship and Poindexter merely a bridge officer who had fouled up his watch. In the case of North, mere resignation was deemed to be insufficient. In the few weeks since the story broke, the volatile Marine had been portrayed in the press as the mastermind behind the covert policies, and to help calm matters, he would have to be fired as an act of public repudiation. Yet on the day the firing took place, Reagan called North and adopted a curiously sympathetic tone toward the man whose misguided zeal had brought so much grief to his administration. "Ollie," he said, "you're a national hero," praise he would repeat on several occasions in the months that followed. Then, drawing from his favorite frame of reference, Reagan offered a cryptic message of solace: "This is going to make a great movie one day."

Operation Damage Control then moved on to other fronts. The day after he announced that Poindexter and North had been let go, Reagan appointed a three-man commission to probe into what had gone wrong with his national-security apparatus. Each member of the bipartisan trio—John Tower, Edmund Muskie, and Brent Scowcroft—had years of experience in Washington. Meese, in the meantime, tried to keep the criminal investigation under his control at the Justice Department, but he soon discovered he could not get away with that. In response to outside pressure, the attorney general reluctantly appointed an independent counsel, Lawrence E. Walsh, and the entire investigation was turned over to him. And on Capitol Hill, both houses of Congress were launching their own detailed inquiries into the scandal.

Yet even as he moved to stave off a disaster that could have destroyed his presidency, Reagan continued to insist in private conversations that it never had been his intention to swap arms for hostages, and to assert that the motives behind the covert operations were deserving of praise, not condemnation. Even his public statements were notable for their lack of chagrin or regret. To Reagan, the chief culprit was the press. In late November, he revealed those feelings in an interview with *Time* magazine's veteran Washington correspondent Hugh Sidey. "There is a bitter bile in my throat these days," he told Sidey.

> I've never seen the sharks circling like they are now with blood in the water. What is driving me up the wall is that [the arms sale to Iran] wasn't a failure until the press got a tip from that rag in Beirut and began to play it up. . . . This whole thing boils down to a great irresponsibility on the part of the press.

But on this issue, the majority of Americans were not inclined to blame the messenger. They felt that it was the President who had been guilty of "great irresponsibility." In early December, a CBS News–New York Times poll disclosed that Reagan's overall approval rating had plunged from 67 to 46 percent in a single month, the largest one-month decline in presidential approval ever recorded. Even more alarming, a vast majority—as many as 90 percent, according to one *Newsweek* poll—believed that Reagan was lying, still covering up what he knew about the Iran-Contra affair. In addition, many people said they were angry and disillusioned. The last thing they had expected from this President, who had set such a resolute tone with his hard-line rhetoric, was that he would sanction the sale of U.S. arms to the Ayatollah Khomeini. Those who live by the polls die by the polls, and no one understood that truism better than the PR-conscious operatives in the Reagan White House.

The sharp drop in public support wasn't their only worry as the administration staggered through the final days of 1986. One of the more obvious casualties of the scandal was Reagan's foreign policy, which was now in a shambles. Allies were shocked by the disclosures, and some said the U.S. government could never again be trusted to keep its word or honor its commitments. The Israelis, in particular, were incensed by the maladroit suggestion, during the early phase of the cover-up, that they had acted on their own without Washington's approval. But from the point of view of Casey, North, and the others who had so fervently believed in the enterprise, the most devastating blow of all was the collapse of Project Democracy and related efforts to help the Contras. There was now no chance a Democratic-controlled Congress would comply with the administration's requests on that explosive issue. Thus, for North and his cohorts, the irony was that by embarking on secret missions to circumvent the law, they had, in the end, betrayed the cause to which they were so committed.

Nor was it just a story of disgrace and failure. On a more poignant level there were tragedy and near-tragedy. Bill Casey, employing all his finesse in the art of bureaucratic intrigue, managed to survive the purge. But in mid-December, the seventy-three-year-old Casey was stricken with a malignant brain tumor. At first, the prognosis was encouraging; there was even talk that the old warrior would eventually be able to resume his duties as director of the CIA. But the optimism soon faded, and in late January he resigned. Casey died on May 6, 1987, leaving behind a host of crucial questions that would remain unanswered. But by then, the depth of his involvement in the covert operations had become known. At the congressional hearings the day before Casey died, Richard Secord named him as Oliver North's secret patron, the sinister mastermind of Project Democracy.

Bud McFarlane also had a serious health problem, but in his case the affliction was psychological. During the frantic scramble for survival that characterized the early attempts to prevent the affair from exploding, McFarlane went along with the cover-up. In particular, when it came to explaining the first two arms sales in 1985, the ones in which his own position was so vulnerable, he helped to fabricate the lie that Israel had acted on its own initiative, without the approval or even the knowledge of officials in Washington. During those turbulent days in November, he also had to contend, once again, with his former bête noire, Don Regan, who was spreading the story that the entire enterprise had been cooked up by McFarlane—that he had acted on his own—and therefore should assume the full responsibility for dragging the White House into such a mess. That reckless accusation reopened old wounds from the days when Regan had fanned the gossip that McFarlane was involved in an extramarital affair. In a bitter memo to Poindexter, McFarlane wrote, "This will be the second lie Don Regan has sowed against my character, and I won't stand for it."

McFarlane eventually underwent a kind of epiphany that led him to conclude he had a duty to his country that transcended all other obligations. But after he decided to cooperate with the various investigations, he soon discovered that he was virtually alone on the jagged edge of culpability. McFarlane could abide the fact that the President was disavowing direct knowledge of certain key decisions, for he truly believed that whatever else happened, the Reagan presidency must find a way to survive this crisis. But he had nothing but contempt for the way North and Poindexter were cowering behind the Fifth Amendment, while he, McFarlane, was doing his best to present a full and accurate account of the events in testimony before Congress and the Tower Commission, the three-man panel Reagan had appointed to investigate the scandal. He could hardly believe that North and Poindexter—who, like him, were graduates of Annapolis, with all its scrupulous traditions—were exploiting the Fifth Amendment to save themselves. Appearing before the Tower Commission was an especially excruciating ordeal for McFarlane. Two members of that commission, John Tower and Brent Scowcroft, were former mentors, men he admired to the point of idolatry. Having to admit to them that he had lied to Congress to conceal the facts about the covert operations was an experience that filled McFarlane with an almost unbearable anguish.

The more he testified and implicated himself while the others continued to be silent, the more McFarlane felt he had been abandoned by his former colleagues. It was as if he were acting out Regan's malicious fantasy that he should take the hit for everyone else. By early February 1987, the pressures were taking a dreadful toll on McFarlane's psyche. He was, by then, sliding into the depths of a life-threatening depression. He already had been through two long sessions with the Tower Board and was scheduled for another round of hard questioning on February 9. The night before he was to make that appearance, he wrote farewell notes to his wife and others, then swallowed about twenty Valium pills in an attempt to take his own life.

The next morning, he was rushed to Bethesda Naval Hospital, where he slowly regained the will to live. Months of therapy followed, and nearly two years after that moment of despair, McFarlane discussed his suicide attempt in an interview with *The New York Times*. "No one has ever really understood why I did it because it doesn't fit our tradition of suicide," he explained. He then referred to "a tradition in the Far East that when a public official fails to do his duty, he has an obligation to the state to sacrifice his life. And I thought I had failed the country."

16

Fallout

"Pardon me, but it's not your ass I'm
talking about. I'm talking about the
country."
                    —Michael Deaver

During the early weeks of 1987, when McFarlane was sinking into
his suicidal depression, his former adversary at the White House,
Don Regan, was losing a battle of his own. Regan had become the
target of the same kind of internecine campaign that he had waged
against McFarlane in the summer and autumn of 1985. Leading
the attack against him was Nancy Reagan, who, during the weeks
of turmoil over the Iran-Contra affair, was determined to drive
the chief of staff out of the White House.

For years, dating back to the "Governor Nancy" days in Sacramento, Mrs. Reagan's critics had portrayed her as a harridan
behind the throne, an elegantly coiffed, Rodeo Drive version of
Lady Macbeth. During those early years, when Bill Clark and later
Ed Meese were running the governor's office, they were so concerned about Nancy's meddlesome nature that they assigned the
young Mike Deaver to what soon became known as the "Mommy

Watch." That, as we've seen, turned out to be Deaver's personal ticket to power and influence. Then in 1981, when the Californians descended on Washington, Deaver once again took on the role of buffer between the First Lady and the White House staff, and many recognized the value of Deaver's service on that sensitive front. When Jim Baker was chief of staff, he appreciated all the aggravation Deaver had to put up with to keep Mrs. Reagan in good humor and discourage her from interfering in the day-to-day process of running the Reagan administration. So, too, did Regan when he and Baker swapped jobs. "In my first months as Chief of Staff, I benefited greatly from Deaver's wisdom in these matters," Regan later wrote. "From the viewpoint of his unique knowledge of the First Lady's character and methods, he understood that Mrs. Reagan would place demands on me and my time that I could not foresee."

What he should have foreseen, however, was that once Deaver left the White House, Regan would no longer have that "wisdom" and "unique knowledge" at his disposal. Yet even if he had stayed on, it's unlikely that even Deaver could have smoothed over the frictions that developed in Regan's relationship with the President's wife. For in contrast to the courtly Baker, Don Regan had an abrasive personality that rubbed the First Lady the wrong way.

Their first serious clash occurred in the summer of 1985 when the President was recuperating from his cancer surgery. Mrs. Reagan was understandably worried about her husband's health and recovery. She had always been protective of his time and energy, and now, more than ever, she was determined to shield him from the stress of his duties as President. Regan, in her view, was insensitive to those concerns. He had established a rule that except for the First Lady, he was the only one who would be allowed unlimited access to Reagan's hospital room. Yet as far as she was concerned, there was no one else besides her (except for the doctors, of course) who was entitled to that privilege, and she resented the way Regan always seemed to be in her husband's hospital room, disturbing his rest and pressing him to discuss matters of policy.

Even worse was his arrogance. Mrs. Reagan noticed that Regan almost seemed to welcome the President's illness as an opportunity to demonstrate that he was everything he had proclaimed himself to be: the chief executive officer of the Reagan administration who, now that the chairman of the board was disabled, had taken on the burdens of the Oval Office. "We'll try to make as many decisions as we can without involving him," he assured a reporter from *The Washington Post.* "We'll try to spare him as many of the details as possible." Such talk, even under the circumstances of convalescence, violated the code of loyal Reaganites who, for the most part, were determined to conceal the President's detachment from the decision-making process. Regan also made self-important statements to the press about Reagan's condition. After one of his hospital visits, he jauntily told reporters, "I tried to test him today, to see was he alert."

Such posturing at her husband's expense infuriated Mrs. Reagan, and she let Regan know how she felt. Not long after that angry exchange, Regan delegated the job of "handling" the First Lady to one of his aides. But Regan's surrogate was no Mike Deaver, and when Mrs. Reagan discovered that the chief of staff was trying to cut off her direct access to him, she exploded all over again. Obviously, Nancy Reagan did not regard herself as a nuisance who needed to be "handled." According to Jane Mayer and Doyle McManus, Ed Rollins, who was getting set to leave his post as head of the political office in the White House (largely because he couldn't stomach Regan's overbearing style of management), later recalled that at one point that summer, he told Regan, jokingly, that one of Regan's "burdens in life . . . is to take Mrs. Reagan's shit." The remark apparently hurt. According to Rollins, Regan turned on him in a fury and shouted, "I've never let any broad push me around before, and I'm not about to start now."

The irate response was indicative of Regan's basic attitude, not only toward Mrs. Reagan but, it seemed, toward women in general. Even some of his public statements revealed the swaggering bias of an earlier era when male chauvinism flourished. Once, when asked why the administration wasn't doing more to impose economic sanctions against South Africa because of its apartheid policy, Regan breezily suggested that American women would not want to give up their primary source of diamonds and gold. On another occasion, at the time of the first summit meeting in Geneva, he asserted that the Reagan-Gorbachev talks would be of no interest to women because "they're not going to understand throwweights, or what is happening in Afghanistan, or what is happening in human rights."

For more than a year after Reagan's cancer operation, Regan and the First Lady feuded, and even on those occasions when they made the effort to be civil toward each other, they could not conceal their animosity. There were long periods when Mrs. Reagan would make a point of barely speaking to the chief of staff, except in formal tones of disdain. At other times, she would enrage Regan with her demands, based on the latest astrological portents, that her husband's appointments or travel plans be changed. Nor was it only the signs of the zodiac that prompted her to call with her complaints. According to Regan, if she was unhappy with a speech that had been written for the President, she would call to insist that it be changed; or if she was dissatisfied with a member of the staff, she would badger Regan to get rid of him.

Apparently, such demands even extended to Cabinet officers. Regan later wrote that Mrs. Reagan pressured him to force the resignation of Labor Secretary Ray Donovan in early 1985 when the legal problems from his days as a New Jersey contractor caught up with him. And later that year, she waged a similar campaign to banish Margaret Heckler, the secretary of Health and Human Services. "You know Ronnie will never fire her," Regan quoted the First Lady as saying. "He can't even talk to a woman in a stern voice. She'll just twist him around her little finger."

Such intrusive behavior not only exasperated Regan but puzzled him. He was aware that Nancy Reagan was not the first President's wife who had tried to wield authority beyond her sphere. Eleanor Roosevelt and Rosalynn Carter, to cite just two, were strong-willed First Ladies who were accused of exerting undue influence. But Mrs. Roosevelt and Mrs. Carter generally used their leverage within the context of the marital bond. What Regan found so intriguing about Mrs. Reagan was that instead of appealing directly to her husband, she maneuvered around him and tried to pressure his advisers. That odd approach led Regan to conclude that either she understood that her husband could not be counted on to take decisive action, or that Reagan, believing her views on policy and personnel were not to be taken seriously, merely humored her in his genial way. Of those two possibilities, Regan rather hoped the latter was the case.

The cold war between Mrs. Reagan and the chief of staff lasted until the autumn of 1986, when it turned hot and flared into open hostility. The Iran-Contra scandal exacerbated it. Mrs. Reagan was furious at Regan for his tasteless remark about the "shovel brigade," with its clear implication that Regan and his beleaguered staff had to clean up the garbage that had been left by the President. The First Lady was also contemptuous of his unseemly behavior in the face of the criticisms being leveled at the White House. From the day he took over as chief of staff, Regan had boasted that he was the man in charge. Yet now he was cravenly trying to shift the blame onto McFarlane and others—anyone but himself. Nancy Reagan resented it; as far as she was concerned, Regan had failed in his duty to protect the President and therefore should be fired. Bringing about Regan's ouster became a prime objective in her life that fall, one she pursued unrelentingly.

But Don Regan was tenacious, and he fought hard to keep his job and defend his reputation. Yet it was a battle he practically had to fight alone. His contempt toward Congress and the press left him with virtually no allies in those two vital centers of power. Even within the administration, Regan had few supporters outside his own staff. There, too, his arrogance and autocratic methods had alienated many officials. His most powerful ally in the struggle to resist Mrs. Reagan's efforts to oust him was, oddly enough, her husband. The President still relished the pleasure of Regan's company, the locker-room camaraderie and bawdy jokes that enlivened their daily conversations. Beyond that, he was responsive to Regan's argument that he should be kept on; because of the scandal, the White House already had been rocked, and the President felt that he needed his trusty CEO to help him through the rest of the crisis.

Mrs. Reagan, in the meantime, had summoned Mike Deaver to help pull the rope on her end of the tug-of-war. There was irony in that, for two years earlier it was Deaver who had been recruited by Baker to sell Reagan on the idea of the job swap that put Regan into the White House, which he did with his memorable line "Mr. President, I've brought you a playmate your own age." Yet now, Deaver lent his support to the First Lady's campaign to get rid of Regan.

When Deaver and Mrs. Reagan presented their case to the President in early December 1986, he rejected their arguments. Reagan stoutly defended Regan's performance as chief of staff. He said that all the criticism of Regan's handling of the Iran-Contra affair was a "bum rap." So the next step, Deaver and Mrs. Reagan decided, was to bring in an influential outsider whose judgment the President respected. The man they chose was Robert Strauss, the former chairman of the Democratic National Committee, who was regarded as one of the shrewdest political pros in Washington. In his meeting with Reagan, Strauss went directly to the point, telling him that he had serious problems in two critical areas: Congress and the press. "Don Regan," he said, "has no allies on the Hill, and no friends in the media. You've got to get a fresh face in that job."

Yet again, Reagan was adamant. "Don has been loyal to me," he told Strauss, "and I'm not going to throw him to the wolves." Besides, he said, the worst of the crisis was behind them. It would all blow itself out in a week or so. But of course it did not, and in the weeks ahead, Deaver and Mrs. Reagan persisted in their efforts to change the President's mind. Joining forces with them during this period was Stu Spencer, their ally from the early days in California. Two meetings that December were marked by lively exchanges between Deaver and Reagan. At the first one, when the President blurted out that he wasn't going to fire Regan "just to save my own ass," Deaver replied: "Well pardon me, but it's not your ass I'm talking about. I'm talking about the country."

Reagan bristled at that and took his revenge a few nights later when the Deavers were invited to a Christmas dinner party at the White House. Because it was strictly a social occasion, Deaver went out of his way to avoid talking about Regan and the Iran-Contra affair. But when the conversation turned to the innocuous subject of presidential awards, he casually suggested possible candidates for the Medal of Freedom. Reagan, who was sitting next to Deaver at the dinner table, promptly responded with a pointed put-down that stunned the longtime aide. "Mike," he said, "I've got competent people at the White House who make those decisions." It was as if he were talking to a casual acquaintance instead of a man who had devoted two decades of his life to Ronald Reagan's political welfare. As Deaver later wrote, "It seemed as if the twenty years I had worked for him had vanished in the blink of an eye."

The President's resistance to the anti-Regan lobbying testified to the hold the chief of staff had on Reagan's affections. Rejecting Strauss's advice was one thing, but Deaver and Spencer had been two of the President's most trusted confidants, longtime members of the inner circle who had helped to shape Reagan's entire political career. In addition, his wife's campaign to force Regan's dismissal continued, both behind closed doors and in the press. Her confederates began to spread the word that the First Lady and top officials in the administration wanted Regan out of the

White House. In no time at all, reports to that effect were published in *The New York Times* and *The Washington Post*. By the early weeks of 1987, the feud was out in the open, and the sidebar story was getting almost as much attention as the still-unfolding drama of the Iran-Contra affair.

Yet even then, Regan continued to exude the defiance and self-confidence that had always been his trademark. The former head of Merrill Lynch was still bullish on his prospects for survival as White House chief of staff. He had been under steady attack since mid-November, and he reasoned that the more time that elapsed without any definitive moves made against him, the more he could rely on Reagan's resolve to hold the line in his defense. Mrs. Reagan and the others had taken their best shots at him, and yet he was still there, swapping one-liners with the President. In his arrogance, Regan even began to suspect that for all her presumed influence, the First Lady was a paper tigress. That proved to be his fatal mistake.

The war of nerves extended into February. By now, when Mrs. Reagan bumped into Regan or reached him on the telephone, she would ask in feigned surprise, "Oh, are you still here, Don?" One such call in early February brought on a bitter argument over the petty question of when the President should hold his next press conference. Fury came pouring out in that exchange, and Mrs. Reagan claimed Regan ended the conversation by hanging up on her, slamming the receiver down hard in her ear. (If so, Regan later asserted, it was only because he was a minisecond quicker and beat her to the punch.) When she told her husband about the quarrel and the way it ended, he was shocked. Regan's display of rudeness offended the chivalric instincts that were so much a part of the President's nature, and the next time Reagan was asked by a reporter whether his chief of staff should resign, he simply shrugged and said, "Well, that is up to him."

Not long thereafter, Vice President Bush was assigned to the task of telling Regan he was through. There was one final and awkward conversation with the President, during which Regan lost his temper in the White House for the last time. "You can't do this to me!" he shouted at Reagan. "I deserve better treatment than that!" He went out as he had come in, full of vinegar and gall. On February 27, even before Regan had a chance to submit his formal resignation, it was announced that Howard Baker, the recently retired senator and Republican moderate who had been majority leader during Reagan's first term, had been appointed to the post of White House chief of staff.

Regan had been looking forward to the public conclusions of the Tower Commission's investigation. Because he had not been directly involved in the covert operations, he assumed that the three-man commission would exonerate him and that its verdict, clearing him of all suspicion, would silence his critics. That was another miscalculation. The Tower report was made public the day before Regan's resignation, and in blunt terms it indicted him for dereliction of duty, precisely the charge that Nancy Reagan and her allies had been leveling against him. "More than any other Chief of Staff in recent memory, [Regan] asserted personal control over the White House staff and sought to extend this control to the National Security Adviser," the report said. "He must bear primary responsibility for the chaos that descended upon the White House. . . ."

Nor was the President spared, although the judgment on him was more ambiguous. For the most part, the investigators chose to accept Reagan's assertions of ignorance and amnesia. They believed him when he said that neither Poindexter nor anyone else had told him about the diversion plan. One member of the panel, recalling the interview with Reagan in the Oval Office, later said that he left that session with "a gut sense" that the President didn't know about it, and that visceral feeling "was reinforced by his general sense of confusion." They also believed him when, in response to a question whether he had authorized the first arms sale to Iran in 1985, Reagan insisted, "The simple truth is, I don't remember—period." In its report, the Tower Commission drew a portrait of a disengaged President who "did not seem to be aware of the way in which the operation was implemented and the full consequences of U.S. participation." John Tower put it more crisply in his statement to the press the day the report was released. The President, he said, "clearly didn't understand the nature of this operation, who was involved, and what was happening."

Many Americans found that hard to fathom. Polls continued to indicate widespread belief that Reagan still had not revealed everything he knew about the Iran-Contra affair; that he was, in fact, still covering up. Although the Tower Commission was praised for its integrity and independence, it was noted that the commission had only two months to conduct its investigation. In addition, Poindexter and North had invoked the Fifth Amendment. Their refusal to cooperate with the inquiry left many questions unanswered, and so the focus of attention quickly shifted to the next investigative phase: the congressional hearings into the scandal, which were scheduled to begin in the spring.

One reason for all the skepticism was that most Americans simply could not believe that a President, any President, could be so out of touch with the policies and actions of his own government. They could not understand how Reagan could have forgotten whether or not he authorized the first arms sales, or how he could have signed presidential findings without comprehending what they meant, or how he could not have known about Oliver North's plan to divert funds from the arms deal to the Contras. Their basic perception of the American presidency had been shaped by a tradition that extended back over half a century to the days of Franklin D. Roosevelt. It was FDR who created the modern, activist presidency, transforming the office into the center of action and power in ways it never had been before, except in times of grave national crisis, such as the Civil War. Moreover, the pattern Roosevelt established became the model that his successors sought to emulate. Every chief executive since FDR, from Truman to Carter, had been, in varying degrees, an activist who personally guided the course of foreign policy and set down the legislative agenda for domestic affairs.

But Ronald Reagan was a throwback to the pre-Roosevelt era. His model was Calvin Coolidge, the President who had amused so many of his countrymen with his habit of sleeping twelve hours a day and, when he was awake, saying and doing as little as possible. On those rare occasions when "Silent Cal" did feel compelled to speak in public, he confined his utterances to dry aphorisms, such as the pronouncement that revealed his basic philosophy: "If the federal government should go out of existence, the common run of people would not detect the difference in the affairs of their daily life for a considerable length of time."

Reagan was in high school during Coolidge's reign, but the man's laissez-faire approach to the presidency made an enduring impression on him. It was an act of some significance when, shortly after he moved into the White House, he requested that Coolidge's portrait replace Harry Truman's in the Cabinet Room. Then in the summer of 1985, after his cancer surgery, Reagan spent his convalescence reading a biography of Coolidge. He later told Don Regan one of the many things he admired about that President was his decision to keep the government out of the marketplace. No mention was made of the fact that Coolidge's indifferent policies and tendency to ignore problems simmering beneath the surface of a fragile prosperity were later cited as a chief cause of the Depression.

But most Americans were too young to remember Coolidge and, conditioned by the vigorous examples of Roosevelt and his successors, they could not understand how Reagan could possibly be so passive and disengaged. Although Barry Goldwater was an avowed conservative, he, too, had been schooled in the tradition of the activist presidency, and he spoke for many of his countrymen when he declared that Reagan had to know what had been going on inside his own White House. With customary bluntness, Goldwater asserted that Reagan was "either a liar or incompetent."

Yet, without rushing to embrace Goldwater's alternative, the evidence strongly suggests that Reagan was not lying. His behavior during the events that produced the Iran-Contra affair was consistent with his political character and past performances. No one understood his detached nature better than the group of Californians who first recruited him to run for governor, then advised him to do as he was told and let them run the campaign. The other Californians who worked for him in Sacramento and later followed him to Washington also understood that they were expected to make the key decisions, and he would merely rubber-stamp them.

It was always the newcomers who were startled and had to make the adjustment. Jim Baker was stunned when, in his first major act as White House chief of staff, he presented Reagan with a legislative agenda for his first year in office, and the President promptly signed off on it without raising any questions or even discussing it in any detail. So was Don Regan when he put together a program for the second term, and received a similar response. So was Bud McFarlane when he drew up a blueprint of foreign policy goals in the hope of discovering what Reagan's priorities might be in that area, and the President blithely replied, "Let's do them all!" And finally, so was John Poindexter when Reagan signed crucial Presidential findings without pondering their significance or potential consequences. The incredible thing is how lucky Reagan had been all those years before the Iran-Contra scandal. Until then, his passive approach had always worked like a charm, so it's no wonder that he himself was bewildered when his longtime habit of letting others make critical decisions for him finally led him and his presidency into deeply troubled waters.

The prospect of the televised Iran-Contra drama on Capitol Hill revived memories of the Watergate hearings that had held so much of the country spellbound fourteen years earlier. Indeed, the sudden resurfacing of Howard Baker into national prominence reminded Americans of his performance in 1973 as the ranking Republican member of the Watergate committee and his key question "What did the President know, and when did he know it?" In the late winter and spring of 1987, comedians had had a field day delivering scornful parodies of that question as it presumably applied to Reagan: "What did the President forget, and when did he forget it?" Or, "What did the President *not* know, and when did he decide not to know it?"

The comparisons to Watergate were no comfort to the White House. The people around Reagan knew how that scandal ended, and as they braced themselves for the televised hearings, the word *impeachment* often hung in the air, unspoken, but menacing. One person who was terrified of that prospect was Nancy Reagan. That was one reason why she had gone after Don Regan with such purpose. Mrs. Reagan was determined to create the impression that the President was doing everything he could to clean house and distance himself from anyone who had been involved in the decisions to carry out the covert operations. (Another man to be fired was Bill Casey, but before she had a chance to move against him, he was stricken with the brain tumor that caused his death.) In *Landslide*, authors Mayer and McManus quote a White House official as saying, "Nancy was so worried about impeachment she was ready to trade anything to avert it. She would have brought in a Democrat as Chief of Staff, if that's what it took." A family friend of the First Lady went even further, telling Mayer and McManus that if the threat of impeachment ever became imminent, "she would have done anything to buy Congress off."

Mrs. Reagan's anxiety was not all that unrealistic. Before the hearings were under way, there was talk of impeachment in other quarters as well. Even some people who believed that Reagan was telling the truth took the position that his professed ignorance and inaction did not necessarily let him off the hook. They pointed out that all public officials—but especially Presidents—are responsible for acts of omission as well as those of commission. Reagan had sworn to uphold the Constitution and see that the laws of the land were faithfully executed. The case could be made that through negligence and misjudgment, he had failed to live up to that oath, an impeachable offense.

But impeachment is as much a political act as it is a legal proceeding. Thus, in the Iran-Contra affair, Reagan was able to draw from a deep reservoir of popular affection to see him through. If there had been hard evidence to prove that he was lying or covering up, then the public might have turned against him, as it had against Nixon fourteen years earlier. But failing that, Congress could not have impeached him simply because he had been disengaged. To the millions of Americans who liked Ronald Reagan, mere negligence or failure to execute the law faithfully simply was not an impeachable offense.

The congressional hearings turned out to be an anticlimax. They provoked no startling revelations. There was some drama in the testimony of Oliver North, but in legal terms, the high point was John Poindexter's testimony. Once he publicly assumed full responsibility for approving the diversion plan, the suspense was over. It was understood that the eventual fate of North and Poindexter would be determined in court. But for the moment, North's emotional testimony helped to distort public perceptions of the scandal and recast it in a more favorable light. And although Poindexter's sketchy account of events aroused plenty of skepticism it did succeed in taking Reagan out of jeopardy.

Even before the Iran-Contra storm finally blew itself out, other troubles were bearing down on the Reagan White House. By the autumn of 1987, it was evident that numerous officials who had served in the administration were having difficulty avoiding criminal indictment and/or charges of ethical impropriety. As if Iran-Contra had not been embarrassing enough, the Reagan presidency soon found itself tarnished by a rash of misdeeds that became known as "the sleaze factor."

One of the more celebrated cases involved Mike Deaver. By his own admission, Deaver had left the White House in the spring of 1985 because he wanted to make a lot of money, and he quickly turned that quest into reality. The public relations and lobbying firm he set up in Washington became a highly lucrative enterprise, in large part because Deaver was correctly perceived as a man who had inside connections at the Reagan White House. But a federal conflict-of-interest law prohibits former government employees from indulging in certain lobbying practices for a period of time after leaving office. Deaver's firm began making money so fast that suspicions were aroused, and a congressional committee decided to look into its activities. A special prosecutor also was appointed to delve into the question of whether Deaver had violated the law.

In the spring of 1986, he was formally questioned by the congressional committee, and some of his answers, under oath, were plainly misleading. That testimony became the basis for his prosecution. In March 1987, Deaver was indicted on five counts of perjury. He was accused of lying to both Congress and a federal grand jury about his lobbying activities. Deaver was later convicted, and although he received a relatively light sentence, the notoriety destroyed both his business and his reputation. But he did not suffer alone. In a strikingly similar case, another old Reagan hand, Lyn Nofziger, was indicted in July 1987 on charges of illegal lobbying, and he, too, was later convicted.

Nor was that all. Yet another member of the early California crowd, Ed Meese, barely escaped indictment. Back in 1985, when the Senate finally decided, with considerable misgivings, to confirm his nomination as attorney general, Meese was sent to the Department of Justice with a warning. Even some of the senators who had voted to confirm cautioned him that in light of his dubious financial dealings, which had prompted so many investigations, he henceforth would have to be completely clean. Meese either forgot that admonition or chose to ignore it.

In the spring of 1987, Meese was implicated in a mushrooming scandal involving Wedtech, a New York–based defense contractor that had become the target of numerous federal and state investigations. Some of the trails in those inquiries led directly to Meese, and he was forced into the ignominious position of having to appoint an independent counsel to investigate his role in the scandal. It wasn't long before other charges against him began to surface, most of them centering on his longtime friendship with Robert Wallach, a San Francisco lawyer whose clients included

Wedtech and others who were doing business with the government. Meese was accused of exerting undue influence on behalf of Wallach and his clients. One could only conclude that Ed Meese had not learned his lesson, after all. From the time he appointed the independent counsel to investigate himself until the day he finally resigned as attorney general in July 1988, Meese had to conduct his duties under a constant fire of allegations and rising criticism that he was an ethical blemish on the administration. Even under the lax moral standards of the Reagan administration, his continued presence as the nation's chief law-enforcement officer was an embarrassment.

Many critics were quick to observe that Meese, Deaver, and Nofziger were all longtime Reaganites. The activities that got them into trouble left the sour impression that they had gone to Washington not to serve the country so much as to use their special connection in the White House to promote their own interests. Their presumed ethics raised disturbing questions about Reagan's ability to judge character, and even questions about Reagan himself. No one ever accused Reagan of being venal or corrupt, but his permissive attitude sent a message to those who, from the beginning, had been his most intimate political associates. He was not one to impose high standards of conduct, and although it could hardly be said that he encouraged his cronies to cut shady deals, he didn't go out of his way to discourage them, either. Besides, those who knew him best were well aware that he had more respect for men of means than he did for men of selfless dedication.

But the Californians weren't the only ones who erred. Toward the end of Reagan's presidency, some zealous reporter compiled a list of transgressors. The final tally revealed that more than a hundred members of the administration had been accused of either criminal or ethical misdeeds. That record invites comparison not with Watergate—which was essentially an exercise in the abuse of power—but with the excesses of the Teapot Dome scandal that occurred during the term of Warren G. Harding.

The sleaze epidemic, coupled with the Iran-Contra affair, had a corrosive effect on Reagan's power and prestige, and nowhere was that more evident than on Capitol Hill. During the first six years of the Reagan era, the Democrats in Congress had been on the defensive. They simply did not have the strength or resources to prevail against a highly popular President. But when the 100th Congress convened in January 1987, the Democrats controlled both houses for the first time since Reagan became President. Their days of compliance were over. Now it was Reagan who was on the defensive. Wasting no time, the Democratic leadership quickly set out to defy his authority and seize control of the legislative agenda.

The first significant test of strength came in late January. Ignoring the President's threat of a veto, Congress voted in favor of a $20 billion extension of the Clean Water Act. When Reagan did veto the bill, claiming that it was "loaded with waste and larded with pork," the legislators overrode it, establishing a pattern that would continue throughout the last two years of Reagan's presidency. In March 1987, the House, clearly reacting to the Iran-Contra scandal, voted to suspend further aid to the Contras until the White House provided an accounting of funds the rebels had received from private sources within the United States and elsewhere. (Not only was Project Democracy dead, but its secret donors were about to be exposed.) The following month, Congress enacted an $88 billion highway and mass transit bill over the President's veto, a particularly bitter defeat for Reagan, because he had chosen that measure as the test of his remaining influence.

Reagan was unaccustomed to such setbacks. He began looking for an opportunity to regain the initiative, and he was sure he had found one in the summer of 1987 when Supreme Court Justice Lewis Powell announced his retirement. Since coming to power, Reagan already had elevated William Rehnquist to chief justice and had appointed two associate justices, Sandra Day O'Connor and Antonin Scalia. Those appointments had strengthened the court's conservative bloc, and the President now had a chance to shift the ideological balance decisively to the right. In recent years, Powell, a judicial moderate, had played the "swing" role on the court, often casting the deciding vote in five to four decisions. Were he to be replaced by a rigid right-winger, the Supreme Court could be set on a solidly conservative course for many years to come.

To fill the vacancy, Reagan named Robert H. Bork, an outspoken conservative and a figure of considerable controversy. Bork had served as solicitor general in the Department of Justice during the Nixon administration and later, in 1982, he was appointed by Reagan to the U.S. Court of Appeals for the District of Columbia. He also had taught constitutional law at Yale, and it was the reputation he acquired as a legal scholar that aroused vehement opposition to his appointment. Bork was a strong advocate of a legal doctrine known as "original intent." According to that doctrine, courts can protect only those liberties that are guaranteed as rights under the Constitution; all other liberties are subject to limitation by the legislative branch. Bork argued that in deciding which liberties are constitutional rights, the courts must be guided by the "original intent" of the Founding Fathers who framed the document. Translated from the legalese, it meant that Bork had opposed a host of major Supreme Court decisions on such volatile social issues as civil rights, abortion, censorship, and right to privacy. As far as his critics were concerned, such unorthodox views made Bork not merely a conservative in the traditional sense but a dogmatic radical.

If his appointment had come one year earlier, at the time of the Rehnquist and Scalia nominations, Bork almost certainly would have been confirmed. But the Senate he had to confront in 1987 was a different body from the one Rehnquist and Scalia had faced, and Reagan no longer had the solid public support he had enjoyed in 1986. From the moment of Bork's nomination in early July until the Senate Judiciary Committee commenced its televised hearings in mid-September, opposition to his appointment steadily gathered strength. There was, of course, ample precedent for repudiation; the last time it occurred was 1969 and 1970, when the Senate successively rejected two of Nixon's nominees. By the time the hearings began, Bork already was on the defensive and his confirmation was in doubt.

From that point on, his prospects declined. In his testimony, Bork declared that he had changed his mind about a number of previously held opinions that had been shaped by his belief in the doctrine of original intent. But most members of the committee were skeptical. One Democrat, Patrick Leahy of Vermont, bluntly asked Bork whether his newfound moderation on certain sensitive issues represented a "confirmation conversion." Although Bork insisted it did not, a majority of the senators found his testimony unpersuasive. J. Bennett Johnston of Louisiana said Bork's attempt to renounce his lifelong legal philosophy reminded him of "a story they like to tell back home about the wife who finds her husband in bed with another woman. Caught red-handed, all the poor man could say in his own defense was, 'Honey, who are you going to believe? Me or your lying eyes?' " In early October, the Judiciary Committee voted nine to five to reject Bork's nomination, and later that month the full Senate followed suit with a fifty-eight–forty-two vote for rejection.

The day after Bork was repudiated by the Senate, an angry Reagan vowed, "My next nominee for the court will share Judge Bork's belief in judicial restraint—that a judge is bound by the Constitution to interpret laws, not make them." Then, on the advice of Ed Meese, Reagan proceeded to nominate one of Bork's colleagues on the U.S. Court of Appeals, Douglas H. Ginsburg.

Ginsburg was deemed to be a safe choice, mainly because he was not weighed down by the welter of controversial opinions that Bork had brought to his nomination. But then the trouble began. First came the disclosure that Ginsburg's wife had performed abortions during her medical training, a practice that offended the right-to-life advocates who formed such a militant part of Reagan's conservative constituency. And that was followed by the revelation that Ginsburg had smoked marijuana in the past, not only in his youth but as a member of the faculty at Harvard Law School. Presented with the evidence, there was only one decision the mortified Reagan White House could make: just say no. Judge Ginsburg promptly withdrew his nomination.

Reagan now managed to steer the process back onto a more dignified course. His third nominee for the seat that had been vacated by Powell was another federal judge, Anthony Kennedy, who had been serving on the U.S. Court of Appeals in California. Kennedy was a mainstream conservative with impressive credentials, and the Senate unanimously confirmed his nomination. Many legal scholars, in fact, predicted that the appointment of Kennedy would achieve the original objective of shifting the ideological balance of the Supreme Court decisively to the right. But the rejection of Bork and the Ginsburg fiasco had been frustrating and embarrassing experiences for the White House, and they reinforced suspicions that Reagan was losing his grip and power to command the course of events. There was no doubt that his influence over Congress had waned. *Congressional Quarterly* reported at the end of 1987 that the percentage of legislative issues on which the President had taken a stand and triumphed had plunged to the lowest point since the rating system was established in 1953. The previous low had been Richard Nixon's record in the Watergate year of 1973.

In October, as the Bork hearings were drawing to a close, one of the last members of the Judiciary Committee to reveal how he intended to vote was Howell Heflin, the portly and colorful senator from Alabama. On the day he finally decided to declare his intentions, Heflin did so with relish and in the down-home language of his Dixie roots. He compared Bork's chances of getting confirmed to "a Christmas turkey that has been in the oven four hours too long. No matter where you put your thumb and push," he said, "it's done."

Ornithological metaphors were in the air that season. One of them offered evidence that even some of the true believers who had formed the hard core of Reagan's support had reached the conclusion that the Reagan era was prematurely over, more than a year before the formal end of his presidency. "Reagan's not just a lame duck," asserted conservative spokesman Howard Phillips, "he's a capon."

Such sentiments did little for the morale of the Republicans as they looked ahead to 1988 and the presidential campaign that would determine who would follow Ronald Reagan into the White House. Among that dejected group, no one found the state of affairs more distressing than the man who, for the past seven years, had been quietly and dutifully playing the role of crown prince.

17

The Great Red Hope

"The man is a PR genius!"
—Washington spectator

For all the trouble and turmoil of Reagan's second term, one member of the Reagan team remained all but invisible. As Deaver, Meese, McFarlane, North, and Poindexter dueled at center stage with the demons of sleaze and Iran-Contra, George Bush was fighting his own demons in the wings. Bush's part in the administration had never been a major one. Reagan hardly knew him in the beginning, and he had never become a Reagan confidant. Bush was like a minor character in a play, neither hero nor villain but one who passes across the stage from time to time on errands that have little to do with the main storyline.

Even the decision to put him on the ticket in 1980 had been an afterthought, a decision made principally, said a Reagan friend, because "there was no place else to go." Reagan's advisers really had no one in mind as a possible running mate when they arrived in Detroit for the convention that summer. It had been some of Gerald Ford's people (notably Henry Kissinger) who came up with the novel idea of putting Ford on the ticket and for a day or so,

Reagan seriously considered that idea. What finally convinced him that it wouldn't work was Ford's trip to the CBS News anchor booth to discuss the idea on television with Walter Cronkite. The Reagans watched the interview in their Detroit hotel room, and to them Ford seemed to be saying that he was the one who would decide whether or not he joined Reagan on the ticket. As Cronkite continued to draw him out, the former President—to the Reagans, at least—seemed to be describing some sort of co-presidency of divided responsibilities. The longer the Reagans watched, the angrier they became and there was plenty of time for the anger to build. Cronkite had an inexhaustible supply of questions and Ford seemed eager to answer them all. To the Reagans, it seemed the interview would never end and they were growing progressively irritated.

That part was not entirely Ford's fault. Cronkite realized he had come upon the only real story at the convention; he was going to hold Ford in that booth as long as possible and the gentlemanly Ford was too polite to leave. Besides, Ford was enjoying himself. He liked to talk on television almost as much as the avuncular Cronkite. Executives at the other networks were furious, and underlings in the control rooms of NBC and ABC were in a state of high anxiety. The only story at the convention was being held hostage in the CBS anchor booth and everyone could see it. Not only *could* everyone see it, everyone *was* seeing it—the ultimate disaster for competitors in the world of network news ratings. As word of Ford's whereabouts swept the Joe Louis Arena, everyone who had a television set was trying to tune it to Cronkite. Through the huge window at the front of the booth, delegates on the floor and reporters from the other networks could see Ford chatting earnestly with the CBS anchorman.

Even those without access to a television set stared as if transfixed, content to watch even if they couldn't hear. There was bedlam in the press gallery. Newspaper reporters were scrambling to find television sets. What had Ford said to Cronkite? Had he confirmed that he was going on the ticket or not? At the entrance to the CBS anchor booth, there was real trouble. Reporters trying for their own interviews were pushing, shoving, and shouting to be in position to snag Ford when he finally left the booth. No one was more furious about Cronkite's scoop than ABC's tenacious Barbara Walters. There is no more formidable competitor in all of journalism, and Walters was trying to talk her way past a security

guard and get into the CBS booth herself when an equally formidable female aide to Cronkite blocked the entrance and bel-
lowed, "Listen, bitch, it's about time you showed a little fucking
courtesy and professionalism."

Humors were only slightly better in Reagan's suite. As the
interview finally concluded, Reagan summoned Deaver and instructed him to "tell Ford I want to talk to him." The interview
had convinced Reagan that a Reagan-Ford ticket wouldn't work,
and he told Ford as much when Deaver finally brought him to
the Reagan suite. That meeting came late in what had been a long
evening. Mrs. Reagan was already in a bad mood after watching
the interview and Reagan was growing weary. It was getting to
the time of night when Ronald Reagan just wanted to get some
sleep; still a decision on the vice president had to be made.

He had never been all that impressed by Bush. He knew little
about him, and friends said that what he did know he didn't
particularly like. After their celebrated primary debate earlier that
year in Nashua, New Hampshire, Reagan told some of his people
that Bush had seemed to "choke" during the encounter and that
was what bothered him. There was an upside to Bush, of course.
The polls suggested he would attract more votes for the ticket
than anyone except Ford and Reagan wanted to get the issue
settled once and for all. Unless someone had a better idea, he
said, why not Bush? When no one spoke up, a person in the suite
remembers that Reagan said, "Well, Bush it is."

In a final bit of irony that night, Bush had also watched
Cronkite's interview with Ford. He came to the same conclusion
that many others at the convention had: Ford would not have
talked so openly about being on the ticket unless he had already
been selected. To the cautious Bush, it was inconceivable that such
a subject could even be broached in public without clearance from
Reagan. Even after Jim Baker, then Bush's campaign manager,
had received a phone call from the Reagan camp and reported
that the Ford-Reagan deal was falling apart, Bush couldn't believe
he was still being considered. Nor did he let himself believe he
had a chance when the Secret Service called a few minutes later
and reported that its agents were occupying a suite just below "in
case anything is needed." When the call from Reagan finally came,
Bush had already decided to go to bed. The message was brief.
Reagan said he wanted to go to the convention hall and announce
that Bush would be his running mate, "if that was all right." Of

course it was all right, the startled Bush responded. He told Reagan he was honored to accept, and from that moment on he performed in the way he always did when given an important political assignment: he pledged his loyalty to his superior and promised to work hard and cheerfully at whatever tasks were given him.

Bush campaigned tirelessly for the ticket, and, once in the White House, he made a concerted effort to win Reagan's confidence. He was intensely loyal to the President, careful never to intrude in the limelight that he believed rightfully belonged to Reagan. He went to such lengths to avoid saying anything even mildly critical of Reagan that some on the staff wondered whether Bush actually held strong views of his own. Even his friends sometimes thought his loyalty bordered on obsequiousness, but that was Bush's way. When political opponents would taunt him about it he would say, "In my family loyalty was considered a virtue."

There was another side to it as well. In George Bush's political career, loyalty had been very good politics. His greatest political rewards had always come as a result of currying favor from those in positions of power. Such men did not hand out rewards to those who had been disloyal or disrespectful. Bush's second run for the Senate in 1970 had been a case in point. He made the race at the urging of Richard Nixon, who wanted to cleanse the Senate of liberal Democrats. Bush was then serving his second term as a congressman from a predominantly Republican district in Houston. When Nixon summoned him to the White House, he said that he recognized that a run for the Senate would mean giving up a safe congressional seat, a seat that Bush could expect to hold for as long as he wanted it. But, Nixon said, there was a real chance that Bush could win the coming Texas Senate race, and if he lost there would also be a reward: he would be considered for a high post in the administration. It was a deal Bush was happy to accept; he was confident he could beat his likely opponent, the liberal incumbent Democrat Ralph Yarborough.

As an unabashed liberal in an increasingly conservative state, Yarborough's political survivability was always tenuous, and he appeared more out of step than ever with the then-powerful conservative wing of the Texas Democratic party. Bush's analysis was more correct than he could have realized. Yarborough was so out of step with the conservatives that he was beaten in the Democratic primary by a little-known, conservative former congressman from south Texas named Lloyd Bentsen. Bentsen had no trouble beating Bush in the general election. He pictured the Ivy League–educated Texas transplant as an Easterner too liberal for Texas taste. Once it became clear that the liberal Yarborough would not be returning to the Senate, Nixon lost interest in that race and gave Bush virtually no help.

True to his word, however, once the election was over he offered Bush a job in the White House. Bush accepted graciously but with reservations. Working in the White House would have put him under the direct control of Nixon's two imperious deputies, H. R. Haldeman and John Ehrlichman, and that was a prospect Bush did not find inviting. He told Nixon that he was happy to serve in any way the President thought best but believed his talents could be put to better use at the United Nations. There, he said, he could be of real service to Nixon because the UN job would allow him to circulate in New York social circles, a territory where Nixon's political base was weakest. It was not the kind of argument that a person interested in foreign policy would normally make to get a diplomatic post, but it was the kind of reason that made real sense to the pragmatic Nixon and Bush got the job. (Bush's arguments were discovered in a memo that was found years later among Nixon's personal papers.)

Although Bush may have secured the UN post for reasons that had nothing to do with foreign policy expertise, he handled his diplomatic duties in credible fashion. His political maneuvering must have impressed Nixon as well. When Watergate turned nasty, it was the untainted Bush who was brought back to Washington to head the Republican National Committee. It was an assignment he accepted with his usual unabashed display of loyalty. "When the President asks you to do something, in my kind of system of civics, you ought to do it," he said. Nixon's confidence in Bush had been well placed, and Bush stuck with the beleaguered President until the end. He took the line that the Watergate hearings were "show biz" proceedings and repeatedly said that it was his belief that Nixon was telling the truth. It was not until the "smoking gun" tapes finally surfaced that Bush reversed himself and told congressional leaders, "The jig is up. . . . I would have voted to impeach."

*   *   *

Other appointive posts followed. During the Ford administration, Bush served as U.S. envoy to China and later as Director of the CIA. Then, as before, he carried out his duties in the good-soldier tradition of a faithful loyalist. The loyalty to his superiors that had always worked so well for Bush worked once more in the Reagan White House. He never really made Nancy Reagan's favorite list and the two couples never socialized, but Reagan came to enjoy Bush's company around the office. He especially liked the "joke of the day" that Bush always brought along to lighten up staff meetings and he appreciated Bush's deference. Some might make fun of Bush's efforts to keep a low profile, but the President was not among them.

For Bush, cultivating Reagan's goodwill came naturally. It was how he had been brought up and he was a genuinely thoughtful person, but staying on Reagan's good side was also central to his own strategy for capturing the presidency. Reagan's popularity in those early years surpassed anything that Washington had seen in modern times. If some of the magic rubbed off on Bush, there was no way it could hurt and he campaigned as enthusiastically for Reagan in 1984 as he had in 1980. For Bush, however, the 1984 landslide had an entirely different meaning than it did for Reagan.

Even though the Reagan-Bush ticket won going away, in the weeks after the election Bush himself felt that somehow he had come out a loser. He was unhappy with his performance in the debate with the Democratic vice presidential nominee Geraldine Ferraro, and made matters worse the following day when a network microphone picked up his voice telling a small group of construction workers that he had "kicked a little ass last night." Although Mrs. Ferraro was unable to swing a significant number of voters to her ticket and in the end was probably a liability to the Democrats, friends said that Bush felt he had suffered badly in the comparisons that had been inevitable in a campaign that had produced the first woman ever on a national ticket. "The whole thing just burned him out," said a friend. "He was in a no-win position from the start and he really wondered whether it was time to start thinking about giving up politics altogether, once the second term was over." Another acquaintance said that Bush was looking forward to the second term as one might look forward to a prison sentence: counting the days until it would end.

Bush's depression turned out to be no more than a case of postelection blues, and it was Jim Baker and New York investment banker Nicholas Brady, his two oldest friends, who convinced him things were not nearly so bad as they appeared. The comparisons with Ferraro were sure to pass, they argued. After all, Mondale and Ferraro lost and besides, Bush had already invested too much of his time and effort into a presidential race even to consider giving it up. Maybe Bush had come off a bit shrill during the campaign, but that was a problem of perception, and like everything else it could be overcome by work. Bush had struggled to get to where he was, his friends told him, and now was the time to make all the hard work pay off. By mid-December the gloom had lifted, as his friends knew it would. Before Christmas, they had convinced him that it was time to start laying the groundwork for campaign '88.

At Baker's suggestion, Craig Fuller was selected to run the vice presidential office. Fuller had once worked in Deaver's California public relations firm and later became one of the few aides to presidential counselor Ed Meese who maintained a good working relationship with the Baker wing of the White House. Bush's second key appointment went to Lee Atwater, the scrappy South Carolinian who had been the number-two man on Reagan's 1984 campaign team. He was chosen—again on Baker's recommendation—to be the chief campaign strategist. It was agreed that Baker would take over the campaign once the primary season had passed, but that was still years in the future and Atwater struck a deal that no one else would be layered between him and Baker. By May 1985, Atwater had established a political action committee called Fund for America and within two months had raised $800,000. That was only seed money, and by October, Bush had more than $2 million in the bank. Atwater planned to build another race around the Southern strategy that had worked so well for Reagan in 1984. He would construct another electoral college fortress across the South and would buttress it by holding together the blue-collar ethnics and law-and-order conservatives of the industrial states who had formed the Reagan coalition in 1980 and again in 1984. It was a good strategy, but Bush's first steps to implement it were not auspicious.

Like Atwater, Bush recognized that he was weakest where Reagan had always been strongest: among the ultraconservatives of the party. He tried to correct this with a series of overtures to the Right. Bush had never been ashamed to paper over differences with old enemies if there were political advantage to be gained, but he surprised some of his supporters when it became clear just how far he was willing to go. He voluntarily took part in a tribute to the late William Loeb, the vitriolic publisher of the *Manchester Union Leader*, a man who just five years earlier had accused Bush of being "a hypocrite, an incompetent, and a spoon-fed little rich kid who was soft on communism and unfit to be President." A month later, Bush praised a hero of the fundamentalist Religious Right, television evangelist Jerry Falwell, founder of the Moral Majority. After Falwell endorsed his presidential aspirations, Bush complimented him for his "moral vision." Bush's reach to the Right had an air of such blatant pandering about it that friends said that even Mrs. Reagan found it offensive. It was after a lunch with the First Lady that conservative columnist George Will wrote a column in which he observed, "The unpleasant sound Bush is emitting as he traipses from one conservative gathering to another is a thin, tinny arf—the sound of a lap dog."

George Will's column gave no joy to Bush and his campaign strategists, but as the second term produced one Iran-Contra revelation after another, they realized there might be more serious problems ahead than accusations of being a lap dog. There was now the real possibility that all of Bush's hard work, all the support he had given Ronald Reagan, all the mundane and sometimes distasteful tasks he had performed over the years might go for naught. In fact, his support of Reagan might even prove to be counterproductive.

In public, Bush said that he could never separate himself from Ronald Reagan, even if it meant the end of his own career, and in view of the loyalty he had always shown to his superiors, he was taken at his word. But some of his closest advisers were now telling him that he ought to do just that. At the very least, they said, he ought to think about how he should go about opening up some space between himself and the President should things get worse. Iran-Contra was bad enough, they said, but there was more than that. The stench of the sleaze factor was now everywhere.

For Bush, it was a different dilemma. He had stood so staunchly with Reagan that people had accused him of being a lackey rather than a loyalist. Now, with things going badly for

Reagan, he risked even more. There was now the real threat of being dragged down with Reagan. At just the time when he should have been in the best position or his life to make a real run at the presidency, the opportunity was slipping away because of events over which he had no control.

For George Bush and his campaign team, the only sustenance in the stormy year of 1987 was provided by the Democrats. In April, Gary Hart, the front-runner for the Democratic nomination, had bused several hundred journalists to a park west of Denver to record his official declaration of candidacy. It was an odd event in that reporters and photographers were invited, but no members of the public. A CBS News producer named Randy Wolf observed that Hart had excluded actual voters because he feared they might wander in front of the television cameras and mess up the pictures. The session was a harbinger of the TV-image-above-everything campaign that the 1988 race would prove to be, and the site's red rock crags provided a backdrop that would have done justice to John Wayne. That had been just the point. Hart wanted to convey a rugged, outdoor image, which he thought would serve him best during the primaries and even better in the general election. Like Bush's people, Hart expected a Hart versus Bush contest in the general election, and he wanted to draw a striking contrast to His Preppiness—George Herbert Walker Bush. By May, however, all that had been forgotten because of a Miami model named Donna Rice. Even the Iran-Contra hearings, which had become a fixture on television, had to settle for second billing for a few days.

Most Republicans were delighted, but it was indicative of how badly things were going for Bush that spring and summer that for him, even Hart's escapade had a downside. The story had rekindled media interest in the so-called character questions, and because of that, old rumors that Bush had been conducting a longtime affair with one of his female staff members resurfaced. No evidence ever came to light to verify the reports, but the story generated so much interest that a staffer at Bush's campaign head-quarters told us he received 113 inquiries about it in one five-day period. The rumors died as quickly as they had sprung up, but for Bush it was just one more thing to be concerned about in a difficult year.

The autumn of 1987 brought more trouble as Bush set out on a tour of Eastern Europe. The trip was designed to show off

Bush's foreign policy expertise, but that purpose was lost when Bush remarked offhandedly that Detroit could use the kind of expertise that Soviet mechanics employed to keep Russian tanks operating. As might have been expected, auto workers and auto industry executives did not appreciate the put-down and Bush was roundly criticized and ridiculed, especially in Michigan, where he was already expecting stiff opposition in the coming Republican caucuses.

Bush officially declared his candidacy in October. Financially the campaign was doing well: it had already raised a record-breaking sum of almost $10 million, but before the month was out, there was yet another setback. This time the trouble had cropped up in Iowa, where the first contest of the 1988 campaign would be held. Bush had beaten Ronald Reagan in the Iowa caucuses in 1980, and he had every intention of making a good showing in Iowa in 1988. His thinking changed abruptly, however, when results came in from an Iowa straw poll. Bush was not only beaten by Bob Dole but finished behind Pat Robertson, a television evangelist. Robertson had also beaten Bush a month earlier in a test vote for Michigan delegates. Stunned by the outcome, Bush made a lame attempt to explain it away, but, as usual, the explanation only made things worse. As reporters snickered, he suggested that his supporters hadn't taken part in the straw poll because they had "been on the golf course or at their daughters' coming out parties."

Iowa is not a state known for elaborate cotillions, and the remark played perfectly into Dole's strategy of picturing Bush as an effete, country-club snob who had nothing in common with the good farm folk of the Midwest. As Democrats poked fun at Bush's latest slip of the tongue (a slip of the mind, one called it), some Bush backers urged him to fold the Iowa effort in order to concentrate his resources elsewhere. As bleak as Bush's chances in Iowa looked, Atwater decided that the campaign had to stay there and Bush agreed. But Atwater had concluded as well that Iowa was lost. A few weeks later he told New Hampshire's governor John Sununu, "We've got to win New Hampshire; Iowa is going to be bad."

What happened next would make it no easier. *Newsweek* magazine published what came to be known as its "Wimp Issue." In a cover story the magazine declared that Bush suffered from "a potentially crippling handicap, a perception that he isn't strong enough or tough enough for the challenges of the Oval Office. That he is, in a single, mean word, a wimp." The word *wimp* even appeared on the magazine's cover. Bush and his family were outraged by the article, and in that hard year of 1987, even the normally unflappable professional politicians around George Bush were beginning to wonder whether a Bush candidacy would really work. In the words of his longtime friend Jim Baker, George Bush's journey to the White House was looking "like a real steep hill to climb."

Back at the White House, Reagan and his advisers had a lot more to worry about than George Bush and his image problems: They had to cope with the burden of trying to revive a stricken presidency. The man who was shouldering a large share of that burden was the new White House chief of staff, Howard Baker.

Baker, who had been an unsuccessful presidential candidate in the past, had been giving serious thought to challenging Bush and Dole for the 1988 Republican nomination when he was abruptly summoned to replace the banished Donald Regan. Mike Deaver and one of Reagan's other old friends, Senator Paul Laxalt, had recommended Baker for the job. It was a wise choice. During his years in Washington, no one enjoyed a better relationship with the press and his colleagues than the easygoing senator from Tennessee. Baker's forte was the art of conciliation, and he was so good at it that he acquired a reputation for being a modern-day version of the "Great Compromiser," Henry Clay. Baker prided himself on being a flexible moderate who always tried to appreciate both sides of an issue. His stepmother once said of him: "Howard is like the Tennessee River. He flows right down the middle." In agreeing to move into the Reagan White House, Baker sensed that his political skills would be put to the test more severely than they ever had before.

By the autumn of 1987, after six months on the job, he could boast that at least some progress had been made in a few areas. The Iran-Contra affair was no longer the crisis that it had been during the first few weeks of his tenure. (Baker had come aboard at the worst possible time: the day after the Tower Commission released its report, with its scathing portrait of a confused President who had only a vague understanding of the secret policies that had been carried out in his name.) The congressional hearings had served to dispel most of the anxieties, and there was no longer any talk about the President's being impeached or urged to resign. Internally, Baker could claim credit for having restored order and civility to a White House operation that had been floundering in rancor and chaos. Another positive sign was vastly improved relations with the press. Reporters found Baker's calm professionalism and quiet candor a welcome contrast to Regan's abrasive manner.

But the White House still had to deal with the perception of a weak and inattentive President. Nor was Reagan's image helped by the sleaze factor stories. Baker was getting tired of fielding questions on that subject, yet he had to admit that they were relevant. He realized that each new indictment or investigation of a longtime Reagan aide raised doubts about the President's own judgment and character. Still, the worst news of all, from Baker's point of view, was the steady string of defeats on Capitol Hill. Selling the President's program and decisions to his former colleagues in Congress was supposed to be his strength, the main reason that he had been appointed chief of staff. But like other former senators before him, Howard Baker discovered that once you leave the club, you lose much of your clout and influence.

The rejection of Judge Bork had been a particularly brutal setback, which, more than anything else, convinced Baker that for Ronald Reagan at this stage of his presidency, battles with Congress were destined to be losing ones. The Democrats were in no mood to negotiate. They, as well as many others in Washington, had come to regard Reagan as a lame duck so severely crippled that his presidency was sliding into paralysis. They saw him as a listless leader who was merely marking time until his reign ended in January 1989.

Such concerns eventually led Baker to conclude that if Reagan were to have any chance of revitalizing his presidency, he could not do so through tests of strength with Congress. Baker decided that Reagan's best chance to reassert his leadership was in the field of U.S.-Soviet relations. For the past several months—to borrow a phrase the other Baker used to describe George Bush's presidential prospects—U.S. and Soviet negotiators had been climbing "a real steep hill" of their own toward another Reagan-Gorbachev summit meeting. But this time, Howard Baker and other Reagan advisers agreed, it could not just consist of cosmetics and showmanship, as the first one in Geneva had; and this time, it could not get bogged down in confusion and stalemate, as the second

one in Iceland had. This time, it would have to produce a substantive achievement: a major agreement on arms control.

In his enthusiasm for a third summit meeting, Baker had plenty
of allies. There was George Shultz, who, along with Bud Mc-
Farlane, had sold Reagan on the idea of going to the summit in
the first place back in 1985. Shultz had emerged vindicated from
his "battle royal" with the Iran-Contra conspirators and had regained his role as the chief architect of foreign policy. In fact, he
was now in a stronger position than ever, partly because most of
his former rivals had been swept out of power by the Iran-Contra
scandal.

Replacing the fallen Poindexter was Frank Carlucci, who had
been Cap Weinberger's top deputy at Defense. Although he was
a Weinberger protégé, dating back to the years when they first
worked together in the Nixon administration, Carlucci's views
toward the Soviet Union and other East-West issues were far less
rigid than those of his former boss. He had even served in the
Carter administration, as deputy director of the CIA, a display of
nonpartisanship that clearly separated him from Weinberger. The
man who succeeded Bill Casey was FBI Director William Webster,
another pragmatist. During the ten years Webster ran the FBI
(he, too, had been a Carter appointee), he disciplined or got rid
of agents who, under previous directors, had been accused of
exceeding their legal authority. Webster promised to practice the
same vigilance in his new job. The day he was sworn in as CIA
director, he pledged "fidelity to the Constitution and the laws,"
an avowal that he was not driven by the kind of quixotic ambitions
that had motivated Casey.

By the autumn of 1987, the only conservative hard-liner left
in a position of high authority was Weinberger, and in November
he announced his resignation. It was commonly believed that the
main reason for Weinberger's decision was he knew that now he
was the one who was out of accord with the centrist thrust of the
administration's foreign policy. His departure put an end to Carlucci's brief stint as national security adviser, for he was picked to
succeed Weinberger as secretary of defense. Replacing Carlucci
in the national security post was Lieutenant General Colin Powell,
a flexible military man in the tradition of Brent Scowcroft and
Bud McFarlane.

Baker, Shultz, Carlucci, Webster, and Powell were all mod-

erates, by and large, and in varying degrees, they all were in favor
of negotiating a new arms treaty with the Soviet Union. Because
they were assertive men, and each of them had his own agenda,
they had their disagreements; but these rarely escalated into ideological confrontation. For the first time since the start of the
Reagan presidency, foreign policy was being shaped in an atmosphere of relative harmony.

Finally, there was Nancy Reagan, whose influence on her
husband's decisions should not be underestimated. She, too, believed that a successful summit meeting would enable the President to regain his prestige and popularity. She saw it too as an
opportunity to achieve the kind of diplomatic triumph that would
earn him an honored place in history. A major arms control agreement with the Soviet Union would overshadow the blunders of
the Iran-Contra affair and would be recognized as the main legacy
of the Reagan administration in foreign policy. So the First Lady
lent her considerable support to the campaign for a third summit
meeting.

But the kind of summit that Reagan's advisers envisioned—
one that would deliver on substance as well as image and public
relations—could not simply be willed into existence. To begin
with, the two leaders had to be amenable to the idea. When last
seen together in October 1986, Reagan and Gorbachev were bidding frosty farewells to each other in Iceland. Because of the
stalemate over Star Wars, their conversations had ended in an
angry exchange of allegations. Each man had accused the other
of negotiating in bad faith.

Under other circumstances, that might well have been the
last U.S.-Soviet summit meeting of the Reagan era. Given his
ideological mind-set, Reagan had always been ambivalent about
the idea of sitting down at the negotiating table with his Soviet
counterpart. If, in the aftermath of Iceland, his presidency had
continued on a placid and untroubled course, he just might have
chosen to retain a hard-line posture, and he would have had a
perfect excuse for doing so. Reagan could claim that he had made
the effort to be a good summiteer, but his Soviet counterpart had
made demands that could not be accepted.

Yet because of the problems that now afflicted his presidency,
Reagan needed to give it another try, or so his top advisers believed, and they eventually were able to persuade him that a third
summit meeting was in his best interest. As for Gorbachev, he had

compelling reasons of his own for continuing to pursue an early breakthrough in arms control. His dramatic new program for domestic reforms, the twin remedies of *glasnost* and *perestroika*, were predicated, in part, on his vow to ease Cold War tensions. To solidify his position of leadership at home, Gorbachev needed to demonstrate his skill and strength in foreign affairs, and the sooner the better. Moreover, the pressure from Washington and Moscow to work out an agreement that would justify a third summit was felt where it mattered the most: in Geneva, where negotiators from the two superpowers were debating the fine points of the complex arms control issues.

U.S.-Soviet arms talks had been in progress, off and on, since the early 1970s when Richard Nixon and Leonid Brezhnev ushered in the era of détente. Those early negotiations led to the first SALT agreement and the ABM treaty to limit each nation's number of antiballistic missiles. By the late seventies, the major problem was the presence of a new class of intermediate-range missiles the Soviet Union had arrayed against potential targets in Western Europe. The Carter administration's response to that threat was to pursue what it called a "dual-track" strategy. The United States would deploy its own new generation of medium-range missiles in Europe, while making a good-faith effort to negotiate an agreement that would require both sides to scale back their new weapon systems.

This was the policy Ronald Reagan inherited when he became President, and he did not agree with it. A longtime critic of détente, he objected to the SALT treaties of the 1970s mainly because they merely limited the supply of nuclear weapons instead of eliminating certain categories altogether. What he wanted was not arms control so much as arms reduction. Or, as Reagan put it to his first national security adviser, Richard Allen, in the autumn of 1981: "Give me a proposal that can be expressed in a single sentence and that sounds like real disarmament." One of his arms experts in the Defense Department, Richard Perle, promptly came up with just the right description: "zero option." A speech was framed around that concept, and in November Reagan presented his proposal. The United States, he said, "is prepared to cancel its deployment" of the new Pershing missiles in Europe "if the Soviets will dismantle" their new class of intermediate-range missiles.

The suggestion seemed to be a blend of naïveté and cynicism; it was hardly an offer that Moscow could be expected to take seriously. The United States was asking the Soviets to scrap real weapons, already deployed at enormous expense, and in return, Washington would merely tear up a piece of paper. One arms control strategist, who also happened to be a football fan, said it was as if the Washington Redskins had asked the Dallas Cowboys to trade their star running back, Tony Dorsett, for a future draft choice—that is, an unproven talent. In private arguments with other administration officials, Secretary of State Alexander Haig bitterly denounced the zero-option scheme as cynical, with the sole purpose of sabotaging honest negotiations for a realistic com- promise. Soviet leaders agreed with that assessment. In Geneva, the arms talks languished, and when the U.S. Pershing missiles were deployed in Europe in late 1983, talks broke off altogether.

In early 1985, however, conciliatory moves in both Moscow and Washington led to the resumption of arms control negotia- tions. Moreover, in March of that year, Gorbachev came to power, and not long after that the talks began to accelerate in the direction of real progress. The Soviets expressed a willingness to consider the zero-option proposal. Because the United States had by now deployed its medium-range missiles in Europe, the mutual elim- ination of those weapons could be viewed as a legitimate quid pro quo. But the Soviets insisted that an agreement to do away with the intermediate-range nuclear forces (INF) would have to be part of a larger agreement that would encompass reductions in long- range missiles and other strategic weapons as well as concessions on Washington's experimental new project: the Strategic Defense Initiative. That "linkage" proved to be the main barrier to a con- crete agreement at the summit meetings in Geneva and especially in Reykjavík.

The impasse remained when the negotiators resumed their deliberations in Geneva. But during the early months of 1987, it became increasingly obvious that both the Kremlin and the White House wanted a tangible, substantive agreement that could be signed by the two leaders at a third summit meeting. In February, Gorbachev announced a major concession: the Soviet Union would be willing to accept a separate INF treaty that did not include agreement on the larger questions of strategic arms re- ductions and the future of SDI. The issues that had been bound by linkage were now delinked. Over the next several months, both sides made other, minor concessions.

By the end of October, the negotiators were so close to an agreement that both governments felt it safe to schedule the next summit meeting. It was announced that Gorbachev would visit Washington in early December. Then in late November came the news from Geneva that the last obstacle, the issue of on-site inspections and other verification procedures, had been resolved. The United States and the Soviet Union had agreed to the terms of an INF treaty banning all intermediate-range and some shorter-range missiles, and the document would be ready for the two leaders to sign when Gorbachev arrived in Washington. For the first time since the beginning of the nuclear age, the two superpowers had agreed to the elimination of two classes of weapons systems.

In the midst of the euphoria over that achievement, some of Reagan's advisers gloated that the INF treaty was an unequivocal victory for the United States. They reminded us that it was Reagan who had proposed the zero-option terms back in 1981, and since then the Soviets kept yielding and yielding until they finally accepted them. In addition, the U.S. team had held firm on SDI, and the agreement did not jeopardize the plans to develop Star Wars. Reagan himself claimed, both then and later, that it was the combination of his massive defense buildup, including the deployment of the Pershing missiles in Europe, and the future threat of SDI that induced the Soviets to negotiate on his terms. Much of this was true as far as it went, but it wasn't really all that one-sided.

The basic goal of the Russians was not only to get rid of the American missiles in Europe, which were poised to strike Moscow and other Soviet cities, but to *keep* them as far away from Soviet territory as possible, and the INF treaty accomplished that objective. Also, any agreement to reduce or eliminate nuclear weapons worked to the advantage of the Soviet Union. As far back as 1977, Leonid Brezhnev gave a speech in which he made precisely that point. Decrying the arms race, he called the pursuit of nuclear superiority "dangerous madness." The Soviet Union, Brezhnev said, only needed nuclear forces that were "sufficient" to hold those of the United States in check. The clear implication, which he did not spell out, was that a standoff in nuclear arms would shift the emphasis to conventional weapons, where the Soviets and their Warsaw Pact allies enjoyed an overwhelming advantage. Although Brezhnev's speech aroused little attention in the West, its message was clearly understood by his successors, and Mikhail Gorbachev had the will and energy to convert it into policy.

That was yet another Soviet edge in the equation: the dynamic presence of Gorbachev himself. Unlike the lame-duck President, Gorbachev could concentrate on the future. Thus, from his point of view, the INF treaty (or, for that matter, almost any kind of arms agreement) was merely the first step in a new era of East-West cooperation.

It was important to take that first step as quickly as possible, and it was especially advantageous to take it while Ronald Reagan was still in the White House. Gorbachev was aware of Reagan's ideological background, and he had a shrewd understanding of domestic politics in the United States. Hence, he knew that forging a nuclear agreement with Reagan would have an impact on the President's successors, no matter who they were. Future Presidents would find it difficult to reverse a trend that had been set in motion by Ronald Reagan. And when the time came for further negotiations, they would have to deal with the man who had shared the summit with Reagan. For Mikhail Gorbachev had every intention of remaining in power for many years.

Gorbachev's understanding of American politics—as well as his own formidable political skills—was on display during his triumphant visit to Washington in early December. His reputation had preceded him. For the past two years, there had been a spate of stories about his visits to the capitals of Western Europe. There, according to all reports, he had dazzled leaders and commoners alike with his vigor, his charm, and his seeming candor about such sensitive matters as political repression in the Communist bloc and the failures of the Soviet economy. Reagan, having already been exposed to the Gorbachev persona on other occasions, knew what to expect. "I don't resent his popularity," the President quipped a few days before the Soviet leader arrived. "Good Lord, I co-starred with Errol Flynn once."

In Washington, Gorbachev became an instant star, and in the process, Reagan was once again relegated to playing the second male lead. At the Soviet Embassy, Gorbachev hosted a meeting

with cultural luminaries, a group that included Paul Newman and
Yoko Ono as well as Henry Kissinger and John Kenneth Galbraith.
He thanked the members of that audience for coming but then
added a gentle barb aimed at the two professors and their ilk,
"Some of you, though, do write long books." Then later, at a State
Department luncheon, he entertained Georgia's Sam Nunn and
Tennessee's Howard Baker with good-old-boy remarks about the
dubious virtues of moonshine whiskey.

While Gorbachev was courting official Washington, most of
the declared presidential candidates in both parties were hustling
caucus votes in Iowa. Their efforts to draw attention to their
campaigns were almost totally eclipsed by Gorbachev's performance, and there was a reference to that at his meeting with
business and corporate leaders. One executive informed the Soviet
visitor that the latest polls showed him running second in Iowa,
"and closing fast." Gorbachev said he appreciated that, then noted,
"I already have a job."

There were, to be sure, some darker moments. During a two-
hour news conference and, again, at a smaller meeting with pub-
lishing executives, Gorbachev bristled at persistent questions
about human rights and the Soviet presence in Afghanistan. He
was not accustomed to the aggressive tactics of a free press, and
on those occasions, the American public caught a glimpse of the
steel that lay beneath the smiles. But those were exceptions that
barely detracted from his overall message of goodwill. The most
enduring impression of Gorbachev's visit was a spontaneous gesture he made on his last day in Washington. On his way to the
White House for a final meeting with Reagan, Gorbachev suddenly ordered his bulletproof limousine to a halt, then bounded
out of the car and into a group of onlookers. "I want to say hello
to you," he gushed in English. The startled crowd adored it. One
woman, obviously schooled in the values of Ronald Reagan's
Washington, bestowed on the Soviet glad-hander the ultimate ac-
colade: "The man is a PR genius!"

Reagan, too, was charmed by Gorbachev, and vice versa.
Their discussions were marked by sharp disagreements on a number of issues, such as the lack of human rights in the Soviet Union,
racial discrimination in the United States, and regional conflicts
in Afghanistan and Central America. But they never allowed the
disputes to flare into the kind of anger that had disrupted their

talks in Reykjavík. By now, they were on a first-name basis, and observers at their meetings were struck by the growing rapport between the two leaders.

"There is good chemistry between us," Reagan later acknowledged. He said he first became aware of it during their initial summit meeting in Geneva when, at one point, the two men went off by themselves to a private cottage, accompanied only by their interpreters. For several minutes, they just sat in front of an open fire and chatted. Reagan recalled that on their way back to join their delegations, "I turned to him and said, 'You've never been to our country. I'd like you to see it.' And he said, 'All right, I'll go to Washington for a summit. But then let's have another one in Moscow and you can see our country.' When we went back and told the others about the two summits, they nearly fell out of their chairs."

One of the few hard news items to come out of the 1987 summit in Washington was the announcement that the two leaders would be meeting in Moscow the following spring. The formal signing of the INF treaty and the triumph of personal diplomacy helped to obscure the fact that in other important areas, Summit III was a disappointment. Little progress was made on the shared goal of reducing long-range missiles and other strategic weapons. So, the arms experts were sent back to their negotiating tables and instructed to do their best to work out a strategic arms agreement in time for Reagan's visit to Moscow in the spring. In the meantime, the INF treaty woud not become law until it was ratified in the Senate by a two-thirds majority.

That was no sure thing. A number of senators, both Republicans and Democrats, had serious reservations about the treaty. Indeed, some of them had never been enamored of the zero-option formula. They remembered that when it was first proposed back in 1981, there was a suspicion that Reagan's arms people had come up with the concept as a maneuver to stall the negotiating process. Thus, on Capitol Hill, questions were raised that went something like this: Okay, sure, that's the deal we asked for, but is it the deal we *should* have asked for? Did we *really* want it then? And do we want it now?

Others were concerned about the issue of on-site inspections and other verification procedures. Could the Soviets be trusted? Did we really want Russian inspection teams snooping around the top-secret sites of U.S. missile facilities? Reagan and his advisers assured the skeptics that the treaty was sound in every respect. Thus, in the late winter and early spring of 1988, Washington was entertained by the spectacle of Ronald Reagan, the anti-Communist crusader, using his powers of persuasion to sell a revolutionary arms agreement he had signed with the Soviet Union. And in the end, it was Reagan's sturdy conservative reputation that saved the INF treaty. A liberal Democratic President might not have been so fortunate. But there weren't many critics who were willing to accuse Ronald Reagan of selling out to the Russians.

There were a *few*, however, and as one might expect, they were to be found among his core constituency. Many of the Reagan fundamentalists already had become disenchanted with their hero over other issues. They were not amused to discover that he was not using his power to enact legislation on such issues as abortion and school prayer. His rhetoric was cheap; where was the commitment? Then there was the matter of the deficits. Such fiscal transgressions were supposed to be the exclusive and unforgivable sins of Democrats. Yet when it came to mortgaging the future, Reagan seemed to be worse than his rivals.

But this latest perfidy—this signing an arms agreement with the Soviets—was the ultimate betrayal. In their rage, many of the conservatives pinned the blame on Reagan's new group of advisers, flaccid moderates such as Howard Baker, who were now clustered around the Oval Office. Others believed that the most insidious influence had been the First Lady. They even came up with a term to describe the President's new posture of accord with the Soviets: "creeping Nancyism."

In terms of substance, Summit IV of the Reagan era fell short of expectations. The two sides failed in their efforts to reach a significant agreement on the reduction of strategic weapons. The negotiators simply were unable to resolve their complex differences on that issue in time for Reagan's visit to Moscow in the late spring of 1988. But this did not mean that the Moscow summit was irrelevant. The two leaders did sign agreements on a number of minor issues, such as nuclear-testing procedures, fishing rights, and exchanges of students and cultural events. More to the point, Reagan's presence in Moscow had symbolic importance.

In terms of style, the Moscow visit was a triumph for the President. Having been upstaged by Gorbachev on his home turf, the old actor now returned the compliment. Once he learned that there was not going to be an agreement on strategic arms reduction, Reagan shifted the focus to a subject on which he, the visitor from America, had a moral and psychological edge: human rights. At the ancient Danilov Monastery, which had recently been returned to the Russian Orthodox Church, Reagan preached about the values of religious freedom: "We pray that the return of this monastery signals a willingness to return to believers the thousands of other houses of worship which are now closed, boarded up or used for secular purposes," he said. At Spaso House, the U.S. ambassador's residence, he hosted a highly publicized meeting with dissidents and "refuseniks" who had protested political repression in the Soviet Union. The President told them that he wanted to "convey support to you that you might in turn convey to others, so that all those working for human rights throughout this vast land . . . might be encouraged and take heart."

Most impressive of all was his speech to students and intellectuals at Moscow State University. The theme of that speech was not just human rights, but the concept of liberty that had defined the American spirit for more than two centuries. Standing in front of a huge bust of Lenin, Reagan told his audience:

> Political leadership in a democracy requires seeing past the abstractions and embracing the vast diversity of humanity, and doing it with humility; listening as best you can, not just to those with high positions, but to the cacophonous voices of ordinary people, and trusting those millions of people, keeping out of their way. . . . And the word we have for this is "freedom."

He later revealed, in an interview with Hugh Sidey of *Time*, how much that moment meant to him. "I wasn't speaking to the American Legion," Reagan said. "I wasn't speaking to the Chamber of Commerce. I was trying to explain America and what we are all about."

Gorbachev resented the sermonizing. In a toast to Reagan at a state dinner, his host sharply asserted, "We want to build contacts among people in all forums . . . but this should be done without interfering in domestic affairs." Yet for the most part, Gorbachev let Reagan talk, and chose to respond with a posture of patronizing tolerance. In his own conversations with Western reporters, he implied that the President simply didn't understand the reforms that were taking place in the Soviet Union. Reagan also went out of his way to strike a balance; his criticisms were interspersed with words of praise for *glasnost* and the other moves Gorbachev had initiated. Thus, as in Washington, the rapport between the two leaders enabled them to slide through the snags of irritation and disagreement.

The Moscow summit also featured an appealing public event. Toward the end of Reagan's visit, the two men went for a walk in Red Square, where they quickly drew a crowd of well-wishers. At one point, as they strolled just a few feet away from Lenin's tomb, Reagan put his arm around Gorbachev's shoulder. That simple and spontaneous gesture of affection made them look like two old friends. The Soviet equivalent of a campaign advance man even managed to produce a small child for the occasion. Seizing the moment, Gorbachev picked up the youngster and, with a broad smile, urged him to "shake hands with Grandfather Reagan." Grandfather Reagan promptly reached out *his* hands and cuddled the kid. Just a couple of old pols engaging in the time-honored ritual of baby-kissing. Witnessing that scene, one American reporter suggested that the Moscow visit should be christened "the Photo Opportunity Summit."

Even Reagan himself seemed to be awed by the dramatic events. He admitted as much that spring when he stopped off in London on his way back to Washington. It was understood that this was to be his final appearance in Europe as President of the United States, and in a moving speech, British Prime Minister Margaret Thatcher thanked Reagan for all that he had done to improve East-West relations and reduce the threat of nuclear war. Reagan responded with a few words of his own. He said that the last two summit meetings with Gorbachev produced "a strategy of vigorous diplomatic engagement" between Washington and Moscow. Then, in a more personal vein came an observation that many construed as a final and formal break with his ideological past: "To those of us who remember the postwar era, all of this is cause for shaking the head in wonder. Imagine, the President of the United States and the General Secretary of the Soviet Union walking together in Red Square, talking about a growing personal friendship." He then all but declared that the forty-year cold war with the Soviet Union was over.

Reagan came home that spring as a hero. Conservatives could

carp about perfidy and betrayal, but their complaints were drowned out by public acclaim. Reagan's popularity had begun to climb at the time of Gorbachev's visit to Washington, and after his trip to Moscow, his public approval rating soared to around 70 percent, back to the level it had reached during the early days of the first term and the summer of 1986. Just when it looked as if Reagan's presidency were permanently stricken, the old actor proved that given the right kind of script and team of advisers, he could still deliver a superb performance.

18

As New Hampshire Goes...

"Hide the forklift, Mama, George Bush
is a comin'."
—campaign reporter

In some important respects, Reagan's recovery was deceptive. Although his triumphs at the summit had enabled him to regain most of his prestige and popularity, this did not translate into political power. The Democratic leadership on Capitol Hill continued to regard Reagan as a lame-duck President whose veto threats could be treated with disdain. In fact, one of the more remarkable performances in Washington during the last two years of Reagan's reign was that of the 100th Congress. In terms of social legislation, the basic issues of liberal Democrats, it put together the strongest and most activist record since the Great Society programs of Lyndon Johnson and the 89th Congress.

The trend was clearly established in the early months of 1987 when Congress voted to extend the Clean Water Act and enacted a multibillion-dollar highway and mass transit bill. From then until it adjourned in the autumn of 1988, the 100th Congress passed legislation on a number of other controversial issues, including a civil rights restoration bill banning federal funds for an entire institution if one of its divisions is guilty of discrimination, a plant-closings bill requiring employers to give sixty days' notification of shutdowns or layoffs, and the Omnibus Trade Law calling for retaliation against foreign unfair trade practices. All those measures were passed in defiance of Reagan's veto or strong objections.

Nor was that all. The 100th Congress passed laws in fair housing and welfare reform; enacted bills to aid the homeless, expand the food-stamp program, provide protection against catastrophic illness, and bolster elementary and secondary education. House Speaker Jim Wright said that the social legislation was the direct result of "pent-up needs too long deferred." His counterpart in the Senate, Majority Leader Robert Byrd, offered a similar explanation: "We were too long in the desert. It seemed like forty years." As for Reagan, his influence on the Hill had diminished to the point that there was nothing he could do to stop the Democrats, and there were times when he became so discouraged he didn't even bother to impose a veto he knew would be overridden.

Congressional leaders who had business at the White House during those last two years were often struck by Reagan's remoteness and seeming inability to understand the issues. They knew that he had never been a man for specifics, but now they encountered gaps in his knowledge that, as one of them put it, made him seem "more out of it than ever."

One bizarre episode occurred when Lloyd Bentsen, the chairman of the Senate Finance Committee, went to the Oval Office to discuss pending trade legislation. Bentsen and Reagan were seated side by side, while Secretary of the Treasury Jim Baker and ranking members of the White House staff were seated in front of the two men in chairs that had been arranged in horseshoe fashion. Bentsen spoke first, outlining the points that had been worked out on the bill during the Senate debate. When he finished, Reagan said nothing until he reached into his breast pocket and produced several typewritten pages. Reagan seldom spoke with Oval Office visitors without referring to notes on index cards, but in this instance, aides had given him full-size manuscript pages. Even though he was seated so close to the courtly Bentsen that their knees were almost touching, he began reading to him from the papers, stating that he had some objections to the bill as currently drawn. He then proceeded to spell out his objections by number. Once he had finished, he put the papers back in his lap and sat in silence while members of his staff picked up the discussion. The conversation was highly technical and Reagan did not speak again until it was time for the meeting to break up. Even those who were used to dealing with Reagan were taken aback by what happened next.

"I don't know how many of you read the Sunday want ads in *The Washington Post* as I do," a person in the room quoted the President as saying, "but when I see all those ads, I can't understand how there can be a trade deficit." Since the remark seemed to be directed at Bentsen, it was up to him to respond. "What an interesting observation," he said. He then quickly excused himself and returned to the Capitol.

Lloyd Bentsen's experience at the White House brought to mind a similar incident that had occurred some two years earlier. It involved a visit to the Oval Office by the ranking members of the Senate Armed Services Committee, Republican Barry Goldwater and Democrat Sam Nunn. They had gone there to map strategy on a budget proposal. An automatic reduction in the Pentagon budget was about to be triggered by the recently enacted Gramm-Rudman-Hollings budget reduction law unless Congress and the administration could agree on plans to reduce the deficit.

Nunn and Goldwater were worried about the effect of an across-the-board cut in defense spending that would be mandatory under the law if the deficit reduction goals were not met. They had gone to the White House to work out a program of selected cuts that would not impair national defense. Secretary of Defense Weinberger was also at the meeting; he had been complaining throughout the discussion about the Gramm-Rudman law and how it was hamstringing defense efforts. At one point, Nunn reminded Weinberger that Reagan had been an active supporter of the Gramm-Rudman legislation. That observation elicited a response from the President. Yes, Reagan admitted, Nunn was right. He had indeed urged that Gramm-Rudman be passed. But, Reagan went on to say, no one had told him the budget reductions the legislation called for were mandatory.

There was an embarrassed silence in the room. The whole point of the legislation had been to force mandatory cuts on the federal budget if Congress were unable to meet deficit reduction goals, and it had been one of the most highly publicized and fiercely debated bills in recent congressional history. Yet Reagan, who had signed the legislation into law, was unabashedly taking the position that he had not understood its purpose. Reagan showed no sign that he had shared in creating the problem. As was so often the case, the problem had to be someone else's fault.

Such tales had been making the rounds since the early days of the Reagan era. But in 1988, more and more stories about the President's obtuse approach to issues began cropping up in the public domain, some of them from the most unlikely sources: former officials in his own administration. The spate of memoirs had begun a few years earlier with the publication of Alexander Haig's *Caveat* and David Stockman's *The Triumph of Politics*. But both Haig and Stockman were generally perceived to be disgruntled men who had more loyalty to their own ambitions than they ever had to the President they served. In the early months of 1988, however, books were published by three men who had been high-ranking members of the White House staff and therefore were in a position to reveal intimate accounts of Reagan's day-to-day performance: *Behind the Scenes* by Michael Deaver, *Speaking Out* by Larry Speakes, and *For the Record* by Donald Regan. All three books drew portraits of Reagan as a pliant and disengaged President who was out of touch with his own government. They could have been read as companion pieces to the Tower Commission's report on the Iran-Contra scandal.

Of the three books, the most gentle was Deaver's, yet even it portrayed Reagan as a rather cold and uncaring man, who accepted devoted service to him as his due and exhibited almost no loyalty in return. The most devastating, of course, was Regan's book, with its revelations about the First Lady's meddling in government business and her secret obsession with astrology. His memoir was also the most spiteful and self-serving. When it was published, the gag around Washington was that Regan suffered from a peculiarly Irish form of Alzheimer's disease: he remembered only grudges.

The books by Deaver, Speakes, and Regan came out at the time when Reagan was enjoying the fruits of his achievement at the summit. Yet those who read them saw another side of Reagan that bore little resemblance to the high-minded President who had made such an inspiring speech at Moscow State University.

One man who desperately hoped that the illusion, Reagan's special magic, would continue to overshadow the less attractive realities was George Bush, who had built his own presidential aspirations around his dutiful role as heir apparent. At the same time, the very strength of Reagan's public image imposed a difficult burden on Bush, who had problems in that area. When we last looked in on the vice president, in the late autumn of 1987, he was committing social gaffes in Iowa, gaffes that his chief rival for the GOP nomination, Robert Dole, was exploiting. In addition, Bush and his advisers were struggling to combat the widespread view of him as a "wimp," a stigma that *Newsweek* magazine had recently elevated to cover-story status. Such a perception only widened the gulf between him and the man he hoped to succeed in the White House. For no matter how remote and inattentive Reagan seemed to those who had worked closely with him, America's first Acting President was going to be a tough act for George Bush to follow—and he knew it.

What truly irritated Bush's friends was that he was so many things that the old actor only pretended to be. Reagan had played war heroes in the movies, but at nineteen, Bush had been the youngest American pilot to see combat in World War II, and he had almost lost his life when his plane was shot down over the Pacific. Reagan had become a standard-bearer of the free enterprise system by extolling it on the dinner circuit. Bush, on the other hand, had started his own business and had met a real payroll for many years before going into politics. Even so, he had never really been trusted by many of the businessmen who had supported Reagan. The contrast was even more striking in their personal lives. Reagan preached strong family values, but his own family life was full of discord and neglect. Bush was an authentic family man, a father of five successful offspring who "still come home," as he often said with obvious pride. Somehow, the good things about Bush just didn't get through. *Newsweek* had been on target with its article, no matter how much the Bush people hated to admit it. Many people still perceived Bush to be a wimp. One Washington wag called him the sort of man who washed his hands *before* going to the bathroom. Ann Richards, the witty Texas state treasurer, said that he seemed like the guy back in high school that the girls hoped would never ask them to dance.

In an era when television reached millions of people, first impressions were often burned into the public consciousness instantly, and the wimp image had been a hard one for Bush to shake. Fairly or unfairly, Bush came off poorly on television, and

Reagan's mastery of the medium for two terms only made the comparison worse. The photographers were right when they said that Ronald Reagan had "never taken a bad picture." That was not the result of happenstance. The President was always "on." It wasn't a conscious effort; it was second nature, the payoff from all those years in Hollywood. Bush, in contrast, always seemed tentative, never sure whether he were onstage or off.

Television has a way of exaggerating even the smallest imperfections. Chubby people look fat on television; middle-age people look old. In Bush's case, the enthusiastic, eager-to-please man that his friends admired came across as frenetic, nervous, and unsure of himself. He had a habit of speaking rapidly and in incomplete sentences, and his penchant for slips of the tongue left an impression of one who was high-strung and at times almost silly. He was left-handed, and on TV even that gave an impression of awkwardness that one tended not to notice when seeing him in the flesh.

It was their candidate's milquetoast television image that concerned Bush's people more than anything else as the primaries of 1988 drew nearer. Bush's chief strategist, Lee Atwater, had concluded by mid-January that the disclosures of Iran-Contra were not going to be the problem he had once feared. Once the campaign in Iowa was under way in earnest, Dole had tried to make an issue of it, but it just wasn't sticking. People had made up their minds about Iran-Contra. Some were uneasy about it and some were not. But whatever they felt, it did not seem to be hurting Bush in any significant way. The televised hearings into the scandal had gone on at such length and had bogged down in so much detail that Atwater was convinced that the public's interest in that subject had already dissipated. Besides, the highly successful December summit with Gorbachev had caused Reagan's popularity to climb again. It was almost as if people were so pleased with the improved superpower relations that they were now in a mood to forgive Reagan for whatever he did or did not do in connection with the Iran-Contra affair. It was not Iran-Contra but getting the wimp business behind them that bothered Atwater in those early weeks of 1988.

The New Year brought the usual bad weather to Washington, and in Iowa, where the first delegates would be selected, it was even worse. CBS News and the other networks had dispatched scores of reporters, producers, camera crews, and editors to Iowa along with a caravan of moving vans loaded with technical gear. But as Janet Leissner, a producer in the CBS contingent, reported for work during that first week in January she knew that the most valuable thing that she had taken to Iowa was her down-filled coat. At Bush's campaign headquarters in Des Moines, Bush operative Rich Bond had similar thoughts. As he watched a howling wind blow snow down Tenth Street, Bond figured this was going to be a long January.

Bond had more problems, however, than the weather. He had been sent out from Washington to salvage what he could of Bush's Iowa campaign effort. Bond had signed on with the Bush team to serve as deputy to his old friend, Atwater, and that was his title on the headquarters roster. But after Bush had fared so poorly in the October straw poll of Iowa Republicans, Atwater decided to put his best man on the case and Bond was the man; it was he who had engineered Bush's Iowa victory over Reagan back in 1980. Iowa was familiar territory, but once he had settled in, he realized that Iowa in 1988 was a different deal from Iowa in 1980. Bond's first reports to headquarters confirmed Atwater's fears: Iowa was already gone. Bond told Atwater that things were so bad that Bush would be lucky to beat evangelist Pat Robertson, let alone Bob Dole.

All that matters in a caucus state such as Iowa is which candidates are able to round up the most people and convince them to go to a precinct meeting on a cold winter's night. Whoever induces the most people to show up and announce their allegiance wins. Bond knew that in a state where the weather is as bad as Iowa's, persuading people to go to a caucus in subzero weather is not always easy. As the weather grew worse, the more likely it became that Robertson's zealots might be the ones who would wade through the snow to be counted on caucus night, while the less committed stayed home.

Dole had put together a more traditional campaign team than Robertson, but it was no less formidable. Dole's national strategy depended on winning Iowa. He had said as much when he officially launched his campaign on a blustery winter's day in Russell, Kansas, the tiny town where he grew up. All roads in the Dole campaign lead to Iowa, he said, and Iowa was so important to Dole that even this was understatement. Dole had no real organization in places across the South as Bush did, and even in New

Hampshire, the second stop of the primary season, Dole's forces were no match for the well-financed Bush team. The Dole plan was simple. He would stagger Bush with a big win in Iowa. The momentum from that victory would have a steamroller effect, and Dole could then go on to New Hampshire and deliver the knock-out. Dole believed that if he scored back-to-back wins in Iowa and New Hampshire, the "electoral fortresses" that Atwater and Bush had spent so much time building across the South would collapse before the campaign moved below the Mason-Dixon line.

By the second week of the New Year, Dole's Iowa operation was moving well. Dole's people believed that Bush's Iowa win in 1980 had been an "anyone-but-Reagan-vote" and that Bush had little in common with Iowans. There were few Old School Ties of Bush's stripe in Iowa, and the strategy was to keep it that way. The core of the Dole campaign was heavy emphasis on Dole's midwestern roots. He was Neighbor Dole, the boy who had grown up on the farm just down the road in Kansas. Dole is "one of us," said his campaign literature, the implication being that Bush was a part of the dreaded "them," just one more wealthy Easterner who knew nothing of Iowans and their problems.

Even Dole's decision to refuse Secret Service protection had been part of the strategy. As vice president, Bush was heavily guarded wherever he went, but what was best for security was not always the best politics. To move Bush around Iowa on his frequent campaign trips, the Secret Service assembled long motorcades of armored government limousines (flown in by Air Force transport planes from Washington), ambulances, and station wagons loaded with guns and communications gear. It was standard security procedure for a vice president, but the motorcades grew to such lengths that they took on a regal look. One Iowan commented dryly, "Bush's motorcade looks like the caravan of an Eastern potentate." They also became a source of amusement for reporters traveling with Bush. Bush was seldom available for press conferences, and reporters joked that the best chance they had to shout questions at him was when the line of cars snaked around highway clover leafs and Bush's limo could be spotted from the press buses that trailed several hundred yards to the rear. "It was the closest we ever got to him," said one.

In contrast, Dole rode in rental cars, accompanied only by campaign workers and several members of the U.S. Capitol police force. When he emerged from his car, his aides seldom tried to hold back well-wishers who crowded in to see him, and he mixed easily with voters and reporters, making wisecracks, teasing the journalists, and answering questions from whoever happened to be close by. Dole can be brutal with staffers and colleagues when his humor turns sour, but to reporters he appeared in high spirits throughout the Iowa campaign. His easy way with well-wishers contrasted with Bush's style as much as the differences in their motorcades.

Bush's security forces discouraged him from plunging into crowds, and he almost never answered questions that were shouted at him from reporters, who were generally kept at least thirty feet away. Bush's people had such an affinity for keeping ropes between him and the public that when he had marched in one Iowa parade back in July and there was not enough rope to cordon off the entire parade route, a group of young volunteers lined up on each side of the street and jogged along beside him holding long lengths of rope so that, as Bush moved along the thoroughfare, there was always a barrier between him and the spectators.

It was more than security. Bush's advisers didn't want him to mix with the crowds, and they were especially wary of too much contact with reporters. Jim Baker felt that one reason Bush had fared so poorly in the comparisons with Ferraro in 1984 was that he held daily sessions with the press. There was the danger of what the staff called the "chucklehead factor," Bush's penchant for slips of the tongue.

Even so, Bush's standoffishness had as much to do with his nature as it did with either the dictates of security or the concerns of the staff. Bush was a man of two distinct sides. The side the public usually saw was one of caution and courtesy. He was somewhat self-conscious, and his friends said that he abhorred confrontation. It was that part of Bush that made it easy for him to stand back from the crowds when his people requested it. Old-line politicians like Hubert Humphrey couldn't resist plunging into a crowd any more than a hound could resist a hunt. It was something that seemed bred into them. There was no such compulsion within George Bush. Reporters who followed him throughout the campaign remembered times when he would visit factories employing hundreds of workers without shaking hands with any of them except those who had been chosen in advance to pose with him for photos. He was a friendly man, but he wasn't one to force himself on others. In the circles where he had grown up, it just wasn't done.

The other side of Bush was the part the public seldom saw. Nevertheless, it was his defining side. In spite of his reserved nature and his tendency to stand back, he was above all a survivor, as his entire career attested. He had not always reacted well to surprises, but he had a dogged inner grit, and those who had known him longest believed that he was at his best when he knew in advance that he was facing a crisis. It was then, they said, that his survival instincts overcame his caution and he found ways to save himself. It was when he had been caught unaware or when he had to perform a routine function, they believed, that he was most prone to mistakes. They cited two examples: When Reagan had surprised him in the New Hampshire debate back in 1980 by grabbing a microphone and declaring that he had paid for it, Bush had been so taken aback that Reagan had believed he "choked." And, his silly mixup later in the 1988 campaign about when the Japanese attacked Pearl Harbor had come during a routine speech before a friendly audience of American Legionnaires. It was at such times, when little was at stake, that Bush's attention was most likely to wander.

Bush bridled at suggestions that aides could manipulate him, even when it was done to his advantage. But several people who held ranking positions in Bush's campaign hierarchy were convinced that the best way to keep Bush focused was to be certain that he understood the dangers ahead (they were not above overstating them from time to time) and to convince him that his survival was on the line. Only then, they believed, did his competitive mettle reveal itself. You had to "get his back up," one told us, to get the best from him.

The way Bush was prepped by his staff for the celebrated interview with Dan Rather illustrated the strategy. Bush had been looking forward to the interview when CBS News had first requested it in early January. When some of his advisers advised caution, Bush said that he wasn't worried. He and Rather had known each other since the days when he lived in Houston, and Rather was the news director of a Houston television station. The advisers remained wary, however. Dole had been trying to stir up Iran-Contra again, and that could be a problem. In addition, they were worried about the "image thing," as they called it. Rather was a tough questioner. If he threw Bush off, Bush might just wind up looking more like a wimp than ever. Even Bush had reached the conclusion that he had an image problem. It was not his favorite topic, but he was straightforward about it. He remarked to several on the team that he had to improve and he was already trying to do something about it. He approached it the way an executive would approach any problem. He hired an expert.

The expert was Roger Ailes, a New York advertising man. Ailes had been brought in to handle the campaign advertising, but his responsibilities went far beyond designing ads. Ailes had polished Richard Nixon's television technique after his disastrous debate with John Kennedy, and after Ronald Reagan had stumbled badly in his first debate with Walter Mondale in 1984, it was Ailes whom Mike Deaver had brought in to get Reagan better prepared. Ailes was a political gut fighter, and he became Bush's voice coach, adviser, alter ego, and motivator. He became a fixture in Bush's office. He showed Bush how to take some of the shrillness out of his voice, by speaking in more measured tones. The two would watch videotapes of Bush's appearances, and Ailes would show Bush how to look more forceful by slowing down his sometimes awkward gestures. He coached him on how to take charge of interviews. Never let the other guy dominate the interview; control it yourself, he would lecture Bush.

But for all the coaching, the people around headquarters knew that if they were going to get the results they wanted from the Rather interview, they had to be certain that Bush understood just how crucial it was and what potential pitfalls lay ahead. If he became riled up about it, that wouldn't hurt a thing. Whether they really believed it themselves is open to question, but in ways large and small they used every opportunity available to tell Bush that Rather was out to get him. The whole thing, they told him, was a trap that Rather had set for him. They insisted that the interview be conducted live. They told him that taping the session in advance, as CBS wanted, meant that he would be at the mercy of Rather and his editors. Bush had to be ready for anything, they told him, and when an opening came, he had to pounce.

Ailes did not send his clients off to major interviews with the idea that one simply put one's self at the disposal of the interviewer. Television interviews, especially unedited, were forums where the subliminal message that was delivered—how a person looked, whether he came off tough or weak—was often more important than what was said. The real talent that both Ailes and Atwater possessed was that they had a keen insight into what played well on television. As they saw it, the Rather interview was a high-risk proposition, but Bush had a great deal to gain if he played it right.

The interview was scheduled for January 25, and in the political world there was the atmosphere of a heavyweight championship fight about it. It was to be conducted live via satellite. Rather would be in his anchor chair in New York. Bush would be in his vice presidential suite at the Capitol. Before the day was out, Mary Martin, the CBS News deputy bureau chief in Washington, discovered that she would be squarely in the middle.

Martin was in charge of setting up the cameras and making the logistical arrangements for the interview. Because of a heavy snowfall, Bush and his entourage showed up for the interview a full hour before the broadcast, and Martin sensed immediately there would be trouble. She had been around Bush only sporadically over the years, but she could not remember when he had seemed so testy and nervous. She recalled that Bush kept saying, "Boy, if this turns out to be an interview about nothing but Iran-Contra, you're going to have another seven-and-a-half-minute black hole on your hands." The remark referred to an episode that had occurred a few months earlier. Rather had left his anchor chair in the belief that a CBS telecast of a tennis tournament was going to preempt the Evening News. He had been furious at the thought of the news broadcast's being preempted, but he had been as surprised as others on his staff when the sports department suddenly terminated its coverage. In the confusion that followed, the network had gone off the air for seven minutes. The incident had been especially embarrassing to Rather, who had always prided himself on his professionalism and had a well-deserved reputation for being a hard worker and team player.

That was the incident that prompted Bush's threat, which led Mary Martin to wonder: What is this all about? Is he going to walk off if he doesn't like the questions? As the time for his interview approached, Bush seemed even more nervous and Ailes was not helping matters. "He was like a boxing coach," Martin recalled. "It seemed like he just wanted to keep Bush stirred up. He was waving his arms and telling Bush, 'He's gonna sandbag you.'" The interview was preceded by a taped report in which

Rather suggested that Bush had been present at numerous White House meetings when the covert schemes of Iran-Contra had been discussed, but when the interview itself got under way it elicited virtually no information. As Rather posed his first questions, Bush launched into a discourse in which he charged that CBS News had misrepresented in advance what the interview was about. He said that the taped report that had preceded the interview had been a rehash. The exchange quickly grew contentious and at one point there was this exchange:

> RATHER: I don't want to be argumentative, Mr. Vice-President.
>
> BUSH: You do, Dan.
>
> RATHER: No—no sir, I don't.
>
> BUSH: This is not a great night because I want to talk about why I want to be President, why those 41 percent of the people are supporting me. And I don't think it's fair—
>
> RATHER: Mr. Vice-President, these questions are designed—
>
> BUSH:—to judge a whole career, it's not fair to judge my whole career by a rehash on Iran. How would you like it if I judged your career by those seven minutes when you walked off the set in New York?

At the CBS News Bureau in Des Moines, seasoned reporters were astounded. What could be next? What people in the bureau and viewers at home could not see was that the response had not been entirely spontaneous. As the interview had progressed, the crafty Ailes had stationed himself beside the camera. If Bush seemed to be struggling for a response, Ailes would write out a key word in huge letters on his yellow legal pad and hold it just beneath the camera in Bush's line of vision. Just before Bush had shouted that it was not fair to judge his career on Iran, Ailes had written out on his legal pad the words "not fair to judge career . . . Yours." Three times during the interview, Bush's answers had come after Ailes had prompted him with key words or phrases scribbled on the legal pad.

The session had been tense throughout, and Bush was still furious when it finally concluded. Asked by a member of the camera crew whether he wanted to discuss it with Rather, Bush said no. Then to no one in particular he remarked that Lesley Stahl, who served as moderator on "Face the Nation," was "a pussy compared to Rather." It was unclear what Bush had meant by that, but there was no misunderstanding Bush's mood. He had not wanted to have a postinterview chat with Rather, but he had plenty to say to others in the room. He rose from behind the desk, pointed his finger at the startled Martin, and said, "You ought to be ashamed of yourself, you knew about this in advance. . . ."

Martin was stunned. She had known nothing about the line of questioning in advance or the taped piece that preceded it. It had merely been her responsibility to make sure that the equipment worked. She tried to be polite but Bush was having none of it. "That was the worst thing in all my years of public life," he said as he came around from behind the desk. "But that bastard didn't lay a hand on me. You can tell your goddam network that if they want to talk to me in the future they can raise their hands at a press conference." The daughter of a journalist and a journalist all her adult life, Martin had been around newsrooms long enough to accept most things with equanimity. But she had never been through anything like this. "I tried not to take it personally," she said. "But he really was steamed. He was wound up like a clock when he got there, and he was boiling when he left."

Lee Atwater was not boiling. He had watched the whole episode on television and he was delighted. Bush had stood his ground and slugged it out. Finally, Atwater thought, we are on the road to putting the wimp business behind us. Bush had stood toe-to-toe with some of the biggest toes on television. It didn't matter who won or lost; the good news was that Bush had looked tough in doing it. The strategy had worked.

Overlooked in all the furor over the confrontation was the fact that Bush had succeeded in stonewalling the questions Rather had tried to ask him about his role in the Iran-Contra affair. Not much was made of this at the time, but recollections of that aborted interview came rushing back to mind a little more than a year later when Bush was in the early months of his presidency. In April 1989, government documents submitted by the defense in Oliver North's trial indicated that Bush had been actively involved in the Reagan administration's covert efforts to induce other governments to contribute to the Contra cause. That information ran counter to Bush's repeated assertions during the 1988 campaign that his role in Iran-Contra was minimal. The disclosures at the North trial raised new questions about Bush's role, but these clearly were not the kind of questions he wanted to answer on national television back in January 1988 when he was in the critical early stages of his run for the White House.

After Bush won the presidency, Atwater would claim that the Rather interview had a major impact on firming up Bush's support across the South and marked a turning point in the campaign. If it had any positive impact on Iowa, however, it was not discernible. The earlier predictions by Atwater and Bond that Bush could not win Iowa were more accurate than they would have liked. Dole's regional ties and his strong support among farmers were simply too much for an Easterner to overcome. The surprise was not so much that Bush lost Iowa but that he lost so badly. He was not only beaten by Dole but, as Bond had feared, finished behind Pat Robertson as well. The Bush team took the loss hard, but no harder than Bush himself. They had all prepared themselves for a defeat, but they had not prepared themselves for a humiliation.

If, as Winston Churchill once remarked, "Nothing so exhilarates a man as having been shot at without result," it is equally true that nothing so focuses a man's attention as being shot at and hit. Bush had been hit in Iowa, and hit hard, and it had finally focused his attention.

As painful as it had been, Iowa became the strong medicine the faltering campaign desperately needed. Even Robertson's presence would eventually be seen as beneficial. "Robertson, as odd as it seems, did us a real favor," Atwater said. Robertson provided another benefit as well in Atwater's view. His second-place finish was such a surprise that it drew a lot of press and television attention away from Dole. "If we had finished a weak second, rather than third," Atwater said, "then Robertson would not have been nearly so good a news story. Dole would have dominated the coverage and might have built up such a powerful head of steam that we never could have caught him in New Hampshire."

Whether Atwater was correct when he argued that finishing third was better than finishing second was conjecture, as was his assertion that Bush's performance in the interview with Rather had been a turning point in the campaign, but what no one in the Bush campaign disputed was the impact that the Iowa loss had on Bush. It was in Iowa that George Bush realized he had to change, and, with a little more help from his friends, he became a different candidate.

* * *

Only seven days separated the Iowa caucuses and voting day in the New Hampshire primary. As Dole had calculated, Bush's New Hampshire lead collapsed after Dole's runaway Iowa win. Three weeks earlier, Dole's tracking polls had shown him trailing Bush by eighteen points in New Hampshire. Two days after the Iowa drubbing, however, the Bush lead had shrunk to only five points, and by Friday it had actually flipped. With the primary only three days away, Dole's polling showed him five points up on Bush—the first time he had ever led in New Hampshire.

But when George Bush blew into the Granite State, it must have seemed that he had undergone a personality transplant to those who followed the campaign nightly on television. The always proper, almost prissy candidate in the dark suit and tie who appeared so reluctant to go near the voters of Iowa was replaced in New Hampshire by George Bush the Working Man. Set speeches were suddenly dropped, replaced by unannounced visits to shopping malls, lumberyards, and truck stops. In a newly purchased trucker's cap and windbreaker, Bush seemed to have as his main goal in life operating every piece of heavy equipment in the state. "Hide the forklift, Mama, George Bush is a comin'," a reporter joked.

In reality, George Bush had not changed as much as his tactics. He had finally convinced himself that he had to show a more down-to-earth, personal side, and the scheme his advisers came up with was a truncated version of a proven campaign ploy called the "work day." In recent years, politicians in dozens of Senate and House races across the country have used *work days* to demonstrate their interest in local concerns. It is an easy technique to execute: the politician announces that he wants to find out whether taxpayers are getting their money's worth out of certain city services and if, for example, the politician decides it is garbage collection he will scrutinize, he puts on old clothes, calls in the photographers, and works for a day with a city sanitation crew. On another day, he might choose to work a shift at a construction site for the stated reason of getting an appreciation for the problems of working people. Among other political benefits, such forays generate good television pictures.

Bush's advisers seized on the idea as a way for Bush to shed his preppy image and show himself to be a regular guy. Bush himself had learned from the comparisons that were drawn between him and Reagan. It was not always what you really were

that came through on television; you had to help your image along
as Reagan had never hesitated to do. Reagan and his image makers
also understood something else: In the television age, the setting
in which a person appears weighs heavily on the impressions that
people form.

Mike Deaver had always been a believer in the theory that if
you wanted to make a message stick in the brief time that was
allotted to a television news story, announcing it in the proper
setting was essential. If the message involved the stock market,
Deaver believed, then it was best to announce it with the New
York Stock Exchange in the background. That way, even if the
reporters were shouting questions at the President about other
things, the television viewer was bound to be left with a question
in his own mind, What is the President doing at the stock market?
Deaver knew reporters were obligated to answer such questions
in their stories. He knew as well that the television reporters were
often prisoners of the pictures they had to work with. It was hard
to write a television story about apples when the only pictures
available to illustrate it were of oranges. In Bush's case, his image
makers concluded that the first step in convincing people he was
tough enough to be President was looking the part. After the loss
in Iowa, Bush decided that they were right.

His people searched New Hampshire for heavy machinery
that he could ride. It was hard not to look macho behind the wheel
of a road grader or a big truck. As Bush turned his attention to
the heavy rolling stock, his people made two major changes in the
work-day technique that other politicians had used so successfully.
The pretense that Bush expected to learn anything from the exercise was dropped. No one believed such talk anymore, so why
try to manufacture a reason for the expeditions? If asked, they
said only, "It's a chance to get some good pictures." The second
Bush innovation was to convert the work day into the "work minute." The stunts lasted only long enough for the photographers
to get pictures of them.

The work minutes became the signature of Bush's New
Hampshire campaign, and there were dozens of them. At lumberyards, Bush demonstrated his expertise at operating forklifts.
At a highway truck stop called Cousin Richie's, he posed with
transient truckers having coffee. For a moment it was hard to tell
Bush from the drivers. (But only for a moment. When the waitress
asked who wanted seconds, one trucker said, "Hit me." Bush said,

"Just a splash, please.") The most celebrated work minute of the campaign took place at Cousin Richie's, where it was arranged for Bush to drive one of the big rigs himself. He climbed into the cab of an eighteen-wheeler and as the regular driver showed him how to shift it into the lowest gear, he chugged off onto the highway with a toot of the air horn.

With two Secret Servicemen hanging off the running boards, and the ambulance and armored limousine that always accompanied Bush following along behind the tractor trailer, it was such a startling sight that even veteran photographers stood transfixed. Mike Marriott, a onetime Vietnam combat cameraman for CBS News, who had been traveling with Bush for months, was so dumbfounded that he momentarily forgot to take pictures. Once they recovered their wits, the journalists traveling with Bush decided that the occasion deserved to be marked by a special gesture. They went to the truck stop curio shop and bought out the entire stock of billed trucker's hats. As the man who would be President turned his rig into the truck stop parking lot a few minutes later, airhorn still blaring, he was greeted by a dozen grown men and women who represented some of the nation's largest newspaper and television outlets. Each of them had donned the newly purchased head gear—black caps embroidered across the front with pink Day-Glo lettering, which read, "SHIT HAPPENS."

As Bush polished up his image at the truck stops, his operatives were working just as intensely on Dole's. On the Friday before the election, Atwater told Bush that drastic action was still needed. Dole was running television commercials that suggested that Bush had left no visible imprint on any of the important government jobs he had held. Bush had to counterattack, Atwater argued. Bush agreed and Ailes came up with a weapon, a new television ad. It would be known later as the "straddle ad" because it pictured Dole as a wishy-washy legislator who was trying to straddle the issues. It accused Dole of taking both sides on Pentagon spending and on an import fee on foreign oil. Finally, and most important, it suggested that Dole secretly favored a tax increase.

New Hampshire's governor John Sununu, later to become Bush's White House chief of staff, played a key role in convincing the local television station to find time in its programming schedule to run the commercial (no small task at that late hour), and it played all day on the Saturday before the primary. By Primary

Day on Tuesday, Atwater could see from his tracking polls that voters were finally moving back to Bush. The last survey showed the two men even, but Atwater took heart in that because every time there had been movement in the numbers it had been toward Bush. Thus he was no more surprised at the result than he had been in Iowa on the night Bush lost. Bush wound up getting 38 percent of the vote, beating Dole by ten points, a victory tantamount to a landslide. The others finished so far behind that they were now out of the race.

Both Bush's people and Dole's camp agreed that it had been the straddle ad that had turned it around. Call it "negative campaigning," call it "attack campaigning," call it "comparative campaigning" (the Bush team's euphemism): by whatever name it was given, it got results and that was a lesson that Bush would remember well in the coming months.

For Dole nothing went right in New Hampshire, and he exacerbated his defeat during an election night postmortem on national television. NBC's Tom Brokaw had just concluded an interview with the victorious Bush, and Dole could be seen on a television monitor waiting to be interviewed next. Brokaw asked Bush whether he had anything to say to his opponent. "Only to wish him well and to say I look forward to meeting him in the South," the happy Bush said graciously. When Brokaw turned to Dole and asked whether he had a message for Bush, the glowering Kansan blurted, "Yeah, tell him to stop lying about my record."

To Atwater and the other members of the Bush inner circle, it was hard to imagine anything that Dole could have done to hurt himself more seriously. Dole's worst liability, the Bush people believed, was that voters perceived him as having a dark, angry, almost quirky side. The incident had reinforced that impression in a way that no amount of negative advertising ever could. As the professional politicians around Bush assessed it, the incident had hurt Dole as badly as Bush had himself been hurt back in the Nashua debate in 1980 when he seemed unable to speak as Ronald Reagan seized the microphone. Dole's reaction on election night in New Hampshire was an episode that all of the Bush people would recall when the time came for Bush to choose a running mate. Some would later say that, had Dole not spoken so harshly that night, he and not Dan Quayle would have become vice president.

* * *

Atwater had good reason to feel confident about the coming Super Tuesday primaries, which were mostly in the South. The South remained the region where Reagan was most popular, and where Reagan was strongest Bush always ran best. Not for nothing had Atwater listened to his mentor, South Carolina's Strom Thurmond. Atwater had been in Southern politics all his life, and he knew what played in the South and what didn't. Even more important, it was the region where he and Bush had worked the hardest. From the beginning, Atwater's aim had been to duplicate the successful strategy that had worked so well for Reagan in 1980 and 1984, one built around an appeal to Southern voters. Bush had made hundreds of trips into towns and cities of the region for seven years. He had written thousands of thank you notes and autographed thousand of photos and forwarded them to key people from Florida to Texas. One of his sons had become a political figure in his own right in Florida and, with his Mexican-born wife, had helped Bush build a strong base among the vehemently anti-Castro Cuban community. (Whereas the majority of Hispanic voters in Texas and California tend to vote Democratic, the Cubans of Florida lean to Republicans in national races.)

At the urging of Atwater, Bush was determined to solidify his chances among voters across the South. As part of that, Episcopalian Bush had begun in 1985 to devote more and more attention to the fundamentalist Christians in the region. Bush and Atwater had concluded then that Robertson might mount a dangerous challenge in the South, and they had set out to preempt it, if at all possible. By some estimates, one of every five votes that Ronald Reagan received in 1984 had come from born-again Christians. It was a voter group too large to be neglected, and Bush had no intention of doing so. This had been the reason for his early overtures to Moral Majority founder Jerry Falwell, and Falwell's endorsement was a major part of the Bush strategy to blunt Robertson's effectiveness. What was not so widely known at the time was that Bush had also tried to establish a political relationship that year with Jim Bakker, the host of "PTL Club," the most widely watched religious broadcast on television. Bush made a trip to Charlotte, North Carolina, to visit Bakker in November 1985, and Bakker's wife, Tammy Faye, was Mrs. Bush's guest in Washington some months later. (It has never been determined just what the two discussed.)

Bush's people have since denied it, but some of Bakker's aides were under the impression in those days that Bakker might wind up with a White House job. The meetings all took place before the Bakkers' religious empire collapsed amid disclosures of his trysts with church secretary Jessica Hahn and rumors of homosexual encounters. After the election, Bush spokesman Marlin Fitzwater said that there had been nothing improper about Bush's meetings with Bakker and that Bush held similar meetings with hundreds of people. That was true. The attention that Bush gave to Bakker was only a small part of his effort to cultivate born-again Christians. Doug Weed, who served as guest host on Bakker's television program, eventually took a paid position in the Bush campaign and served as liaison with the born-again community across the South. Weed organized hundreds of fundamentalists who kept weekly tabs on Robertson's political activities and arranged for Bush to meet privately with many born-again Christian leaders, sessions that were convened so that Bush could tell them that he had "accepted Jesus Christ as his Lord and personal Savior."

The effort across the South paid off. The cultivation of the Religious Right, the thousands of thank you notes, the nights of mashed potatoes and ham with raisin sauce at one testimonial dinner after another in small towns and large resulted in a landslide Bush win. As Atwater had expected, Bush swept the Super Tuesday contests, but the victory was even greater than had been anticipated. He won every state except Washington, and because results were so late arriving from the Pacific Time Zone, that news was missed by many Americans.

For Bob Dole, it was no longer a question of whether to give up the fight, but when. For the Bush people, it meant the fight for the nomination was over. There were still primaries ahead, but Bush had crushed Dole and his other opponents so thoroughly that there was no chance they could prevent him from getting the Republican nomination. The Democrats still didn't have a candidate, although it was looking more and more as if Michael Dukakis would be Bush's opponent in the fall.

19

As Paramus Goes...

"We couldn't have done it without them."

—Lee Atwater

By all conventional standards, the late spring of 1988 should have been a joyous time for George Bush and his campaign. His rout of Dole and the other rivals in the Super Tuesday contests carried him to the brink of the Republican nomination and he clinched it with a one-sided victory in late April in Pennsylvania. It had been the earliest in recent history that a candidate in either party had wrapped up the nomination in a contested race. As Bush was finallly taking control of his party, he also seemed to be getting the kind of boost he needed from the White House. The pictures of the Reagan-Gorbachev summit that were beamed back to American voters from Moscow were helping Reagan recapture much of the popularity that had been lost during the Iran-Contra troubles, and that could only help Bush's prospects in the coming battle with the Democrats.

But these surface impressions were misleading. While Reagan and Gorbachev spent Memorial Day weekend "campaigning" in

Red Square, Bush convened a summit of his own at his vacation home in Kennebunkport, Maine—and the mood there was somber. A series of polls taken that spring indicated that voters preferred Michael Dukakis to Bush by substantial margins. A Gallup survey had Bush trailing his Democratic rival by fifteen points, and that was not the worst of it. On the question of "likability," the polls showed that for every voter who liked Bush, there was one who disliked him. In contrast, voters who said they "liked" Dukakis outnumbered those who didn't by five to one. (One of the most sobering assessments came from a private poll that showed that Americans even held Gorbachev in higher esteem than Bush—but then the Soviet leader had been spending more time with Reagan lately than Bush had.) It was looking so bad that some of Bush's senior advisers were taking bets that he would still be trailing Dukakis even after the Republican convention in August and would remain behind even after the autumn campaign began on Labor Day.

The problem, as they saw it, was still the "image thing." To many voters, Bush just didn't come across as tough enough to handle the job, and, added to that, wrapping up the nomination so early had produced its own set of complications. The top command had always understood that Bush would have to relinquish the spotlight to the Democrats at some point, but as the Democratic race boiled down to a two-man contest betwen Dukakis and Jesse Jackson, not only were the Democrats getting all the attention but Dukakis was slowly shedding his liberal reputation. There were not many Democrats in the United States whose politics were to the left of Dukakis's, but Jackson was one of them. Every time the two went head-to-head in a primary, the comparison made Dukakis appear more of a centrist. To Atwater and Stu Spencer, the longtime Reagan adviser, nothing could have been worse for Bush. Atwater had built his whole strategy around winning the votes of Southern conservatives and blue-collar ethnics. There was no way that Bush would ever command the kind of affection from voters that Reagan did, so it was mandatory that he appear more in line with traditional values than his Democratic opponent. At the very least, Bush had to be seen as the lesser of two evils.

One of the great strengths that Bush's campaign team possessed was that all of them were able to judge their man in a dispassionate way. Atwater and Bush were not particularly close, but Bush and Baker were longtime friends. Yet, they never allowed personal feelings to intrude on the judgments they were forced to make on Bush's electability. Stu Spencer, one of the few people who could look Nancy Reagan in the eye and tell her what was wrong with Ronald Reagan, shared Baker's and Atwater's objectivity. Less experienced strategists might have rationalized that the big lead was the result of a statistical fluke or Dukakis's relative "newness" to voters and would eventually fade. But the group that convened at Kennebunkport had two successful Reagan campaigns behind them and years of experience even before that, and their findings alarmed them.

They were now convinced that if Bush were to have any chance to win, he would have to adopt a high-risk, highly unconventional strategy for the general election and it had to be launched immediately. They no longer had the luxury of waiting until the traditional Labor Day starting time. Dukakis was bound to go up in the polls after his own nominating convention in August, and if he entered that convention with the kind of lead he already had, it would be all but impossible to catch him. Dukakis was shedding his liberal image so rapidly, Atwater felt, that they had to begin by attacking him immediately. Normally a candidate laid out his own program and what he stood for before attacking his opponent, but Atwater felt that Bush was too far behind to present a detailed program of proposals. Nor was there time to plan and execute a campaign to improve Bush's image. The recent polling suggested that negative feelings about Bush had reached such high levels that the only way to offset them was to drive up negative feelings about Dukakis. In other words, it was faster and quicker to tear down Dukakis than to build up Bush. This was the technique they had used so successfully on Reagan's behalf against Carter and Mondale.

In the months after the plan was put into action, several people on Bush's staff tried to convince reporters that Bush himself had misgivings about "going negative." But two people in the inner circle told us that the only reservations they heard Bush express about the strategy had to do with whether or not it would be effective. "As far as I could tell he had no qualms about it," said one of them. "It was just the facts of life. He realized that as far behind as he was it was the only way to win."

Hired gunslingers seldom travel unarmed and Bush's political advisers had arrived in Kennebunkport with an attack plan already in hand. It had several broad objectives. If voters perceived Bush as weak, then they would make Dukakis appear even weaker. If Bush sometimes came off as shrill, Dukakis would be painted as impractical. If Bush did not come off as the flag-waving, God-fearing Fourth of July patriot that Ronald Reagan did, well, just wait until the voters got a load of what Dukakis represented.

The advisers believed they had discovered a potent tool that would forever change America's mind about what Michael Dukakis stood for. It was the Massachusetts prison furlough program, an issue that had first been broached during one of the debates the Democrats held before the New York primary in April. Al Gore, the young Tennessee senator, had been groping for an issue to keep his candidacy alive and had tried to embarrass Dukakis by bringing up the case of Willie Horton, a convicted Massachusetts murderer who had brutally beaten a Maryland couple and then raped the woman while he was out on a pass from prison. The question had no impact on the New York race and Gore's campaign collapsed, but Dukakis seemed nettled by the question. As the Bush campaign's research chief, Jim Pinkerton, watched the debate, he noted the incident and called it to Atwater's attention. Atwater thought that it had real possibilities, and three days before the Kennebunkport summit, the campaign arranged a market test in much the same way a manufacturer might test public reaction to a new product before producing it in large quantities.

The fieldhands who worked for the campaign's pollster, Robert Teeter, rounded up thirty people in Paramus, New Jersey, to see how voters would react to the Horton case. The technique they used is what is known in marketing as *focus-group testing:* Pollsters assemble a cross section of people and test their reactions by asking them questions. In some cases, the group is simply asked to discuss a certain issue. In others, they are connected to machines similar to lie detectors, which measure their pulse and perspiration rate as they are asked questions. In Paramus, the group of thirty people Teeter had assembled represented what the advisers believed would be swing voters in the coming election. All of them had been Democrats at one time in their lives, but each had voted for Ronald Reagan. Now, however, each of them had decided to return to the Democratic party and support Dukakis. The group was split in half and tested separately. Seated in a small, comfortable room, they had been told that their responses were being

videotaped, but they were not aware of who was paying them or
that they were being watched through a two-way mirror by the
Bush campaign's high command: Atwater, Teeter, Bush's vice
presidential chief of staff Craig Fuller, TV expert Ailes, and
Bush's old friend Nick Brady.

In a voice that was purposely free of emotion, one of Teeter's
employees told the group about the Massachusetts furlough program and the story of Willie Horton. Several other issues that
were little known outside Massachusetts were also raised: that
Dukakis had once vetoed state legislation that would have required
Massachusetts teachers to lead their students in the Pledge of
Allegiance each morning; that Dukakis was a member of the
American Civil Liberties Union; that he opposed the death penalty; and that Boston Harbor was polluted and Dukakis had not
moved quickly to clean it up.

Atwater believed from the beginning that the Willie Horton
case had promise, but he and the others were astonished by what
they saw unfolding on the other side of the two-way mirror. As
the evening wore on, fifteen voters in the groups, half the people
who had been assembled, reached the conclusion that they would
not vote for Dukakis after all. It almost defied belief. Fifty percent
of a group of people who had planned to vote for one candidate
for President had decided, in the space of an evening and in the
presence of strangers, to vote instead for his opponent. They
found the Pledge of Allegiance issue disconcerting, and they were
surprised to learn how dirty Boston Harbor was, but most of all
it had been the furlough program for convicts such as Willie
Horton that disturbed them. The Bush people had known that
support for both Dukakis and Bush was soft, but not until the
Paramus test had they realized *how* soft. And not until then would
Lee Atwater tell others that despite Bush's trailing Dukakis in the
polls, he was now confident that he had found an issue to turn
the bleak situation on its head.

Videotapes of the session were taken to Kennebunkport, and
after watching them, Bush decided to go along with his advisers'
recommendation. A new attack speech was written, and Bush
unveiled it later that month at the Republican state convention in
Houston, his adopted hometown, and he repeated it at every
opportunity. By the end of June, Atwater was telling Republican
audiences that Willie Horton was going to be one of the most

famous men in America. He jokingly suggested at one gathering that Horton might wind up as Dukakis's running mate.

What happened next was almost as amazing as the transformation the advisers had witnessed in the Paramus market test. From the moment that Bush first mentioned Willie Horton, Dukakis's lead in the polls began to shrink: By the time the Democrats opened their convention in Atlanta, it was down to eight points, still a formidable margin to be sure, but at a level that Atwater considered manageable.

Dukakis got the expected "bump" from his convention exposure, as Atwater had predicted, and that sent his lead climbing again. But even with the boost, Dukakis was at exactly the place in the polls where he had been three weeks before the convention. It was still going to be tough, but as Dukakis rested after his Atlanta triumph, the Bush people were finally coming to believe that they could win the election. They had changed the minds of half the people in the Paramus focus groups, and they had done it by telling them about Dukakis, not about Bush. Atwater was convinced that they could do the same with voters in the general election.

Bush and Jim Baker went fishing together during the Democratic convention, but once it concluded, Bush returned to the attack and Baker, in line with the plan that had been agreed to four years earlier, resigned his Cabinet post to devote full time to managing the campaign. (To no one's surprise, Reagan appointed Bush's *other* old friend, Nick Brady, to succeed Baker as secretary of the treasury.)

The interval between conventions is usually "down time" for both parties, but as Bush's attacks on Dukakis grew sharper, a curious rumor that swept political Washington in late July kept both camps busy. It was a rumor that Dukakis had been treated for severe mental depression after the hit-and-run death of his brother in 1973. Reporters from several newspapers and television networks had checked into the story. But when they found nothing to substantiate it, it seemed destined to die until a reporter for one of political extremist Lyndon LaRouche's publications asked President Reagan about it in the White House Press Room. To the surprise of those present, Reagan said that he "was not going to pick on an invalid" by commenting. When a President speaks on a subject—any subject—it becomes news and the re-mark touched off a furor. Later that afternoon, the President apologized, but Dukakis could take little solace in that. The net-work news programs all included the story in their broadcasts that night, and it was on the front pages of many newspapers the next day.

Had the rumor been the work of the Bush campaign? Was it yet another part of the attack strategy? No, Atwater stated em-phatically. He said that he had asked his people whether they had started it and they denied it. Furthermore, he told reporters that if any of them could prove that someone in the Bush campaign had been responsible for the story he would fire him. Several reporters who had been tipped on the story said that they had no proof Atwater's operatives had actually started the rumor. Even so, the Bush people did not hesitate to circulate it. Whatever its origin, the rumor bore a striking parallel to another report that had circulated years earlier during a state campaign in which Atwater had been involved. In that case, it was alleged that the opponent of one of Atwater's clients had undergone shock ther-apy. When the man accused Atwater of circulating the story, he responded, "I'm not going to comment on what was said by some-body who has been hooked up to jumper cables."

Nothing was ever revealed to suggest that the story concern-ing Dukakis's mental health was true, but the way in which Dukakis dealt with it was so awkward that the handling itself raised new questions as to whether it might have some validity. Dukakis had refused—"as a matter of principle"—to release his medical rec-ords for several days. By the time he finally did release a detailed statement from his doctor that showed he had an excellent medical history, the incident had been blown into a major controversy. It was the kind of thing that would have had little impact on a politician with a national reputation, but Dukakis was a relative unknown, and from the day it first surfaced, his popularity began to slide. Because of it, the attacks that Bush had been leveling at Dukakis's values and patriotism proved even more potent. It would now be only a matter of days until Bush surged ahead of Dukakis in the polls, and once he got the lead he never lost it.

Ironically, the turnabout came within days after the Repub-lican convention, the only point when the campaign seemed to go off track and one of the few junctures when Bush had rejected the advice of both Baker and Atwater. That unusual disagreement had resulted over Bush's selection of a running mate. Roger Ailes, who had become increasingly influential in the inner-circle deliberations after Bush's victory in New Hampshire, had suggested Indiana's Republican senator Dan Quayle as a possible vice presidential candidate. It was a natural choice for Ailes because Quayle had hired him as a consultant during a previous Senate campaign. Ailes took the line that Quayle would appeal to very conservative Republicans as well as young voters. Teeter had also done some work for Quayle in the past and had not objected when Quayle's name had been added to the list of possible running mates, but Quayle's only other real champion was Craig Fuller. Quayle had virtually no support from other members of the team or from Bush's family and friends.

Despite speculation at the convention that Dole was the favorite choice of the top command, most of them later disputed that. In fact, one of the inner circle told us that just the opposite was true. "The real worry," said one adviser, "was making sure that Bush didn't choose Dole. He was just too erratic. He was guaranteed to get pissed off at least a couple of times during the campaign and with an election that we thought at that time was going to be very close, it was just too big a risk to take." Dole apparently thought that he was in the running until the last. Several hours before Bush announced that Quayle was his choice, Dole told us that he had called Baker some weeks earlier with a request that if Bush did not want him on the ticket he let him know quietly so he could publicly take himself out of the running and avoid the embarrassment of rejection. But, Dole added, no such call ever came.

Even though there was no enthusiasm for Dole, there was more support than generally believed at the time for his wife, Elizabeth. Atwater, for example, cited her as his first choice in the list of potential running mates he submitted to Bush. The cagey Baker considered Quayle a "lightweight," but he never disclosed his own favorite to anyone but Bush. After the selection became known, however, he did not hesitate to stress in an interview with us that the choice had been Bush's alone.

Quayle's selection and his disjointed answers at his first press conference set off a furor among the thousands of reporters covering the convention. Asked about his military service, Quayle left open the possibility that he had avoided military duty in Vietnam by using the connections of his wealthy family to gain admission to the Indiana National Guard. "Calls were made," he told one interviewer.

Quayle's first impressions on an electorate to whom he was largely unknown could not have been worse and sent the advisers into emergency damage-control planning sessions. Removing Quayle from the ticket was never given serious thought, but Baker became so concerned about the controversy that he convened an all-night session of the inner circle to probe more thoroughly into Quayle's past. Once they had questioned Quayle extensively and concluded that the story of how the young Indianan had wound up in the Guard was no worse than what had already come to light, they began to lay out plans to keep him under control during the campaign. Quayle gets angry quickly when provoked and he bristled about the treatment, but for nearly all of the campaign he was kept out of the major cities and the areas where the ticket was being seriously challenged.

At junctures in the campaign, Bush would go for days without mentioning Quayle by name, and on the morning after the vice presidential debate when Lloyd Bentsen had branded him "no Jack Kennedy," Bush addressed a gathering in Fort Worth, Texas, without once mentioning him. (The advisers came up with a crafty plan to avoid charges that Bush was ignoring Quayle altogether. For weeks after the debate, Bush would not mention Quayle at all during appearances scheduled during the morning and mid-day. Because of broadcast deadlines, the comments in those speeches were the ones most likely to generate stories on the networks' evening news broadcasts. He would, however, sometimes mention him briefly in the late afternoon and evening speeches. In that manner, the campaign could say that Bush talked about Quayle "all the time." But, it also ensured that whatever Bush had to say would be more likely to show up on the morning news programs, which attracted far smaller audiences than evening broadcasts.)

Quayle's selection stunned the inner circle, but Bush never really explained what led him to pick the young senator who was neither a Bush intimate nor a favorite of the party. The most likely explanation, even to many of Bush's friends, was that Bush wanted someone who would be the kind of vice president he had been: quiet, loyal, and nonthreatening. Quayle never recovered from the controversy, and surveys showed that he remained a drag on the ticket throughout the campaign, but he never proved to be the major liability that some on the team had feared during the convention.

It was Bush himself who finally got the convention—and the campaign—back on track when he delivered his acceptance speech, which many around him called "the best speech of his life." It was in that speech that he talked about America's being "a thousand points of light," but it was the promise of no new taxes, and the trademark attacks on Dukakis's values (it was one of the few times he did not mention Dukakis by name) that provoked the biggest cheers from the partisan crowd. By the following Monday, Atwater had the evidence to show that his attack strategy had been correct. After trailing Michael Dukakis by seventeen points just three weeks earlier, George Bush had not only pulled even but now led Dukakis by a healthy margin, forty-six to forty. It was an astonishing turnaround. In less than a month, almost one person in four had changed his or her mind about the choice for President.

Labor Day fell late in 1988, leaving eighteen days between the end of the convention and the traditional starting date of the autumn campaign, and Dukakis used the respite to make his annual tour of western Massachusetts. Bush, however, stuck to the schedule that had been mapped out at the Memorial Day summit in Kennebunkport. For the Bush team, the autumn campaign had really begun in June, and the last days of August were a period in which the campaign was stepped up, not toned down. In those first days after the convention, Bush flew to California for a joint appearance with Reagan, and his words there were illustrative of the line he now took routinely against Dukakis. "What is it about the Pledge of Allegiance that upsets him so?" Bush asked an audience. "It is very hard for me to imagine that the Founding Fathers—Sam Adams and John Hancock and John Adams—would have objected to teachers' leading students in the Pledge to the flag of the United States."

The pattern for the Bush campaign was now set—it was to be nonstop attacks—and for all practical purposes, the race for the presidency was settled in those weeks before Labor Day, the date when campaigns of the past had usually begun. As the style of the Bush campaign had jelled, so too, in a sense had Dukakis's. Not until the last weeks would Dukakis finally realize that Bush's attacks had to be refuted. But that realization came too late. Over the objections of many in his party and even his own running mate, Lloyd Bentsen, Dukakis had declined to respond to most of Bush's attacks. The Harvard technocrat found it difficult to believe that voters would be seriously influenced by Bush's words and felt that trying to answer them would only give them credibility. If one were to draw an analogy with a boxing match, it was as if Dukakis had gone down for a count of eight before the bell had rung but had not realized until much later that he had even been hit.

In an insightful analysis published in *The New Yorker*, journalist Elizabeth Drew argued that Dukakis misunderstood the difference between campaigning and governing, where a leader tries to fashion positive solutions to problems and does not have to repeat himself. It seems equally clear, in hindsight, that the Dukakis people had very little understanding of what Bush was really doing when he brought up the Pledge and furlough issues. As Drew wrote in *The New Yorker*,

> "His life—being a law student, a process-oriented governor, a teacher at the Kennedy School—had been the life of reason. He thought that negative campaigning had to do with attacking the other person's proposals, or record, but not his values; he didn't comprehend the importance of symbols.

Nor, it might be added, did he understand what Bush's advisers had learned from their long association with Ronald Reagan: symbols could be used with devastating force on television, where they can be repeated constantly in campaign commercials.

The Bush people, of course, knew precisely what they were doing and made no secret of it. They recognized that the Pledge of Allegiance, the prison furlough issue, and the repeated references to Dukakis's being a "card-carrying member of the American Civil Liberties Union" were only code words for much deeper concerns. One of the advisers told *The Washington Post* that each of the issues "would have been three-day wonders if Dukakis had not failed to grasp that they were tapping something deeper and more significant that he needed to address." As the adviser explained it, the Pledge of Allegiance "went to the symbol of the Nation and essentially raised the question whether Dukakis believed we were a special nation, with a special role and responsibilities." The furlough issue and the ACLU issue were designed, the adviser said, "to paint Dukakis as the kind of liberal who would use the legal system to protect aberrant behavior, rather than stamp it out."

From a tactical standpoint, it was Dukakis's failure to understand the value of repetition that was the most serious flaw in his approach to rebutting Bush's criticism. The charge that Dukakis failed to respond to Bush's charges is accurate only to a point. In truth, he did respond. His mistake was in failing to repeat his response. Once he dealt with an issue, he considered the matter closed and sought to move on to other things. The Bush team had no such illusions. When Dukakis responded to a charge, the Bush campaign simply repeated the accusation and kept repeating it, refusing even to acknowledge that Dukakis had tried to rebut it. The differing approaches illustrated the striking contrast that marked the two campaign teams.

A television reporter who used the word *disciplined* to describe the Bush organization remembered being complimented the next day by two of the senior strategists in separate telephone conversations. The Bush campaign took great pride in being disciplined. More than anyone else, it was Baker who gave discipline to the campaign, a discipline that kept it focused where he wanted it focused. After eight years of polishing their techniques of campaign symbolism and pageantry during the Reagan era, Baker and Atwater understood that the winning campaign was the campaign that dominated the agenda. Baker had a formula to ensure that. First, extensive polling to identify themes that made an impact on voters was ordered; once those themes were identified, a candidate stuck with them, continually repeating them.

Eleanor Clift, a veteran White House correspondent for *Newsweek*, wrote after the election that Reagan's "Presidency ushered in the era of the packaged candidate." But it had really begun long before. The techniques that Baker, Atwater, Teeter, Ailes, and Spencer used to elect Bush were just a refinement of the same methods that Spencer and his old partner, Bill Roberts, had developed when they had been hired in 1966 by a group of California millionaires to turn a fading movie actor named Ronald Reagan into a salable political commodity. One of the first things that Spencer and Roberts had done back then was commission a study of what issues voters cared most about. The two behavioral scientists who had made the study had used it as the basis for developing the set of themes that Ronald Reagan campaigned on for most of his life. It was these original marketing concepts—plus the early appreciation for the value of symbols that Reagan and his handlers had devised—that Baker and Atwater had refined as they shaped the two winning campaigns that brought Ronald Reagan to Washington and kept him there for eight years.

As Baker, Meese, and Deaver had convened for breakfast in the early days of the Reagan presidency to thrash out what would be the "White House story of the day," Baker now convened the top officials of the Bush team at the campaign headquarters each morning to decide on the emphasis that day. It was a highly sophisticated process. The team would lay out broad long-range strategies that called for emphasizing one theme per week, such as the environment, the economy, or crime. If the plan for the week were to focus on the economy, for example, then all activities that week would be built around it. Bush usually spoke only in generalities, but all of the set speeches, all of the television ads, and all of the messages being delivered by surrogate speakers would involve some facet of the same subject. Even Bush's own informal comments, and the answers that he might or might not give in the rare instances when reporters got close enough to shout questions, were equally carefully coordinated and thought out in advance, as were the other pronouncements issued by the campaign. That was the crucial thing: to make certain that Bush and the people traveling with him did not say something that drew attention away from the main message. To prevent that, Bush seldom held news conferences and avoided being in a position where reporters could ask questions that invariably changed the subject.

Baker came up with another simple plan to ensure that aides traveling with Bush did not reveal unauthorized news. He simply told them very little. As Larry Speakes, Reagan's longtime press secretary, had written in his memoir, it was the same technique that Baker had used at the White House. If he didn't want unauthorized news leaks coming out of the White House press office, he just made certain the press office was kept ignorant of what was happening in the White House.

The main focus of the daily early-morning meetings that Baker convened at the campaign headquarters was to review how the plan of the week was progressing and what needed to be changed or modified and to review what Dukakis was doing and where he was putting the bulk of his television advertising. (The monitoring of Dukakis's activities was so thorough that Bush's people were able to tell on a daily basis where he was placing his ads, a procedure that had been developed by setting up a phone bank that kept in contact with television stations around the country and checked daily on what commercials had been purchased that day.)

Although Bush never again fell behind Dukakis once he overtook him in late August polls, the size of his lead did fluctuate. Whenever Dukakis seemed withing striking distance, however, or when danger signals flared, the advisers refocused attention on the crime issue—Willie Horton and the furlough program—and Bush again began to pull away. In the days before the first debate with Dukakis, for example, Baker ordered a two-track contingency plan. If Bush did well in the debate, then the campaign would concentrate on economic issues in the days afterward. If Bush did poorly, they would roll out Willie Horton and crime again. When neither Dukakis nor Bush was decisively superior, Baker took no chances. He understood that by just holding his own with an incumbent vice president, Dukakis had been the de facto winner of the encounter and tracking polls showed that Baker's hunch had been right. So for the next week, the campaign put heavy emphasis on the crime topics and in a matter of days, movement in the polls was again going in Bush's direction.

Ronald Reagan's long-awaited endorsement of Bush had come in May, but it had been so tepid that it set off considerable speculation about whether the President would actively campaign for his loyal veep. (At one point he even seemed to mispronounce Bush's name, rhyming it with lush.) As it turned out, however, Bush could not have asked for more than he got from the Reagan White House. Reagan had read the endorsement as it had been written by his staff, and when the Bush people complained the next day that it had not been strong enough, another one was prepared and Reagan happily read that one, too.

As autumn began and the weather turned cooler, Reagan campaigned hard for Bush all across the country, and polling showed that wherever he went, Bush's standing rose. The greatest favor that the White House did for Bush, however, was to coordinate Reagan's activities carefully to fit the strategies that the campaign was following. As Dukakis tried to sell himself as a Democrat in the tradition of Franklin Roosevelt and Harry Tru-

man, Reagan was asked to rebut that assertion and his response
showed the old actor still knew how to deliver a punch line. "If
he's Harry Truman, I'm Roger Rabbit," Reagan quipped. The
White House also agreed to postpone several unpleasant and
highly unpopular actions until after the election. Foreclosure, for
example, on more than eighty thousand farmers who had fallen
behind on paying back government loans was put off until after
the election, as was the Justice Department decision to petition
the U.S. Supreme Court to overturn the decision legalizing abortion.

For the Democrats, however, it was their own candidate, not
Ronald Reagan, who had become the problem. By late September,
party professionals were beginning to understand the seriousness
of what was wrong with the Dukakis campaign. One group of
outside advisers made a weekend trek to Boston to see what could
be done to rescue the effort and left dismayed and discouraged.
One of them said that it appeared that Dukakis and his team were
not familiar enough with the workings of the government to offer
serious criticism of the Reagan administration or to rebut the
criticisms that Bush was leveling at them. Dukakis had been taking
a heavy pounding from Bush at the time for being against the
Midgetman missile program, yet the Massachusetts governor had
apparently been unaware that it had been the Reagan administration that had tried to cut funding for the weapon. It was a
situation that arose over and over throughout the campaign.

For example, one person who had tried to help the campaign
was amazed to discover after the election that the prison furlough
program had not come into being under Dukakis but during the
administration of a previous governor. "Sure it was in operation
when Dukakis was governor," the adviser said with some exasperation, "but the damn thing had been started by a Republican
governor. Somehow in their arrogance, they just figured everybody knew that."

No group of politicians had been more surprised by Dukakis's
reticence to answer Bush's criticism than the people in Bush's
inner circle. "We couldn't have done it without them," Atwater
was fond of saying. His attack strategy had been devised as much
out of desperation as anything else, and no one had expected it
to sustain the entire campaign. The result was that Bush never
did lay out a comprehensive program of his own. There was never
any real need.

Reagan had won the presidency in 1980 by running as a strong ideological candidate who promised to cut taxes and build up national defense, and he had recaptured it on the strength of his personality, but Bush had won with neither a message nor any particular core of affection among the electorate. His victory was the triumph of a powerful new force in modern American politics: the professional campaign managers. In politics, 1988 would be remembered as the year of the handlers, and Bush's win was the ultimate marketing success. Bush had not stressed his own qualifications for the job. Instead he had emphasized his opponent's lack of qualifications—and it worked. By historical standards, it was not a dirty campaign, but it was one of the shallowest of modern times, an exercise that was largely irrelevant to the problems facing the nation.

In his first official act on the morning after the election, Bush revealed that he intended to nominate his old friend Baker to be his secretary of state. For Baker, the Cabinet post was the realization of a long-held goal. As he had said so often during his White House days, foreign policy was the one area the administration "just never could get right." Now, he was finally getting the chance he had always wanted: the opportunity to influence it directly. In addition, his most valuable aide at the White House and later at Treasury, Richard Darman, was picked to become the administration's new budget director.

In the weeks after the election, there had been speculation that the acrimony of the campaign would carry over into the new administration, but the period proved to be a peaceful interlude. Although Bush had promised an administration of new faces, what his appointments amounted to, instead, was the return of the Baker wing of the old Reagan White House. It was the Reagan administration without Reagan and the California crowd.

Although campaign tempers cooled by late January, there was still some expectation that Democrats on the Foreign Relations Committee would try to dust up Baker at his confirmation hearing. It did not happen. As usual, Baker had done his homework. In the Reagan White House, Larry Speakes had derided Baker's habit of spending hours at a time preparing for brief television interviews, but the technique worked. He prepared for the hearings by spending a lot of time with key committee members. "If you spent as much time with everybody on the committee as you did with me, it was a Herculean effort," quipped Christopher Dodd, the liberal Connecticut Democrat.

What guaranteed Baker's confirmation, however, was an appearance before the committee by Texas Senator Lloyd Bentsen, who had been Dukakis's highly praised running mate. The patrician Bentsen had dropped by the committee to introduce Baker, as senators often do when residents of their home states are nominated to high federal office. What Bentsen said, however, went far beyond courtesy.

"Jim Baker is my friend," he told the committee, "but he is also highly qualified. The nation will be in good hands with Jim Baker as Secretary of State." Coming as it did from a Democrat and especially from a person who had been on the losing ticket, the praise was something of a shock to outsiders. But to those who had dealt with the Reagan administration over the years as Bentsen had, it was not at all surprising. What Bentsen understood, after dealing with Reagan in private, was that Ronald Reagan had very little to do with his administration and the issues that came before it. No matter whose name had been on the marquee, when the Reagan administration was at its best it had been people like Baker and Darman who had kept the White House running.

20

Final Curtain

"I guess that's about it."
—Michael Deaver

In the first days after Ronald Reagan had defeated Jimmy Carter in 1980, Rosalynn Carter had been hurt to hear that Nancy Reagan was telling her friends that the Carters had turned the White House into a pigsty and that if they had any class they would move out immediately so that her decorators could begin redesigning.

When the story finally surfaced, Reagan aides said that Mrs. Reagan had never had such thoughts, let alone expressed them. But if Nancy Reagan had not been as eager to move into the White House as the gossip of the time suggested, she was more than ready to go when the time came to leave. Her friends said that the embarrassment over the astrology disclosures, the friction during Donald Regan's tenure as chief of staff, and a new spate of criticism in 1988 that grew out of her practice of "borrowing" designer gowns at no cost had wearied her. By 1988 Nancy Reagan was ready to go home.

Long before the November election, she began shipping the Reagans' personal belongings back to the new home that friends had purchased for them in Los Angeles. By inauguration day, the White House had been stripped of their personal belongings, and when the Reagans arrived in Los Angeles that night everything in the home was in place: no dishes to unpack, no waiting for a favorite armchair to arrive. It was a home ready to be lived in. The house had been purchased by, among others, what was left of that original group of old California millionaires: the men who had first heard Reagan on the banquet circuit and decided that he could be molded into a political candidate who could sell their views to the country.

The Reagans would be living in the house under a lease arrangement. It was fitting that the group of purchasers was led by Holmes Tuttle, the California auto magnate who had been one of the very first to recognize the actor's political potential. Along with seventeen others, most of whose names were never released to the public but who identified themselves as "independently wealthy," the group quietly purchased the seven-thousand-square-foot California home that sat on a one-and-a-quarter-acre lot in Bel-Air, the most fashionable of the Los Angeles suburbs. The price was $2.5 million. By the time the Reagans moved in, the lot alone had appreciated to $3 million.

The home was more than just a monument signifying the Reagans had come full circle; it was another testament to Reagan's unique ability to escape criticism for actions that would have landed other politicians in severe trouble. At a time when congressmen were being criticized for accepting honoraria for speeches to special interest groups, Reagan received virtually no criticism for being the sole beneficiary of a multimillion-dollar transaction that had been financed by a largely anonymous group, each of whom had put at least $150,000 into a deal that had been consummated two and a half years before he left office.

As the Reagans settled into their new home, their retirement years held the promise of being just as happy as their days in the White House. (Now that they were back in California, the question arose whether the former President would regale his Hollywood friends with old Washington stories.) One week after the inauguration Simon & Schuster announced that it would publish Reagan's memoirs and a volume of selected speeches as part of a package deal that would reportedly pay the Reagans more than $5 million dollars. The next day, a booking agency announced that it would represent the Reagans on the lecture circuit and expected the President to get fees in the neighborhood of $40,000 to $50,000 a talk. Reagan said he would lecture on what he had always talked about, the runaway growth of the federal government, freedom, and the value of optimism.

After eight years in office, polls showed that Reagan was leaving office as popular with voters as when he had arrived in 1980. Ronald Reagan and Company, it was fair to say, had been one of America's longest-running hits, and even after its successful stay at the White House had come to an end one could not help noticing its almost eerie show business parallels. Like many new acts, it had been developed in the backwaters of the after-dinner circuit; as was so often the case with new productions, which are fine-tuned in regional theaters, it had then been honed in the governor's mansion in Sacramento; and finally, when the timing was right, it arrived at the Broadway of politics, the national capital of Washington. Once the long and successful run was completed there, Ronald Reagan geared up to do just what Yul Brynner had done after *The King and I* had completed its run on Broadway: take the show back on the road for a national tour.

Reagan had traveled a long way, but the trip to the White House had been only one part of the actor's journey. He had been back in Hollywood only a month when he got the first feelers about returning to the movies. The suggested role was a natural: a cameo appearance as President Ronald Reagan in a film about former White House press secretary James Brady.

The widely held view as Reagan left office was that his legacy was one of good news and bad news. He was widely praised for reviving the nation's morale and for driving down inflation and unemployment. But many said that the feeling of economic well being rested precariously on a mountain of debt, the enormous deficits that resulted from his economic policy.

We should not make too little of the way that Reagan's indomitable good humor and confidence revived the nation's morale and its confidence in the presidency. Indeed, it was a measure of just how low expectations of the presidency had fallen that toward the end of Reagan's term, some commentators were congratulating him for simply finishing his assignment in good humor and health. As Jimmy Carter had captured the American fancy for a moment by promising never to lie—a trait that had once been the least Americans expected of their public officials—so it was that after five Presidents had been overwhelmed in one way or another by the presidency in the 1960s and 1970s, Ronald Reagan was considered remarkable because he was still standing after shouldering the burdens of the office for eight years. For the first time since the Eisenhower era, a President had not been conquered by the office he had held. The question of course was whether after eight years of Reagan's reassuring words, the nation might be lulled into such complacency that it failed to recogize serious problems such as the deficit while there was still time to address them. After the stock market crash in 1987, Reagan had cheerfully brushed it off "as profit taking," nothing to worry about. In that case, Reagan had been partially right. There was plenty to worry about but nothing had happened. The market eventually recovered. Even George Will, the commentator who was a friend of the Reagans, would write in a widely quoted *Newsweek* essay published at the end of Reagan's presidency that his cheerfulness had been "a narcotic that numbed the nation's senses to the hazards over the horizon."

Much was written in those months about the ironies of the Reagan era and how Reagan had so often confounded critics and supporters alike by doing the unexpected. In retrospect, however, one might just as easily conclude that Reagan's behavior patterns were remarkably consistent in that he had always been willing to change with the times. He had been a New Deal Democrat in the days when Roosevelt was popular, but later he was just as proud to represent the right wing when he was being paid by business interests to espouse their cause. He had refined his free-enterprise, anti-Communist philosophy in those days when the backlash to the antiwar movement was at its peak and the core of his financial support came from the California millionaires who had discovered him. In Washington, his policies generally mirrored the philosophy of those who controlled his staff. In the first term when the pragmatic James Baker and Richard Darman's tight control over White House operations was at its peak, policy generally followed a moderate course except in the case of Defense, where the hard-line and highly independent Weinberger ruled. When Baker was replaced by Donald Regan and a more conservative group of advisers, policy took a turn to the Right. (It is true that it was on Regan's watch that the President had been prepared at one point to negotiate away the nation's entire nuclear arsenal, but clearly that seems more the result of misunderstanding than ideology.) When Donald Regan was finally ousted as chief of staff in favor of the moderate Howard Baker, policy shifted even more to the center, culminating in the far-reaching agreement with the Soviet Union to ban medium-range nuclear missiles in Europe: the first arms control agreement with the Soviets that Ronald Reagan had supported in his entire political career.

Perhaps the greatest irony, however, was Reagan's impact on the programs that were dearest to the Far Right. As it turned out, it was this group and their causes that suffered most under Reagan. On that night back in 1980 when they had gathered at the Plaza Hotel to celebrate the twenty-fifth anniversary of Bill Buckley's *National Review*, they had seen Reagan's election as the final confirmation of the virtue of the cause. But few of their champions wound up in positions of authority in the Reagan White House or in his Cabinet, and it was their cherished issues such as school prayer and the banning of abortion that fell early. Nor would they have dreamed that one of theirs would eventually promote an even warmer relationship with the Soviet Union than the hated détente of Henry Kissinger. In a roundabout way, it had also been Reagan's election that finally cleared the way for the takeover of the White House by the Eastern Republican establishment, the most hated species of all to those on the Far Right. George Bush may have claimed to be from Texas, but the roots of his Republicanism could be traced directly to the party of Tom Dewey, Nelson Rockefeller, the Tri-Lateral Commission, and all the rest of the Eastern establishment, the people who had poked fun at Ronald Reagan back in the very early days of his political career.

On a late autumn day in those first weeks after Bush had been elected, Michael Deaver sat in the sunny kitchen of his home in the Wesley Heights section of northwest Washington and talked of these and many other things with a visitor. Wesley Heights nestles in the wooded, rolling hills above Georgetown and is one of Washington's most beautiful areas. From the windows of Deaver's kitchen one could see the garden where in warmer weather Deaver spent much of his time. Unlike Ronald and Nancy Reagan, the couple he had served so faithfully for so many years, Deaver was not going home to California as he had once hoped to do. He was broke and he did not know where he was going. His wife, Carolyn, had only recently qualified as a licensed real estate agent, but she had not yet sold a house and so they had borrowed against the mortgage on their home to get enough money together to keep the family going. With one daughter at Brown University and a younger child in a Washington prep school, it was difficult. Shortly before the election, Deaver had finally heard the verdict on his perjury conviction. He had gotten off lightly. He would serve no time in prison, but there was a large fine and he would have to spend much of the next few years doing public service work with alcoholics. To support himself and his family, he was trying to form some kind of consulting business, but so far very little had come together and he said that he and his wife had just decided to play it by ear for a while. For the onetime piano player who had spent most of his adult life in selfless devotion to the Reagans, there was no other way to play it. He had been one of the most influential people in the United States during his years in the Reagan White House and had made an enormous amount of money in those first months after he left the White House and formed his own public relations firm. But now, he had already spent a million and a half dollars on legal fees, he owed a million more, and the Reagans were not a part of his life. In many ways, he felt better knowing that he was no longer an appendage of someone else, but where life would now take him, he could not say. It was only after he left the White House that it became known he had suffered from alcoholism. In those months after the 1988 election, however, he considered himself a recovered alcoholic and said the cure had caused him finally to take control of what was left of his life.

"I feel better about myself than I have ever felt," he told the visitor as he poured more coffee. "And a lot of it has to do with my recovery from alcohol. I have come to grips with all of that."

Deaver said that part of his problem through the years had been that he had always considered himself an extension of the Reagans and that everything he did was weighed in his own mind in terms of how it might affect them.

"I always thought my only worth was being associated with them and I found out that's not true," he said, "and that's wonderful. It is not meant with any animosity."

But if Deaver feels no animosity toward the Reagans, it also seems clear that he has been hurt by the way they have ignored him since he fell into disgrace. Despite Reagan's image as a fatherly and caring person, Deaver knew—as did most of the people around

Reagan—that Reagan had few real friends except his wife and seemed to lose interest in anyone who was not around him daily.

During the conversation in Deaver's kitchen that morning, many topics were touched, among them the strange case of Carl Rowan, the liberal columnist who had recently been put on trial after shooting a teenage intruder who had wandered into his backyard, a case that had ended in a hung jury. But always the talk returned to the Reagans, whom Deaver had served so long and so loyally. At one point the visitor asked what sort of relationship Deaver now had with the couple and he replied that he really didn't know.

"I haven't seen them in—gosh—I guess a couple of years," Deaver said. "I have talked with Nancy on a couple of occasions over the last year. I guess that's about it."

He said that he assumed that the Reagans had been told by legal counsel not to contact him, but Mrs. Reagan had called after a newspaper printed excerpts from his book in the months before it was published. She had been exercised because the excerpts painted a particularly unflattering portrait of the Reagans, but Deaver had told her at the time that it had been taken out of context and that she should not worry. There had been no other contacts with her until several hours after he had received his suspended sentence and she had spoken with him briefly by telephone.

When the visitor asked whether he felt hurt by this, Deaver began to speak of himself in the third person, as if he were analyzing the feelings of a friend.

"Oh, I'm sure it hurts," he said. "But I don't dwell on that kind of stuff—it's not healthy—but I'm sure deep down it hurts."

The hardest part, he said, had been the previous Christmas.

We had always been at the White House for Christmas and it was only two weeks after I had been convicted and we learned that we weren't going to the White House for Christmas.

I didn't expect it, but we learned about it through Mrs. Reagan's interviews and I thought, Gee, why couldn't they have dropped a note to the kids.

These kids grew up with Ronald and Nancy Reagan as kind of their idols. They were very close.

He said that there had been no contact at all with Reagan himself except for one time when Reagan had called to say thanks for a note of congratulation that Deaver had written to him on his return from the Moscow summit.

"But he didn't call you during the trial," the visitor asked.

"No," said Deaver.

"Or afterward?"

"No," said Deaver. "He called Carl Rowan, but he never called me."

Two months later, Ronald and Nancy Reagan watched George Bush being sworn in as the forty-first President of the United States, and then as Bush and his family prepared for their inaugural lunch under the Capitol Rotunda, the Reagans boarded a helicopter for one last trip to Andrews Air Force Base, where the big blue and silver jetliner would be waiting to take them to California.

As they made their way to the helicopter, its huge rotors already whirring, a reporter tried to ask a question above the roar, as so many reporters had tried to do over the past eight years. "Isn't that cute?" said Mrs. Bush as she waved goodbye. "They're giving him his last official shout." The big Marine helicopter—no longer designated Marine One, because Reagan was now a former President—finally lifted off the Capitol parking lot and made one last pass across the great Mall that stretches between the Capitol, the Washington Monument, and the Lincoln Memorial. Ronald Reagan was finally going home to California, and in many ways he was leaving as much an outsider as the day he had arrived. To many in the old federal city he was still an enigma. No one, those who had served him loyally for years, such as Deaver, or those who had known him only as President, really professed to understand him or to comprehend the secret of his popularity fully. But it was still as hard as ever for even his enemies to say that they disliked him. His old friend Stu Spencer had once said that Americans had not just loved Ronald Reagan but had been entertained by him. Perhaps that was it. After two decades of turmoil, Ronald Reagan had not only given the country a rest; he had entertained it as well. It was as fine a compliment as an actor could receive.

Index